CONTENTS

Etruscan Craftsmanship in Italy

THE ROMANS

The Effects of Romanisation in Italy

Roman Exports to the North

Roman Financial Systems

Tableware as a Sign of Romanisation

FOREWORD

The sixteenth British Museum Classical Colloquium was held on 8-10 December 1992. That was the year of the Economic Union of EEC countries, and it seemed appropriate to mark the occasion by recalling the trade between Italy and other parts of Europe in antiquity. The theme falls naturally into two periods, the first dealing with the products of Etruscan workshops and the routes by which they reached customers north of the Alps, and the second with production and trade in Roman times, including the economic background and the relationship between commerce and Romanisation within and beyond the northern boundaries of the Empire.

Although there were participants and speakers from several countries, the Colloquium exemplified that special collaboration between the British Museum and our Italian colleagues that has been so fruitful in recent years. It owed much of its success to the joint organisers, Dr Susan Walker and Dr Judith Swaddling. They have also jointly edited the papers with the assistance of Dr Paul Roberts. I should like to thank them and all the speakers, especially Andrea Carandini, for contributing to the success of the last Colloquium that it was my pleasure to introduce as Keeper of Greek and Roman Antiquities.

B.F. Cook
December 1994

ABBREVIATIONS

Where possible periodicals and journals are cited according to the abbreviated form used in *Archäologischer Anzeiger*. When not listed in *Archäologischer Anzeiger* the abbreviation and its full title are listed before individual bibliographies.

INTRODUCTION

L'ITALIA COME GENERATRICE DEL MERCATO IN EUROPA

Andrea Carandini
Via 24 Maggio 14, Rome

Ci vorrebbe il più miope antiquario per trattare un argomento così impegnativo da un punto di vista esclusivamente antichistico, come se non fossimo moderni Europei e come se non ci trovassimo a Londra, capitale del paese che per primo ci ha salvati da un pericolo pari, se non peggiore, dell'invasione persiana. E' infatti solo dopo questa salvezza, costata alla Gran Bretagna il dissanguamento, che possiamo dirci liberamente Europei e possiamo sperare, come io spero, in una unione Europea, capace di sfidare le tempeste che si preparano, di fronte alle quali i singoli stati mi paiono ormai deboli fuscelli. In particolare noi Italiani soffriamo in questo momento cosi particolarmente difficile, giovane nazione quasi sull'orlo del dissolvimento, ma che proprio sull'orlo del baratro potrebbe ritrovare la tempra morale per risorgere, e ci aspettiamo che i legami millenari che uniscono il Mediterraneo all'Europa non si infrangano. Senza il Mediterraneo l'Europa perde le sue più profonde radici culturali e la sua solidarietà e potrebbe ricadere nel veleno di qualche mito Nibelungico. Senza l'Europa il Mediterraneo si trova privo di riforma e quindi dell'essenza stessa della modernità.

Giunti alle soglie del 1993, anno simbolico che potrebbe rivelarsi più importante dello stesso 2000, bisogna ripensare a quell'età, l'età Romana, nella quale si raccoglie come in un imbuto tutto il patrimonio di esperienza delle civiltà piccole e grandi che hanno gravitato sull'Egeo e quello delle genti barbare, in una sorta di ricapitolazione di tutto il mondo antico, consegnata al Medioevo, che la trasmetterà rielaborata e digerita a noi figli dell'attuale disincanto. Fra i tanti beni che ci giungono da lontano grazie alla creatività e alla mediazione dei Romani, dalla tecnica alla bella forma ellenistica, è senz'altro quella realtà materialissima e al tempo stesso impalpabile che è il mercato. Certo non il mercato del capitalismo industriale o post-industriale, ma quello che ne ha costituito l'humus: il mercato di uno sviluppatissimo capitalismo commerciale. Non è forse proprio questa la nostra peculiarità, origine di tutti i nostri beni e mali?

Non sono mancate tendenze che hanno guardato al mercato soprattutto come fonte di tutti i mali, come una forza di gravità irresistibilmente seduttiva, dalla quale bisognava cercare di affrancarsi. Ma con il crollo del socialismo reale è ormai chiaro, ciò che accade quando il mercato è deliberatamente distrutto: miserie fino alla fame e soppressione della democrazia fino alla tirannide. Se saggiamente regolato dalle comunità, il mercato appare invece come un bene prezioso e, abbiamo scoperto, straordinariamente fragile, tanto che dove è stato soppresso, sembra non riuscire più ad attecchire, in mancanza di quell'humus di cui si è parlato. Se il mercato è innanzi tutto una programmazione cerebrale in direzione del mercato, sarebbe difficile negare che il suo fiorire, specie nell'Europa occidentale, ha una sua radice, prima di tutto culturale, proprio nei Romani e nella loro fortuna nei ragionamenti e negli archetipi delle nostre collettività.

Il tema della Romanità si è bruciato per l'uso immondo e ridicolo fattone dal Fascismo, per cui alla gente comune sentir parlare di Romani piace, ancora oggi, non molto. La saga della Romanità in chiave tutta centralistica, colonialistica, autoritaria e retorica fu celebrata in occasione della mostra Augustea della Romanità. Dopo la liberazione dal nazi-fascismo nessuno ha osato riproporre una lettura dei Romani espressione della nostra epoca, che fosse di pari impegno e di pari impatto dell'infausto precedente. Mostre archeologiche si tengono ovunque, anche nella prestigiosa sede di

Palazzo Grassi a Venezia. Etruschi e Fenici impazzano, ma di Roma e del suo impero si tace, quasi che le civiltà maggiori fossero per noi oppressive, come un grande padre-padrone.

Eppure un enorme lavoro è stato fatto e va facendosi, di revisione critica degli antichi preconcetti, di ripensamento di quell'età così formidabile, ma l'organismo da indagare, l'imperialismo e l'impero Romano, è talmente complesso, che non si trova ancora la forza per proporre una sintesi, una chiave di lettura così persuasiva e semplice da valer la pena di esporla per il grande pubblico. Eppure quanto sarebbe necessario un nuovo 'grand tour', che ci riportasse sanamente, criticamente, anche ironicamente, al nostro passato comune, oggi che masse d'uomini sempre più crescenti sembrano fluttuare come isole galleggianti, senza più consapevolezza dei legami profondi che ci riconducono anche ai Romani.

Arriverei quasi a dire che se non riuscissimo a raccogliere una tale sfida, sfida di una mostra innanzi tutto immaginaria, il nostro stesso essere storici, filologi e archeologi del mondo antico perderebbe gran parte del suo senso, perchè il nostro ricercare sarebbe completamente staccato dal mondo di oggi, quindi da ogni sorgente di vitalità e di memoria vivente.

Nel concepire l'ossatura della mostra, una mostra sulla comunicazione e sul mercato, non ci aiuterà nessun Rostovzev o Braudel. Serve un lavoro comune fra studiosi del centro e della periferia. Mai si chiariscono le idee agli specialisti come quando si devono spiegare realtà complesse alla gente comune. Le resistenze non mancano e prima di tutto le scissioni, che in ogni campo travagliano la vita dell'uomo.

L'ostacolo principale è rappresentato dalla divisione fra Mediterraneo e Europa, fra archeologia classica e archeologia provinciale. Bisognerebbe prevedere soggiorni in provincia per i classicisti e saturare il cuore di Roma di studiosi del limes per ottenere qualcosa di buono. Servirebbero occasioni periodiche di scambio, come la felice iniziativa dei prossimi giorni in questo British Museum.

Un secondo ostacolo, almeno per gli archeologi, è il modo diverso di concepire la disciplina: prevalentemente storico-artistico e storico-antiquario nell'archeologia classica e prevalentemente stratigrafico-tipologico nell'archeologia provinciale. Anche qui bisognerebbe integrare i metodi della tradizione umanistica con quelli della tradizione indiziario-scientifica, tanto in sviluppo nell'ultima generazione da aver ingenerato molta paura nel Mediterraneo presso gli studiosi più conservatori. Sarebbe interessante fare un confronto e un bilancio: sono meglio note le città e le campagne dell'Italia centrale tirrenica o le più estreme periferie dell'impero? Non sarebbe diplomatico rispondere a questa domanda.

Altri pregiudizi riguardano una concezione meramente politica del mondo Romano, per cui l'antichità terminerebbe nei nostri paesi con la caduta dell'impero Romano di Occidente e sarebbe confinata entro i suoi limiti amministrativi. Insigni medievisti stanno ormai dimostrando quanto durino gli effetti dell'antichità, almeno per tutto il primo millennio e insigni antichisti delle province hanno dimostrato quel rotolare di mondi, quelle onde successive che si propagano proprio a partire dal limes: quasi un secondo impero Romano immateriale eppure presentissimo al di fuori di quello difeso dalle legioni. Sistemi economici di carattere indigeno sono noti entro il limes cosi come condizioni di mercato oltre di esso.

Il compito da affrontare sarebbe davvero immane. Sembra di addentrarsi nel corpo umano, dove la nostra ignoranza non ha mai fine. Certo, ci si puó accontentare di sintesi rassicuranti e superficiali, ma non appena si lavori intensivamente e sistematicamente, ecco sorgere complicazioni inaudite.

A partire da un certo momento, si potrebbe forse dire dalla nascita delle proto-città, prima ancora delle città, tra la fine del X secolo e la fine dell'VIII nell'Italia centrale tirrenica, comincia quel gioco fra centro e periferia, prima limitato a territori e a regioni e poi esteso a un intero universo, dove finisce per moltiplicarsi ai più diversi livelli, come in un caleidoscopico sistema fra Mediterraneo latinizzato ed Europa barbarica.

L'immensa abilità di Roma, che l'ha resa più potente di tutte le altre potenze, sta proprio nell'aver capito come nessun altro le leggi che governano questo gioco: il Campidoglio si é esteso ai montes nel bronzo recente, i montes hanno dominato i colles nella prima età del ferro, e poi avanti nel Lazio, in Italia, nelle province vicine, in quelle lontane e oltre i limiti, sempre usando lo stesso vantaggioso e iniquo meccanismo. E' come se una stessa esperienza venisse ripetuta, dove la città vince il chiefdom e il chiefdom l'insediamento tribale, fino a che la tribalità non prende le sue rovinose rivincite, giungendo a incendiare la stessa Roma, dai Galli della prima repubblica ai Barbari del tardo impero.

Nessuno ha saputo raccontare questa storia in modo semplice, sintetico e avvincente come Barry Cunliffe, in *Greeks, Romans and Barbarians* (1988). Noi classicisti al centro riusciamo a spingere il nostro sguardo fino alla 'periferia interna' dell'impero: la Gallia, la Spagna e l'Africa. Gli studiosi della 'periferia esterna', lungo la frontiera, si fermano spesso anch'essi a quella periferia interna. Ma la sfida sta nel riuscire a intravedere se non a vedere tutto insieme. E' un poco come Dante alla fine della Commedia che cerca di vedere Dio, quasi accecandosi nel cercare di risalire i raggi che da lui discendono.

Ma questo ossessivo ripetersi della voracità di Roma, il cui esito è la prima omologazione conosciuta dalla nostra storia, il primo germe di modernità nel mondo antico, finisce sempre per adattarsi alle situazioni locali più varie, articolandosi in modi diversi di fascinazione e di sfruttamento, tanto che quasi anche la sostanza del dominio sembra mutare e di qui quel senso di confusione ordinata che l'intero insieme non smette di trasmetterci.

Gli esordi su grande scala si datano alla fine del VI, con l'azione per allora sconvolgente delle città-stato, prima di tutto greche ed etrusche, ad esempio nei confronti della cultura di Hallstatt, fra Friburgo e Würzburg, e la conclusione si ha col tardo impero, quasi se si fosse trattato di un seguito ciclico di paci e turbolenze appartenente ad uno stesso unico fenomeno.

Ma non è cosi, se siamo ancora in grado di cogliere le differenze fondamentali, già intraviste da Marx quando distinse un modo di produzione 'antico' e uno 'schiavistico', dimostrando la profonda differenza fra questi modi dal punto di vista dell'economia politica.

Se è vero che la maniera di lavorare delle città-stato è il presupposto di quella dell'imperialismo Romano nel suo epicentro, quest'ultima ha moltiplicato l'intensità, gli spazi e la velocità di sfruttamento nell'economia a un punto tale, da generare una differenza qualitativa capace di cancellare le precedenti esperienze e di giganteggiare sulla scena materiale e fantastica del mondo, fino a raggiungere la nostra età. L'immagine di Roma che travaglia il Medioevo è la Roma degli schiavi e dell'impero. Se possiamo parlare oggi di un sistema di interdipendenze mediteraneo-europeo lo dobbiamo alla fase imperialistico-schiavistica della storia di Roma. Senza metalli e schiavi rapinati nella periferia e filtrati, per canali marittimi e fluviali, attraverso le turbolente zone tribali di approvvigionamento dominate da guerrieri, le zone di scambio controllate dalle aristocrazie dei chiefdoms, le zone intermedie già pervase dall'economia di mercato all'interfaccia della frontiera e ai suoi ports of trade, fino alle province della periferia 'interna' e al vecchio centro dell'Italia e di Roma - rimando nuovamente alla sintesi di Cunliffe - nulla si sarebbe dato del mondo di cui si tratta. E come bisogna distinguere i mercati delle città-stato dai mercati dell'imperialismo schiavistico, che è tutto un mondo, cosi bisogna distinguere fra un mercato poco più che interregionale di beni di lusso per una élite e un mercato mediterraneo-europeo di beni di largo consumo destinati a vasti strati sociali, per la prima volta in grado di comprarli. La distribuzione delle merci, non dovunque in questo mondo, ma sulle rive del Mediterraneo e nelle zone privilegiate attraversate dai grandi canali di comunicazione, è tale, da trovar confronti solo nell'epoca moderna e da sconfiggere gli ultimi bastioni del primitivismo, che in Gran Bretagna hanno trovato un sicuro rifugio, per ragioni che ancora non conosco. Fra le pericolose scissioni di cui sopra ho parlato avevo dimenticato proprio questa, fra primitivismo e modernismo, che andrà pur sciolta se vogliamo dare una immagine coerente e adeguata dello stato delle cose dei Romani.

Si, la mostra immaginaria sulla romanizzazione dell'Europa su cui vado fantasticando potrebbe incentrarsi proprio sui canali di comunicazione, risalendo per diversi rami dalle città, agli oppida pseudo-urbani, ai villaggi tribali, come in un viaggio attraverso i diversi mondi, che sempre più si allargano, fino a raggiungere i Germani, e ciò visto a diverse scale, dalle più ampie visioni fino a cogliere con la lente anche qualche particolare molto significativo, come Hengistbury in Britannia, di cui a Roma nulla credo si sapesse, eppure importante come alcuni nostri piccoli organi vitali di cui ignoriamo l'esistenza, ma di cui ci preoccupiamo quando si ammalano. Questo mi pare il modo migliore per sconfiggere la visione classicistica dei Romani, diversa ma non meno fuorviante di quella legata ai Greci, questi ultimi sempre i primi e i Romani sempre i più forti.

In questo complicato organismo costituito dall'imperialismo Romano, l'Italia si è trovata all'inizio in una posizione di grande vantaggio, dal momento che dominava un mercato i cui accessi erano sostanzialmente proibiti. Quale condizione migliore? Io ti do ventisei litri di vino e tu mi dai uno schiavo. In questa situazione sono i produttori a comandare, non i consumatori. Ci si trova davanti a un monopolio e di qui il carattere altamente speculativo delle transazioni. Se il vino viene sovrastimato, qualsiasi costo di produzione può essere coperto e l'aristocrazia Romana fa tanti soldi senza dover troppo calcolare. Siamo nel II e I secolo a.C. Ma quando la fluidità antiburocratica dell'imperialismo si cristallizzerà in uno stato imperiale, l'offerta potrà finalmente allargarsi, crollerà la situazione e si potrà parlare per la prima volta di una forma di concorrenza. Di concorrenza parla Braudel, nei suoi *Giochi dello scambio* (1981) per l'economia pre-capitalistica dei secoli XV-XVIII, ma solo a proposito di questo secondo genere di mercato, dove più sorgenti concorrono a saturare l'offerta. Le garanzie date dallo stato imperiale hanno normalizzato il mercato e comincia la stagione dei vini dell'Italia settentrionale, della Betica, della Tarraconese e infine della Gallia. Le zone marginali e sottosviluppate (il terzo mondo di allora) si sposta ancor più verso settentrione e occidente, troppo lontano rispetto all'Italia, ormai circondata da ordinate e laboriose province, che la adorano, la imitano, la superano. Servono ora merci di qualità medio-bassa, per accontentare un pubblico vasto e modesto e di gusti e mezzi sempre più urbani. Avanzano le aristocrazie provinciali e i sistemi lavorativi periferici. L'Italia settentrionale, la Spagna e la Gallia, l'Europa avanzata di allora, sono ormai diventati il centro economico dell'impero. L'Italia meridionale è persa da questo punto di vista e quella centrale slitta impercettibilmente in una condizione di semiperiferia. Più tardi sarà l'Africa a svolgere il ruolo principale, con un brusco movimento verso meridione dell'apice economico dell'impero. Il Mediterraneo si dimostrava in tal modo ancora più forte dell'Europa, tanto che l'Europa centro-settentrionale non diventerà mai il centro economico di questo sistema mondiale. L'opposto di quello che è avvenuto nell'Età moderna.

Nell'introduzione al XIV libro della *Storia naturale* di Plinio, dedicato alla viticoltura, si legge: 'chi non ammetterebbe che il condividere l'unità del mondo, resa possibile dalla maestà dell'impero romano, abbia fatto progredire le nostre condizioni di vita e ciò grazie alla circolazione delle merci, alla partecipazione alle gioie della pace e al fatto che quanto un tempo era riservato a pochi ora è accessibile a tutti?' L'Italia settentrionale, la Spagna e la Gallia partecipano ormai delle 'gioie' della pace, sono diventate il centro produttivo dell'impero e hanno quindi accesso al grande mercato prima riservato agli Italici. In una *Epistola* (8.2) di Plinio il Giovane i mercanti sperano in prezzi alti che non si verificano perchè sono qui i consumatori, il mercato concorrenziale, a dettare i prezzi e non più i produttori in condizione di sostanziale monopolio. L'Italia ha fatto da maestra all'Europa sua alunna. Ha reso seducente il grande mercato e ne ha innestato il desiderio, la capacità di affrontarlo, nelle menti dei provinciali più inciviliti. Ma garantendo pari diritti di accesso al mercato, Roma ha determinato la crisi del suo habitat, l'Italia, che non era stata allevata per resistere a un così ampio confronto concorrenziale.

Se vogliamo capire le ragioni di questa crisi Italica, meglio definendola di quanto non fossimo in grado un tempo, bisogna prendere la lente e guardare ancora una volta alle ville della Penisola, che erano le manifatture agricole di quel tempo. Con Traiano si consuma la decadenza dell'arboricoltura. Alcune ville si riconvertono, come Settefinestre, all'allevamento di schiavi e maiali, ma non riescono a sopravvivere oltre l'età antonina, ancora una volta come Settefinestre. Altre, invece, sopravvivono deperendo gradualmente nel corso del tardo impero. Se dovessi cercare un sintomo della crisi non tanto a livello della circolazione quanto a quello dei centri di produzione, quindi a livello delle ville, non sarei tanto alieno dal dar ragione a Plinio sul suo '*latifundia perdidere Italiam*', dando a *latifundia*, ardua impresa, un significato determinato.

E'stato dimostrato (si vedano R. Martin, *Recherches sur les agronomes latins et leurs conceptions économiques et sociales*, 1971) che nel I secolo d.C. si usava il termine *latifundium* per proprietà grandissime, ma anche per proprietà assai meno grandi. Ma se latifondo finisce per significare una qualsiasi azienda che non sia una piccola proprietà o possesso contadino, l'utilità di questa parola e del relativo concetto svanisce del tutto. Evidentemente fra le aziende di media dimensione dovevano esisterne alcune che non erano considerate latifondi ed altre che invece lo erano. E' possibile apprezzare questa differenza e, se è possibile, quale potrebbe essere la connessione tra la media proprietà latifondistica e la crisi economica dell'Italia? Sulla base delle ricognizioni topografiche di carattere sistematico svolte in Etruria siamo finalmente arrivati a capire che non esiste mai 'la' villa, ma una tipologia di ville basata sulla economia politica, che troviamo negli agronomi e che siamo riusciti a rinvenire sul terreno, analizzando le ville non in sé, ma in relazione ad eventuali case rurali e villaggi. I tipi fondamentali che siamo riusciti a identificare sono due, che ho chiamato 'villa centrale' e 'villa periferica'. Come vedete il tema centro-periferia immancabilmente ritorna. Quello che si è sperimentato prima di tutto nelle periferie di Lazio, Campania ed Etruria verrà poi sperimentato a raggio sempre più ampio nei successivi contesti periferici.

La 'villa centrale'è tipica della *suburbana regio Italiae* e delle altre zone di tipo centrale della Penisola. E' vicina a città, porti o grandi vie di comunicazione. Si trova su terreni fertili e in ambiente salubre. E' indirizzata verso colture intensive (le prime quattro elencate da Catone). I fondi non sono molto grandi. E' facilmente sorvegliabile dal proprietario. Usa precipuamente schiavi *soluti*, cooperanti fra loro, con rare integrazioni di coloni insediati in rare case coloniche satelliti. Si serve anche di *operae* esterne, ma solo quando proprio non può fare a meno. Tipiche ville centrali sono, ad esempio, quelle della Valle d'Oro nel Cosano, fra cui quella di Settefinestre.

La 'villa periferica' (assai meno conosciuta di quella centrale, anzi quasi del tutto sconosciuta) si trova solo nella *longinqua regio*. E' più lontana da città, porti e grandi vie di comunicazione. E' posta su terreni meno fertili e in condizioni meno salubri. Implica minori investimenti di capitale (per cui il settore capitalistico-commerciale è più ridotto). E' rivolta verso colture estensive (le ultime cinque elencate da Catone). I fondi sono più ampi (almeno quattro volte quelli delle ville centrali). E' più difficilmente sorvegliabile dal proprietario. Si avvale qualche volta di schiavi anche *vincti* alloggiati nella villa, ma precipuamente di coloni accolti in case rurali (come nell'Hebano) o in rare case rurali e soprattutto nel vicino villaggio (come nel Saturnino e nel Volterrano).

Più la villa è di tipo centrale, più l'agricoltura è separata dall'artigianato, che si trova incorporato nel villaggio di riferimento (il villaggio è una città in miniatura, ma più immersa nella sfera rurale). Più la villa è centrale, più è una struttura economicamente progredita, ma assai meno solida e duratura. Alle ville centrali va il merito essenziale della fortuna economica dell'Italia. Esse normalmente scompaiono in età antonina o più raramente si convertono in ville periferiche. Ad esse è legato il concetto di crisi italica. Le ville periferiche tendono invece gradualmente a sparire nel corso della tarda antichità e costituiscono l'aspetto della lunga durata. E' evidente che, man mano che le ville spariscono o diminuiscono, i fondi diventano sempre più grandi, fanno riferimenti a ville sempre più distanti e a direzioni aziendali sempre meno dirette. E' il risultato della *pulchritudo iungendi*. Scrive Plinio il Giovane in una *Epistola* (3.19): 'sono in vendita dei terreni vicini ai miei poderi, anzi addirittura incastrati in essi. Mi fa gola innanzi tutto la stessa soddisfazione dell'annettere, per la considerazione che non è meno utile che piacevole poter visitare entrambi i possessi con una stessa fatica ed uno stesso viaggio, amministrare con uno stesso *procurator* e quasi con gli stessi *actores*, attrezzare perfettamente e abbellire una sola delle due ville e l'altra mantenerla soltanto in buone condizioni'. Così il proprietario risparmiava in arredamenti, arnesi e personale. E' soltanto l'inizio di un fenomeno, che finirà per aggravarsi con il tempo: le seconde o terze ville, prima appena mantenute, finiranno poi per essere abbandonate, con conseguente accorpamento delle terre che da esse dipendevano.

La villa periferica non è meno antica di quella centrale (le tendenze estensive sono già della tarda repubblica). Ma mentre all'origine devono aver economicamente prevalso le ville centrali, a partire dal I secolo d.C., al tempo della villa Columelliana e Pliniana, devono aver prevalso quelle periferiche. Come che sia, le ville periferiche hanno sempre avuto fondi più *lati* e sono verosimilmente quelle che hanno continuato a durare, spegnendosi gradualmente nel corso della tarda antichità, il tempo tipico del latifondo. Nella lontana periferia, come nel meridione d'Italia, il fenomeno della dominanza della villa periferica deve essere stato ancora più vistoso. I due tipi di villa, sopra descritti grazie agli agronomi e alle ricognizioni, emergono chiaramente anche in un passo di Cicerone, *Pro Roscio*, 132-133: '(villam) *aptam et ratione dispositam se habere existimant, qui in Salentinis aut in Bruttiis habent, unde vix ter in anno audire nuntium possunt*', dove le ville per eccellenza periferiche della Penisola vengono confrontate per contrasto con quelle vicine e amene del suburbio di Roma, che abbiamo chiamato per convenienza centrali.

Se le ville centrali, cioè a dire pienamente schiavistiche, sono tipiche del *diligenter colere* - per questo furono prese a modello degli agronomi, che dedicano a esse la stragrande maggioranza dei loro sforzi normativi - allora, proprio per l'intensività delle loro colture, rotazioni e allevamenti, dovremmo tenerle distinte da quelle periferiche, dal carattere nettamente più estensivo e dalle proprietà considerevolmente più ampie. Ed infatti gli agronomi non definiscono mai queste ville 'classiche' come latifondo. Sarebbero invece le ville periferiche, cui gli agronomi riservano pochi cenni ma certamente molto diffuse, a rappresentare i *lati fundi* dell'Italia. Nel loro prevalere a scapito delle ville centrali è forse una importante ragione della decadenza economica della Penisola. Se poi è vero che è proprio la villa periferica ad essere stata replicata nelle province e che ad essa è principalmente dovuto il loro successo produttivo ciò significa che i provinciali hanno saputo usare tale strumento insediativo e produttivo in modo diverso, per le diverse condizioni sociali, politiche e ambientali, su cui non è qui il caso di soffermarsi. Si potevano impiantare in provincia manifatture artigianali e anche delle ville (Mazzei non impiantò forse una fattoria toscana presso Monticello in Virginia, che era la piantagione di Jefferson?), ma la traduzione in quei luoghi così diversi di queste invenzioni economiche dell'Italia finiva per implicare una loro adattamento, una loro trasformazione per cui finivano per apparire tutt'altra cosa.

Cercare di capire perchè le ville periferiche non funzionarono nella viziata Italia e funzionarono invece, una volta adattate alla nuova situazione, nelle attivissime province potrebbe essere un tema di ricerca interessante, che si potrebbe ora cercare di affrontare, per avvicinarsi al profondo mistero della riproduzione economica dell'impero Romano.

THE ETRUSCANS

EXPORTS NORTH OF ITALY

LEAVEN IN THE DOUGH: GREEK AND ETRUSCAN IMPORTS NORTH OF THE ALPS - THE CLASSICAL PERIOD

Brian B. Shefton

Department of Classics, The University of Newcastle, Newcastle upon Tyne

For Wolfgang Kimmig in gratitude

It is generally accepted that in the early fifth century BC there was a radical change in both the character and the ways of access of Mediterranean material to Europe north of the Alps. Broadly speaking it appears that a 'wine trade', proceeding via Marseilles up the Rhône valley into the western Hallstatt world during the last third of the sixth century, was superseded for reasons which we do not entirely understand by an Etruscan push through northern Italy across the Alps into the Rhine valley and beyond. This thrust is most clearly recognisable in the novel appearance *en masse* of Etruscan beaked flagons of bronze *(Schnabelkannen)* in the area of the middle Rhine, the Moselle and particularly in the Hunsrück range. This appreciation of a changed situation is surely broadly correct. We can however now look at the evidence provided by the southern imports in a more differentiating way than has been possible until very recently and it is really to this aspect that I propose to devote my attention in this paper.

The route across the Alpine passes must have been in use since very early times.[1] Yet there can be little doubt that the situation changed at the end of the sixth or early fifth century in the sense that this Alpine route became, perhaps for the first time, the premier and regular route by which southern luxury and prestige goods reached the North. This was most probably connected with the settlement of Etruscans in the subalpine regions north of the river Po.[2] Here the excavations near Mantua under the direction of Raffaele de Marinis during the past decade or so have opened up new perspectives.[3]

The route across the Alps is perhaps most clearly delineated by the distribution map of the beaked flagons, the Etruscan product which during the first half of the fifth century reached the North in the greatest density.[4] It is revealed not only through the finds of the flagons, but also through local imitations in bronze and clay. All this is nowadays common knowledge ever since the pioneer work of Paul Jacobsthal in 1929, work which was then continued by other scholars, notably Otto-Herman Frey in Germany and also Bernard Bouloumié in France. Less attention has however been paid to the fact that near the turn of the sixth and fifth centuries - and distinctly earlier than the main current which brought the beaked flagons - the presence of Etruscan prestige objects can already be discerned, objects which had evidently made their way through northern Italy and the Alpine passes into the French Jura range.[5] This presence is traceable as far as central France (Bourges) and perhaps even further north, if the reported provenance of Meulan, near Paris, is at all reliable. It is worth looking at the relevant material a little more closely.

What is available to us here is Etruscan material of considerable variety, all of bronze and, as far as we can judge, predominantly (but not entirely) produced in Vulci. There is the stamnos handle from the scrap metal deposit in Arbedo near Bellinzona (Ticino), at the southern end of the route to the St Gotthard pass, which has to be dated to the last quarter of the sixth century BC.[6] The next object going north is the small-sized Etruscan, surely Vulcian, amphora from Conliège (Jura) now in Lons-le-Saunier.[7] This important piece may still belong to the first quarter of the fifth century. Now as we move further west we find that the track of this new Etruscan surge inevitably crosses the older import route of the later sixth century up the Rhône and the Saône by which the Massaliote wine import and the connected imports of Attic black-figured vases reached inland into the Hallstatt world. This much is dictated by geography and nowhere is it more strikingly illustrated than in the princess's grave at Vix, below the Hallstatt hill fort of Mont Lassois in Burgundy (just north of Châtillon-sur-Seine). This grave, uniquely so far, contains precipitations of both import streams. The Attic Droop cup of about 520 BC[8] and the black Attic cup type C, which is datable to the end of the sixth century,[9] if not even a little later, are the precipitation characteristic of the wine import activity emanating from Marseilles and going upstream along the river valleys as far as Châtillon in the North and the Heuneburg on the Danube further east, a trade which can be traced not only through the Attic symposion pottery but also through Greek transport amphorae, which brought the wine to these destinations.[10] This Greek material is in the Vix grave associated with the new-fangled Etruscan imports (including an early beaked flagon) of the very end of the sixth century, which we take to have come over the Alpine passes.[11] We are here already at a period roughly contemporary with the Arbedo deposit and the amphora from Conliège. I have advisedly not mentioned here the great and much earlier bronze krater, for it represents yet another facet of the Vix grave to which we shall allude later.

We can consolidate this picture by other finds, all of them fragmentary, which belong to this same period and may be considered as part of the same phenomenon under review. There is the fragment of a bronze handle in London (Fig. 1) which is reported to have come from Bourges.[12] It once belonged to the collection of Léon Morel, Receveur des Finances, the nineteenth-century investigator of the Marne graves in the Champagne. This handle seems to me to have come from the same type of Vulcian amphora as the one from Conliège, even though the handle is not affixed to the neck of the vessel by the expected rivet, but by means of solder. Finally we ought to mention here the frequently cited bronze attachment from Meulan (Yvelines), a little downstream from Paris (Fig. 2). This attachment is kept at Saint Germain-en-Laye. Though considered by Jacobsthal, Frey and others including Bouloumié as belonging to some kind of vessel (stamnos-situla or oinochoe), it is in fact one of a pair of brackets serving as crest-holder on a Vulcian helmet of the early fifth century.[13] I understand from Alain Duval that the provenance of Meulan rests on the statement by the previous owner and there is of course no knowing how reliable that information is. Yet even if we regard the Meulan helmet with some caution - in any case it can hardly have been an import in the usual sense of the term - the picture emerging here of a series of Etruscan, largely Vulcian, imports of the latest sixth and early fifth centuries is of considerable interest and importance (map Fig. 5).[14] It shows that there was an overlap when, simultaneous with the latest wine trade emanating from Marseilles to penetrate the interior of the continent via the Rhône valley during the final Hallstatt period, we already have evidence which points to a new and systematic thrust of Etruscan import across the Alps and the Jura range into this same area of Burgundy (Vix) with a penetration further into the Northwest.[15] We do not know if these two streams, where they crossed, gave rise to rivalry and even conflict in the areas served simultaneously by Greek and Etruscan imports, each from a different direction.

It is now time to consider the well-known stream of Etruscan mass import to the Rhine, Mosel and Hunsrück areas which, as we hinted at, seems to be appreciably later than the first appearance of the Etruscan import just examined. This material has been studied for almost a century and we are bound to recall the great names of the past, Reinecke (who took the flagons to be Greek), Déchelette ('Italo-Greek'),[16] Jacobsthal and more recently the prematurely deceased Driehaus. We note the dense concentration of these flagons, but also the presence of Etruscan bronze basins of several varieties, some of which have been studied by Ulrich Schaaff.[17] Much rarer are the big bronze stamnoi, mostly of Vulcian origin. Yet the importance of these impressive vessels is out of proportion to their small number, seeing that there is a significant distribution of this shape both in Italy and north of the Alps, which can be considered together. Moreover, the chronology of these stamnoi has recently been clarified and they can therefore serve as markers, whose development and workshop affiliations can be surveyed over a period of almost two centuries.[18] Thus they serve as indicators of Etruscan import more reliably than the infinitely larger number of beaked flagons, which cannot as yet be classified or dated closely. Nor have the flagons in the north as yet been systematically linked with the finds in Italy. Here there is still work to be done, where Otto-Herman Frey and his school will, it is to be hoped, point the way.[19]

To judge by the presence of stamnoi north of the Alps, the Etruscan import is concentrated in the second quarter of the fifth century, with a noticeable decline in the third quarter. Beyond that there is silence. How far this pattern of development fits in with that of the imported beaked flagons we cannot, as we have just noted, at present say with any confidence.

I have already indicated the distribution pattern of the Etruscan beaked flagons beyond the Mediterranean basin, that is northern Italy, southern Switzerland, the scatter along the upper Rhine, followed by a leap north to the Moselle-Rhine confluence and to the Hunsrück in the West, where the quantity becomes very considerable indeed.[20] This is the great thrust northwards into the world of the Celts. This central thrust, to which we propose to devote our main attention, is flanked both in the East and in the West by lesser thrusts, in the East through Austria and Bohemia and in the West into France.[21] We should note that these two lateral penetrations, though they too are characterised by beaked flagons (in lesser quantities) and basins of bronze, also produce some southern material of a kind which has not so far been found in the central penetration.[22]

The distribution pattern of southern imports within the central area is now radically different from that which we knew earlier in the Hallstatt period. This is conditioned partly by the difference in approach routes, as we have indicated, but also by changes in the location and the power structure of the recipients. The major Hallstatt hill settlements with their evident centralised sway over sizeable surrounding areas, which had previously been the main destinations of the wine trade and the connected import of Attic black-figured pottery,[23] had in many cases ceased to exist. Instead a multiplicity of new, smaller centres more on a par with each other had taken their place and were situated in regions some distance away from the previous seats of power.[24] These new centres can be identified by a great number of relatively modestly furnished warrior-graves.[25] In the Hunsrück especially, the new concentration, clearly discernible in the distribution maps of the beaked flagons, has been explained by Jürgen Driehaus in terms of the exploitation of iron ore resources and the consequent wealth generated by this activity.[26] This development is usually put into the second quarter of the fifth century.

There are a number of particularly important finds which stand out from the somewhat monotonous homogeneity of beaked flagons, bronze basins and stamnoi.[27] They are also earlier than the second quarter of the fifth century. Here we have to mention first of all the Etruscan, Vulcian tripod from Bad Dürkheim and also the exceptional stamnos from the same grave.[28] Both are with the rest of what remains of the grave contents in Speyer - with some fragments pertaining to both in Budapest. The tripod belongs to the Vulcian group of outstanding pieces, which are found in some quantity within Etruria and are assigned to the early fifth century (Fig. 3a,b).[29] They are now scattered in many of the major collections, the Vatican, the Louvre, the British Museum, St Petersburg and elsewhere, not least in the United States. Only a few are from known excavated contexts, among them a fragment from the Athenian Acropolis and also, by chance, an intact one from a grave in Spina, now in Ferrara,[30] part of a rich grave of the advanced fifth century and therefore an 'heirloom' out of its proper chronological ambience. Seen geographically the Spina tripod is the closest neighbour to the one from Bad Dürkheim, together with one recovered by divers some years ago off the coast of southern France near Agde (Marseillan),[31] now in the Maritime Museum at Cap d'Agde. All these belong to the Vulcian group, but none apart from the Dürkheim tripod is known to have crossed the Alps.

The big stamnos from the same grave of Bad Dürkheim is early, still belonging to the first quarter of the century.[32] It is a particularly elaborate piece well beyond the norm of the stamnoi which were to cross the Alps subsequently (Fig. 4). It is clear that these exceptional objects are early imports to this region and should belong to the first wave of Etruscan goods reaching the region of the middle Rhine; they are contemporary with or only very little later than the stream of Arbedo, Conliège and the Etruscan elements in the grave inventory at Vix, which were crossing the Jura into France at the end of the sixth or in the early fifth century. Perhaps the Dürkheim pieces had taken the same route and subsequently gone downstream along the Moselle through Lorraine into the Rhine valley (cf. the map Fig. 5). Again contemporary with these, though not as splendid, is the early, Etruscan '*Plumpe Kanne*' now in Colmar, from Hatten in the Alsace a little north of Haguenau. Its significance was spelled out several decades ago by Otto-Hermann Frey.[33]

The more splendid pieces from Bad Dürkheim do not stand alone, for they are rivalled by the impressive pointed bronze amphora from Schwarzenbach (distr. Birkenfeld) in the Hunsrück, which, together with the famous openwork Celtic gold bowl,[34] was recovered from a grave in 1849 and is now kept in the Charlottenburg Antikenmuseum of Berlin. This bronze amphora (Fig. 6a,b) is commonly regarded as western Greek work. This was the opinion of Anton Neugebauer in his pioneering paper in the 1920s,[35] a view still widely accepted nowadays.[36] More recently, however, voices have been raised in favour of an Etruscan origin. The Schwarzenbach amphora has a number of close relatives, including the well-known one in the Vatican, and together they give several clues which point to Etruscan manufacture.[37] Most striking in this respect perhaps is the hitherto unpublished pair of handles from such an amphora in the Louvre, which should lend further support for this view (Fig. 7a-c).[38] The Louvre pair is in fact somewhat later and is likely to date well into the second quarter of the century.

All these three prestige items (and the *Plumpe Kanne* from Hatten) are singletons north of the Alps, very much in contrast to the homogeneity, noted already, of much of the later import. This special status requires explanation. I have elsewhere suggested that such prestige vessels at the beginning of new and significant enterprises can perhaps most plausibly be interpreted as 'introductory gifts' to local potentates on whose goodwill the future of such contacts would depend.[39] For the Vix krater and the cauldron of Hochdorf in the third quarter of the sixth century a similar view can be proposed. Then it was the very beginning of the wine trade and the accompanying Attic symposion pottery coming via Marseilles. Now these exceptional pieces are the immediate precursor of the mass importation of the Etruscan beaked flagons and other bronze vessels. Whether this trade was accompanied by wine import (in wooden casks or in skins, rather than in clay amphorae, which would have left evidence) or other perishable goods we cannot say.[40] What however must be stressed is that similar phenomena have been observed in other periods of antiquity. I quote Bondi, writing of the earliest Phoenician imports in the eighth and seventh centuries to primitive regions, '*I primi contatti sistematici fra Fenici ed élites locali furono caratterizzati ... dall'offerta di prodotti artigianali di pregio, il cui possesso divenne verosimilmente uno status symbol per i partners indigeni del commercio fenicio*'.[41] We cannot, incidentally, say that similar 'introductory gifts' have so far been identified among the material in the flanking streams, either East or West.

As we have remarked already we cannot unfortunately fix the date when the great flood of stereotypical Etruscan import goods, such as the beaked flagons, begins. Nor can we as yet determine the chronology of most of this material with assurance. However, a date early in the second quarter of the century will hardly be far off the mark. Perhaps we can find more precision by considering the stamnoi, whose chronology and workshop connections have been worked out in recent study.[42]

The earliest stamnoi north of the Alps, apart from the singular Dürkheim piece, belong to the second quarter of the fifth century, some of them perhaps quite late in it. The bulk of these imports consists of a number of vessels manufactured in Vulci. In the north they show a distribution in the latitude ranging from the northern bend of the Loire near Orléans to Stuttgart (Kleinaspergle) in the East.[43] The stamnos from Altrier in Luxemburg, near the Moselle, is an outlier to the North. These vessels tend in the North to serve as ash containers for cremated remains just as they frequently do in Italy,[44] though they were hardly imported for that purpose. In several instances, such as on the Kleinaspergle stamnos, the obvious traces of wear on the handles argue for extended use before they came into the grave, either as containers for the ashes or as banqueting equipment for the departed in the hereafter.[45]

We should add here in passing a few remarks on a puzzling feature in the distribution of these stamnoi, for we notice a surprising absence of finds between the Etruscan sites in Italy and those north of the Alps. This absence is in marked contrast to the almost linear continuity which we can observe in the distribution of the beaked flagons. I confess that I have no explanation to offer for this void in the evidence which occurs even in Italy north of the Apennines. There too there is a total absence of relevant finds.[46]

I should also add here that the two Etruscan stamnoi in the British Museum from the famous Basse-Yutz find near Thionville in Lorraine, though produced in workshops different from those of the Vulcian products so far mentioned, also belong to the same period,[47] that is to say the second quarter of the fifth century. Their findspot on the Moselle, a little north of Metz, really belongs to the same area as the Luxemburg stamnos from Altrier. This region then comes closest to showing a concentration of these stanmoi, particularly as the rather later stamnos from Weiskirchen, now in the Landesmuseum of Bonn, also comes from the same parts. The Weiskirchen stamnos[48] it should be said, is a later product of the same Vulci workshop which had earlier produced the Kleinaspergle Group, to which the bulk of the stamnoi found north of the Alps belongs. It is presumably the latest imported stamnos so far known in the area under review here and belongs well within the third quarter of the century.[49] Probably this same later period would also cover Alfred Haffner's finds at Bescheid, east of Trier, in the Hunsrück. Here there is a kyathos from a workshop in the mid-Tiber valley, and a beaked flagon of special shape with a lower handle-attachment, of a kind which is connected with stamnos attachments of the San Ginesio Group at an early stage, and should therefore date to near the end of the fifth century.[50] A close match to this handle, also from a beaked flagon and no doubt a product of the same workshop comes from Maurizio Gualtieri's excavations at Roccagloriosa (prov. Salerno) in southern Italy.[51]

Such pieces are late and rare witnesses to the by now declining material links between Italy and areas north of the Alps, in so far as they can be gauged through the imported material recovered. How are we then to assess the significance of this decline and subsequent cessation in the second half of the century? We do not know. What is certain, however, is that it was not caused by the cessation in the Etruscan centres of the production of prestige objects suitable for export to the North. A glance at the distribution map of the Weiskirchen Group demonstrates this clearly enough,[52] particularly since it represents products emanating from the same Vulci workshop which had fabricated the bulk of the earlier stamnoi in the North. The map shows that there was within Etruria an active production and distribution, of which however only one example reached the North, namely the eponymous stamnos from Weiskirchen, southeast of the confluence of the Moselle and Saar. It seems thus entirely justified to speak of a noticeable decline in the import of available Etruscan bronze prestige vessels after the middle of the fifth century, as by this time the flood of beaked flagons also appears to have subsided. Let us however recall once more that the chronological indicators provided by these flagons are by no means secure; nor do we know as yet how long and in what measure they continued in production in their homeland.

It is now time to step back a little from the material and reflect on the effect which such intensive import of goods from the South had on local art. Here after Jacobsthal, scholars like Otto-Herman Frey, Georg Kossack, Venceslas Kruta and, for the later periods of Celtic art, Martyn Jope have shown the way in the appreciation and analysis of these influences.

We know that the shape and decorative elements of the Etruscan beaked flagon made an impact upon local creativity. We allude here to masterpieces of Early Celtic art, and I hardly need to recall that we stand here at the birth and beginnings of the first sophisticated art in continental western Europe, the so-called La Tène art. We can witness, as it were, a direct and immediate influence of imported artefacts upon Early Celtic art at the time of its inception. Leaven from the south then in the dough of the north? One could quote the striking Celtic recreation of an Etruscan beaked flagon from Kleinaspergle.[53] However perhaps an even more significant example of the effect of imported pieces upon the creative urge of the local craftsman is provided by the Celtic flagon from Dürrnberg, just south of Salzburg,[54] possibly somewhat later than the Kleinaspergle piece. Here too the influence of the Etruscan model is plain to see, both in the small head, and in the Celtic wallowing in the decorative elements of the prototype which are here, in consonance with Celtic predilections, heightened to the *nth* degree.[55]

However, we must go beyond individual cases of direct southern influence upon specific Celtic objects, and note that there was an even more fundamental factor at play, namely the reception into the Celtic ornamental vocabulary of certain Etruscan motifs which possibly carried a magic content and which became known to the Celtic craftsmen through the imports from the South. Let us look once more at the handle-attachments of the Kleinaspergle Group of stamnoi, which were widely dispersed in the western Celtic area round the middle of the fifth century. The Etruscan eye motif on these attachments,[56] itself taken over from earlier Greek imports, was adopted in Celtic art. There it developed an autonomous existence in that it was transformed into a very important element of the Early La Tène ornamental vocabulary as the so-called 'bladder' motif.[57] This is, however, only one of many such motifs where the classical world can be shown to have provided the impulse,[58] though the means of transmission are not always as evident.

The foregoing enumeration of the import of Etruscan bronze vessels has by no means exhausted the inventory of what came to the North at this period. It would have been hard to encompass them all within the confines of this paper.[59] Nevertheless I take this opportunity to point to two important pieces of the second half of the fifth century which are perhaps less well known than some of those discussed so far. There is the interesting Etruscan bronze oinochoe shape 9 from Kappelen, south of Mulhouse and now in the museum there (Fig. 8a,b).[60] The shape is very Hellenic and is not unknown in the Aegean, even in Attic pottery. Examples in bronze, where it is not always easy to distinguish between the genuine Etruscan article and Greek work, even got as far as Macedonia, Sardis, Southern Russia, Colchis (Georgia) and Syria.[61] The Kappelen oinochoe is, however, the only one known for certain to have crossed the Alps. The second piece is the basin-handle in the shape of a pair of wrestlers from Borsdorf (Hessen), now in Darmstadt (Fig. 9a,b). This handle has recently been vindicated by Wolfgang Kimmig as a genuine find from a Celtic grave context.[62] We may recall that a related but appreciably later handle of the same shape comes from near Angers on the Loire.[63]

Without exception then all the bronze prestige objects under discussion here have turned out to be Etruscan. Not a single import can be shown to be Greek. They range from the splendid early 'introductory gifts' of the end of the sixth and early fifth centuries down to the sparse, yet still interesting - even outstanding - pieces in the final decades of the fifth century. Then, however, these imports appear to cease altogether.

If we look now at the pottery imports from the South during this same time-span the picture, to our astonishment, is totally different. Not a single piece is known to be Etruscan or Italic; they are all without exception Greek, though no doubt coming via Italy. There could be no more telling illustration of the availability of Attic decorated pottery in Italy as commercial objects used by non-Greek traders in their own dealings. What reached the North was Attic red figure, not in great quantities and predominantly cups or mugs. Paul Jacobsthal in a paper entitled 'Bodenfunde griechischer Vasen nördlich der Alpen' (1934) counted but seven pieces.[64] This number has increased only a little since then. However, the recent finds in Bourges are changing this picture considerably, at least for the western current of imports and we await their publication with great interest and expectation.[65] For the more central current let me take this opportunity to draw attention to some interesting fragments found during the last few years in Jörg Biel's excavations on the settlement site of Hochdorf, near Stuttgart. As an example I may cite the recently published fragment of a cup by the Marlay Painter (or the Lid Painter) (Fig. 10).[66] It belongs to a stemless cup with lozenge pattern on the outside and tiny silhouette figures under the handle, a pattern found in that Athenian workshop during the late thirties or perhaps rather the twenties of the century (cf. Fig. 11a-c).[67] In some ways this group is related to the St Valentin class of kantharoi of which a good example had been known from long ago in the Rodenbach grave now in Speyer.[68] The Hochdorf fragment actually raises an important and potentially critical point, as its nearest siblings are found in some numbers along the coastal sites of the Languedoc and the Gulf of Lions and also in Marseilles.[69] It could therefore serve to undermine our dogmatic insistence that the Attic pottery at this time came in its entirety across the Alps. But perhaps it is premature to draw conclusions from one piece, and the situation of the Stuttgart region may have its own special features.

With these pieces we have practically exhausted the spectrum of Attic pottery imported to the North during the fifth century, always setting aside the important new material from Bourges to which we have just alluded. With this proviso we may say that most of the material is of moderate quality and restricted to drinking vessels. The finest piece so far is perhaps a lip fragment, also a recent find from Hochdorf.[70] It is from a surprisingly thin-walled (therefore vulnerable) cup with a fine drawing of a peplos-clad woman (as she must surely be) running to the right, ungirt and thus exposing her bare flank, just like the girl on the Parthenon Frieze who passes the new peplos to the Archon Basileus.[71] The date of the fragment should be well on in the third quarter of the century.

What is so glaringly missing are the jugs (oinochoai), the jars (amphorae), the water-carrying vessels (hydriai), the basins for wine (dinoi) and the elaborately fashioned sophisticated mixing vessels (kraters) for the symposion which, during the preceding Hallstatt period, were so characteristic an import to the great centres on their hillforts, such as the Heuneburg on the Danube or Mont Lassois in Burgundy.[72] With the possible exception of the red-figured krater (?) fragment from Yverdon at the southern end of Lake Neuchâtel the contrast to the much greater availability of shapes during the Hallstatt period could not be more striking.[73] A greater egalitarianism of the society seems to have left its mark upon the range of imports and possibly upon their use too!

On the one hand, we have the bronze vessels, Etruscan throughout, available in some quantity - though in a limited range of stereotype shapes - during the first half of the century and a little beyond, but declining sharply in the second half, even though we encounter then some rare instances of shapes not hitherto met with in the North. On the other hand, we have the pottery imports, Attic throughout and mostly of the second half of the century, limited in quantity and range of shapes. What can be the significance of this astonishing and unexpected lack of congruity? Is it that in the early fifth century there was a direct contact between the Etruscan centres and the regions north of the Alps, even though the precise modalities of these contacts are as yet unknown? This direct contact brought the early Vulcian 'introductory gifts' to the north, then the stamnoi, the basins and the beaked flagons and a very small amount of Attic pottery. This Attic pottery seems to have had only a minor function in the choice of prestige or luxury imports, though evidently the owner of the Kleinaspergle set of cups thought otherwise![74] Perhaps he was an exception. This direct contact with Etruria decreased in the second half of the century and was redirected to the Italic centres north and east of the Apennines, that is Picenum and the Romagna. There are certain indications supporting such a scenario. Already in 1934 Jacobsthal showed that the closest parallels to the Attic pottery imported to the north were to be found in these areas, thus the St Valentin kantharoi. Also the later imported bronze vessels, the kyathos from Bescheid and the basin from Borsdorf, have their kin predominantly in Picenum, that is the Adriatic/north Italian regions east of the Apennines.[75] Such a hypothesis does not by any means solve all the problems and one will have to see how far future work will bring new insights here.

Is this now the end of our story? Yes and no. It does indeed seem that there is a gap of almost a century before another prestige bronze vessel from the south made its appearance. But this time the object was no longer Etruscan but Greek. I refer to the bronze situla in the Landesmuseum, Bonn from Waldalgesheim near Bingerbrück, and the confluence of the Nahe and the Rhine.[76] This famous princely grave also contained the gold torque which is eponymous for the Second Early Celtic, the Waldalgesheim style.[77] I have argued elsewhere that this situla does not originate in southern Italy, where it is almost universally placed in modern scholarship, but that it was produced in the Aegean Greek area, and that it is to be dated to the advanced fourth century BC.[78] I also attempted to show that situlae of this special technique had not only reached the area of the Marche of eastern Italy (Montefortino cemetery) but also Etruria, where they led to local imitations, even in pottery. It is therefore entirely conceivable that this Aegean Greek situla came to the north via Etruria, or at any rate northern Italy. Nor was it the only one *sui generis* in the north for we know of at least one other situla of the same technique which got as far as Keldby on the Danish island of Møn and is now in the National Museum in Copenhagen.[79] However there is no helpful grave context here and we can form no view as to how this piece came to the Far North. Did it get there secondarily after an initial arrival in the Rhine region?

The Etruscan element then has disappeared from the southern import of the fourth century directed to the central regions at any rate to which we have devoted our attention. Greek luxury products have displaced them, even if these were reaching the North via Etruria or at least northern Italy. We can hardly generalise from two objects only, but it looks like an astonishing development for which it would be good to have an explanation.[80]

I want to conclude by an observation which may possibly shed some light upon this problem. Inspection of the eponymous Waldalgesheim gold torque strongly suggests that its master knew Greek (and perhaps Etruscan) models for its ornamentation,[81] yet not as goods imported to the North but through familiarity acquired in the South, presumably in the celticised areas of northern Italy east of the Apennines. I take it that he had worked there for a time at any rate, a view also hinted at in other recent literature. An analogous case can be made out for the third important constituent of that same Waldalgesheim grave, the spout-flagon ('*Röhrenkanne*').[82] It seems to me that the dignified, hellenising face on its lower handle-attachment (Fig. 12) betrays familiarity with models such as the face on the handle-attachment of an Etruscan stamnos of the San Ginesio Group in its early phase (Fig. 13).[83] Contrast this classical face with that of the starkly grotesque mask on the fifth-century Kleinaspergle beaked flagon of Celtic production, inspired by an Etruscan model but worked in the North.[84] Now the crucial point is that to our knowledge no stamnos of the San Ginesio Group ever reached the area north of the Alps, but considerable numbers crossed the Apennines to precisely the Picene areas which were to see the Celtic settlement in the advancing fourth century BC.[85] It is thus by no means inconceivable that a Celtic metalsmith in this Celtic part of Italy would have gained familiarity with stamnoi of the Group, or similar representations of the human face, and taken his inspiration from there when he fashioned the Waldalgesheim masterpiece, either there or in the North after his return.[86] There are strong reasons then to think that much of the southern influence discernible in the North during the fourth century was no longer brought solely through the medium of imported artefacts, but rather through direct experience of the South in the South. If this is so, then the choice of what was to go North could easily have changed radically from what had gone there before, chosen as it had then been, if not also brought, by alien preference. But here we are still groping in the dark.

Postscript: Otto-Hermann Frey very generously looked over this piece, supplied me with additional references and also saved me from some errors. Elements of this lecture were also given in December 1992 in Speyer in connection with the exhibition of Masterpieces of Celtic Art (Catalogue Trier 1992). I am grateful to Dr Grewenig, the Director and Dr Sperber of the curatorial staff at the Historisches Museum der Pfalz for their invitation.

NOTES

1. Above all Pauli 1971 and now id. 1993, 163 ff. By implication for very early Italic material passing north across the Alps: von Hase 1989a, 1031 ff.; id. 1992; id. 1993, 189 ff. with maps. Cf. also Frey 1988a, 33 ff.; id. 1989, 5 ff. (both especially for the Iron Age).

2. It is usual in this context to refer to the establishment of Adria (though Attic imports had been getting there for two generations earlier!) and Spina at the head of the Adriatic as the crucial factors in the exploitation of the North and as the entry point for imports from the South. (Such a view is reflected in Pauli's various maps of cross-Alpine traffic at this period, for which most explicitly in Vienna 1992, 486 f. with plate volume 125-6 esp. figs. 3-4; and id. 1993, 166 figs. 42-3; cf. also id. 1988, 26 figs. 200, 202.) This must be true to a large extent, as seems certified by the rich presence in Mantua/Forcello of Greek transport amphorae for wine from a range of Aegean centres (summary of evidence in Malnati and Manfredi 1991, 234 - with bibl.). Were these then the naturalia destined for the North, of which otherwise no traces are left? Cf. also n. 40 below. All this however does not alter the fact that much of what went north across the Alps came direct from Etruria, rather than via the caput Adriae; cf. also Shefton 1989b, 217 n. 47; also id. 1988, 118 n. 40.

3. De Marinis (ed.) 1988a, I, 124 ff. (on Mantua); id. *et al.* ibid, 140 ff. (on Forcello) esp. 211 f. (on transport amphorae); 225 ff. (on Attic red-figure (Paribeni)). Cf. also De Marinis 1988b, 45 ff.; id. 1989, 27 ff. For a good illustrated selection of material from earlier seasons Moscati 1984, II, 50-3. In general also Malnati and Manfredi 1991, 228 ff.

4. Amongst the latest maps Frey 1989, 15 fig. 5; Kimmig 1983a, 41 fig. 32; id. 1988, 101 fig. 29 (the last map has entries also for imitations in clay); Frey 1988b, 15 fig. 191. The primary work was done in Jacobsthal and Langsdorff 1929 (Fundkarte).

5. See however also n. 15 below.

6. Shefton 1988, 108; 119 no. 7.

7. Conliège amphora: Lerat 1958, 89 ff.; id. 1962, 19 no. 128, pls. 7-10; Trésors 1987, 203 ff. - with bibl. also on the site (Roulière-Lambert); cf. also Steyr 1980, 12.34 (illustr); Kimmig in Vienna 1992, 318. The amphora with its internal neck sleeve belongs to a well-defined group with other examples in Hamburg (already cited by Jacobsthal and Langsdorff 1929, 48f. n. 3 no. 5), Copenhagen, New York, Rome (Villa Giulia) and an elaborate precursor in the Vatican (Raccolta Guglielmi). I shall have more to say on these elsewhere. I do not see the specially close connection with the Schwarzenbach amphora (here n. 34) advocated by Rolley 1982, 27 f. (note however his observations on the internal neck sleeve on the Vatican amphora; cf. also the description in Dohrn 1963 no. 686) and repeated in the catalogues

Trésors 1987, 203 and those of the recent Etruscan exhibitions in Paris, Grand Palais (1992) and in Berlin, Altes Museum (1993) under no. 325.

8.   Joffroy 1954, pl. 26, top; Steyr 1980, 12, 2 (illustr.).

9.   Joffroy 1954, pl. 25 below; profile of cup (with commentary) now in Rolley 1987, 415 f.; id. 1988, 100 fig. 9.

10.   See references in Shefton 1989b, 216 f. n. 43.

11.   The material also includes Etruscan bronze basins with characteristic handles, Joffroy 1954, pl. 28; Trésors 1987 nos. 138-39.

12.   British Museum (Prehistoric and Romano-British) ML 1620: Morel 1875-90, pl. 25, 2 'handle of oinochoe'. On Morel cf. Déchelette 1927, 527 f. n. 1. My suggestion that it belonged to a Conliège type amphora was first reported in Bouloumié 1986, 67 with n. 52. I am worried though by the absence of rivets which would have secured the internal neck sleeve.

13.   Musée des Antiquités Nationales, Inv. 8509: Jacobsthal 1944, I, 140; Frey 1960, 148 no. 114; Bouloumié 1978, 11 'oinochoe attachment' pl. 3, 5; id. 1986, 74 n. 79 'furniture attachment'. For this type of helmet attachment, Adam 1984, 114 f. (on no. 144). Seen in place on the helmet from Vulci, Tomba del Guerriero, now best in Proietti 1980, figs. 49-51. The Meulan attachment seems more slender, but has the requisite sharp angle where the upright finial turns into the attachment and accommodates itself to the descending slope of the helmet wall. For a good match in the Vatican, Guarducci 1936, 25 f. pl. 8, 11.

14.   Key to the 'Selective map of imported etruscan bronze vessels by periods' (Fig. 5) (note that apart from the case of Vix the standard beaked flagons and basins are not entered):
Squares mark Etruscan imports at the end of 6th and the first quarter of 5th centuries across the Alps and the Jura in the sequence South to North: Arbedo; Conliège; Bourges; Vix; Meulan, as they have been discussed in the text. This sequence is continued West to East by Schwarzenbach and Bad Dürkheim (twice) for the exceptional pieces to be discussed below. **Solid circles** mark the distribution of the Kleinaspergle Group stamnoi (second quarter and middle of 5th century). **Open circles** mark other groups of stamnoi of second quarter of fifth century (note 47). **Triangles** mark bronze vessels of second half of fifth century (West to East: Weiskirchen (note 48); Bescheid (note 50); Kappelen (note 60); 'Wiesbaden' (note 49); Borsdorf (note 62); Dürrnberg-Hallein.

15.   An overlap arising out of strong impulses across the Alps was already documented largely with epichoric material in Frey 1957, 243 ff. and more recently id. 1988a, 33 ff. with map 1 (Etruscan imports north of the Alps at the end of the Hallstatt period, including several of the objects discussed here and others not here treated).

16.   Déchelette 1927 also calls them Greek. An Etruscan attribution had however already been advocated in the nineteenth century, cf. ibid. 575 n. 3; also Szilágyi 1953, 424 ff. with n. 16.

17.   Schaaff 1969b, 187 ff., esp. 189 fig. 2; 192 fig. 3 (distribution maps). They are predominantly mid-fifth century and the third quarter. For other, somewhat earlier, basins cf. Adam 1993, 366.

18.   Shefton 1988, 106 ff.

19.   Meanwhile Frey 1984, 293 ff. also Dehn and Frey 1979, 495 f.; 503 (on some of the problems involved).

20.   The inventory of Etruscan imports to the North, not only beaked flagons, by Frey 1960, 147 ff., though inevitably no longer entirely up to date is still most useful; cf. also id. 1969, 85 fig. 49 (map); 115 ff. (for list of beaked flagons, including Italy). It is incorporated with additional material in the later list of southern imports in general: Schaaff and Taylor 1975, 312 ff., whence the map of bronze vessels of Etruscan origin in the north, Frey 1985, 239 fig. 2. See also the selective mapping of beaked flagons, inclusive of southern Italy and Carthage,

in von Hase 1989b, 380 fig. 32. A general map of Early La Tène 'princely tombs' with imported Greek and Etruscan objects also in Frey 1976, 147 fig. 7, which can now be supplemented by some few subsequent finds. For a wide ranging and densely documented panorama (now inevitably dated) of these phenomena in their Mediterranean context the classic study is Szilágyi 1953, passim.

21.   For the eastern flank also Bouzek 1985, 17 ff.; id. in Vienna 1992, 361 ff.; cf. also Pauli 1974, 116 ff. for the approach routes and the metal resources at the destination; cf. also Frey 1985, 245 for salt imports northwards along the same route. For the western flank see the series of studies by Bouloumié, and now for Bourges by Gran-Aymerich (n. 65 below). For the eastern flank in a wide context cf. Bouzek and Kästner 1988, 387ff (with bibl.). For the eastern flank now J. Bouzek and Z. Smrz, Drei Fragmente attischer Keramik aus Drouzkovice in Nordwestböhmen, *Germania* **72 (2)** 1994, 581-86. Ibid, fig. 6 shows the latest distribution map of mediterranean imports to Bohemia and adjoining regions. This embraces the area due north of Dürrnberg, beyond the Danube and thus complements our map Fig. 5 here very fittingly. The map also shows the provenances of the few and very fragmentary Attic imports (and the intriguing local imitation of a red-figured cup) found so far, probably all within the fifth century. For the only datable piece, the stemmed palmette cup from Kadan, see also Shefton 1989b, 217, n. 45 (with comparanda in datable contexts: second quarter fifth century). More in: author, *Heuneburgstudien* forthcoming, (Greek imports at the Heuneburg - with E. Böhr) nn. 56-58. These imports should presumably be considered together with the Castulo cup in Dürrnberg, grave 44/2; cf. n. 74 below.

22.   For specific examples cf. for the East the material in n. 80 below, for the West the Bourges material n. 65 below.

23.   For the literature on the 'Fürstensitze' cf. Shefton 1989b, 216 nn. 42, 44; the concept has been criticised, so Eggert 1989, 53 ff.; cf. also the discussion in Pauli 1993, 110f.

24.   This change, if not contrast, is graphically illustrated by a comparison of the site distribution on the maps, e.g. Kimmig 1990, 80 fig. 5 (Late Hallstatt princely seats) as against ibid. 79 fig. 4 (Early La Tène warrior-graves). The geographical disposition and spacing of the sites make the point on their own very tellingly! Cf. also Pauli 1993, 112 f.

25.   Warrior-graves: see the inventories in Jacobsthal and Langsdorff 1929 *passim*. The iron weapons in the graves have often left little for recovery by nineteenth century techniques, the time when the bulk of them were found. For recent excavation with the panoply of modern techniques e.g. Haffner 1992, 25 ff. (Hochscheid, Hunsrück).

26.   Driehaus 1965, 32 ff. For similar resources on the eastern flank see Pauli, cited in n. 21 above; also Frey 1985, 243 f.

27.   Cf. the lists in Driehaus 1966, 47.

28.   On the Bad Dürkheim find of 1864 now Frey and Polenz 1985, 263 ff. (s.v. Dürkheim); also Hallein 1980, no. 29 (Pauli). On the material in Budapest now, Szilágyi 1988, 390 ff. I 5 and I 6 (from tripod - with illustr.). Part of the figural handle of the stamnos is also there, id. 1979, 30, fig. 22.

29.   Speyer Historisches Museum der Pfalz inv. B99. Neugebauer 1943, 224 f. figs. 13-16 (before subsequent restoration in Mainz; for present state Hallein 1980 no. 29 with illustr. on p. 220); also Cristofani 1985, 238 illustr.; 239 commentary 8.12, 2 with bibl. For the type cf. the old studies by Riis 1939, 22 ff.; Neugebauer 1943, 210 ff.; Fischetti 1944, 9 ff. Many more have turned up since; cf. also S. Haynes 1985 no. 53 commentary, and bibl., to which add Jannot 1977 for interpretation of the mythological figures.

30. Aurigemma 1960, I, pls. 39-42; cf. also Malnati and Manfredi 1991, 226 ff.; fig. 55 (grave 128 Valle Trebba; tomb contents in part). The contents are predominantly third quarter of the fifth century, but the deposition, indicated by the latest objects, was in the last quarter.

31. Cap d'Agde: Gallia Information 1, 1987-8, 7 (Sète, Tour du Castellas); Fonquerle and Torelli 1986, 111 f.

32. Speyer, Historisches Museum der Pfalz. Dürkheim stamnos: Neugebauer 1943, 242 fig. 30 (shape); Jacobsthal 1944, pl. 253 top (handle). Shefton 1988, 108 n. 19, 136. (I take it that the handle pair, Dresden inv. ZV 30 42 comes from an earlier stamnos of the same kind, *Welt der Etrusker* 1988, 190, B7, 28-9, illustr.) The piece needs modern restoring, including the removal of the nineteenth-century base ring. Our Fig. 4 shows the nineteenth-century reconstruction by Lindenschmit.

33. Frey 1957, 229 ff.; cf. Steyr 1980, 12.25 (illustr.).

34. Gold bowl cage Frey 1971, 85 ff. Recent colour illustr. in Venice 1991 135. The Schwarzenbach amphora (Berlin Fr. 674): Gehrig *et al.* 1968, 95 (with bibl.) pl. 14, 2; Haffner 1976, pls. 145-6; Banti 1960, pl. 58 - excellent detail of drinking satyr on matching Vatican amphora; Banti 1973 pl. 45a - the same but inferior reproduction; Del Chiaro 1975-6, 79 ff., figs. 6-8. Detailed description in Neugebauer 1923-4, 365 ff.

35. Neugebauer 1923-4, 341 ff.

36. Thus Gehrig *et al.* 1968, 95 - 'South Italian': Heilmeyer *et al.* 1988, 8 f. no. 7 (on amphora) - 'South Italian'; but ibid. 294 f. (on Celtic gold from grave) refers to the amphora as 'Etruscan'; cf. also the summary of past opinions in Driehaus 1972, 341 n. 33 and the discussion with references to previous views in Riis 1941, 85 f. ('Vulcian').

37. Del Chiaro 1975-6, 75 ff.; Rolley 1982, 28 n. 29 (but cf. n. 7 above); cf. also Driehaus 1972, 328. The Schwarzenbach amphora belongs to a group of which the body survives only on this piece in Berlin and on the Vatican amphora from southern Etruria ('excavations in Vulci and Bomarzo 1834-1836'; cf. also Dohrn 1963, no. 686). (There is a closely related and intact piece, also with internal neck sleeve, Brit. Mus. GR 1976.5-1.1 (Bouloumié 1986, 66 f., figs. 5-6) but with simple double reed handles and palmette attachments; perhaps not Etruscan; cf. the bail amphora from Ukrainian Pishchanoye (= Peschanoye in Russian south of Kiev, Ganina 1970, fig. 37. For an evidently Greek amphora of related shape from Pishchanoye, cf. conveniently Galanina and Grach 1986, pls. 102-3; Fuchs 1978, 115 '460-450 BC' with pl. 22). There are however a number of detached handles, pairs and singletons, none with provenience, which clearly belong (list with illustrations in Del Chiaro 1975-6, 75 ff.). Of recent discussions an Etruscan origin has been argued in some detail by Krauskopf 1980, 8f.; cf. also Rolley (as above), while Adam 1993, 361 f. restates the case for manufacture in southern Italy (Magna Graecia or Campania; cf. also Vokotopoulou 1975, 134; 186 Nos. 19, 20). There is in fact on the analogy of the Campanian dinoi from Capua, much to be said for an Etruscan production in the southern dependency of Campania under the influence of nearby Greek workshops. However, there are powerful arguments for manufacture closer to Etruria proper. The shell motif as the finial below the squatting satyrs (vestigially seen on the Schwarzenbach amphora, more distinctly on other members of the group, such as the one in Boston) is a characteristic feature over a long time-span on bronze vessels which appear to have been produced in the mid-Tiber region cf. Krauskopf 1980 *passim*; Shefton 1988, 136 (thus: oinochoai shape 6 - Beazley, such as Newcastle University, Shefton Museum inv. 561 (loan Dr and Mrs Malcolm Weller); stamnos-situlae from Todi, Bendinelli 1917, 857 figs. 9-10; from Spina, Arias 1955, 152 f. figs. 90-91, cf. ibid. fig. 93). Note also its presence in Macedonia at Stavroupolis on an Etruscanising shape 6 oinochoe, Treasures 1980 no. 271 cf. Shefton 1985a, 287). This same motif is also found on the amphora handle pair in the

Louvre, here Fig. 7 and n. 38 below, which I take to be from the same workshop, but somewhat later. Here in addition to changes in the decorative elements the satyrs are replaced by frontal sirens with spread wings. These siren heads are clearly Etruscan, as is the rendering of the plumage, and the piece may already be mid-fifth century. With all this in mind it is difficult to detach the Schwarzenbach amphora from Etruria proper or its immediate vicinity. That these pieces are under an unusually direct Greek influence hardly requires demonstration. The frontally squatting satyr, thighs impudently parted without any inhibitions, is taken straight from Attic-vase painting, where he may have been introduced by Epiktetos (Cohen 1978, 411 f.; cf. also Hirschmann Collection 1982, 101, on no. 26 with references (Lezzi-Hafter)). For more Etruscan instances of the motif cf. an Etruscan strainer from Todi, Bendinelli 1917, 855, fig. 8. On Greek bronze vessels the invention tends to be modified with thighs positioned somewhat differently (cf. von Bothmer 1979, 63 ff., esp. 66 f.; pls. 18, 3; 22, 2; cf. also pl. 23; there also illustrations of some of the Greek models for the beading along the handle-shaft. So also the Hermitage oinochoe from Nymphaeum with a similar motif, Silant'eva 1959, 80 fig. 44, now also Galanina and Grach 1986, fig. 104). There is however at least one bail-amphora handle which shows at its lower end a satyr squatting much like the ones on our Etruscan amphorae, Rossbach 1889, 42 f. pls. 2,3, once Breslau University; cf. also Neugebauer 1923-4, 370. As to the Louvre siren the motif is commonplace on Greek bronze hydriae of the period, to a lesser extent on oinochoai too and occasionally also on amphorae (thus Venedikov and Gerassimov 1975, pls. 102. 104 - bail-amphora, Sofia from Rouets).

38.   I am most grateful to Alain Pasquier and Françoise Gaultier for photographs (phot. Chuzeville) and for permission to illustrate this important pair (Br. 4396 - 4397) 'ex coll. Baron de Turckheim; entered the Louvre 1965; no provenance; height 16.5cm.' (information F. Gaultier). See the preceding n. 37. (I append some observations on the originals made in 1982: the handles are very heavy; uncertain whether cast solid or filled with lead. The two rivets at the top are carefully pushed through the centre of the volutes; at the bottom they pass through the wings, where cold work assimilates them to the pattern of the plumage. The wing span is 9.5cm for 4396; 8.9cm for 4397.)

39.   For the notion of introductory gifts cf. Shefton 1989b, 218 n. 50 (with the Bondi quotation; note especially *Iliad* XXIII, 743 ff., cited in Shefton 1982a, 351 n. 37); id. 1987, 140; cf. von Hase, in Vienna 1992, 264 with nn.; also Morel 1992, 22.

40   For the probability of wine imports cf. Frey 1985, 252.

41.   See previous n. 40.

42.   See n. 18 above.

43.   See the map in Shefton 1988, 109 fig. 31, and here map Fig. 5.

44.   Shefton 1988, 119 no. 6 (Marzabotto); 121 no. 6 (St Geneviève-des-Bois); 122 no. 34 (Altrier).

45.   For traces of wear on the Kleinaspergle stamnos, Shefton 1988, 106.

46.   This applies particularly to the crucial Kleinaspergle Group; see map in Shefton 1988, 109 fig. 31. For the much less acute problem with beaked flagons, Kimmig 1988, 102 f.

47.   Now Megaw and Megaw 1990. For the attribution, Shefton 1988, 136 no. A1; 149 no. 1; for their date ibid. 136.

48.   Shefton 1988, 125 no. 6.

49.   For an unplaced stamnos without certain provenance in Wiesbaden, presumably from our area cf. Schaaff 1969a, 62 ff.; id. 1969b, 202 no. 13. It is also likely to date to the third quarter of the century.

50.   For the Bescheid finds, Haffner 1981, 17 ff. (kyathos from mound 9, a burial which is actually dated there to the mid-fourth century; cf. also n. 75 below).   More now in Trier 1992, 44, fig. 18 o; 26 fig. 1; 88 no. 12 (phot.) - kyathos.   Ibid. 78 fig. 17; 63 r. - beaked flagon; in general cf. Venice 1991, 160 ff. (Haffner).   For the San Ginesio Group of stamnoi, Shefton 1988, 113 ff.; 130 ff.

51.   Roccagloriosa (material in Pontecagnano).   For the rich tomb 6 and the flagon (inv. 48144), Gualtieri 1984, 307, fig. 9; id. 1993, 195 fig. 97 (view of attachment).

52.   Shefton 1988, 112 fig. 32.

53.   For the flagon now Kimmig 1988, 87 ff.; cf. also Trésors 1987, no. 233; Trier 1992, 124 fig. 2.   On the grave also Venice 1991, 178 f. (F. Fischer).   The mask on the lower handle-attachment is often illustrated, e.g. Venice 1991, 179 below; Hallein 1980, 77 fig. 2.

54.   Dürrnberg flagon, known since 1932: Jacobsthal 1944 pls. 184-6; cf. also Hallein 1980, no. 141 and above all Lessing's brilliant photograph in Kruta and Szabó 1979 pl. 28 (and pl. 56); Venice 1991, 171 (illustr.); cf. Megaw 1970, no. 72 (commentary); Kimmig 1988, 96 ff.; Moosleitner 1985 (monograph with good illustrations).

55.   For the Etruscan imports inspiring see e.g. Jacobsthal and Langsdorff 1929, pl. 2; 3 - lower row; 5 - head above stacked spirals.   Convenient assembly of relevant material in good pictures also in Schaaff 1971 pl. 11.   Note ibid. fig. 7 showing that the presumed Etruscan models for the Dürrnberg pattern were all found in the Rhine, Hunsrück, Moselle region.   Is this indicative of the original home of the Dürrnberg flagon?

56.   For the eye motif on the stamnos handle-plates and its Greek origin Shefton 1981, 117 ff.; id. 1988, 110.   The combination of satyr head and pair of eyes is confined to examples in the Kleinaspergle and the Weiskirchen Groups, the two groups of stamnoi available for inspection and copying in the critical areas north of the Alps!   Maps in Shefton 1988, 109 fig. 31, cf. also ibid. 112 fig. 32.   Examples of the eye motif are figured in Jacobsthal 1944, pl. 220a and d.

57.   Bladder motif: Shefton 1989a, 727; id. 1989b, 220 n. 57.   The Celtic adaptations include some of the best-known pieces of Early Celtic art (some of them conveniently gathered in Kruta and Szabó 1979, pls. 8 (Dürrnberg bronze face); 9 (Pfalzfeld stone pillar); 11 (Waldalgesheim spout-flagon attachment, see n. 82 below)), thus also the gold foil heads from Schwarzenbach, Venice 1991 136; Bescheid bronze pommel, ibid. 161.   It will be noticed that the eyes on the Etruscan stamnoi point upwards above the head on either side.   The Celtic master turned the outlines of the eyes upside down to hug the head, on either side too.   (The motif has been interpreted in Celtic terms as a crown of mistletoe for a deity, Kruta and Szabó 1979, 36; Hatt in Hallein 1980, 59 ff.; also Kruta 1989, 13 ff.; Frey 1993, 155 with references incl. Pliny *Nat. Hist.* XVI, 95.)   Examples could be multiplied and the question arises whether certain more developed motifs such as are found on the Berlin Schwarzenbach open-work gold cup (n. 34 above) can also be derived from this source; cf. somewhat differently Frey 1971, 85 ff. and Verger 1987, 287 ff., esp. 323 ff.

58.   Much of this in Jacobsthal 1944 and in studies by Frey and Kruta; cf. also Kossack 1993, 138 ff. esp. 147 ff. (elucidating the ornament in its own terms).   Note also Kruta's essay 'Etruscan influences on Celtic art' in the exhibition catalogue *The Etruscans and Europe* Grand Palais, Paris and Altes Museum, Berlin, 1992/3, 206 ff..

59   For a stimulating discussion of a wide range of these bronze imports and their reception, Adam 1993, 361 ff. - occasionally Roman-period imports are in the literature misassigned to the fifth-fourth centuries BC, thus Bouloumié 1983, 217 with pl. 5 (Clermont-Ferrand); also Guillaumet and Szabó 1985, 73 f. with figs. 4-6 (Chalon-sur-Saône, from the Saône near Tournus; can the handle really come from an amphora as claimed?); also the Roman-period

bronze oinochoe and aryballos, ibid. figs. 2-3 - I take these to be examples of the early Imperial Roman fashion for the 'classical' inspired by the 'Necrocorinthia' and the parallel finds at Capua and no doubt elsewhere.

60. Mulhouse, Musée Historique, Inv. 2281. Werner 1921, 31, fig. 2, 1 - find of 1910. For shape Weber 1983, 176 ff. (lists on 411 ff. - which do not include this piece). Distribution maps ibid. 181, 182. The Gorgoneion is close to British Museum GR 1867.5-8.724; Weber 412, b. 18.

61. Shefton 1985a, 287. For Georgia (Kobuleti-Pitchvnari), Kakhidze 1987, 47 ff., pl. 36; cf. also Shefton forthcoming c. For Syria (Al Mina) now Weber 1990, 445 no. 4. For 'possibles' in Slovakia and Hungary cf. Szabó 1988, 385 ff. figs. 8-9 (Abraham) and 10-11 (Szombathely) cf. Weber 1983, 417 d3; more sceptical view in Szilágyi 1965, 386 ff. with pl. 91, 1.

62. Darmstadt, Hessisches Landesmuseum inv. IV A.K. 18. Kimmig 1990, 75 ff., with list of related pieces (Gauer and von Freytag - Löringhoff). To the bibl. of the British Museum (warrior) handle add S. Haynes 1985 no. 153 (commentary) '400-350'. (The 'new' pair of handles in Cleveland, Ohio mentioned in Haynes' commentary had in fact been stolen from Bologna and has since been returned there - information Arielle Kozloff.)
Menke 1991, 389 f. ignoring any stylistic criteria, rather cavalierly makes the Borsdorf handle contemporary with the basin from Filottrano grave 2. Though the chronology of these basins and their handles is not as securely established as one would wish, I cannot follow this procedure. I agree though with his late date for the deposition of the Filottrano grave, which however contains much earlier material too and cannot be used for close dating of the Filottrano basin, as becomes evident from Shefton 1988, 149; id. 1989c, 100 (mistakenly referring to the warriors as wrestlers!) with n. 39. Menke's argument rests on thin ice. I have incidentally abandoned as unnecessary my guess (Shefton 1985b, 410) that the Borsdorf basin, though late fifth century in date, had not reached the north until the advanced fourth century.

63. On this group of basin handles Boucher 1986, 107 ff. with good illustrations of all of them (Borsdorf: 113, figs. 10-11; near Angers: ibid. figs. 8-9); to her bibl. of the Angers handle add Provost 1983, 211 ff.

64. Jacobsthal 1934, 18 did not know of, or chose to ignore, the few mid-fifth century red-figure fragments from Camp du Château, Salins, of which there are new pictures in Villard 1988, 336 figs. 4-5. They should have been added to his list, as they might well have come across the Alps and the Jura, unlike the earlier, black-figured material from the site. The published fragment from Weissenturm - Urmitz (Jacobsthal 1934, 17 no. 5 with fig. 1; Beazley 1963, 901 no. 6) is presumably fairly close in time and workshop affiliation. For these cf. Frey 1985, 249.

65. Meanwhile Gran-Aymerich 1992a, 345 ff.; id. 1992b, 28 ff. and this volume; id. and Almagro 1991, 315 ff. (some illustr.; attributions by J-J Maffre).

66. Stuttgart, Landesdenkmalamt, Baden-Württemberg. Biel 1991, 100 fig. 64.

67. Laon, Musée Archéologique Municipal. CVA Laon 1, pl. 50 (Here Fig. 11a-c). (Beazley 1963, 1279 no. 51 *bis* - Marlay Painter). cf. CVA Sèvres pl. 20, 1-3; 5; 8 (Beazley 1963, 1282 no. 12 - Lid Painter). CVA Los Angeles County Museum 1, pl. 39, 3 (Beazley 1963, 1279 no. 51 - Marlay Painter; Beazley Addenda [2], 357).

68. Rodenbach kantharos: Jacobsthal and Langsdorff 1929 pl. 40a; Hallein 1980, 219 no. 28 (illustr.). For a St Valentin kantharos with lozenge pattern all over, from Sasso Marconi (near Marzabotto) Malnati and Manfredi 1991, pl. 48, 4; another partially covered with lozenge

pattern from Este, Frey 1969, pl. 38, 2; more from Spina, Alfieri 1979, 58ff., figs. 134-5; cf. also ibid. fig. 138 (skyphos).

69. Jully 1983 II/1, 455, under no. 55 points out that these cups are not rare in the mediterranean Languedoc; cf. ibid. II., 2 pl. B 38, 55, 56 (Mailhac). Further references there include Montlaurès and La Monédière (Hérault). Jully 1973, 138 no. 448 (with commentary), pl. VI, 20; pl. 18, 6. Note also the fragment from Marseilles, Villard 1960, 30 n. 6; pl. 16, 18. There is also the inside fragment of a stemless cup possibly similar to the inside roundel of the Laon cup (here n. 67 above) from Bourges (Saint Martin-des-Champs); exhib. cat. Châteaudun 1985, 23 fig. 8 top left (to be rotated by 90° to the left!). I owe an extract of this catalogue to the kindness of Alain Duval. [=*RACentre* **24**, 1985, 103 fig. 1 (Ruffier and Troadec)].
   The Bourges material may however well have come via the Alps and the Jura ranges rather than the Rhône valley. In favour also of the Alpine route note the fragment from a lozenge cup, no doubt of our kind, in Mantua/Forcello, De Marinis 1988a I, 158 fig. 75d.
   We may too consider against the Rhône route some observations on the very restricted evidence for any pertinent traffic northwards along the mid-Rhône valley and further inland during the fifth century, cf. Bellon and Perrin 1990, 247 ff.; eid. 1992, 419 ff. esp. 425 with discussion on 475; also Flouest 1990, 253 ff.

70. Biel 1990, 93 fig. 53 top.

71. Robertson and Frantz 1975, East V 35 - (unnumbered) pls. 14, 17. On the question whether girl or boy on the Parthenon East frieze see now J. Boardman in *Kanon, Festschrift Ernst Berger,* Basel 1988, 9 f. (pro girl); contra: Chr. Clairmont, *ArchAnz* 1989, 495 f. (pro boy).

72. For this phenomenon note the reflections by Villard 1988, 333 ff.; cf. also Shefton 1989b, 216 ff. It will be recalled that Attic imports of the Hallstatt period tend to come from habitation sites, whereas during the fifth century they are found in both habitations and graves.

73. Yverdon: Kaenel 1984, 94 ff. fig. 3. A red-figured cup has also been hypothesised from a black lip fragment from the Marienberg, Würzburg (Zahn and Boss 1986, 21 fig. 6). More red-figure is claimed for the Münsterberg, Breisach, but there are no details available (Bender and Pauli and Stork 1993, 87). In all these cases the authors take the material to be late Archaic, associated with late black-figure pieces, therefore part of the Late Hallstatt 'wine trade' up the Rhône valley. In that case the material is of no direct relevance to our theme and the fact that there is some rare red-figure included is interesting rather than significant.

74. Now Boehr 1988, 176 ff. Note also Biel's 1990, 93 suggestion that the head on a cup fragment from the settlement site at Hochdorf had been specially saved. Thinking of the fine Attic black stemless cup from Kleinaspergle it is noteworthy and probably significant that no Castulo cups have so far turned up in this central sector, nor for that matter in the western flank, i.e. the interior of France. This is in interesting contrast to what happened in the eastern flank, where we find one in the princely grave Dürrnberg, Hallein tomb 44/2, Hallein 1980, 228, below left; Trésors 1987, 232 ff. no. 198. On Castulo cups Shefton 1982b, 403 ff.; id. forthcoming b. (See n. 21 above.)

75. For St Valentin kantharoi cf. some quantity indications for north-east Italy in Bouloumié 1978, 20; but they are not entirely unknown from the recent excavations in Milan either. For bronze kyathoi: Husty 1990, 7 ff. esp. 17 fig. 8 (distribution map). Borsdorf basin: note the basin with wrestlers' handles from Picenum, in Boston.

76. Waldalgesheim situla: Zahlhaas 1971, 115 ff. (with review of earlier opinions, but virtually ignoring the important contribution by Riis 1959); pls. 2-3; Schiering 1975, pls. 6-7. Hallein 1980, 85 fig. 21; 225 f. no. 34 (on the grave - Pauli; the full publication of the grave by Driehaus remains unpublished; see abstract in Jankuhn 1990, 247 ff.). Jope 1971, pl. 23

reproduces the originally published drawing, which renders the ornament very clearly. The publication is now in the hands of H. E. Joachim.

77.   Cf. also Jope 1971, 167 ff.

78.   Shefton 1985b, 399 ff.; 407 ('late in the third quarter of the fourth century'). Rolley 1987, 418 now suggests a Macedonian origin and operates with a general drift of Macedonian material across Celtic Europe, if I understand him correctly. For a reinforcement of the arguments for an Aegean origin of these situlae, Shefton forthcoming a

79.   Riis 1959, 17 ff. Zahlhaas 1971, pl. 4 (side A); Schiering 1975, pl. 4 (side B). Cf. Shefton 1985b, 407 ('quite late in the second half of the fourth century'); id. forthcoming a.

80.   There are though Etruscan imports on the eastern flank in fourth-century grave contexts, thus the Mannersdorf (Austria) situla Hallein 1980 no. 50; also Kruta 1988, pl. 209; cf. Frey 1985, 256. Another, a situla from the Salzach near Laufen is presumably earlier. (Heger 1973, 52-6 - excellent treatment; Hallein 1980 no. 42; Maier 1993, 204 fig. 170; cf. also Dehn and Frey 1979, 502; Frey 1985, 245. Its match though in the Ticino is apparently in a fourth-century context, so Heger 55 f..) On Mannersdorf also Venice 1991, 298 f. with illustr. (J-W Neugebauer). Bouloumié 1986, 70 considers the Mannersdorf situla as much earlier than the date of the grave. Note also Szabó 1988, 393 f. with similar conclusion.

81.   Waldalgesheim torque: For drawing of the ornament Hallein 1980, 85 fig. 20 (Frey); also Kruta 1988, 303, pl. 3B; Venice 1991, 202 (Kruta); colour picture of its cuff decoration: Duval 1977, figs. 70-1; Kruta 1988, 271 pl. 207; Venice 1991, 213 (Kruta). The related torque in the British Museum PRB 1930.4-11.1 : Jacobsthal 1944 no. 45; Duval 1977, figs. 109 (phot.) (here reproduced as Fig. 14); Kruta 1988, 303 pl. 3A; Venice 1991, 203, below (drawing and commentary - Kruta) makes the point even more cogently, always assuming it to be ancient. (Doubts have been expressed, and the piece is now being reexamined as Ian Stead informs me.) Note that Jacobsthal 1944, 87; 197 and subsequently Jope 1971 suggested that the Waldalgesheim torque's ornament was directly influenced by decorative elements of the Greek situla from the same grave, an idea also taken up by Frey 1976, 149; id. in Hallein 1980, 85, but rejected by others; thus Kruta and Szabó 1979, 46. In general note the discussion after Frey 1976, 160 ff.

82.   Bonn, Rheinisches Landesmuseum. Spout-flagon: Jacobsthal 1944, pls. 189-90; Kimmig 1988, 99 fig. 238 (profile drawing): fine photograph of the attachment by Lessing in Kruta and Szabó 1979 pl. 11; also Megaw 1970 pl. 78 (here Fig. 12); Venice 1991, 676 (illustr.): Trier 1992, 17 fig. 2, 5 (Frey). For the shape, Kimmig 1983, 44 f. with bibl. For the face as that of a Celtic deity, Kruta 1989, 18.

83.   Vienna, Kunsthistorisches Museum inv. 635. For the type Shefton 1988, 130 f. Nos. A4 - A11 [ours here = ibid. no. A7.] The long moustache of the satyrs on these attachments would naturally appeal in view of the Celtic habit of wearing theirs long too, cf. Diodorus V, 28, 3. If this juxtaposition (first suggested in Shefton 1989a, 728) is tenable it would argue for a date not later than the early fourth century for the flagon as against the much later date of the grave deposition, dictated by the imported Greek situla (for which see n. 78 above). Such an early date would be an interesting reversal of the common position where the imported object tends to be the relic from an earlier age. For the early dating of these spout-flagons Kimmig 1988, 97 f.; for the date of the Waldalgesheim piece Jacobsthal 1944, 143; also Megaw 1970 no. 78; Driehaus 1971, 102; also Frey 1976, 148, 158 - 'decoration is pure Early Style'; id. in Hallein 1980, 85.

84.   See n. 53 above; also the convenient juxtaposition in Trier 1992, 16 f. figs. 2, 5. In its hellenising features the face on the Waldalgesheim spout-flagon stands alone, as the contrast with the corresponding face on the Reinheim piece in Saarbrücken clearly demonstrates, Keller

1965, pl. 23; Megaw 1970, no. 73 (plates); cf. however Frey 1992, 260 with n. 151. For the Reinheim grave Hallein 1980, no. 33 (Pauli).

85. Shefton 1988, 114 fig. 33, 113 ff. esp. 115. The San Ginesio handle (ibid. 131 no. A9) shows that already quite early in the fourth century stamnoi of this group crossed the Apennines to the Adriatic side.

86. We recall the case of Helikon, the Helvetic Celt craftsman, who is reported by Pliny (*Nat. Hist.* XII, 5) to have been active in Rome ('fabrilem ob artem' (metal or wood)) presumably at about this time; cf. Köves-Zulauf 1977.

BIBLIOGRAPHY

Editor's Note: Superscript numbers indicate the edition of the volume.

Adam, A-M. 1984. *Bronzes étrusques et italiques.* Paris, Bibliothèque Nationale, Dept. des monnaies, medailles et antiques

Adam, A-M. 1993. Importation et imitation de bronzes mediterranéens en milieu celtique: quelques problèmes de méthode. *ArchMosellana* **2** (= *Actes XIe colloque AssFrEtudAgeFer*, Sarreguemines 1987) 361-73

Alfieri, N. 1979. *Spina.* Museo archeologico nazionale di Ferrara I. (Musei d'Italia Meraviglie d'Italia) Bologna

Arias, P. 1955. La tomba 136 di Valle Pega. *RIA*, n.s. **3**, 95-189

Aurigemma, S. 1960. *La necropoli di Spina in Valle Trebba.* Rome

Banti, L. 1960. *Die Welt der Etrusker.* Stuttgart

Banti, L. 1973. *Etruscan cities and their culture.* London

Beazley, J.D. ARV² 1963. *Attic Red-figure Vase-painters².* Oxford

Beazley Addenda² 1989. Additional references to ABV, ARV² and Paralipomena², compiled T.H. Carpenter *et al.* Oxford

Bellon, C. and Perrin, K. 1990. La circulation des amphores massaliètes dans la moyenne vallée du Rhône au VI - V s. av. J.-C. In, *Les amphores de Marseille grecque,* ed. M. Bats (*Etudes Massaliètes* **2**) 247-52. Lattes

Bender, H., Pauli, L. and Stork, I. 1993. *Der Münsterberg in Breisach II (Hallstatt und Latènezeit).* Munich (= *Münchner BeitrVoruFrühgesch.* 40)

Bendinelli, G. 1917. Tomba con vasi a bronzo del V secolo avanti Cristo scoperte nella necropoli di Todi. *MonAnt* **24**, 841-914. Rome

Berlin, Altes Museum 1993. *Die Etrusker und Europa*. Exhib. Cat. Paris and Milan

Biel, J. 1990. Fortsetzung der Siedlungsgrabung in Eberdingen-Hochdorf, Kr. Ludwigsburg. *Archäologische Ausgrabungen in Baden-Württemberg* 1990, 87-93

Biel, J. 1991. Weitere Grabungen in Eberdingen-Hochdorf Kr. Ludwigsburg. *Archäologische Ausgrabungen in Baden-Württemberg* 1991, 97-102

Boehr, E. 1988. Die griechischen Schalen (Kleinaspergle). In, W. Kimmig 1988, 176-190

Bothmer, D. von 1979. A bronze oinochoe in New York. In, *Studies in Classical Art and Archaeology. Festschrift P.H. von Blanckenhagen*, eds. G. Kopcke and M.B. Moore, 63-7. Locust Valley, N.J.

Boucher, S. 1986. Problèmes concernant une anse étrusque. In, J. Swaddling (ed.), 107-15

Bouloumié, B. 1978. Les stamnoi étrusques de bronze trouvés en Gaule. *Latomus* **37**, 3-24

Bouloumié, B. 1983. Les documents étrusques et grecs du Second Age du Fer en Auvergne et leur signification. In, *Le deuxième Age du Fer en Auvergne et en Forez*, eds. J. Collis, A. Duval and R. Perichon, 214-22. Sheffield and St Etienne

Bouloumié, B. 1986. Vases de bronze étrusques du service du vin. In, J. Swaddling (ed.), 53-79

Bouzek, J. 1985. Gli Etruschi e la Boemia. *StEtr* **53**, 17-25

Bouzek, J. 1992. Die Etrusker und Böhmen. In, *Vienna 1992*, 361-9

Bouzek, J. and Kästner, V. 1988. Der etruskische Norden und die Auswirkungen der etruskischen Kultur auf Mitteleuropa. In, *Die Welt der Etrusker*, Exhib. Cat. (East-) Berlin, Altes Museum, 387-9

Châteaudun 1985. Céramiques d'importation de Saint-Martin-des Champs, Bourges (Cher). In, *La civilisation gauloise en pays Carnutes,* Exhib. Cat. Châteaudun, 21-4

Cohen, B. 1978. *Attic bilingual vases and their painters*. New York

Cristofani M. 1985. *Civiltà degli Etruschi*, Exhib. Cat. Florence, Museo archeologico. Milan

De Marinis, R. 1988a. *Gli Etruschi a nord del Po²* (ed.). Exhib. Cat. Mantua

De Marinis, R. 1988b. Nouvelles donnés sur le commerce entre le méditerranéen et l'Italie septentrionale du VIIe au Ve siècle avant J-C. In, *Princes Celtes* 1988, 45-56

De Marinis, R. 1989. Problemi e prospettive della ricerca protostorica nel Mantovano. In, *Gli Etruschi a nord del Po*, ed. E. Benedini, Atti Convegno, Mantua 1986, 27-47. Accademia Virgiliana, Mantua

Déchelette, J. 1927. *Manuel d'archéologie préhistorique celtique et gallo-romaine IV. Second Age du Fer ou époque de La Tène²*. Paris

Dehn, W. and Frey, O-H. 1979. Southern imports and the Hallstatt and Early La Tène chronology of Central Europe. In, *Italy before the Romans: the Iron Age, Orientalizing and Etruscan periods*, eds. D. and F. Ridgway, 489-511. London

Del Chiaro, M.A. 1975-76. Archaic Etruscan amphora handles. *RendPontAcad* **48** [1977], 75-85

Dohrn, T. 1963. In, *Die päpstlichen Sammlungen im Vatikan und Lateran*, ed. H. Speier, (= Helbig, *Führer durch die öffentlichen Sammlungen klassischer Altertümer in Rom⁴* I) 518-19. Tübingen

Driehaus, J. 1965. 'Fürstengräber' und Eisenerze zwischen Mittelrhein, Mosel und Saar. *Germania* **43**, 32-49

Driehaus, J. 1966. Zur Verbreitung der eisenzeitlichen Situlen im mittelrheinischen Gebirgsland. *BJb* **166**, 26-47

Driehaus, J. 1971. Der Grabfund von Waldalgesheim. *HambBeitrA* **1(2)** (Frühlatène-Studien), 101-13

Driehaus, J. 1972. Der absolut-chronologische Beginn des frühen Latène-stils (LTA; Early Style) und das Problem Hallstatt - D3. *HambBeitrA* **2 (2)** (1978), 319-47

Duval, P-M. and Hawkes, C. 1976. *Celtic Art in ancient Europe: Five protohistoric centuries*. Colloquy Maison Française, Oxford 1972. London, New York and San Francisco

Duval, P-M. 1977. *Les Celtes* (coll. *'L'Univers des formes'*). Paris

Eggert, M.K.H. 1989. Die "Fürstensitze" der Späthallstattzeit. Bemerkungen zu einem archäologischen Konstrukt. *Hammaburg NF* **9**, 53-66

Fischetti, G. 1944. I tripodi di Vulci. *StEtr* **18**, 9-27

Flouest, J-L. 1990. Inventaire des amphores massaliètes des régions Berry, Bourgogne et France-Conté. In, *Les amphores de Marseille grecque*, ed. M. Bats (Etudes Massaliètes **2**) 253-8

Fonquerle, D. and Torelli, M. 1986. Le trépied étrusque et le mobilier d'accompagnement dans le gisement sous-marin de 'La Tour de Castellas'. *DialHistAnc* **12**, 111-21

Frey, O-H. 1957. Die Zeitstellung des Fürstengrabes von Hatten in Elsass. *Germania* **35**, 229-49

Frey, O-H. 1960. Importazioni etrusche dalla fine del VI a tutto il V sec. nei territori a nord delle Alpi. In, *Mostra dell' Etruria Padana e della città di Spina II*, Exhib. Cat. Bologna, 147-152.

Frey, O-H. 1969. *Die Entstehung der Situlenkunst*. Berlin

Frey, O-H. 1971. Die Goldschale von Schwarzenbach. *HambBeitrA* **1(2)** (Frühlatène-Studien), 85-100

Frey, O-H. 1976. Du premier style au style de Waldalgesheim. Remarques sur l'évolution de l'art celtique ancien. In, Duval and Hawkes 1976, 141-63

Frey, O-H. 1984. Zur Bronzeschnabelkanne von Besançon. In, *Hommages Lucien Lerat* I, 293-316

Frey, O-H. 1985. Zum Handel und Verkehr während der Frühlatènezeit in Mitteleuropa. In, *Untersuchungen zum Handel und Verkehr der Vor-und frühgeschichtlichen Zeit in Mittel- und Nordeuropa* I, eds. E Düwel *et al.*, 231-57. Göttingen

Frey, O-H. 1988a. Les fibules hallstattiennes de la fin du VIe siècle au Ve siècle en Italie du Nord. In, *Princes Celtes* 1988, 33-44

Frey, O-H. 1988b. I rapporti commerciali tra Italia settentrionale e l'Europa centrale dal VII al IV secolo a.C. In, De Marinis ed. 1988a II, 11-17

Frey, O-H. 1989. Como fra Etruschi e Celti: Rapporti con il mondo transalpino. *RivArch dell' Antica ProvDiocesiComo* **171**, 5-26

Frey, O-H. 1992. Zum Stil der Beschläge von Brno-Malomerice. In, *BerRGK* **73**, 247-60

Frey, O-H. 1993. Die Bilderwelt der Kelten. In, *Das keltische Jahrtausend*, ed. H. Dannheimmer and R. Gebhard, Exhib. Cat. Munich, 153-68. Mainz

Frey, O-H. and Polenz, H. 1985. In, *Reallexikon der germanischen Altertumskunde*[2] Vol. 6, 263-6. Berlin

Fuchs, W. 1978. Bronzegefässe in Kiev. *Boreas* (Münster) **I**, 113-15

Galannia, L. and Grach, N. 1986. *Scythian Art*. Leningrad

Ganina, O.D. 1970. *Antichni bronzi z Pishchanogo*. Kiev

Gehrig, U., Greifenhagen, A. and Kunisch, N. 1968. *Führer durch die Antikenabteilung, Staatliche Museen*, (West Berlin)

Gran Aymerich, J. 1992a. Les matériaux étrusques hors d'Etrurie. Le cas de la France et les travaux en cours à Bourges-Avaricum. In, *Vienna 1992*, 329-59

Gran Aymerich, J. 1992b. Un site princier à Bourges: Importations étrusques et grecques. *Les Dossiers d'Archéologie* No. 175 (Oct), 28-35

Gran Aymerich, J. and Almagro-Gorbea, M. 1991. Les fouilles récentes à Bourges et les recherches sur les importations étrusco-italiques. *BSocNatAntFr* 1991, 312-39

Gualtieri, M. 1984. Two Lucanian burials from Roccagloriosa. In, *Crossroads of the Mediterranean: papers delivered at the International Conference on the Archaeology of Early Italy at Brown University*, eds. T. Hackens, N.D. and R.R. Holloway, 301-32. Providence (R I) and Louvain-la-Neuve

Gualtieri, M. 1993. *Fourth Century BC Magna Graecia. A case study*, eds. M. Gualtieri and S. Bökönyi. Jonsered

Guarducci, M. 1936. I bronzi di Vulci. *StEtr* **10**, 15-53

Guillaumet, J-P. and Szabó, M. 1985. Sur quelques vases en bronze d'importation du Musée de Chalon-sur-Saône. In, *Les Ages du Fer dans la vallée de Saône* (= *Actes VIIe colloque AssFrEtAgeFer at Rully*, 1983), 71-6. *RAEst* 6th Supplement

Haffner, A. 1976. Die westliche Hunsrück-Eifel Kultur (= *R-G Forschungen* vol, 36). Berlin

Haffner, A. 1981. Ein etruskischer Bronzebecher aus einem keltischen Kindergrab des 4. Jhd v. Chr. Funde und Ausgrabungen im Bez. Trier 13 (= *Kurtrierisches Jb* **21**) 17-23

Haffner, A. 1992. Die frühlatènezeitlichen Fürstengräber von Hochscheid im Hunsrück. *TrZ* **55**, 25-23

Hallein 1980. *Die Kelten in Mitteleuropa*, ed. L. Pauli. Exhib. Cat. Hallein. Salzburg

von Hase, F-W. 1989a. Etrurien und das Gebiet nordwärts der Alpen in der ausgehenden Urnenfelder- und frühen Hallstattzeit. In, *Atti Secondo Congresso Internazionale Etrusco* (Firenze 1985) II 1031-51. Rome

von Hase, F-W. 1989b. Der etruskische Bucchero aus Karthago: Ein Beitrag zu den frühen Handelsbeziehungen im Westlichen Mittelmeergebiet. In, *JbZMusMainz* **36(1)** (1992), 327-410

von Hase, F-W. 1992. Etrurien und Mitteleuropa. Zur Bedeutung der ersten italisch-etruskischen Funde der späten Urnenfelder- und frühen Hallstattzeit in Zentraleuropa. In, *Vienna 1992*, 235-66

von Hase, F-W. 1993. Die transalpinen Beziehungern - Norddeutschland und Polen. In, Berlin, Altes Museum, 189-95 (equivalent section in Paris, Grand Palais 1992)

Haynes, S. 1985. *Etruscan Bronzes*. London

Heger, N. 1973. Ein etruskischer Bronzeeimer aus der Salzach. *BayrVorgBl* **38**, 52-56

Heilmeyer, W-D. *et al.* 1988. *Antikenmuseum Berlin. Die ausgestellten Werke. Staatliche Museen.* (West Berlin)

Hirschmann Collection 1982. *Greek Vases from the Hirschmann Collection*, eds. H. Bloesch, H.P. Isler and C.W. Hirschmann. Zurich

Husty, L. 1990. Ein neuer etruskischer Gefäßtyp aus der frühlatènezeitlichen Adelsnekropole Bescheid 'Bei den Hübeln' Kreis Trier-Saarburg. *TrZ* **53**, 7-54

Jacobsthal, P. and Langsdorff, A. 1929. *Die Bronzeschnabelkannen: Ein Beitrag zur Geschichte des vorrömischen Imports nördlich der Alpen.* Berlin

Jacobsthal, P. 1934. Bodenfunde griechischer Vasen nördlich der Alpen. *Germania* **18**, 14-19

Jacobsthal, P. 1944. *Early Celtic Art.* Oxford

Jankuhn, H. 1990. Waldalgesheim, Studien zum Problem frühkeltischer 'Fürstengräber'. In, *Gedenkschrift Jürgen Driehaus*, eds. F.M. Andraschko and W-R. Teegen, 47-9. Mainz

Jannot, J-R. 1977. Décor et signification: A propos d'un trepied de Vulci. *RA*, 3-22

Joffroy, R. 1954. Le trésor de Vix (Côte d'Or). *MonPiot* **48(1)**, 1-68

Jope, E.M. 1971. The Waldalgesheim Master. In, *The European community in later prehistory. Studies for C.F.C. Hawkes*, eds. J. Boardman, M.A. Brown and T.G.E. Powell, 167-80. London

Jully, J.J. 1973. *La céramique attique de La Monédière, Bessan, Hérault; ancienne collection J. Coulouma, Béziers. (Coll. Latomus vol. 124).* Brussels

Jully, J.J. 1983. *La céramique grecque ou de type grec et autres céramiques en Languedoc méditerranéen, Roussillon et Catalogne* (Annales Litteraires, Besançon). Paris

Kaenel, G. 1984. A propos d'un point sur une carte de répartition. *Arch Schweiz* **7(3)**, 94-9

Kakhidze, A. Yu 1987. Examples of ancient metalwork from Pitchvnari (Georgian with Russian summary). In, *Pamyatniki Yougozapadnoi Gruzii* **16**, 47-50. Tbilisi

Keller, J. 1965. *Das keltische Fürstengrab von Reinheim.* Mainz-Bonn

Kimmig, W. 1983a. Die griechische Kolonisation im westlichen Mittelmeergebiet und ihre Wirkung auf die Landschaften des westlichen Miteeleuropa. (= first Mommsen-Lectures cycle) *JbZMusMainz* **30**, 5-78

Kimmig, W. 1983b. Das Fürstengrab von Eigenbilzen. Neue Überlegungen zu einem alten Fund. *BullMusRoyauxArtHist* (Brussels) **54(1)**, 37-53

Kimmig, W. 1988. *Das Kleinaspergle; Studien zu einem Fürstengrabhügel der frühen Latènezeit bei Stuttgart.* Stuttgart

Kimmig, W. 1990. Zu einem etruskischen Beckengriff aus Borsdorf in Oberhessen. *AKorrBl* **20**, 75-85

Kimmig, W. 1992. Etruskischer und griechischer Import im Spiegel westhallstättischer Fürstengräber. In, *Vienna 1992*, 281-328

Kossack, G. 1993. Hallstatt- und Latèneornament. In, *Das keltische Jahrtausend*, eds. H. Dannheimer and R. Gebhard, Exhib. Cat. Munich, 138-52. Mainz

Köves-Zulauf, T. 1977. Helico, Führer der gallischen Wanderung. *Latomus* **36**, 40-92

Krauskopf, I. 1980. La 'Schnabelkanne' della collezione Watkins nel Fogg Art Museum e vasi affini. *Prospettiva* **20** (January 1980) 7-16

Kruta, V. 1988. I Celti. In, *Italia omnium terrarum alumna*, (coll. Antica Madre, dir. G. Pugliese Carratelli) 263-311

Kruta, V. 1989. La fibule 'à masque' de Port-à-Binson. *EtCelt* **26**, 7-22

Kruta, V. 1992/3. Etruscan influences on Celtic art. In, Paris, Grand Palais 1992, 206-13 (= Berlin, Altes Museum 1993)

Kruta, V. and Szabó, M. 1979. *Die Kelten* (pictorial documentation E. Lessing). Freiburg/Br.

Lerat, L. 1958. L'amphore de bronze de Conliège (Jura). In, *Actes du colloque sur les influences helléniques en Gaule, Dijon 1957*, 89-98. Dijon

Lerat, L 1962. In, *Catalogue des collections archéologiques de Lons-le-Saunier II (Les antiquités de l'Age du Fer)*, eds. J. Millotte and M. Vignard, (Annales Litteraires, Besançon), 19-21. Paris

Maier, F. 1993. Fernhandel und Kulturbeziehungen in der zweiten Jahrtausendhälfte. In, *Das keltische Jahrtausend*, eds. H. Dannheimer and R. Gebhard, Exhib. Cat. Munich, 203-8. Mainz

Malnati, L. and Manfredi, V. 1991. *Gli Etruschi in Val Padana*. Milan

Megaw, J.V.S. 1970. *The Art of the European Iron Age*. Bath

Megaw, J.V.S and Megaw M.R. 1990. *The Basse-Yutz Find*. London. Soc. Ant.

Menke, M. 1991. Borsdorf-Filottrano-Waldalgesheim. *Germania* **69**, 389-99

Moosleitner, F. 1985. *Die Schnabelkanne vom Dürrnberg. Ein Meisterwerk keltischer Handwerkskunst*. Salzburg

Morel, J-P. 1992. Marseille dans la colonisation phocéenne. In, *Marseille Grecque et la Gaule*, eds. M. Bats *et al.* (Etudes Massaliètes **3**) 15-25. Lattes

Morel, L. 1875-1890. La Champagne Souteraine. Châlons

Moscati, S. 1984. *Italia Ricomparsa II: Etrusca - Italica*. Milan

Neugebauer, K.A. 1923-24. Reifarchaische Bronzevasen mit Zungenmuster. *RM* **38/39**, 341-440

Neugebauer, K.A. 1943. Archaische Vulcenter Bronzen. *JdI* **58**, 206-78

Niemeyer, H.G. 1982. Phönizier im Westen. International Symposium *Die phönizische Expansion im westlichen Mittelmeerraum*, Cologne 1979 (ed.) (= *MB* vol. 8). Mainz

Paris, Grand Palais 1992. *Les Etrusques et l'Europe*. Exhib. Cat. Paris, Grand Palais, Réunion des Musées Nationaux, Paris. (Pagination and catalogue numbers as in Berlin, Altes Museum 1993)

Pauli, L. 1971. Die Golasecca-Kultur und Mitteleuropa. Ein Beitrag zur Geschichte des Handels über die Alpen. *HambBeitrA* **1(1)**

Pauli, L. 1974. Der Goldene Steig. Wirtschaftsgeographisch-archäologische Untersuchungen im östlichen Mitteleuropa. In, *Studien zur Vor-und Frühgeschichtlichen Archäologie* (Festschrift J. Werner) (= *MünchBeitrVorFrühgeschichte*, Supplementary vol 1), 115-39. Munich

Pauli, L. 1988. La società celtica transalpina nel V secolo a.C. In, De Marinis ed. 1988a II, 18-30

Pauli, L. 1992. Discussion contribution, in, *Vienna 1992*, 486-8

Pauli, L. 1993. See Bender, Pauli and Stork 1993

Perrin, F. and Bellon, C. 1992. Mobilier d'origine et de filiation méditerranéennes dans la moyenne vallée du Rhône, entre Alpes et Massif Central. In, *Marseille Grecque et la Gaule*, eds. M. Bats *et al.* (*Etudes Massaliètes* **3**) 411-18. Lattes

Princes Celtes 1988. *Les Princes Celtes et la Méditerranée*. Rencontres de l'Ecole du Louvre, Paris. La Documentation Française, Paris

Proietti, G. 1980. *Nuovo Museo Etrusco di Villa Giulia*, eds. M. Pallottino and G. Proietti and G.B. Battaglia. Rome

Provost, M. 1983. Une anse de chaudron étrusque à Sainte-Gemmes-sur-Loire (Maine-et-Loire). *Gallia* **41**, 209-15

Riis, P.J. 1939. Rod-tripods. *ActaArch* **10**, 1-30

Riis, P.J. 1941. *Tyrrhenika. An archaeological study of the Etruscan sculpture in the archaic and classical periods*. Copenhagen

Riis, P.J. 1959. The Danish Bronze vessels of Greek, Early Campanian, and Etruscan manufactures. *ActaArch* **30**, 1-50

Robertson, M. and Frantz, A. 1975. *The Parthenon Frieze*. London

Rolley, C. 1982. *Les vases de bronze de l'archaisme récent en Grande-Grèce*. Naples, Institut Français

Rolley, C. 1987. Deux notes de chronologie celtique. *RAEst* **38**, 415-19

Rolley, C. 1988. Importations méditerranéennes et repères chronologiques. In, *Princes Celtes 1988*, 93-101

Rossbach, O. 1889. *Griechische Antiken des Archäologischen Museums in Breslau.* (Festgruss Versammlung Deutscher Philologen und Schulmänner, Görlitz. Breslau

Schaaff, U. 1969a. Zwei etruskische Bronzegefässe aus der Rheinpfalz? *MittHistVerein Pfalz* **67**, 61-3

Schaaff, U. 1969b. Versuch einer regionalen Gliederung frühlatènezeitlicher Fürstengräber. In, *Marburger Belträge zur Archäologie der Kelten. Festschrift W. Dehn*, ed. O-H. Frey, 187-202. Bonn

Schaaff, U. 1971. Ein keltisches Fürstengrab von Worms-Herrnsheim. *JbZMusMainz* **18**, 51-117

Schaaff, U. and Taylor, A.K. 1975. Südimporte im Raum nördlich der Alpen (6 - 4 Jhd v. Chr.). In, *Ausgrabungen in Deutschland* III, 312-16. Mainz, Röm.-German. Zentralmuseum

Schiering, W. 1975. Zeitstellung und Herkunft der Bronzesitula von Waldalgesheim. *HambBeitrA* **5**, 77-97

Shefton, B.B. 1981. Das Augenschalenmotiv in der etruskischen Toreutik. In, *Die Aufnahme fremder Kultureinflüsse in Etrurien und das Problem des Retardieren in der etruskischen Kunst*, ed. W. Schiering (= Kolloquium, Mannheim in *Schriften des Deutschen Archäologen Verbandes* 5) 117-23

Shefton, B.B. 1982a. Greeks and Greek imports in the South of the Iberian peninsula. The archaeological evidence. In, Niemeyer 1982, 337-70

Shefton, B.B. 1982b. Discussion contribution. In, Niemeyer 1982, 403-5

Shefton, B.B. 1985a. Round table discussion 'le strutture del commercio'. In, *Il commercio Etrusco arcaico. Atti Incontro di Studio, Rome 1983*, ed. M. Cristofani, 285-88, 298. Rome

Shefton, B.B. 1985b. Magna Grecia, Macedonia or Neither? Some problems in 4th century BC metalwork. In, *Magna Grecia, Epiro e Macedonia. Atti 24° Convegno di Studi sulla Magna Grecia, Taranto*, 399-410. Naples

Shefton, B.B. 1987. Discussion contribution, to, '*Grecs et Ibères au IVe siècle avant J-C. Commerce et iconographie*'. *Table ronde Bordeaux 1986*. *REA* **89**,**(3-4)**, 134-8, 140

Shefton, B.B. 1988. Der Stamnos. In, W. Kimmig 1988, 104-52

Shefton, B.B. 1989a. Etruscan bronze stamnoi. In, *Atti Secondo Congresso Internazionale Etrusco (Firenze 1985)* II, 727-8

Shefton

Shefton, B.B. 1989b. Zum Import und Einfluss mediterraner Güter in Alteuropa. *KölnJbVFrühgesch* **22**, 207-20

Shefton, B.B. 1989c. The Paradise Flower, a 'Court Style' Phoenician ornament; its history in Cyprus and the Central and Western Mediterranean. In, *Cyprus and the East Mediterranean in the Iron Age*. 7th B.M. Classical Colloquium 1988 (dedicated to V. Karageorghis), ed. V. Tatton-Brown, 97-117. London

Shefton, B.B. forthcoming a. The Waldalgesheim situla: Where was it made? In, *Festschrift O-H. Frey*, ed. K. Dobiat. Marburger Studien zur Vor - und Frühgeschichte **16**, 583-93

Shefton, B.B. forthcoming b. The Castulo Cup: An Attic shape in black-glaze of special significance in Sicily. In, *Atti Convegno Internazionale 'I vasi attici ed altre ceramiche coeve in Sicilia' Catania and Camarina 1990*

Shefton, B.B. forthcoming c. Castulo cups in the Aegean, the Black Sea area and the Near East with the respective hinterland. In, *Proceedings of the 1990 Vani (Georgia) conference*. Besançon

Silant'eva, L.F. 1959. Necropoleis of Nymphaion (in Russian). *MIA* **69**, 5-107

Steyr 1980. *Die Hallstattkultur. Frühform europäischer Einheit*. Exhib. Cat. Schloss Lamberg. Steyr

Swaddling, J. (ed.) 1986. *Italian Iron Age Artefacts in the British Museum. Papers of the Sixth British Museum Classical Colloquium 1982*. London

Szabó, M. 1988. La vaiselle métallique dans la cuvette des Karpates à l'époque des princes celtes. In, *Princes Celtes* 1988, 384-96

Szilágyi, J.G. 1953. Zur Frage des etruskischen Handels nach dem Norden. *ActaAntHung* **1**, 419-57

Szilágyi, J.G. 1965. Trouvailles grecques sur le territoire de la Hongrie. In, *Le Rayonnement des civilisations grecque et romaine sur les cultures périphériques*, 386-90. (= 8th International Congress of Classical Archaeology, Paris 1983) Paris

Szilágyi, J.G. 1979. *Antik Müvészet*. Budapest, Szépmüvészeti Múzeum (Museum of Fine Arts)

Szilágyi, J.G. 1988. Catalogue entries. In, *Die Welt der Etrusker*, Exhib. Cat. (East-) Berlin, Altes Museum. Berlin

Trésors 1987. *Trésors des princes celtes*. Exhib. Catal. Paris, Grand Palais.

Treasures 1980. *Treasures of Ancient Macedonia*, ed. K. Ninou. Exhib. Cat. Thessalonike.

Trier 1992. *Hundert Meisterwerke keltischer Kunst. Schmuck und Kunsthandwerk zwischen Rhein und Mosel*. Exhib. Cat. Trier and elsewhere. Trier

Venedikov, I. and Gerassimov, T.D. 1975. *Thracian Art Treasures*. Sofia and London

Venice 1991. *The Celts*. Exhib. Catal. Palazzo Grassi. Venice

Verger, S. 1987. La genèse celtique des rinceaux à triscèles. *JbZMusMainz* **34(1)**, 287-239

Vienna, 1992. *Etrusker nördlich von Etrurien. Etruskische Präsenz in Norditalien und nördlich der Alpen sowie ihre Einflüsse auf die einheimischen Kulturen*, ed. L. Aigner-Foresti. Symposion Wien - Schloss Neuwaldegg. Akademie Verlag, Vienna

Villard, F. 1960. *La céramique grecque de Marseille (VI-IV siècle): essai de histoire économique*. Paris

Villard, F. 1988. Des vases grecs chez les Celtes. In, *Princes Celtes* 1988, 333-41

Vokotopoulou, J. 1975. *Chalkoi korinthourgeis prochoi: symvole eis ten meleten tes archaias hellenikes chalkourgias. (Athens Arch. Society Series* vol **82**). Athens

Weber, T. 1983. *Bronzekannen. Studien zu ausgewählten archaischen und klassischen Oinochoenformen aus Metall in Griechenland und Etrurien*. Frankfurt and Bern

Weber, T. 1990. Etruskisches Bronzegerät in Syrien. *AA* 435-48

Welt der Etrusker 1988. Exhib. Cat. (East-) Berlin, Altes Museum. Berlin

Werner, L-G. 1921. L'Age du Fer dans le Sud d'Alsace. *BullAComTravHist* 1921, 22-38

Zahlhaas, G. 1971. Der Bronzeeimer von Waldalgesheim. *HambBeitrA* **1(2)**, 115-29

Zahn, E. and Boss, M. 1986. Griechische Vasen auf dem Marienberg in Würzburg. *Mainfränkisches Jahrbuch für Geschichte und Kunst* **38**, 15-25

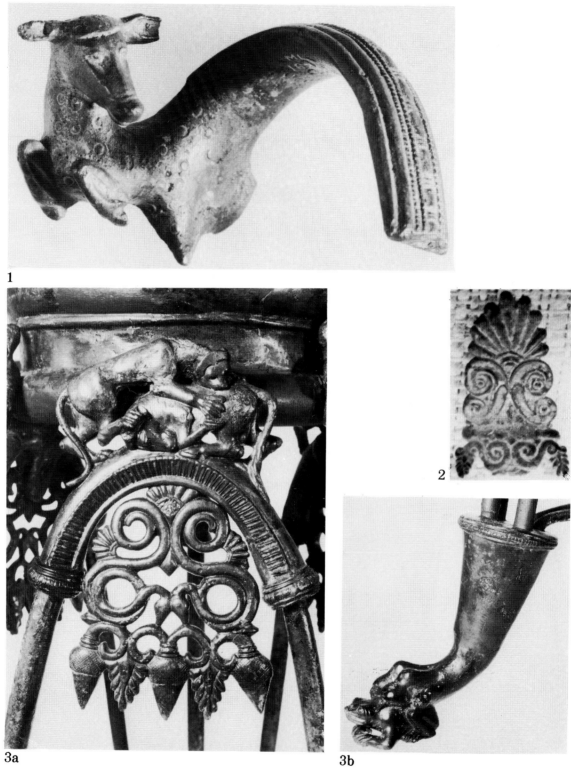

Fig. 1   Handle of bronze amphora 'from Bourges', Etruscan. London, British Museum (see note 12). Photo: courtesy of the Trustees

Fig. 2   Crest holder of bronze helmet 'from Meulan' (near Paris), Etruscan. Saint Germain-en-Laye, Musée des Antiquités Nationales (see note 13). Photo: author

Fig. 3a,b   Bronze tripod from Bad Dürkheim, Etruscan. Speyer (see note 29)
Photo: courtesy Römisch-Germanisches Zentralmuseum, Mainz

Fig. 4   Bronze stamnos from Bad Dürkheim, Etruscan. Speyer (see note 32). Photo: author

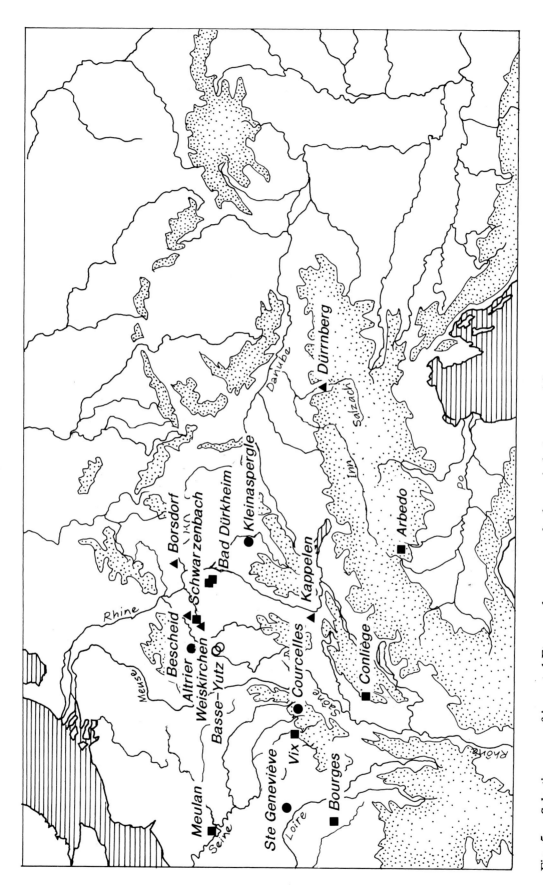

Fig. 5   Selective map of imported Etruscan bronze vessels, by periods (see note 14)

■ : imports at end of 6th - beginning of 5th century BC   ● : Kleinaspergle group of stamnoi - second quarter to mid-5th century

○ : other groups of stamnoi, second quarter 5th century   ▲ : vessels of second half of 5th century

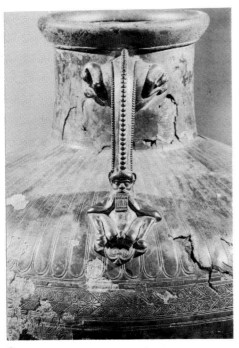

6a

6b

7a

7b

7c

Fig. 6a,b   Bronze amphora from Schwarzenbach, Etruscan. Berlin, Antikenmuseum (see note 34)
             Photo: Jutta Tietz-Glagow, courtesy Museum
Fig. 7a-c   Handle pair of bronze amphora, (shape as Fig. 6), no provenance, Etruscan. Paris,
             Louvre (see note 38). Photos: a) author; b) and c) Chuzeville, courtesy Museum

40

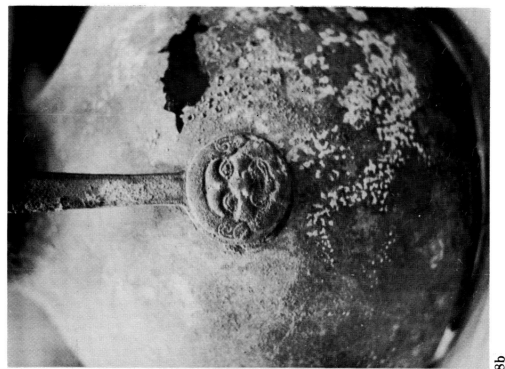

8b

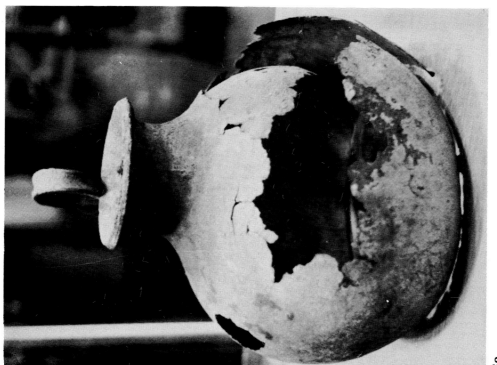

8a

Fig. 8a,b   Bronze oinochoe from Kappelen, Etruscan. Mulhouse (see note 60). Photo: author

41

9a

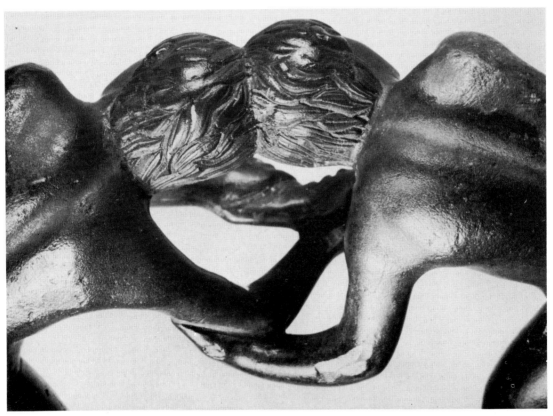

9b

Fig. 9a,b   Handle of bronze basin from Borsdorf, Etruscan. Darmstadt (see note 62)
Photos: a) author; b) courtesy of the Hessisches Landesmuseum

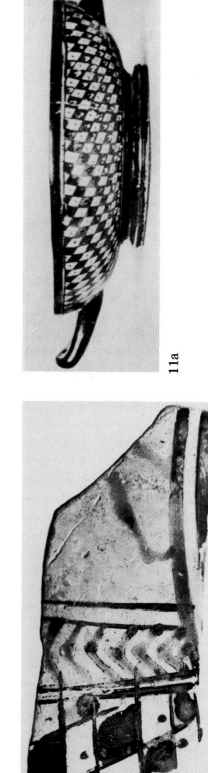

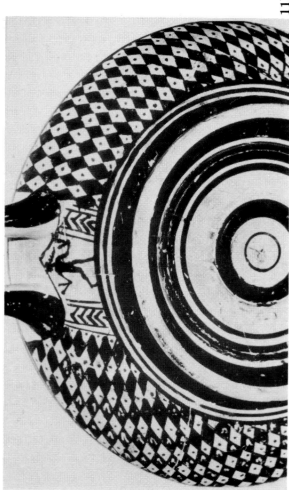

11a

10

11b 11c

Fig. 10   Fragment of cup similar to Fig. 11 from Hochdorf, Attic.   Stuttgart (see note 66).   Photo: courtesy of Landesdenkmalamt Baden-
Würtemberg

Fig. 11a-c Cup decorated by the Marlay Painter, no provenance, Attic. Laon (see note 67).   Reproduced from CVA Laon 1, pl. 50

43

12

13

14

Fig. 12   Lower handle attachment of bronze spout-flagon from Waldalgesheim, Celtic. Bonn, Rheinisches Landesmuseum (see note 82). Photo: Megaw, reproduced from Megaw 1970, pl. 78

Fig. 13   Handle of bronze stamnos, no provenance, Etruscan. Vienna, Kunsthistorisches Museum (see note 83). Photo: the author

Fig. 14   Gold torque, no provenance, Celtic. London, British Museum (see note 81) Photo: reproduced from Duval 1977

LES IMPORTATIONS ETRUSQUES AU COEUR DE LA GAULE: LE SITE PRINCIER DE BOURGES ET LES NOUVELLES DECOUVERTES A LYON ET BRAGNY-SUR-SAONE

Jean Gran-Aymerich

Département des Antiquités Grecques, Etrusques et Romaines, Musée du Louvre, Paris

Les recherches menées, à partir des années 1950, sur la tombe de Vix, les habitats du mont Lassois et de la Heuneburg, ou d'autres sites analogues, ont considérablement contribué à relancer les études sur les échanges entre d'une part les Etrusques et les Grecs, et d'autre part les peuples au nord et à l'ouest des Alpes. Les fouilles sur les rares ensembles du monde proto-celtique occidental à comprendre un habitat et ses nécropoles, par exemple le mont Lassois, la Heuneburg, ou Bourges (Fig. 1), confirment le caractère multiple des importations et des voies d'influences culturelles méditerranéennes, sur les centres de pouvoir d'une Europe en gestation, ouverte simultanément aux échanges continentaux et maritimes.[1]

Le centre de la Gaule est traversé par la Loire et par les voies qui relient son embouchure au couloir Rhône-Saône. Cette région Centre, que les anciens plaçaient au coeur de l'isthme gaulois (Fig. 1), constitue le verrou occidental de l'un des principaux réseaux de communication qui irriguent l'Europe: celui qui relie la façade atlantique au continent (échanges est-ouest), et au monde méditerranéen (échanges nord-sud). Ces longs parcours terrestres connaissent une phase d'intense activité, au Premier Age du Fer et au début du Second, et concernent les populations proto-celtiques et celtiques, ainsi qu'une partie du mouvement commercial et colonial étrusque et grec. La richesse des aristocrates locaux s'expliquerait par leur situation aux points de contrôle des voies terrestres, en particulier celles qui conduisaient à l'arc alpin et celles de l'axe Rhône-Saône.[2]

La présence sur la butte de Bourges, qui domine la confluence de deux affluents de la Loire, d'une résidence princière et ses nécropoles aristocratiques est suggérée par deux riches séries d'importations: d'une part, dans les tombes périphériques, les objets de parure ou les vases métalliques étrusco-italiques (Figs. 3-18); d'autre part, sur l'habitat, les amphores grecques de transport et les vases attiques de banquet (Figs. 19-29). La position de Bourges, au coeur de la Gaule, est exceptionnelle pour un habitat et des nécropoles aux caractéristiques identiques à celles d'autres sites importants du cercle hallstattien occidental. En effet, jusqu'ici, le mont Lassois marquait la limite occidentale des centres riches en importations méditerranéennes; aujourd'hui, il faut reconsidérer leur extension vers l'ouest, à la lumière des travaux récents à Bourges, et dans la nécropole de Gurgy près d'Auxerre (Fig. 1).[3] D'autres nouveautés importantes sont à signaler, en particulier la présence d'amphores étrusques de transport, ou de gobelets de Golasecca, à Bragny-sur-Saône près de Chalon (Figs. 30-32), d'amphores étrusques à Lyon (Figs. 33-35), ou de canthares en bucchero et ses imitations dans le nord du département de l'Ardèche, au sud de Lyon (Figs. 36-38).[4]

LES MATERIAUX ETRUSQUES AU COEUR DE LA GAULE

Les importations étrusco-italiques attestées au coeur de la Gaule, du 8ième au 5ième siècles avant J.-C., sont dans un premier temps en majorité des objets de parure, de toilette ou des armes (Figs. 3-8), puis des vases de banquet métalliques (Figs. 11-18): les tombes avec vaisselle de bronze étrusque se généralisent avec la fin du 6ième siècle, au moment où se confirme, pour les habitats, la présence d'amphores de transport marseillaises et de vases attiques liés au banquet aristocratique (Figs. 19-29). On décèle d'autres importations, comme le corail et l'ivoire, ou encore, parmi les denrées périssables, le vin et vraisemblablement les tissus.[5] Le monde des images fait irruption sur le continent, et joue un rôle important dans la formation du premier art celtique, de la fin de l'époque de Hallstatt au début de la première phase de La Tène.[6] On connaît le témoignage, discret encore et entravé par l'absence de contextes précis, des statuettes étrusco-italiques,[7] dont Bourges aurait peut-être livré un exemplaire du Mars italique nu (Fig. 10a,b). Plus sûrs sont les témoignages iconographiques des bronzes d'applique étrusques, tels que celui des protomes de l'amphore de Conliège, ou de l'anse du British Museum, qui vient de Bourges par la collection Morel (Fig. 9).

Les découvertes étrusco-italiques, au nord et à l'ouest des Alpes, se sont considérablement multipliées depuis les travaux pionniers de Henri Schuermans en 1872 et Hermann Genthe en 1874.[8] La corrélation entre importations étrusques et importations grecques s'est confirmée, de même que le rôle actif des populations proto-celtiques et celtiques, que Joseph Déchelette avait souligné dès 1909.[9] Dernièrement, les recherches dans les régions de l'axe de la Loire sont renouvelées, par la réévaluation des découvertes anciennes, et par l'apport des fouilles sur l'habitat de Bourges: ainsi W. Kimmig a-t-il ré-examiné la plaque de ceinture villanovienne du Musée Dobrée de Nantes, et J.-R. Jannot les fibules d'or à *sanguisuga* de Saint-Aignan, de la même zone de l'embouchure de la Loire;[10] l'épée à antennes de type tarquinien d'Amboise a été revue par G. Cordier, et R. Chevallier a inclus l'étude de l'oenochoé de Saint-Etienne-de-Chigny, près de Tours, dans son analyse de l'axe de la Loire, qu'il définit comme une 'troisième route de l'étain en Gaule'.[11] Enfin, les bronzes trouvés, en une extraordinaire concentration, à Bourges et dans ses environs, ont été l'objet des premières études d'ensemble. Le programme d'archéologie urbaine sur Bourges, engagé par le Service archéologique municipal, en étroite collaboration avec d'autres institutions dont le CNRS, fournit actuellement les preuves de la présence sur ce site d'un riche habitat proto-historique. Cette nouvelle résidence 'princière', avec importation de céramiques grecques de grande qualité, de la fin du Hallstatt et du début de La Tène (Figs. 19-29), vient compléter le panorama des tombes aristocratiques, découvertes au siècle dernier autour de la ville (Fig. 2), et qui ont livré les importations étrusco-italiques conservées à Bourges, Paris et Londres.

LES BRONZES ETRUSCO-ITALIQUES DE BOURGES

Dans un rayon d'environ 3km autour de Bourges, ont été localisées quatre concentrations de riches importations: à l'Est, dans les secteurs de la Route de Dun, aux Fonds Guaidons, et dans les Etablissements ou Quartiers militaires, dits aussi la Fonderie des Canons, se situe, à proximité immédiate de la ville, la zone funéraire la plus importante du Berry,[12] d'où proviennent au moins quatre vases étrusco-italiques de bronze (Fig. 2.B, Figs. 11, 14-16); au nord, dans le secteur de la Gare SNCF, ont été recueillis des armes et des objets de parure, dans un environnement fluvial marécageux (Fig. 2.C, Fig. 3), et, à une dizaine de kilomètres plus au nord, à Saint-Eloy-de-Gy, un fond de ciste à cordons (Fig. 17); au sud-ouest, dans le secteur de Mazières ont été signalées deux fibules à disque, dont une est conservée (Fig. 2.D, Fig. 5); plus loin, à Morthomiers et Le Subdray ont été trouvées une oenochoé et une ciste à cordons (Figs. 12, 18); au sud de Bourges, à Lazenay (Fig. 2.E), de nombreuses tombes et enclos cultuels ont été mis à jour depuis 1987, et offrent une continuité remarquable jusqu'aux nécropoles d'époque gallo-romaine: on note la présence exceptionnelle de céramiques d'importation, dans ce secteur hors de l'habitat.

Une fructueuse collaboration de notre équipe avec le Musée du Berry, le Musée des Antiquités Nationales de Saint-Germain-en-Laye, et des collectionneurs privées, a permis de réunir à Paris, l'important lot de bronzes étrusco-italiques de Bourges. De 1990 à 1992, des analyses ont été effectuées par le Laboratoire de Recherches des Musées de France, et conduites par Loïc Hurtel, sur

17 objets, parmi lesquels huit vases, cinq objets de parure ou toilette et une statuette conservés en France; il faut y ajouter l'anse du British Museum, que nous avons pu examiner à Londres en 1992.

1.   Oenochoé à long bec (*Schnabelkanne*) provenant de la tombe découverte, en 1849, dans les travaux de la route de Dun, face au Petit séminaire de Saint-Célestin (Fig. 2.B, 21). Conservée au Musée des Antiquités Nationales à Saint-Germain-en-Laye, inv. 49 511, (moulage déposé aux Musées du Berry à Bourges) (Fig. 11).

De cette tombe à incinération ont été recueillis un grand torque, plusieurs bracelets et des pendeloques, dont l'un représente un petit personnage accroupi en ronde bosse, avec nombreux parallèles connus dans le monde hallstattien.[13] Le principal mobilier est constitué par cette oenochoé et le stamnos-situle n. 4, avec restes d'ossements brûlés, que nous verrons plus loin. L'oenochoé a perdu l'anse et son attache inférieure, qui aurait permis de préciser le type et la chronologie. Par comparaison avec les deux autres oenochoés de Bourges, n. 2 et 3, ce vase a été daté du milieu du 5ième siècle, bien que le contenu de la tombe, de même que les petites dimensions de l'oenochoé, son profil ramassé et le col à nette tendance tronconique, suggèrent une chronologie plus ancienne, vers le début du 5ième siècle.[14]

2.   Oenochoé à long bec (*Schnabelkanne*) de la nécropole de Morthomiers, commune de Prunay, dans les faubourgs à l'ouest de Bourges. Conservée aux Musées du Berry à Bourges, inv. 950.1.269 (Fig. 12).

L'un des tumulus explorés en 1880 a livré, dans une tombe à inhumation, cette oenochoé. Les précisions sur son lieu de trouvaille, et son excellent état de conservation, avec l'attache du type à volutes, en font le meilleur jalon chronologique des trois exemplaires de Bourges. Cette pièce se situe vers le milieu du 5ième siècle.[15]

3.   Oenochoé à long bec (*Schnabelkanne*) de Bourges ou ses environs (sans précision). Conservée aux Musées du Berry à Bourges, inv. 892.25.2 (Fig. 13).

Achetée en 1894 par l'intermédiaire de L. Aufort, antiquaire à Bourges, auprès d'un ouvrier agricole; le vase présentait encore les traces d'extraction et de son séjour sous terre; l'objet pourrait provenir des tumulus de Dun-sur-Auron.[16] Cette pièce, peu commune par le registre de fleurs et bourgeons incisés sur le col, est à rapprocher de son double trouvé en Belgique, près de la frontière hollandaise, à Eigenbilsen, ou, à l'autre extrémité du monde hallstattien au Hradiste de Pisku; d'autre part, le 'déhanchement' au niveau de l'épaule se retrouve sur l'oenochoé des Bercias, dans le Puy-de-Dôme.[17] Les trois exemplaires de Bourges-Bercias-Eigenbilsen correspondent aux points extrêmes de la diffusion vers l'Occident de ces oenochoés étrusques.

4.   Stamnos-situle, de la même tombe que l'oenochoé n. 1, dans la nécropole de la route de Dun à Bourges. Conservé au Musée des Antiquités Nationales à Saint-Germain-en-Laye, inv. 49 512 (et inv. 49 512 pour les anses et leurs attaches, qui ne sont pas fixées au vase). Restauré en 1966 au Musée du Fer à Nancy (Fig. 14a,b).

Ce vase se caractérise par sa paire d'anses terminées en bourgeons, et les plaques d'attache ornées de palmettes simplifiées à 'tête de chouette'; à noter encore la finition du rebord en bourrelet, décoré d'incisions disposées trois par trois, selon le même schéma que sur le bassin à ombilic de la tombe de Vix. Il appartient au type C de G. Pomes, et a été daté, comme l'oenochoé n. 1 qui complétait le service, vers le milieu du 5ième siècle:[18] cependant, B.B. Shefton a tendance à rehausser la chronologie de ces stamnoi vers la première moitié du 5ième siècle, ce que semble confirmer le contexte du stamnos, presque identique, du grand tumulus V de Gurgy, dans les environs d'Auxerre.[19]

5. **Stamnos-situle d'une tombe de la nécropole des Fonds Guaidons, dans les faubourgs à l'est de Bourges.** Conservé aux Musées du Berry à Bourges, inv. 892.25.1 (Fig. 15a,b).

Ce vase a été recueilli avec des os calcinés, deux anneaux de bronze et une paire d'anses avec attaches, plus frustes et d'origine vraisemblablement locale.[20] L'objet est daté du milieu du 5ième siècle, et comme l'exemplaire de la Route de Dun, est à rapprocher du stamnos trouvé à Gurgy, près d'Auxerre. La présence d'os calcinés a été retenue comme preuve de son utilisation exclusive en tant qu'urne funéraire, sans rapport avec le service du vin, à la différence des pièces apparues dans la région rhénane.[21] Cependant, la déposition toute proche de la Route de Dun, qui associe clairement le même type de stamnos (n. 4) et une oenochoé (n. 1), contredit, ou du moins nuance, cette hypothèse.

6. **Anse torsadée de ciste à cordons, de la nécropole des Etablissements militaires, la Fonderie des Canons, à proximité des tombes de la route de Dun.** Conservée aux Musées du Berry à Bourges, inv. 907.49.1 (Fig. 16).

Plusieurs dépositions, considérées comme des tombes plates et datées du Hallstatt final à La Tène I-II furent mises au jour en 1868 dans ces faubourgs à l'est de Bourges. Ont été conservés, aux Musées du Berry, plusieurs torques, anneaux et boucles de bronze, parmi lesquels figure cette anse torsadée de ciste à cordons.[22]

7. **Fond de ciste à cordons du bois du Château-de-Dames, commune de Saint-Eloi-de-Gy, des faubourgs au nord de Bourges.** Conservée dans la collection de la Guère, à Bourges (moulage déposé dans les Musées du Berry à Bourges) (Fig. 17).

Ce fond de ciste, recueilli hors contexte dans le bois du Château de Dames, vers 1834, correspond à un vase de grandes dimensions, compte-tenu de son diamètre de 36cm.[23]

8. **Ciste à cordons, d'un tumulus du lieu-dit Le Chaumoy, commune de Subdray, à environ 12km à l'ouest de Bourges.** Conservée aux Musées du Berry à Bourges, invent. 950.1.276 (Fig. 18).

Ce vase complet provient d'un tumulus, exploré en 1889, et contenait des ossements non calcinés, humains et animaux mélangés.[24] D'un diamètre de 22,5cm, cette ciste à cordons fait partie des séries produites dans la zone du Haut-Adriatique (Vénétie-Istrie-Slovénie) au Hallstatt récent et final. Parmi les neuf exemples de ces cistes, que G. Stjernquist avait recensés en Gaule, trois font partie de notre lot de Bourges, auxquels il faut ajouter les découvertes récentes, comme celles de Gurgy près d'Auxerre.[25]

9. **Rasoir villanovien de l'ancienne prairie Saint-Sulpice, près de la Gare de Bourges.** Conservé dans la collection de la Guère, à Bourges (moulage déposé dans les Musées du Berry à Bourges) (Fig. 3).

Cet objet fut recueilli, vers 1888, dans un contexte marécageux,[26] dans le même secteur de confluence de l'Yèvre et de l'Auron que d'autres bronzes, comme une épée de bronze du type à langue de carpe du Bronze final ou un poignard à antennes du Hallstatt final.[27] Il s'agit d'un rasoir villanovien, semi-circulaire avec appendice et anneau de suspension, daté du 8ième siècle.[28] Parmi les très rares rasoirs villanoviens trouvés en Gaule, il faut citer l'exemplaire trouvé à Saint-Pierre-du-Lac, près de Nantes, et de cette même région, la plaque-ceinture villanovienne publiée par W. Kimmig, ou encore dans la basse vallée de la Loire, l'épée à antennes d'Amboise.[29]

10. **Fibule à arc cintré, et porte-ardillon court, vraisemblablement des environs de Bourges (anciens fonds locaux du musée, sans précision).** Conservée aux Musées du Berry à Bourges, inv. 906.4.264 (Fig. 4).

Cet objet, dont on ignore le lieu de trouvaille,[30] appartient à la période du Hallstatt ancien, 8ième siècle, avec parallèles dans la deuxième phase de la culture de Golasecca; le décor d'incisions obliques de l'arc imite les arcs torsadés des prototypes, et semble désigner l'objet comme une imitation nordique, peut-être locale.[31]

11. **Fibule à disque d'une tombe du faubourg Mazières, au sud-est de Bourges.** Conservée aux Musées du Berry à Bourges, inv. 907.47.20 (Fig. 5).

Dans une tombe à double inhumation, découverte en 1885, ont été signalés plusieurs objets en fer, cette grande fibule et une identique, mais plus petite, notre n. 12. Cette fibule, à double ressort et pied à disque, est du type italique largement attesté à Terni, qui survit jusqu'au 7ième siècle;[32] mais, l'absence de décor sur le disque, et la section carrée de l'arc, suggèrent une imitation du nord de la plaine padane, peut-être même du nord des Alpes.[33] Les fibules en général, et celles de type étrusco-italique en particulier, sont rarement attestées dans une déposition funéraire au Premier Age du Fer: dans leur bilan A. Duval, C. Eluère et J.-P. Mohen en ont recensé cinq exemplaires (dont les deux de Bourges), alors que trente-cinq fibules étaient signalées pour les dépôts et dragages, et six pour les habitats;[34] aujourd'hui encore, la découverte en milieu funéraire d'un objet comme la fibule de type italique à navicelle, dans le tumulus I de Colmar-Riedewihr, est un évènement exceptionnel.[35]

12. **Fibule à disque de la même tombe du faubourg Mazières que l'objet précédent.** Lieu de conservation inconnu.

Dans la tombe antérieure fut signalée la présence d'une deuxième fibule, identique à la première mais de dimensions plus petites.[36]

13. **Fibule serpentiforme de Bourges ou ses environs (sans précision).** Conservée aux Musées du Berry, à Bourges, inv. 906.4.263 (Fig. 6).

Fibule serpentiforme en bronze, avec son aiguille fermée dans l'étrier. De l'ancienne collection Lachaussée, trouvée dans les environs de Bourges, vers 1850.[37] Cette pièce et les deux suivantes identiques correspondent à l'un des deux types de fibule italiques les plus communs au nord des Alpes, pendant la période du Hallstatt ancien final, au 7ième siècle avancé.[38] Le second type, celui des fibules à arc cintré renflé, à *sanguisuga* ou navicelle, est représenté, dans le département du Cher, par deux exemplaires, peut-être de Bourges ou ses environs, conservés dans la collection Pouroy à Quincy. Le problème soulevé, depuis le siècle dernier, par les fibules étrusco-italiques de type serpentiforme ou à arc cintré renflé, découvertes lors de dragages dans la Saône à Lyon, ou dans la Seine à Paris, vient de rebondir, en 1991, grâce aux fouilles parisiennes de Bercy: dans un contexte du Hallstatt ancien assuré, où sont attestées des activités métallurgiques ou des échanges métallifères, révélés par la présence d'une barre-lingot d'étain, on a retrouvé une de ces fibules italiques à navicelle avec décor incisé.[39]

14. **Fibule serpentiforme probablement des environs de Bourges (sans précision).** Conservée aux Musées du Berry, à Bourges, 953.X.76 (Fig. 7).

Anciens fonds locaux du Musée.[40] Mêmes remarques typologiques que pour l'objet précédent.

15. **Fibule serpentiforme de Bourges ou ses environs (sans précision).** Conservée dans la collection de la Guère, à Bourges (moulage déposé aux Musées du Berry à Bourges) (Fig. 8).

Fibule serpentiforme en bronze; à remarquer que cet objet se trouve dans la même collection que le fond de ciste à cordons n. 7.[41] Voir les observations typologiques sur les deux pièces antérieures.

16. **Figurine en bronze d'un homme nu debout; provenant vraisemblablement de Bourges.** Achetée en 1892 avec un lot de bronzes d'origine locale. Conservée aux Musées du Berry, à Bourges, inv. 892.36.1 (Fig. 10a,b).

Le personnage de la figurine est représenté debout, la jambe gauche légérement avancée, les bras ouverts latéralement, l'avant-bras gauche replié à angle droit et le droit soulevé, dans le geste d'un lanceur de javelot; d'après l'orientation du poing, la hampe aurait été inclinée vers l'avant.[42] La figurine a été brisée au niveau des chevilles, puis soudée avec un alliage de métal blanc. Les analyses métallographiques effectuées au Laboratoire de recherche des Musées de France ne contredisent pas l'authenticité de l'objet. L'hypothèse de la découverte de cette pièce à Bourges s'insère dans le difficile chapitre des figurines étrusco-italiques en Gaule, sans contexte de découverte pour la plupart (voir note 7). Plus à l'ouest de Bourges, le dépôt de Thorigné-en-Charnie, en Basse-Loire, a livré plusieurs figurines d'origine étrusco-italique, de la fin du 7ième siècle.[43] Cette statuette trouve ses plus proches parallèles en Etrurie centrale, dans les bronzes tardo-archaïques de la fin du 6ième siècle et du premier quart du 5ième siècle.[44]

17. **Anse en bronze, avec attache plastique en forme de faon. Provenant de Bourges, et vraisemblablement d'origine locale.** Conservée au British Museum, ancienne collection Morel, inv. ML 1620 (Fig. 9).

Anse à section intérieure plane et extérieure torique, ornée d'un cordon lisse et deux rangées de perles, de chaque côté d'un bandeau central, où alternent oves et doubles traits courts. L'attache de l'anse est encadrée par deux protomes de faon ou daim, dont seul celui de gauche subsiste, de chaque côté d'un renfort central fini en bas par une pointe. Le rendu plastique de la figurine d'applique est de très bonne facture: les pattes avant sont repliées, le cou est svelte et la tête allongée, de composition triangulaire, marquée par les deux longues oreilles et le museau affiné; ce dernier, ainsi que les yeux, ont été soigneusement complétés au burin. Un semis de petits cercles estampés représente le pelage tacheté, sur le front, le cou et une partie de la surface interne de l'anse.

Cette trouvaille, rattachée à Bourges depuis son entrée dans la collection Morel, est demeurée presque inaperçue.[45] Nous avons pu examiner l'objet au British Museum, lors de ce colloque, et B.B. Shefton en a fait mention dans sa communication. Les anses avec attaches encadrées de protomes sont fréquentes sur les vases de bronze de la fin du 6ième siècle, et, dans les exportations au nord des Alpes; elles figurent sur des objets aussi précieux que l'hydrie de Grächwill.[46] Le parallèle le plus proche de l'anse de Bourges est l'amphore de Conliège, dont le traitement des protomes de chevaux qui encadrent les anses est pratiquement identique.[47] A l'amphore de Conliège et à l'anse de Bourges, qui pourrait appartenir à un vase de même forme, il faut ajouter, parmi les récipients en bronze trouvés au nord des Alpes, l'amphore pointue plus récente de Schwarzenbach, à Birkenfeld en Rhénanie, conservée à Berlin.[48] Parmi les amphores de bronze trouvées en Etrurie, les parallèles les plus proches pour l'amphore de Conliège sont l'exemplaire conservé à Hambourg[49] et celui du Vatican, venant peut-être de Vulci ou de Bomarzo.[50] L'ensemble de ces amphores a été daté dans la première moitié du 5ième siècle, et leur fabrication rattachée d'une manière générale à Vulci; mais on a remarqué que l'amphore de Conliège, et donc l'anse de Bourges, 'date encore du Hallstatt final', tandis que 'l'amphore de Schwarzenbach est de La Tène I'.[51] Il faut certainement considérer que 'ce sont les contextes celtiques qui datent les importations',[52] ou plutôt le moment de leur déposition; ainsi, pour l'amphore de Conliège les fibules qui l'accompagnaient dans le tumulus 6, 'à timbale et ressort bilatéral protégé par une feuille d'or, de type rare.. sont bien dans l'esprit.. du 5ième siècle avant J.-C.',[53] et c'est dans la première moitié du 5ième siècle que l'on peut situer la date de la tombe: cependant, la chronologie de fabrication de ces vases de banquet est bien entendu antérieure et le décalage entre la production et le dépôt final est certainement variable; B.B. Shefton, dans ce même colloque de Londres, a proposé de placer à la fin du 6ième siècle la chronologie, de production et de diffusion, de l'amphore de Conliège et de l'anse de Bourges. Cette datation, dans la fin du 6ième siècle, s'accorde avec celle qui est proposée pour des exemples trouvés en Etrurie, et récemment publiés, comme les deux anses de Cerveteri, conservées à Florence;[54] l'origine cérétane de ces derniers exemples permet d'ouvrir la possibilité d'une diffusion, sinon d'une production, non exclusivement vulcienne; cette piste est appuyée par le fragment d'anse de la même série, conservé au Louvre, issu de la collection Campana et provenant vraisemblablement de Cerveteri.[55]

LES VASES GRECS DE BOURGES

L'étude des céramiques grecques mises au jour, depuis 1984, par les fouilles de l'habitat de Bourges est d'une importance capitale pour le réexamen des importations étrusco-italiques dans les dépositions funéraires, et pour la compréhension globale du site.[56] Le programme d'archéologie urbaine sur Bourges a révélé, depuis 1984, neuf chantiers avec vestiges de l'habitat protohistorique antérieur à l'époque gallo-romaine (Fig. 2.A, 1-9); quatre de ces sites présentent des vestiges de la fin du Premier et du début du Deuxième Age du Fer, les céramiques grecques se trouvant en deux secteurs principaux: d'une part les chantiers Littré et Nation (Fig. 2.A, 1-2), d'autre part le chantier Saint-Martin (Fig. 2.A, 9). Le chantier intermédiaire des Jacobins (Fig. 2.A, 3) a livré des matériaux résiduels du Premier Age du Fer, et des fragments d'amphore de Marseille; le site extra-urbain de Lazenay (Fig. 2.E) a livré deux fragments de céramiques d'importation (attique et à vernis noir étrusco-campanien) en position résiduelle.

Les couches du Premier et du début du Deuxième Age du Fer explorées à Bourges sont encore d'une surface et d'un volume réduits, par rapport aux travaux réalisés à la Heuneburg ou au mont Lassois; cependant, la variété et la qualité, le nombre même des témoignages recueillis, placent dès maintenant Bourges au rang des plus importants sites princiers. A titre d'exemple: la Heuneburg aurait fourni environ 80 fragments de vases attiques et 120 fragments d'amphore de Marseille.[57] Tandis que pour Bourges les comptages, arrêtés à 1992 (ne comprenant pas les découvertes de la campagne de 1993 à Saint-Martin-des-Champs, qui a fourni de nouveaux témoignages d'importations), sont de 75 fragments attiques (correspondant à un minimum de 15 vases) et 47 fragments d'amphores grecques (correspondant à un minimum de 4 vases).

La céramique attique (75 fragments et 15 vases minimum)

Le taux de fragmentation et de dispersion des vases attiques est très élevé, et seuls quelques rares objets (comme la coupe à palmettes du chantier Littré, Fig. 19), auraient été fracturés à proximité immédiate de leur lieu de trouvaille.

Le style des figures noires est attesté par cette coupe à palmettes, trouvée dans le plus ancien horizon du chantier Littré. Le style à figures rouges est présent par un minimum de 5 vases pour les deux chantiers voisins de Littré-Nation (Fig. 2.A, 1-2), et 5 vases minimum pour le chantier de Saint-Martin, à l'autre extrémité de l'habitat (Fig. 2.A, 9), ainsi qu'un fragment en position résiduelle dans le chantier de Lazenay, hors habitat, au sud de Bourges (Fig. 2.E). Les fragments de vases à vernis noir, ou sans décor identifiable, représentent un minimum de 2 vases pour Littré-Nation et 1 pour Saint-Martin.

Les coupes à boire sont attestées, dans leurs différentes variantes (kylix à pied haut type B et C, canthare, skyphos, coupe à pied bas), dans toutes les phases des importations de vases attiques, de la fin du 6ième à la fin du 5ième siècle, et sur les deux secteurs principaux de l'habitat (Littré-Nation et Saint-Martin). Par contre, les vases hauts à col ou vases fermés (amphore, stamnos, hydrie, oenochoé) se retrouvent essentiellement concentrés dans la période 480-460 avant J.-C., et dans le secteur de fouille Littré-Nation (c'est à dire dans l'extrémité nord-ouest de l'habitat, Fig. 2.A, 1-2).[58]

La céramique attique de Bourges se caractérise par la haute qualité du décor des vases à figures rouges (plusieurs maîtres ou écoles sont identifiables),[59] par la variété des formes (kylix à pied haut, skyphos, coupes à pied bas, amphore, stamnos, canthare, vraisemblablement aussi hydrie, oenochoé) et par l'ampleur de l'éventail chronologique, du dernier tiers du 6ième siècle à la fin du 5ième siècle ou même le début du 5ième. Il faut remarquer la présence de formes fermées, comme le stamnos à figures rouges, bien attesté en Etrurie; ou de vases, aussi peu communs que la grande amphore à figures rouges (Fig. 28), pour laquelle l'Etrurie a livré la plus grande concentration d'exemples hors du monde grec, en particulier à Vulci et à Bologne: deux villes qui s'avèrent par ailleurs des points-clés pour la diffusion des vases de bronze étrusques, tels que l'oenochoé à long bec et le stamnos, du type bien attesté dans les nécropoles de Bourges.

Le plus ancien témoignage de vase attique à Bourges a été trouvé sur le chantier de Littré: il s'agit de la coupe à registre de palmettes sous la lèvre, '*floral band cup*', datée vers 530-520 (Fig. 19). Cette forme est bien attestée dans le contexte commercial continental, où elle est diffusée tant par le Haut-Adriatique et la plaine du Pô, que par le cercle colonial de Marseille dans le golfe du Lion. La première moitié du 5ième siècle est la période la plus représentée, pour les vases attiques à figures rouges, dans les chantiers du secteur Littré-Nation: ainsi le fragment, vraisemblablement d'amphore, décoré d'un homme imberbe drapé, qui fait face à un deuxième personnage dont restent les traces de la main et une canne (Fig. 26), oeuvre que l'on peut attribuer au peintre de Harrow, vers 480-470; un stamnos avec visages d'éphèbes (Fig. 27.a-f) se rattacherait à Cléophradès (vers 480-470), ou à un peintre proche comme Syriskos et le peintre de Copenhague; un médaillon de kylix avec tête coiffée de pétase (Fig. 20), de 470-460, serait de Brygos ou de son école. De Saint-Martin-des-Champs, provient un fragment de médaillon de kylix, avec les pieds d'un personnage masculin qui se rattache aux successeurs de Macron, vers 470 (Fig. 21). Parmi les pièces de Saint-Martin-des-Champs, qui couvrent la période du milieu à la fin du 5ième siècle, on remarque un vase à figures rouges, du type '*owl skyphos*', avec tête de chouette (Fig. 22), et plusieurs fragments d'un canthare de la catégorie de Saint Valentin (Fig. 23). Le dernier témoignage de ces importations de céramique attique est celui d'une coupe (peut-être deux) de la '*delicate class*' à pied bas, décorée à l'intérieur d'une double rosace incisée, du dernier quart du 5ième siècle ou début du 4ième siècle (Fig. 25).

Les amphores de Marseille (47 fragments et 4 vases minimum)

On observe également un très fort indice de fragmentation et de dispersion, avec un seul fragment d'anse et col assez grand, avec embouchure à lèvre repliée, de type Py 4, ou Bertucchi 2B, recueilli à Saint-Martin (Fig. 29a). Les pâtes sont de couleur jaune-rosé, de texture feuilletée et, dans la plupart des exemples, très fortement chargées en plaquettes de mica. Plusieurs fragments de panse, de bord et d'anse, ainsi qu'un fond, ont été recueillis dans les chantiers de Littré-Nation, les Jacobins et de Saint-Martin (Fig. 29b-d).

Amphores grecques sans identification précise

Dans le premier horizon du chantier de la Nation, ont été signalés deux fragments d'amphores de transport, à pâte rougeâtre et engobe blanchâtre extérieur, dont l'origine reste à déterminer.

Céramique á pâte claire peinte du Midi

Deux fragments ont été identifiés dans le chantier Littré, dont une écuelle à bord lisse légèrement rentrant, à pâte claire très fine, vernis rougeâtre et large bande rouge-noirâtre près du bord.

Céramique grise monochrome

Un fragment de panse provient du chantier de la Nation, d'un vase fermé de dimensions moyennes, à pâte grise fine, avec sillons de tournage à l'intérieur.

Céramique à enduit noir, sans identification précise

Trois fragments du chantier Littré et un autre du chantier Saint-Martin appartiennent à deux bols et deux vases fermés de petites dimensions. La pâte grisâtre est couverte d'un enduit noir, épais et satiné, sur les deux surfaces pour les vases ouverts et à l'extérieur pour les vases fermés, qui présentent des fines traces de tournage à l'intérieur.

La première céramique à vernis noir étrusco-campanienne

Après les dernières importations de céramique attique, attestées par la coupe à pied bas avec rosace incisée de la fin du 5ième ou le début du 4ième siècle du chantier de Saint-Martin (Fig. 25), aucune importation n'a été relevée avant le milieu ou la deuxième moitié du 3ième siècle, auquel correspond le plus ancien vase de céramique étrusco-campanienne, provenant du chantier Lazenay, campagne de 1991: il s'agit d'un fond de bol, décoré d'un double cercle guilloché, entourant des palmettes radiales à longues feuilles, avec au centre une estampille en croix portant l'inscription *NIKIA*. Ces séries de vases *NIKIA.ION*, attribués aux ateliers d'Ampurias ou Rosas, ont été amplement diffusés dans l'arc catalano-languedocien, et auraient pu parvenir jusqu'à Bourges par l'axe de la haute Loire, des importations de céramique grise ampuritaine ayant été relevées en Auvergne et jusqu'en Armorique.

SITES ET PHASES D'IMPORTATIONS ETRUSCO-ITALIQUES EN GAULE INTERNE

Dans la Gaule interne, ont été identifiés trois grands types de sites avec importations étrusco-italiques: les dépôts, isolés ou non, qui peuvent correspondre à des zones fluviales ou marécageuses, comme le site de la Prairie Saint-Sulpice, au nord de Bourges près de l'actuelle gare SNCF, à la confluence de l'Yèvre et de l'Auron. Les dépositions funéraires princières, avec ou sans résidence identifiée à proximité (les habitats explorés n'ayant fourni jusqu'ici que des témoignages d'importations céramiques grecques, et pas étrusques). Enfin, les sites de passage qui, comme Bragny-sur-Saône ou peut-être aussi Lyon, ne seraient pas des résidences aristocratiques mais des *emporia* ou relais sur les circuits de diffusion, et ont livré tout dernièrement des amphores de transport étrusques (Figs. 30, 33-35), et des gobelets de Golasecca (Figs. 31, 32) (voir note 4).

La diffusion des matériaux étrusco-italiques, au nord et à l'ouest des Alpes, connaît deux périodes principales, subdivisées de façon variable selon les régions. Les premiers contacts entre le monde hallstattien et le monde étrusque, de la fin du 8ième siècle au 7ième siècle, connaissent une première période d'échanges équilibrés, ou 'd'égal à égal', comme l'attestent dans le sens nord-sud les objets métalliques d'Europe centrale trouvés en territoire étrusque, peut-être aussi la présence d'artisans hallstattiens dans des villes étrusques comme Vetulonia, et, dans le sens sud-nord, la diffusion, de plus en plus intense, de produits étrusco-italiques en Europe continentale, dont témoignent tout particulièrement les objets métalliques. Dans cette première phase de diffusion de bronzes étrusco-italiques dans le continent, on remarque tout particulièrement les objets de parure et les armes: par exemple, les rasoirs semi-circulaires du type Benacci, attestés jusqu'en Gaule par les exemplaires de la forêt de Mulhouse et de Bourges; les épées à antennes de type tarquinien comme celle d'Amboise sur la Loire; les casques à crête tels que celui d'Armancourt sur l'Oise; les fibules serpentiformes comme celles de Besançon et de Bourges; les plaques de ceinture comme la pièce de Châtel-Gérard ou celle de Nantes; enfin, les premiers vases en bronze attestés par le biconique de Gerelinghausen, la pyxide d'Appenwhir en Alsace et les bassins côtelés comme ceux de Poiseul-la-Ville.

Une deuxième phase générale d'échanges se développe aux 6ième et 5ième siècles: elle correspond au témoignage de Tite-Live sur la première présence celte en territoire italique, maintenant partiellement confirmée par l'archéologie, qui semble révéler la présence de Celtes complètement étrusquisés en Etrurie (comme peut-être le *Katakina* d'Orvieto). Cette deuxième phase, d'intensification commerciale du sud vers le nord, est marquée par la diffusion dans les régions les plus lointaines, telles que le centre de la Gaule, de vases de bronze formant des services de banquet aristocratique: principalement les oenochoés, et les vases destinés aux mélanges et à la présentation de la boisson, stamnos et cistes à cordons, plus exceptionnellement d'autres éléments du service, tels que amphores, dinoi, louches ou simpula, bassins et trépieds.

LE VIN DU BANQUET ARISTOCRATIQUE ET LES VASES ETRUSQUES

Même si la tendance actuelle est à la réévaluation de la production des boissons alcoolisées locales dans le monde proto-celtique et celtique, il ne fait pas de doute que le vin a eu une place idéologique très importante dans les échanges du monde continental avec Grecs et Etrusques. Le vin, offert ou échangé avec les notables de la Gaule interne aux 6ième et 5ième siècles, par ses qualités spécifiques, mais aussi par son prix élevé, sa rareté, enfin par la parafernalia des vases de service importés avec lui des régions méditerranéennes, confère au repas collectif des chefs les caractères du banquet royal ou aristocratique. Ce vin venu de loin et la vaisselle de prestige sont des symboles d'ostentation et de pouvoir, qui évoquent moins peut-être le symposium grec que les fastes des monarchies orientalisantes.

La Gaule interne a livré un nombre important de vases de bronze utilisés pour le service de banquets aristocratiques, mais pas de vases céramiques étrusques, sauf dans le cas des toutes dernières découvertes de Lyon et de Bragny-sur-Saône (Figs. 30-38, et voir note 4). Par contre, de la Heuneburg sur le Danube, au mont Lassois sur la Seine et à Bourges dans le bassin de la Loire, la vaisselle de bronze étrusque des tombes princières apparaît en association étroite avec les vases céramiques attiques et les amphores marseillaises. Cette complémentarité entre vases métalliques étrusques et vaisselle céramique grecque mérite une étude approfondie qui ne peut être envisagée dans les limites de cette communication.

La plus forte concentration de vases céramiques étrusques (en bucchero, impasto ou céramique peinte) hors d'Italie se trouve dans le Midi de la Gaule, en particulier à Saint-Blaise et Marseille; des quantités importantes de vases ne semblent pas remonter la vallée du Rhône au-delà du sud de la région de Lyon. Le bucchero a été parfois signalé plus au nord, sur le site de Vix, sur l'habitat de Sion, dans les Vosges, et jusqu'à Bourges même, mais les références ont été jusqu'ici démenties. La présence de céramiques étrusques au nord des Alpes serait exceptionnelle, et n'a pas été certifiée dans un contexte de fouille. Cependant, du bucchero a été signalé sur le site de *Lauriacum*-Lorch, près de Linz, sur le Danube, et à Standz, près d'Innsbruck, ou encore, de manière plus fantomatique en Bohème, sur le cours du Danube ou à Koscielec au centre de la Pologne. Pour ce qui est des vases étrusco-corinthiens, sont à signaler, en dehors des pièces du cercle du Midi de la Gaule, deux cas: d'une part l'oenochoé trilobée du tumulus de Sticna, du groupe Dolenisko en Slovénie, qui contenait aussi des harnais en bronze proches de ceux du Circolo del tridente de Vetulonia; d'autre part, la très douteuse olpé 'étrusco-corinthienne' du Musée de Saint-Rémy, à Reims, de l'ancienne collection Payard, et portant la mention 'trouvé à Haguenau. Bas-Rhin', très sujette à caution. Cette absence de vases céramiques étrusques en milieu proto-celtique contredit l'hypothèse d'une influence des formes ou des techniques du bucchero sur les céramiques hallstatiennes locales. Les seuls témoignages connus, d'une influence des canthares en bucchero sur des productions locales internes, sont ceux des canthares en bucchero de Soyons et Bourg-Saint-Andéol dans l'Ardèche (Figs. 36, 37, et note 4), le canthare en céramique grise monochrome de Saint-Paul-Trois-Châteaux dans la Drôme (Fig. 38 et note 4) et l'anse de canthare en céramique grise de Chassey en Bourgogne.[60]

'MONDE CLOS, MONDE OUVERT?' LE CENTRE DE LA GAULE FACE AUX INFLUENCES EXTERIEURES

Christian Goudineau résumait récemment par cette alternative le débat sur le rôle des influences grecques et étrusques dans le Midi de la Gaule; reprendre ces termes pour les appliquer à l'hinterland n'est pas simplement reproduire la réalité des zones littorales: la situation, en cette époque charnière du 6ème au 5ème siècle, n'est certes pas la même pour les régions du Midi, en contact direct avec les colonies grecques et le commerce maritime étrusque, ou pour le monde continental, où les apports des centres littoraux sont relayés par de longs échanges terrestres qui subissent la concurrence des voies transalpines. La question des voies empruntées pour les échanges, ou bien par le Midi de la Gaule et le couloir Rhône-Saône, ou par les multiples voies de l'arc Alpin, ou encore selon les deux grands itinéraires simultanément pendant les périodes d'échanges les plus intenses, ne fait que relancer les problèmes de fond: quelle est la nature des échanges, distribution aléatoire ou concentration de biens de prestige dans les cours de petits royaumes, et quel est le degré de perméabilité technique et culturelle de ces régions continentales.

En Gaule, deux des installations du littoral les plus significatives pour l'importation de matériaux étrusques sont Marseille et Saint-Blaise, tandis que pour les sites princiers de l'intérieur, les ensembles les plus complets sont actuellement la Heuneburg, le mont Lassois et Bourges. Sites d'*emporia* littoraux et sites princiers continentaux apparaissent comme des entités antinomiques, bien qu'économiquement complémentaires, et représentatives de deux mondes qui s'attirent: celui de la Méditerranée occidentale, et celui, à la fois continental et atlantique de l'isthme gaulois (Fig. 1). Il est indispensable de ne pas dissocier l'étude de ces sites, pas plus qu'il ne faut dissocier celle de la diffusion maritime des productions étrusques de celle de leur diffusion terrestre. Les récentes trouvailles de Bourges et les travaux en cours d'inventaire systématique des matériaux étrusques hors d'Italie nous permettent de mieux percevoir la complexité et la complémentarité de ces deux domaines, maritime et terrestre, et de mieux évaluer le rôle joué par les Etrusques à l'aube de l'Europe historique. Ainsi se confirme l'intuition d'un J. Déchelette, qui avait pressenti la richesse d'une recherche comparative sur les deux cultures, qui occupaient une position centrale dans le cadre géo-stratégique du monde antique: l'Etrusco-italique au centre de la Méditerranée, et la Celtique entre la façade atlantique et l'Europe orientale.[61]

NOTES

1. Voir en particulier: Benoit 1965; Kimmig 1983a; Frey 1986; *Actes Paris* 1988; *Actes Marseille* 1992; *Actes Châtillon-sur-Seine* sous presse.
    Pour les importations étrusques en Gaule: Bouloumié 1980; Gran-Aymerich 1992a. Sur les travaux en cours à Bourges, voir Almagro-Gorbea *et al.* 1990; Alvarez-Sanchis et Davila sous presse; Briquel *et al.* 1992; *Bourges* 1988; Collet sous-presse; Gran-Aymerich 1990; 1991; 1992a; 1992b; 1993a; 1993b; 1994a; Gran-Aymerich et Almagro-Gorbea 1993; Gran-Aymerich *et al.* 1993; Troadec 1993a; 1993b.
2. Joffroy 1979; Brun 1987; 1993; *Celti* 1991, *passim*; *Etrusques* 1992, *passim*.
3. Pellet et Delor 1980; *Princes Celtes* 1988, 189-93.
4. Pour Lyon: Bellon et Perrin 1992; Perrin et Bellon 1992, 421, fig. 1.
    Pour Bragny-sur-Saône: Duvauchelle 1993; Flouest 1990.
5. Bouloumié 1983; Mohen 1988; Massurel 1988.
6. Aigner Foresti 1980; Frey 1992. Ce thème a fait l'objet d'un colloque à Berlin, au Pergamonmuseum, au mois de mars 1993, *Etrurien und die Wurzeln der keltischen Kunst*, avec entre autres communications: F.-W. von Hase, Die Kriegerstele von Hirschlanden; A.-M. Adam, Kleinkunst in N-Frankreich und ihr Beziehung zum Kunsthandwerk Etruriens (7.-5. Jh.), et J. Gran-Aymerich, Motifs figurés en Etrurie et dans le domaine occidental de la culture de Hallstatt, voir n. 60 et Gran-Aymerich 1994b.
7. Après les travaux de S. Boucher - en particulier: Boucher 1969; 1970; 1976; 1982; - et le traitement très critique et restrictif de ces documents qui s'en est suivi (par exemple Bouloumié 1980, 144-5) une nouvelle approche, avec examen minutieux cas par cas est en cours: Adam 1989, 384. Pour le cas de Bourges voir la figurine présentée ici même sous le n. 16.
8. Schuermans 1872; Genthe 1874.
9. Piroutet et Déchelette 1909; Déchelette 1914. Sur J. Déchelette voir Gran-Aymerich E. et J. 1983, et Binétruy 1994.
10. Kimmig 1984; Jannot 1990; 1992.
11. Cordier 1985; Chevallier 1976.
12. Willaume 1985, 43.

13. Pour l'ensemble de la tombe voir essentiellement Corot 1901; Willaume 1985, 48sq.

14. Pour l'oenochoé à bec de la route de Dun: Corot 1901, 568, pl. IV, n. 22; Breuil et de Goy 1903; Jacobsthal et Langsdorf 1929, 33, n. 120; Bouloumié 1973b, 3, fig. 7-9; 1973a, 168, 220; Willaume 1985, 48, pl. 9.9; Bailly 1987, 38; Josset 1990, 29-38, 11.18.12, p. 17; Gran-Aymerich 1992a, 349, fig. 8.1; Briquel *et al.* 1992, 182; Gran-Aymerich 1992b, 28, fig. p. 31-2; Gran-Aymerich et Almagro-Gorbea 1993, 321.

15. des Meloizes 1881; Jacobsthal et Langsdorf 1929, 36, n. 34; Bouloumié 1973b, 5, fig. 32; Bailly 1987, 38, fig. 13; Willaume 1985, 98, pl. 29.1; *Bourges* 1988, fig. p. 49; Josset 1990, 19, n. 11.18.22; Gran-Aymerich 1992a, 350, fig. 7; Briquel *et al.* 1992, 182; Gran-Aymerich 1992b, 28, fig. p. 32; Gran-Aymerich et Almagro-Gorbea 1993, 321.

16. de Meloizes 1899; Corot 1901, 568, n. 23, pl. IV; Jacobsthal et Langsdorf 1929, 33, n. 24; Bouloumié 1973b, 3, fig. 10-12; Willaume 1985, 131, pl. 41.1; Bailly 1987, 38, fig.13; Josset 1990, 8.31; Gran-Aymerich 1992a, 350, fig. 6; Briquel *at al.*, 1992, 182, fig. p. 183, fig. p. 185; Gran-Aymerich 1992b, 28, fig. p. 32-3; Gran-Aymerich et Almagro-Gorbea 1993 318, 325, fig. 3.

17. Pour l'oenochoé d'Eigenbilsen: Jacobsthal et Langsdorf 1929, 32, n. 29, pl. 13; Bouloumié 1973b, 6, n. 18, fig. 37-8; Kimmig 1983b; Kimmig 1886. Pour l'oenochoé du Hradiste de Pisku: Bouzec 1992. Pour l'oenochoé de Les Bercias, Puy-de-Dôme: de Longperier 1863; Corot 1901, 571, pl. VI, n. 27; Jacobsthal et Langsdorf 1929, 35, n. 43, pl. 5; Bouloumié 1973b, 4, n. 11, figs. 21-4.

18. Corot 1901, 568; Breuil et de Goy 1903, 165, fig. 5; Bouloumié 1977, 31, fig. 11; Willaume 1985, 48, pl. 9.10; *Bourges* 1988, fig. p. 48; Josset 1990, n. 11.18.12, p. 17; Gran-Aymerich 1992a, 350, fig. 8.2; Briquel *et al.* 1992, 182; Gran-Aymerich 1992b, 28, fig. p. 33; Gran-Aymerich et Almagro-Gorbea 1993, 325.

19. Shefton 1988, 106-18. Pour le stamnos de Gurgy voir note 3 et Rolley 1989, 111, fig. d.

20. Mater 1893; Bouloumié 1977, 4, 32, fig. 11; Willaume 1985, 27, n. 18, pl. 11.14; Bailly 1987, 38, fig. 12; Josset 1990, 18, n. 11.18.16; Gran-Aymerich 1992a, 350, fig. 9.2; Briquel *et al.* 1992, 182, fig. p. 183, fig. p. 185; Gran-Aymerich 1992b, 28, fig. p. 33; Gran-Aymerich et Almagro-Gorbea 1993, 318, 325 fig. 3.

21. Willaume 1985, 254.

22. Willaume 1985, 40; Bailly 1987, 38, fig. 10; Gran-Aymerich 1992a, 350, fig. 10.1; Gran-Aymerich et Almagro-Gorbea 1993, 325.

23. de la Guère 1893; Bailly 1987, 38; Gran-Aymerich 1992a, 350, fig. 12.1; Gran-Aymerich et Almagro-Gorbea 1993, 325.

24. D'abord considérés tous comme des ossements animaux, ces restes ont été analysés par A.-C. Besnard, du Laboratoire Européen d'Anthropologie: dans son rapport, démeuré inédit, sont identifiés: 'treize fragments humains osseux, appartenant au membre inférieur, à l'exception d'une phalange de la main', 'un des os reconstitué n'est pas humain', 'il n'ya pas de trace d'incinération'. Nous remercions P. Bailly, des Musées du Berry qui nous a communiqué ce document.

25. Roger et Ponroy 1889; Bouloumié 1976, 13, n. 7, fig. 14-15; Willaume 1985, 122, pl. 29.2; Bailly 1987, 38, fig. 11; *Bourges* 1988 fig. p. 48; Josset 1990, 18, n. 11.18.20; Gran-Aymerich 1992a, 350, fig. 10.2; Briquel *et al.* 1992, 182, fig. p. 185; Gran-Aymerich et Almagro-Gorbea 1993, 318, 325, fig.3.
     Pour Gurgy: Rolley 1989, 111, fig. a-b.

26. de la Guère 1893, 24, pl. II; Willaume 1985, 238, fig. 14.1; Bailly 1987, 36, fig.5; Josset 1990 , 17, n. 11.18.13; Gran-Aymerich 1992a, 350, fig. 12.2; Briquel *et al.,* 1992, 182, fig.

57

p. 184, fig. p. 185; Gran-Aymerich 1992b, 28, fig. p. 30; Gran-Aymerich et Almagro-Gorbea 1993, 317, 325, fig. 2.

27. Pour l'épée en bronze, du type à langue de carpe, de production atlantique, conservée aux Musées du Berry: *Bourges* 1988, 35, fig. 9.1.

    Pour le poignard à antennes: Guère 1893, 23, pl. I. Ce dernier viendrait de la région du Bad-Würtemberg (opinion confirmée oralement par J. Biel).

28. Gsell 1891, 197-208, fig. 60-1, 64, 70; Falconi Amorelli 1968, n. 42; Bianco Peroni 1979; Fugazzola Delpino 1984, 82, n. 13; Guidi 1993, 17-80.

29. Pour la plaque de ceinture de Nantes et l'épée à antennes d'Amboise voir notes 10 et 11. Pour les rasoirs villanoviens dans le monde celtique, von Hase, 1992, 245-7, pl. 9-10.

30. Breuil et de Goy 1903, 172, fig. 10; Duval *et al.* 1974 9, fig. 4.6; Bailly 1987, 36, fig. 6; Josset 1990, 20, 11.18.32; Gran-Aymerich 1992a, 350, fig. 13.4; Gran-Aymerich et Almagro-Gorbea 1993, 325.

31. Pour le difficile sujet des fibules étrusco-italiques en Gaule: Adam (R.) 1992 et Adam (A.-M.) 1992.

32. de Goy 1887; Willaume 1985, 28, 251, 264; Duval *et al.* 1974, 31, fig. 20.3; Bailly 1987, fig. 4; Guéret 1989, fig. p. 18; Josset 1990, 17, n. 11.18.14; Gran-Aymerich 1992a, 350, fig. 13.1; Briquel *et al.* 1992, 182, fig. p. 184; Gran-Aymerich 1992b, 28, fig. p. 30; Gran-Aymerich et Almagro-Gorbea 1993, 317, 325, fig. 2.

33. A.-M. Adam 1992, p. 389, fig. 6; Tendille 1975, 5, n. 1, pl. 1.

34. Duval *et al.* 1974, 9 sq.

35. Bonnet *et al.*, tombe 22, fig. 21, n. 14.

36. Goy 1887, 14; Willaume 1985, 28; Bailly 1987, 36; Gran-Aymerich 1992a, 353; Gran-Aymerich et Almagro-Gorbea 1993, 327.

37. Breuil et de Goy 1903, 171, fig. 8; Duval *et al.* 1974, 36, fig. 22.2; Bailly 1987, 35, fig. 1; Guéret 1989, fig. p. 18; Willaume 1985, 23, n. 8, pl. 2.11; Josset 1990, 18, 11.18.17; Gran-Aymerich 1992a, 350, fig. 13.3; Briquel *et al.* 1992, fig. p. 184; Gran-Aymerich et Almagro-Gorbea 1993, 325.

38. A.-M. Adam 1992, 389.

39. *Bercy* 1992,, 12, fig. n. 12.

40. Willaume 1985, 238, pl. 14.2; Bailly 1987, 35, fig. 3; Josset 1990, 18, n. 11.18.18; Gran-Aymerich 1992a, 350, fig. 12.3; Briquel *et al.,* 1992, 182, fig. p. 184; Gran-Aymerich et Almagro-Gorbea 1993, 325.

41. Willaume 1985, 238, pl. 14.2; Bailly 1987, 35, fig. 3; Josset 1990, 18, n. 11.18.18; Gran-Aymerich 1992a, 350, fig. 12.3; Briquel *et al.* 1992, 182, fig. p. 184; Gran-Aymerich, Almagro-Gorbea 1993, 325.

42. Note des acquisitions du Musée de Bourges, de 1892-1893, parue dans le journal local, établie par D. Mater, qui signale en particulier sur 5 bracelets gaulois des environs de Bourges (4 en bronze et 1 en lignite), une fibule de bronze, un petit Mercure en bronze trouvé à Bourges et 'une divinité égyptienne, bronze' qui correspond à cette statuette (document archives des Musées du Berry, que nous avons pu consulter grâce à l'obligeance de M. P. Bailly); Bailly 1987, 36, fig. 8-9; Gran-Aymerich 1992a, 356, fig. 14; Gran-Aymerich et Almagro-Gorbea 1993, 317, 325, fig. 2.

43. Térouanne et Boissel 1966; et en dernier avec bibliographie, Piel 1990; R. Adam 1992, 385, fig. 10.

44. Cristofani 1979; Falconi Amorelli 1982, 39, n. 16; Richardson 1983 pl. 138, fig. 467, pl. 215, fig. 725, pl. 216, fig. 726; Tabone 1990, n. 13, pl. IV, p. 35-36, 42.

45.   Morel 1898, pl. 25, fig. 2. Citée dans Bouloumié 1980, 400-1, qui note 'faisant probablement partie d'une oenochoé'; p. 447 le fragment est comptabilisé dans la liste '5ième siècle (indistinctement). Bourges (anse d'oenochoé)', le même auteur ajoute 'bien que nous manquions de pièces de comparaison ... un rapprochement est à faire avec l'anse conservée à Munich publiée par W.L. Brown' (1960, pl. XLV, d.1-d.2), pour le motif, mais le rendu plastique est très différent.

46.   Pour cette dernière et ses attaches latérales, avec deux avant-trains de chevaux, Jucker 1973. Pour ces anses en général, Kent Hill 1958.

47.   Pour l'amphore de Conliège, Lerat 1958; Rolley 1982, 27-8; *Princes Celtes* 1988, 203-7, n. 132-133; *Jura* 1991, 52-3; Cianferoni 1991; *Celti* 1992, n. 325, p. 264.

48.   Gehrig *et al.*, 95, pl. 14; Haffner 1976, 201, pl. 145-6; Rolley 1982, 27-8.

49.   Hoffmann 1973, pl. 44-45; *Mayence* 1968, 192-3, n. 198; Rolley 1982, 27-8.

50.   Rolley 1982, 27; *Etrusques* 1992, 264, no. 325.

51.   Rolley 1982, 28, n. 29.

52.   Rolley 1982, 28, n. 29.

53.   *Princes Celtes* 1988, 204.

54.   Cianferoni 1991, 72-3.

55.   de Ridder 1913 t.2, 107, n. 2650, pl. 96; Cianferoni 1991, 130, qui renvoie encore à une dernière anse complète, conservée dans une collection privée en Suisse, 108, n. 268, pl. 38. Le rendu plastique de l'anse de Bourges au British Museum est très proche des mêmes motifs qui figurent sur d'autres vases de bronze, par exemple encadrant l'attache inférieure de l'anse de l'oenochoé à long bec de Weisskirchen (Jacobsthal et Langsdorf 1929, pl. 18.3; Brown 1960, 96-7, 130, pl. 38b) ou sur les trépieds de la deuxième série vulcienne, Brown 1960, pl. 39 a-b, qui les situe dans '*a date not far from 500 BC*' (*ibidem*, 97).

56.   Pour les céramiques grecques de Bourges voir les publications préliminaires, *Châteaudun* 1985, 23, fig. 8; Villard 1988, 331-41, n. 6; *Bourges* 1988, fig. p. 59 et 62; Almagro-Gorbea *et al.* 1990, fig. p. 32-4; Ruffier 1990, 35, fig. 7; Gran-Aymerich 1992a, 344 sq.; Briquel *et al.* 1992, 182, fig. p. 185; Gran-Aymerich 1992b, fig. p. 33; Gran-Aymerich et Almagro-Gorbea 1993, 318-19, 329-31, figs. 3-4.

57.   Information orale, fournie par W. Kimmig, à qui nous adressons nos plus vifs remerciements.

58.   Il faut relever les exceptions, très notables, des deux fragments de deux vases fermés de dimensions moyennes et à panse arrondie (type stamnos ou hydrie) à figures rouges: le premier a été trouvé en position secondaire dans le secteur funéraire et à enclos rituels de Lazenay, campagne 1992; l'on remarque le bas d'une draperie délimité par un registre de perles disposées en zig-zag; le second a été trouvé dans le secteur de Saint-Martin dans la campagne de 1993 et présente un visage de jeune homme de style sévère, qui serait du dernier quart du 5ième siècle.

59.   Nous avons pu bénéficier de l'avis de MM. J.-J. Maffre, F. Villard et B.B. Shefton que nous tenons à remercier très chaleureusement.

60.   Gran Aymerich 1993a. Pour une oenochoé à têtes plastiques en bucchero de Marseille, et son imitation en céramique grise de l'oppidum de Saint-Marcel, voir Gran-Aymerich 1994b.

61.   Mes plus vifs remerciements vont aux collègues du British Museum, pour leur efficace et courtoise organisation lors du colloque, tout particulièrement Mmes. Judith Swaddling et Susan Walker, responsables de l'édition, et le conservateur Mlle. Val Rigby qui m'a fourni la photographie de l'anse de Bourges de l'ancienne collection Morel qui est publiée ici.

BIBLIOGRAPHIE

Actes Châtillon-sur-Seine sous presse. P. Brun (éd.), *Vix et le phénomène princier*, (1993).

Actes Lons-le-Saunier 1993. *Fonctionnement social de l'Age du fer. Opérateurs et hypothèses pour la France*, (1990). Lons-le-Saunier

Actes Marseille 1992. M. Bats (éd.), Marseille grecque et la Gaule, (1990).

Actes Paris 1988. La Documentation Française (éd.), *Les princes celtes et la Méditerranée*, (1987). Paris

Adam, A.-M. 1992. Signification et fonction des fibules dans le cadre des relations transalpines du 8ième au 5ième siècle avant notre ère. Dans, *Etrusker nördlich von Etrurien,* 389-409, pls. 111-20. Vienne

Adam, R. 1992. Appunti sul repertorio delle importazioni italiche in Francia. Dans, *Etrusker nördlich von Etrurien,* 371-88. Vienne

Aigner Foresti, L. 1980. *Der Ostalpenraum und Italien. Ihre kulturellen Beziehungen im Spiegel der anthropomorphen Kleinplastik aus Bronze des 7. Jhs. v. Chr.* Florence

Almagro-Gorbea, M., Gran-Aymerich, J. et Troadec, J. 1990. Avaricum: un oppidum hallsttático en la cuenca del Loira. *Revista de Arqueología* **110** (juin), 29-36

Alvarez-Sanchis, J. et Davila, A. sous presse. La séquence culturelle du Premier Age du Fer à Bourges. Dans, *Actes XVIIe Colloque de l'Association française pour l'étude des Ages du Fer*, (1993). Nevers

Bailly, P. 1987. L'Etrurie aux Musées de Bourges. *Cahiers d'Arch et d'Hist du Berry* **88-9** (mars-juin), 35-51

Bellon, C. et Perrin, F. 1992. Nouvelles découvertes de l'Age du Fer à Lyon-Vaise (Rhône): le site de la rue du Docteur-Horand. *RAE* **43**, 280, fig. 10.3-5

Benoit, F. 1965. *Recherches sur l'hellénisation du Midi de la Gaule.* Aix-en-Provence

Bercy 1992. *Les pirogues néolithiques de Bercy.* Catalogue de l'exposition. Paris

Bianco Peroni, V. 1979. Die Rasiermesser in Italien. I rasoi nell'Italia continentale, *PBF* **VIII.2**, 139-40

Binétruy, M.-S. 1994. *Joseph Déchelette.* Lyon

Bonnet, Ch., Plouin, S. et Lambach, F. 1991. Le tumulus I de Colmar-Riedewihr (Haut-Rhin). *Gallia* **48**, 2-57

Boucher, S. 1969. Une aire de culture italo-celtique aux VIIe-VIe siècles avant J.-C. *MEFRA* **81**, 37-57

Boucher, S. 1970. Importations étrusques en Gaule à la fin du VIIe siècle avant J.-C. *Gallia* **28**, 193-206

Boucher, S. 1976. *Recherches sur les bronzes figurés de Gaule pré-romaine et romaine.* Rome-Paris

Boucher, S. 1982. Bronzes étrusques et italo-étrusques en Gaule. *MEFRA* **94**, 149-62

Bouloumié, B. 1973a. *Les oenochoés en bronze de type* Schnabelkanne *en Italie.* Paris-Rome

Bouloumié, B., 1973b. Les oenochoés en bronze du type *Schnabelkanne* en France et en Belgique, *Gallia* **31**, 1-35

Bouloumié, B. 1976. Les cistes à cordons trouvées en Gaule (Belgique, France, Suisse). *Gallia* **34**, 1-30

Bouloumié, B. 1977. Situles de bronze trouvées en Gaule. *Gallia* **35**, 4-38

Bouloumié, B. 1980. *Recherches sur les importations étrusques en Gaule du 8ième au 4ième siècle avant J.-C.* Thèse d'état, Université de Paris IV, texte dactylographié

Bouloumié, B. 1983. Le vin et la mort chez les 'princes' celtes. Dans, *L'imaginaire du vin*, 15-24. Marseille

Bourges 1988. *Le site de Bourges. Son territoire aux 'Ages des Métaux' (2,5000 à 50 av. J.-C.).* Bourges

Bouzec, J. 1992. Die Etrusker und Böhmen. Dans, *Etrusker nördlich von Etrurien*, 361-9, fig. 2. Vienne

Breuil, H. et Goy, P. de, 1903. Note sur une sépulture antique de la rue de Dun (Bourges). *MémSocAnt du Centre* **XXVII**, 157-173

Briquel, D., Adam, R. and Gran-Aymerich, J. 1992. Les relations transalpines. Dans, *Etrusques, 1992*, 180-7.

Brown, W. L. 1960. *The Etruscan Lion.* Oxford

Brun, P. 1987. *Princes et princesses de la Celtique.* Paris

Brun, P. 1993. La complexification sociale en Europe moyenne pendant l'Age du Fer: essai de modélisation. Dans, *Actes Lons-le-Saunier*, 275-87

Celti 1991. *I Celti.* Venise.

Châteaudun 1985. *La civilisation gauloise en pays carnute.* Catalogue. Châteaudun

Chevallier, R. 1976. La troisième route de l'étain en Gaule. A propos d'une oenochoé en bronze étrusque trouvée près de Tours: Homenaje a A. García y Bellido, 2. *Revista de la Universidad Complutense* **25.104**, 131-57

Cianferoni, G.C. 1991. Materiali ceretani del Museo Archeologico di Firenze. *Studi e Materiali. Scienze dell'Antichità in Toscana* **6**, 100-35

Collet, S. sous presse. La céramique tournée cannelée. A partir des exemples de Bourges et de Bragny. Dans, *XVIIe Colloque de l'Association française pour l'étude des Ages du Fer* (1993). Nevers

Cordier, G. 1985. 'Nouveaux' objets de l'Age du Bronze tirés de la Loire. *RACAntNat* **24**, 63-8

Corot, H. 1901. Notes pour servir à l'étude de la civilisation celtique en Gaule. Les vases en bronze pré-romains trouvés en France. *BullMonumental* **65**, 531-72

Cristofani, M. 1979. La 'testa Lorenzini' e la scultura tardoarcaica in Etruria settentrionale. *StEtr* **47**, 85-92, pl. XXIV, d-e

Déchelette, J. 1914. *Manuel d'archéologie préhistorique, celtique et gallo-romaine, Note additionnelle* dans t. II, 3e partie. Paris

Duval, A., Eluère, Ch. et Mohen, J.-P. 1974. Les fibules antérieures au 6ième siècle avant notre ère, trouvées en France. *Gallia* **32**, 1-61

Duvauchelle, C. 1993. *Les céramiques d'importation de Bragny-sur-Saône (Saône-et-Loire).* Mémoire de maîtrise, Université de Paris I, texte dactylographié

Etrusques 1992. *Les Etrusques et l'Europe*. Paris

Falconi Amorelli, M.T. 1968. *La collezione Massimo*. Milan

Falconi Amorelli, M.T. 1982. *I materiali archeologici pre-romani del Museo di Pesaro*. Rome

Flouest, J.-L. 1993. Activités métallurgiques et commerce avec le monde méditerranéen au 5ième siècle av. J.-C. à Bragny-sur-Saône (Saône-et-Loire). Dans, *Actes Lons-le-Saunier* (1993), 21-31

Frey, O.H. 1986. I rapporti commerciali tra l'Italia settentrionale e l'Europa centrale dal VII al IV secolo a.C. Dans, R. de Marinis (éd.), *Gli Etruschi a nord del Po*, vol. 2, 11-17. Mantoue

Frey, O.-H. 1992. Beziehungen der Situlenkunst zum Kunstschaffen Etruriens. Dans, *Etrusques* 1992, 93-101

Fugazzola Delpino, M.A. 1984. *La cultura villanoviana*. Rome

Gehrig, U., Greifenhagen, A. et Kunisch, N. 1968. *Antiken-Sammlung. Führer durch die Antikenabteilung. Staatliche Museen Preussischer Kulturbesitz*. Berlin

Gran-Aymerich

Genthe, H. 1874. *Uber den etruskischen Tauschhandel nach dem Norden.* Frankfurt

Goy, P. de, 1887. Sépultures antiques en Berry. *MémSocAnt du Centre* **XIV**-1886, 12-15

Gran-Aymerich, J. 1990. L'exemple de Bourges. Actes Importations italiques en Gaule. Nantes, Musée Dobré 1989. Dans, *Répertoire des importations étrusques et italiques en Gaule* III, *Caesarodunum, Bulletin de l'Institut d'Études latines et du Centre de recherches A. Piganiol,* suppl. **59**, 90-1. Tours

Gran-Aymerich, J. 1991 sous presse. La Méditerranée et les sites princiers de l'Europe occidentale. Recherches en cours dans le cercle du détroit de Gibraltar et dans l'isthme gaulois. Dans, *Actes IIIe Congrès International d'Etudes Phéniciennes et Puniques.* Tunis

Gran-Aymerich, J. 1992a. Les matériaux étrusques hors d'Etrurie: le cas de la France et les travaux en cours à Bourges-Avaricum. Dans, *Etrusker nördlich von Etrurien,* 329-59, figs. 85-97. Vienne

Gran-Aymerich, J. 1992b. Un site princier à Bourges. Importations étrusques et grecques. *Les Etrusques et l'Europe. Les Dossiers d'Archéologie* **175** (oct.), 28-35

Gran-Aymerich, J. 1993a sous presse. Bourges: les importations grecques et étrusques. Dans, *XVIIe Colloque de l'Association française pour l'étude des Ages du Fer.* Nevers

Gran-Aymerich, J. 1993b sous presse. Bourges dans le contexte des importations méditerranéennes. Dans, *Actes Vix et le phénomène princier.* Châtillon-sur-Seine

Gran-Aymerich, J. 1994a sous presse. Les premières relations entre l'Etrurie et la Gaule. Les nouvelles découvertes dans le Midi, en Bourgogne et à Bourges. Dans, *Actes Archäologische Untersuchungen zu den Beziehungen zwischen Altitalien und der Zone nordwärts der Alpen während der frühen Eisenzeit Alteuropas.* Regensburg

Gran-Aymerich, J. 1994b sous presse. Le bucchero et les vases métalliques. *Vaisselle métallique, vaisselle céramique. Rencontre d'étude à propos des vases étrusques.* Nantes

Gran-Aymerich, J. 1995. Vases grecs de Bourges. Catalogue *Luxusgeschirr Keltischer Fürsten.* Würzburg

Gran-Aymerich, J. et Almagro-Gorbea, M. 1993. Les fouilles en cours à Bourges et les recherches sur les matériaux étrusco-italiques. *Bulletin de la Société Nationale des Antiquaires de France* (1991), 312-39

Gran-Aymerich, E. et J. 1983. Joseph Déchelette. *Archeologia* **185**, déc., 71-4

Gran-Aymerich, J., Almagro-Gorbea, M. et Troadec, J. 1993. L'état des recherches à Bourges - Avaricum: le site de hauteur, les tombes aristocratiques et les importations méditerranéennes l'Age du Fer. Dans, *Actes XIIe Congrès de l'Union internationale des Sciences pré- et protohistoriques,* 215-27. Bratislava

Gsell, S. 1891. *Fouilles dans la nécropole de Vulci.* Paris

de la Guère, Comte A. 1893. Notes sur divers objets gaulois trouvés aux environs de Bourges, 1873-1888. Grande ciste de Dames, commune de Saint-Eloy-de-Gy (Cher). *MémSocAnt du Centre* **XIX**-1892, 22-8, pl. I-II

Guéret 1989. D. Vuaillat *et al.* (eds.), *Aspects des Ages du fer en Berry et Limousin.* Guéret

Guidi, A. 1993. *La necropoli veiente dei Quattro Fontanili nel quadro della fase recente della Prima Eta del Ferro italiana.* Florence

Haffner, A. 1976. *Die westliche Hunsrück-Eifel-Kultur.* Berlin

von Hase, F.W. 1992. Etrurien und Mitteleuropa. Zur Bedeutung der ersten italisch-etruskischen Funde der späten Urnenfelder- und frühen Hallstattzeit in Zentraleuropa. Dans, *Etrusker nördlich von Etrurien,* 235-66. Vienne

Hoffmann, H. 1973. *Kunst des Altertums in Hamburg.* Hamburg

Jacobsthal, P. et Langsdorf, A. 1929. *Die Bronzeschnabelkannen.* Berlin

Jannot, J.-R. 1990. A propos d'une fibule étrusque. La fibule d'or de Saint-Aignan (Loire-Atlantique). Dans, *Répertoire des importations étrusques et italiques en Gaule,* III. *Caesarodunum, Bulletin de l'Institut d'Études latines et du Centre de recherches A. Piganiol,* suppl. **59,** 85-6

Jannot, J.-R. 1992. Une fibule étrusque à l'embouchure de la Loire. *Annales de Bretagne et des pays de l'ouest* **99,** 1-12

Joffroy, R. 1979. *Vix et ses trésors.* Paris

Josset, D. 1990. Les importations en région Centre. Dans, Répertoire des importations etrusques et italiques en Gaule, III. *Caesarodunum, Bulletin de l'Institut d'Études latines et du Centre de recherches A. Piganiol,* suppl. **59,** 12-29

Jucker, H. 1973. Altes und neues zur Grächwiller Hydria. *AntK* **9,** 42-62

Jura 1991. *Les Celtes dans le Jura.* Yverdon-les-Bains

Kent Hill, D. 1958. 'A class of bronze handles'. *AJA* **62,** 197-205

Kimmig, W. 1983a. Die griechische Kolonisation im westlichen Mittelmeergebiet und ihre Wirkung auf die Landschaften des westlichen Mitteleuropa. *JbZMusMainz* **30,** 5-78

Kimmig, W. 1983b. Das Fürstengrab von Eigenbilzen-Neue Uberlegungen zu einer alten Fund. *BMusArt* **54,** 37-44

Kimmig, W. 1984. Zu einem getriebenen Bronzeblech aus dem Musée Dobrée in Nantes (Frankreich). *AKorrBl* **14**, 293-8

Kimmig. W. 1986. Eigenbilzen. *Reallexikon der Germanischen Altertumskunde* 6.5-6. 555, pl. 40. Berlin

Lerat, L. 1958. L'amphore de bronze de Conliège. Dans, *Actes du Colloque sur les influences hellénistiques en Gaule*, 89-92, pl. XI-XII. Dijon

Longpérier, A. de, 1863. Nouvelles archéologiques. *RA* **2**, 81

Massurel, H. 1988. Le tissage, technique de pointe à l'âge du fer. Dans, *Actes Paris* (1988), 187-97

Mater, D. 1893. Description d'objets antiques en bronze récemment acquis par le Musée de Bourges. *MémSocAnt du Centre* **XIX**-1892, 31-42, pl. III.3-4

Mayence 1968. *Master Bronzes from the Classical World. Catalogue.* Mayence

Méloizes, A. de, 1881. Note sur la découverte d'un vase de bronze dans un tumulus de la commune de Morthomiers (Cher). *MémSocAnt du Centre* **IX**-1880, 1-10

Méloizes, A. de, 1899. Oenochoé en bronze du Musée de Bourges. *MémSocAnt du Centre* **XXII**-1897/98, 1-5

Mohen, J.-P. 1988. La circulation des matières précieuses: l'ambre, l'étain, le corail et l'ivoire. Dans, *Actes Paris* 1988, 221-7

Morel, L. 1898. *La Champagne souterraine.* Reims

Perrin, F. et Bellon, C. 1992. Mobilier d'origine et de filiation méditerranéennes dans la moyenne vallée du Rhône. *Actes Marseille* 1992, 419-30

Pellet, C. et Delor, J.-P. 1980. Les ensembles funéraires de 'La Picardie' sur la commune de Gurgy (Yonne), étude préliminaire. *RAE* **31**, 7-54

Piel, T. 1990. Les importations dans le Pays de Loire. Dans, *Répertoire des importations étrusques et italiques en Gaule*, III. *Caesarodunum, Bulletin de l'Institut d'Études latines et du Centre de recherches A. Piganiol,* suppl. **59**, 39-50

Piroutet, M. et Déchelette, J. 1909. Découverte de vases grecs dans un oppidum hallstattien du Jura. *RevArch.* **1**, 193-212

Princes Celtes 1988. *Trésors des princes celtes.* Paris

Privatbesitz 1967. *Antike Kunst aus Privatbesitz, Bern-Biel-Solothurn.* Solothurn

Gran-Aymerich

Répertoire des importations étrusques et italiques en Gaule, I-IV, 1987-92. Dans *Caesarodunum, Bulletin de l'Institut d'Études latines et du Centre de recherches A. Piganiol,* suppl. **57-59** et **62**.

Richardson, E. 1983. *Etruscan votive bronzes. Geometric. Orientalizing. Archaic.* Mayence

Ridder, A. de, 1913. *Les bronzes antiques du Louvre.* Paris

Roger, O. et Ponroy, H. 1889. Ciste en bronze à cordons trouvée au Chaumoy, commune de Subdray (Cher) en 1889. *MémSocAnt du Centre* **XVII**, 1-10

Rolley, C. 1982. *Les vases de bronze de l'archaïsme récent en Grande-Grèce.* Naples

Rolley C. 1989. Les Ages du Fer. Dans, *L'Yonne et son passé. 30 Ans d'Archéologie,* 105-112. Auxerre

Ruffier, O. 1990. L'opération archéologique de la rue de la Nation à Bourges. *Cahiers d'Arch et d'Hist du Berry* **103** (sept.), 29-41

Schuermans, H. 1872. Découverte d'objets étrusques faite en Belgique. *BullAcadRoyScsLetts. Belgique* **41**, 513-18

Shefton, B.B. 1988. Der Stamnos. Dans, W. Kimmig, *Das Kleinaspergle. Studien zu einem Fürstengrabhügel frühen Latènezeit bei Stuttgart,* 104-52. Stuttgart

Tabone, G.P. 1990. *Bronzistica a figura umana dell'Italia preromana nelle civiche raccolte archeologiche di Milano.* Milan

Tendille, C. 1975. *Objets métalliques de la protohistoire au Musée archéologique de Nîmes.* Nîmes

Térouanne, P. et Boissel, R. 1966. La trouvaille de Thorigné-en-Charnie (Mayenne). *Annales de Bretagne et des pays de l'ouest* **73**, 187-92

Troadec, J. 1993a sous presse. Le site de Bourges. Dans, *XVIIe Colloque de l'Association française pour l'étude des Ages du Fer.* Nevers

Troadec, J. 1993b sous presse. Bourges et son territoire. Dans, *Vix et le phénomène princier.* Châtillon-sur-Seine

Villard, F. 1988. Des Vases grecs chez les Celtes. Dans, *Actes Paris* 1988, 333-41

Willaume, M. 1985. *Le Berry à l'âge du Fer. HaC - La Tène II.* BAR International Series **247**. Oxford

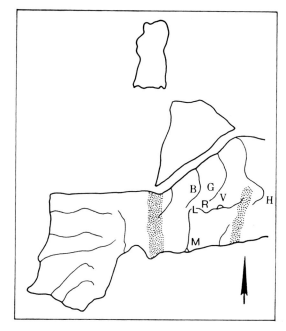

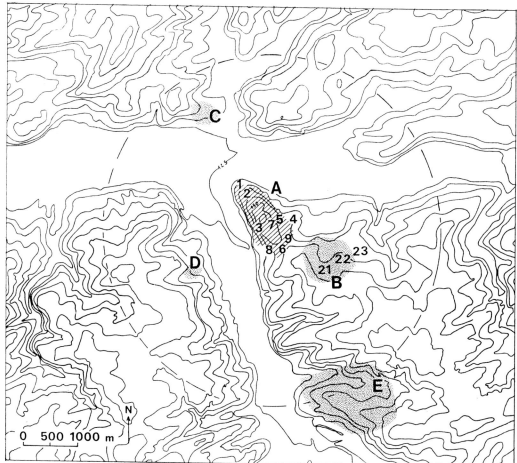

Fig. 1 L'Europe occidentale vue par Strabon. Marseille (<u>M</u>), Lyon (<u>L</u>), Bragny-sur-Saône (<u>R</u>) et les sites 'princiers' de Bourges (<u>B</u>), Gurgy (G), Vix-mont Lassois (<u>V</u>) et la Heuneburg (<u>H</u>)

Fig. 2 Emplacement du site de Bourges, avec l'habitat (<u>A</u>), les nécropoles et les dépôts périphériques (<u>B</u> à <u>E</u>)

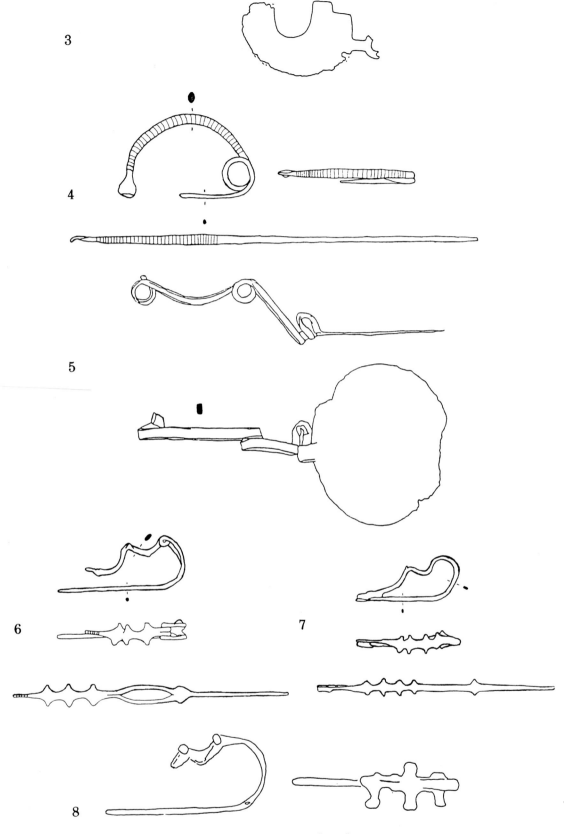

Figs. 3-8   Bourges, importations étrusco-italiques du 8ième-7ième siècle avant J.-C., des nécropoles et dépôts périphériques (Musées du Berry et collection privée, Bourges)

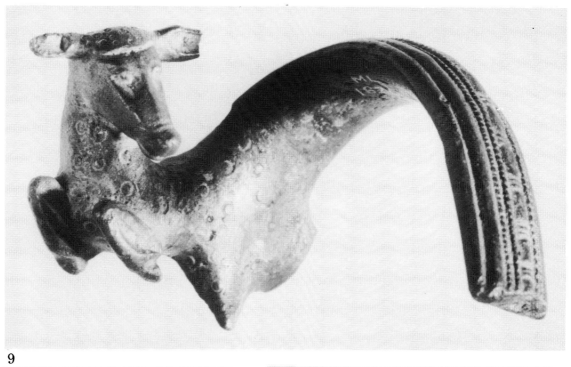

9

10a   10b

Fig. 9   Bourges, anse de la collection Morel (British Museum)
Fig. 10a,b   Figurine en bronze (Musées du Berry à Bourges)

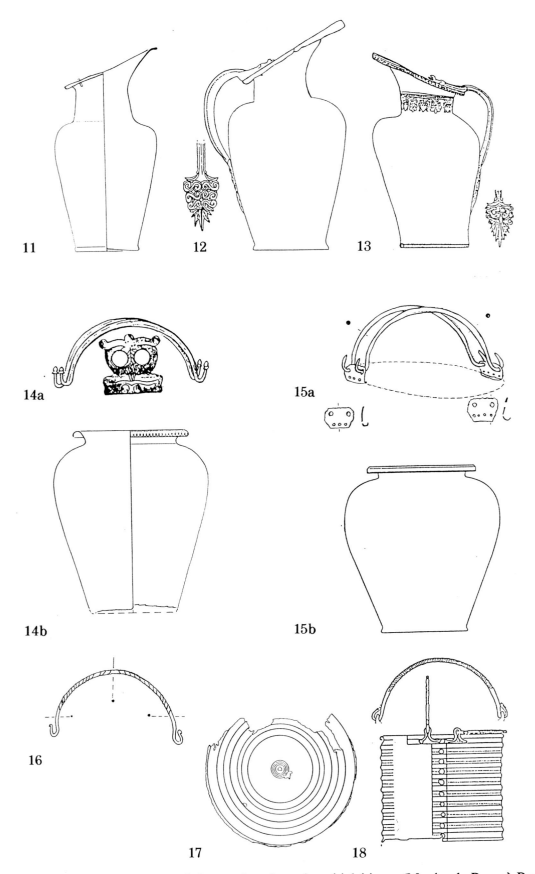

11 **12** **13**

14a **15a**

14b **15b**

16 **17** **18**

Figs. 11-18   Bourges, vases de bronze des nécropoles périphériques (Musées du Berry à Bourges)

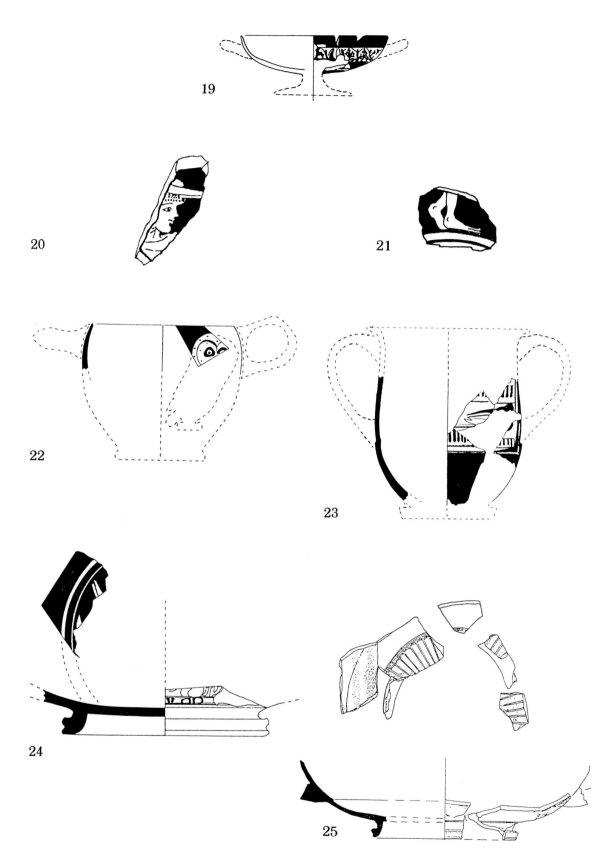

Figs. 19-25   Bourges, vases à boire de céramique attique. Chantiers de l'habitat, Littré, Nation et Saint-Martin, fouilles de 1984 à 1989 (dépôt archéologique de Bourges)

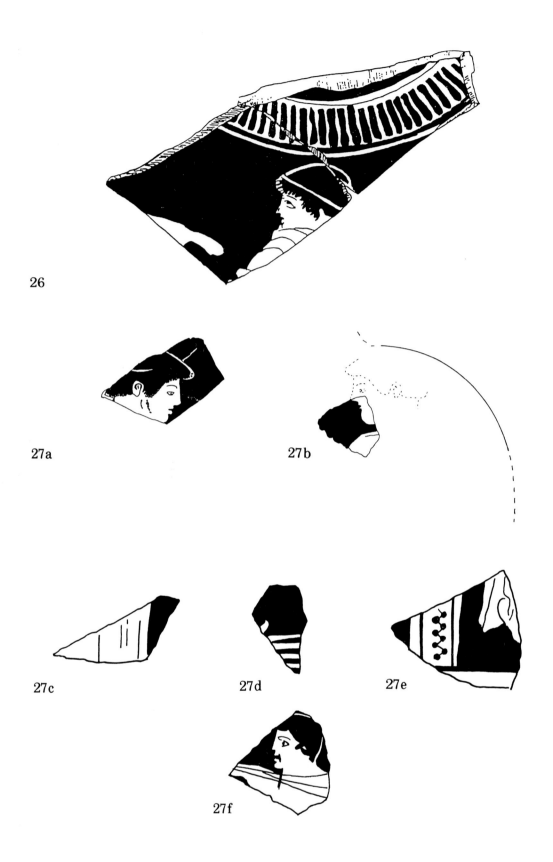

26

27a

27b

27c

27d

27e

27f

Figs. 26,27a-f   Bourges, vases hauts de céramique attique.   Chantiers de l'habitat, Littré et
Nation, fouilles de 1987 et 1989 (dépôt archéologique de Bourges)

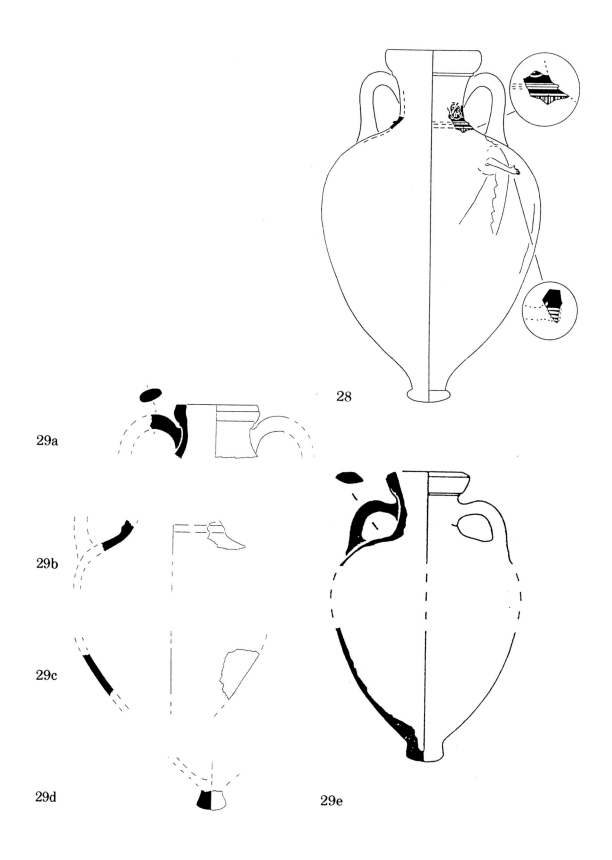

Figs. 28,29a-e   Bourges, amphores grecques de l'habitat: en haut, 28, amphore attique à figures
rouges de la Nation; en bas, 29a-e, amphores de Marseille, restitution typologique,
à partir de fragments des chantiers Littré, Nation, Jacobins et Saint-Martin

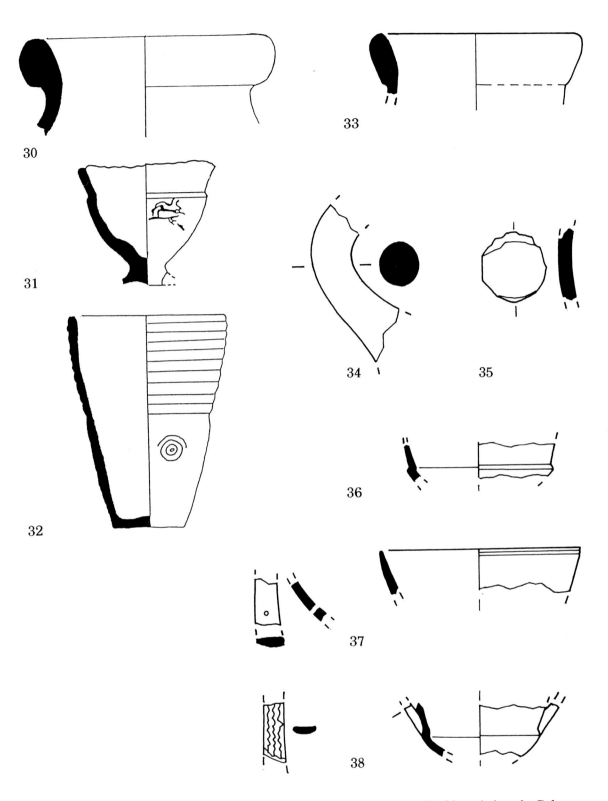

Figs. 30-32   Bragny-sur-Saône: 30, amphore étrusque de transport; 31,32, gobelets de Golasecca
(d'après Ch. Duvauchelle 1993, voir note 4)

Figs. 33-38   Lyon: 33-35, amphores étrusques de transport (d'après Bellon-Perrin 1992). Soyons
(36) et Bourg-Saint-Andéol (37) en Ardèche, canthares en bucchero. Saint-Paul-Trois-
Châteaux dans la Drôme (38), imitation en céramique grise monochrome de canthare
en bucchero (d'après Bellon-Perrin 1992, voir note 4)

Editors' Note: The following papers in this section adopt varying standpoints regarding Etruscan and Italic material found, or said to have been found, in Europe outside Italy. Reference to a number of objects recurs in one or more papers, with the finds being granted differing degrees of credibility.

PEUT-ON PARLER DE COMMERCE ETRUSQUE EN GAULE DU NORD-OUEST?
(FACADE MANCHE-ATLANTIQUE ET ARRIERE-PAYS, DU 8[IEME] SIECLE AU 2[IEME] SIECLE AV. J.-C.)

Jean-René Jannot

Département d'Histoire et Archéologie, Université de Nantes, France

Il semble nécessaire de poser cette question pour deux raisons majeures: d'abord parce que la présence d'objets étrusco-italiques en Gaule de l'Ouest semble, à certains restrictions près qui feront ici l'objet d'une discussion, absolument avérée, d'autre part, parce que leur nature, leur répartition géographique et leur appartenance à certaines périodes relativement délimitées obligent à une réflexion de fond. Les hypothèses proposées à la fin de cette étude sont fragiles et contestables car elles reposent sur des documents archéologiques dont le degré de fiabilité est limité. Pourtant, sauf si l'on dénie toute valeur aux documents archéologiques en notre possession (et dans ce cas il vaut mieux déclarer d'emblée qu'il est impossible de parler de ces problèmes), ces hypothèses peuvent s'intégrer dans un tissu de probabilités qui est loin d'être inintéressant.[1]

LES DOCUMENTS ARCHEOLOGIQUES

Nature des documents

Tous les documents archéologiques évoqués dans cette courte étude sont métalliques. En effet dans la France de l'Ouest, il n'existe, à notre connaissance, aucune mention de trouvaille céramique méditerranéenne antérieur à l'aube du premier siècle av. J.-C.[2] Cette lacune de documentation peut certes refléter seulement une lacune de la recherche, tant il est vrai que la céramique commune n'intéressait guère les érudits locaux du siècle dernier.[3] Mais ce silence peut également correspondre à une réalité historique et témoigner d'un type de relations dans lequel ne circulaient que les objets métalliques d'une certaine valeur, ce qui montrerait une physionomie très différente de ce que nous observons dans la France du centre (région de Bourges[4]) ou dans celle de l'Est (Alsace, couloir Saône-Rhône, Alpes[5]).

Ces objets métalliques sont déstinés à la parure, aux activités militaires et dans une moindre mesure aux activités de prestige comme le banquet. L'imagerie à fonction religieuse, beaucoup plus rare, est cependant présente et les petits bronzes retrouvés dans la région posent des problèmes plus sérieux encore que nous tenterons d'évoquer plus loin.

Chronologie des documents

Les objets d'origine italique dont nous parlerons se regroupent sur deux périodes nettement distinctes et séparées par un véritable hiatus.

La *première période* couvre la fin du 9ième siècle, tout le 8ième siècle, le 7ième siècle et la première moitié du 6ième et fournit dans cette région:
- les fibules villanoviennes et tardo-villanoviennes, ainsi que quelques objets de toilette (rasoirs) datant de l'époque orientalisante ou archaïque;
- les petits bronzes figurés tardo-villanoviennes ou du haut archaïsme représentant des êtres humains et des animaux;
- des éléments ayant appartenu à un mobilier de luxe (chaudrons à tiges);
- des objets de mobilier plus courant (chaudrons du type atlantique) et les armes offensives ou (surtout) défensives.

Dans l'état actuel de notre documentation, aucun objet d'origine étrusco-italique ne semble être parvenu dans la région concernée entre le milieu du 6ième siècle et le milieu du 4ième siècle av. J.-C.

La *seconde période* ne commence qu'au milieu du 4ième siècle et paraît se terminer dans le courant du 2ième siècle av. J.-C. Elle nous a livré:
- des bronzes figurés;
- des éléments de mobilier;
- et enfin des armes principalement défensives.

Répartition géographique (Cartes 1-3)

Nous nous sommes intéressés à la façade Manche-Atlantique, et à l'arrière-pays de ces régions: de la région parisienne à la Loire moyenne et à la vallée de la Garonne. La répartition géographique qui se dessine est relativement claire et, pour les deux périodes majeures que nous avons mises en évidence, les localisations géographiques diffèrent de manière sensible.

En ce qui concerne la *période villanovienne, orientalisante et archaïque*, les objets dont l'origine italienne nous semble probable ou certaine se concentrent sur des zones côtières et sur les routes intérieures qui paraissent y conduire. La baie de Somme, celle du Mont St Michel, l'embouchure de la Loire et le cours de la Garonne sont pratiquement les seuls points de la Gaule du Nord Ouest à recéler des objets de cette origine. Nous tenterons plus loin d'évaluer le sens de cette répartition.

Les localisations de trouvailles de la *période 'tardo-classique' et 'hellénistique'* sont beaucoup plus vagues et se répartissent sur des espaces qui ne semblent pas avoir de rapport direct avec des voies de communications ou des embouchures fluviales. On les trouve souvent hors de tout terminal maritime ou de tout cours fluvial majeur. La répartition semble correspondre davantage à des groupes de populations fixées qu'à des voies de déplacement. La carte de ces répartitions en témoigne d'une manière suggestive.

CRITIQUE DES DOCUMENTS

Il est indispensable de se poser quelques questions concernant les documents évoqués ci-dessus dont il faut rappeler qu'ils sont le plus souvent issus de fouilles anciennes, que leur étude n'a pas toujours été menée de manière scientifique et que leur dispersion dans des collections privées ne facilite pas les recherches.

Ces documents sont-ils de provenance italienne?

LES FIBULES

La quantité de fibules de bronze antérieures à Hallstatt moyen retrouvées en France est considérable. L'étude en a été faite de manière soigneuse.[6] Tous les auteurs ayant traité de ces objets estiment que certaines fibules peuvent parfaitement avoir été fabriquées non pas en Italie, d'où semblent venir les modèles, mais sur le territoire français lui-même. L'hypothèse d'une fabrication dans le secteur alpin a même été plusieurs fois proposée.

A la vérité, ce sont principalement les fibules à arc plein qui semblent pouvoir être des imitations plausibles de modèles italiens. En effet, leur densité est élevée au nord des Alpes alors qu'elle est presque nulle au sud de l'Apennin; ceci permettrait de supposer que leur fabrication n'est pas italienne. En revanche, les fibules à arc très renflé (*a sanguisuga*), les fibules à arc creux (*a navicella*), les fibules à arc lozangé (également creux), qui sont très nombreuses dans nos régions, le sont encore plus en Italie et singulièrement dans les zones dont le développement à l'époque villanovienne est particulièrement avancé et qui deviendront les territoires des cités côtières (surtout sur le site de Tarquinia). De plus, la décoration géométrique gravée de ces petits objets est absolument identique sur de nombreux exemplaires trouvés en Italie et en France. Nous avons donc décidé de ne tenir compte dans cette rapide étude que des fibules qui sont de fabrication italienne probable.

LES RASOIRS

Peu de rasoirs sont parvenus à nous, mais les trois exemplaires existant sont rigoureusement identiques à ceux que nous retrouvons dans l'espace de la culture villanovienne. Il nous semble donc probable que leur origine réelle est italienne.

LES BRONZES FIGURES

Ils sont peu nombreux, mais ceux de Thorigné en Charnie (Mayenne), de Saint Just sur Dives et les petits bronzes animaliers retrouvés sur les routes fluviales de l'isthme breton (par exemple Châtillon sur Seiche ou Saint Grégoire) sont assurément de fabrication italique. Il est aisé de les comparer à toute une série bien connue d'autres objets semblables, étudiés par ailleurs.

LES OBJETS DE MOBILIER

Il faut clairement distinguer entre ceux dont la fabrication est courante et ceux qui, au contraire, par leur haute qualité, appartiennent au mobilier de luxe.

Les premiers, bassins à bord perlés, et fragments de vases en tôle de bronze, sont, pour une bonne part, non des objets d'importation mais des imitations des fabrications italiennes. La date de ces productions doit le plus souvent être abaissée vers la fin du 6ième siècle et ne peut être prise en compte. Pourtant, comme nous le constatons pour les épées dérivées des modèles à antennes, la présence de ces imitations locales témoigne de contacts qu'il faut bien nommer 'culturels' avec le monde étrusco-italique. On doit admettre de la même manière que les fragments de casques de type 'villanovien' provenant du Calvados,[7] témoignent sinon d'importations, du moins de contacts et l'existence d'imitations qui nous semblent culturellement plus significatives que l'importation pure et simple. Ces contacts, dont l'importance, la date, l'origine et la diffusion demeurent impossibles à déterminer, existent pourtant de manière certaine et renforcent l'hypothèse d'une demande locale de produits 'italianisants'.

En revanche, les produits de haute qualité sont de fabrication méditerranéenne certaine. C'est le cas du fameux protome de griffon de St Gemmes sur Loire, attribué à un atelier de bronziers grecs, mais qui est plus probablement étrusque, et qui appartenait à un grand trépied à tiges comparable à ceux des tombes orientalisantes d'Etrurie côtière.

Les objets qui appartiennent à la seconde période, qu'il s'agisse de bronzes figurés comme les Héraclès à la massue, les guerriers en armes, les animaux souvent un peu frustes, ou d'objets de luxe: armes ou mobilier, sont en revanche beaucoup plus difficiles à attribuer avec certitude à telle ou telle origine. Les petits bronzes figurés peuvent être de fabrication locale ou du moins 'gauloise' et ne témoigner que de contacts culturels. Le casque de St Jean Trolimon, l'anse de Chaudron de St Gemmes semblent en revanche provenir de la culture étrusco-gauloise de l'Italie padane.

On le voit, la critique des objets eux-mêmes permet de nuancer ce qui apparaîtrait au premier coup d'oeil comme trop schématique.

Authenticité des origines

A quelques trop rares exceptions près, tous les objets qui sont ici évoqués, proviennent de 'fouilles' ou de trouvailles du siècle dernier. La plupart sont dépourvus de contexte, tous sont parvenus jusqu'à nous dans des conditions qui sont totalement ascientifiques. Le pire des cas est celui d'un groupe de fibules du Musée Dobrée (Nantes) dont nous ignorons jusqu'aux circonstances de l'entrée au Musée![8] Ajoutons que les fouilles récentes de toute cette région n'ont pas livré de nouveaux éléments permettant de confirmer ou d'infirmer la présence de ce type de matériel dans un contexte scientifiquement établi. Un certain nombre de ces objets, souvent de dates peu homogènes, proviennent de 'dépôts' métalliques, c'est à dire que leur contexte est déjà celui d'un remploi. Notons enfin que les trouvailles dans les cours d'eau, par example dans la Loire, sont, comme souvent ailleurs,[9] relativement fréquentes.

Naturellement, en l'absence de toute preuve, on pourrait facilement imaginer que ces fibules, ces fragments de casques ou ces petits bronzes figurés ont été achetés en Italie par des collectionneurs du siècle dernier. Le groupe des fibules de l'Avranchin, partiellement rassemblé par un érudit local,[10] a donné lieu à quelques soupçons de cette nature. Pourtant, une recherche un peu plus approfondie montre que certaines de ces fibules ont des origines géographiques définies[11] et diversifiées. L'hypothèse d'un authentique trouvaille locale de ces objets, hélas invérifiable, nous semble pour cette raison beaucoup plus probable que l'hypothèse inverse qui est tout aussi invérifiable. La présence d'autres fibules ne provenant pas de la même collection et retrouvées dans la région donne aux objets 'douteux' un caractère de vraisemblance. Nous estimons donc que dans ce cas précis, comme dans celui des fibules de Nantes qui n'ont pas d'origine définie mais qui voisinent typologiquement et géographiquement avec des trouvailles attestées, il y a *présomption* d'importation antique.

Il reste le problème assez préoccupant des petites statuettes de bronze de Thorigné en Charnie.[12] Après avoir été considérées comme des importations étrusco-italiques absolument incontestables, le doute sur leur origine s'est installé au point qu'on en est arrivé à se demander si ces trois petits bronzes n'ont pas tout simplement été achetés en Italie comme on le soupçonne pour quelques uns de leurs semblables.[13] Un retour aux documents[14] permet de penser que la trouvaille est parfaitement authentique et doit, par conséquent, trouver une place dans une hypothèse d'ensemble.

S'il est indispensable de traquer le faux, l'imitation antique et l'importation récente, s'il convient de n'avoir pas un confiance aveugle dans les indications des trouvailles du siècle dernier, en revanche il ne nous semble pas de bonne méthode de récuser absolument les données venues de fouilles imparfaites ou des trouvailles invérifiables. C'est pourquoi, chaque fois que leur cohérence avec des données plus précises nous a parue claire, nous les avons fait entrer dans ce travail.

ANALYSES DES DONNEES MATERIELLES, GEOGRAPHIQUES ET CHRONOLOGIQUES

Les fibules (Carte 1)

La répartition des fibules tardo-villanoviennes datable du 8ième et du 7ième siècle et des objets contemporains met en évidence l'importance d'étroites façades maritimes et des voies qui y conduisent. Du Nord au Sud ces objets se regroupent clairement sur les zones suivantes:

A) La baie de Somme, et en arrière-pays jusqu'à la Seine moyenne (+ de 10 fibules).

B) La baie du Mont St Michel et les voies qui y conduisent: vallée de la Sée et de la Vire, haute vallée de la Mayenne et de la Sarthe (+ de 8 fibules, 1 rasoir, 2 fragments de casque(s) villanovien(s)).

C) L'embouchure de la Loire et son arrière-pays jusqu'à la Maine (11 fibules, 1 rasoir, 1 fibule en or).

D) Dans une moindre mesure l'axe de la Garonne et de la Charente, depuis la Gironde jusqu'au seuil de Naurouze (7 fibules).[15]

Notons des trouvailles isolées à la pointe sud de la Bretagne (St Jean Trolimon, 2 fibules) qui ne peuvent être fortuites.

Nous admettons que ces fibules sont d'origine étrusco-italique et qu'elles sont arrivées dans ces zones peu après leur fabrication. Quelle peut être la signification de leur présence en ces points et à cette date?

La réponse à cette question dépend étroitement de ce qu'étaient la fonction et l'usage de ces fibules. Elles ont presque toutes été retrouvées sans contexte exploitable, la plupart du temps, dans des dépôts où, brisées, elles avaient été rassemblées peut-être pour être fondues. Quelques unes portent des traces de réparations antiques. Aucune de celles que nous avons étudiées ne semble avoir une fonction funéraire définie. La fibule de St Aignan de Grandlieu (près de Nantes)[16] a même été retrouvée au milieu d'un petit trésor monétaire du premier siècle!

On a suggéré que ces objets avaient un rôle monétaire et que les fibules, au même titre que les haches à douilles ou les obeloi, s'intégraient dans un système de payement.[17] Nous avons soigneusement pesé toutes celles que nous avons eu entre les mains (22 exemplaires): il nous a été impossible de trouver un dénominateur pondéral commun. Aussi, cette hypothèse, pour ingénieuse qu'il soit, nous semble difficile à admettre.

Il est plus difficile encore d'admettre que ces bijoux de bronze ont pu être portés par ceux-là même qui les fabriquaient et que leur présence témoignerait du passage de commerçants venus d'au-delà des Alpes.

En revanche, l'arrivée de ces objets dans ces confins de l'Europe péninsulaire où ils semblent plus nombreux que leurs imitations, mais aussi leur diffusion très au delà des zones dont nous parlons, et singulièrement en Europe centrale et danubienne, l'usage prolongé de certains d'entre eux, l'usure et les réparations de quelques exemplaires, la fabrication locale d'imitations que nous avons cru devoir exclure de notre étude, leur présence enfin dans des contextes qui, quand ils sont datables, sont toujours plus tardifs que les objets eux-mêmes, suggèrent que les fibules avaient un rôle d'insigne distinctif, une fonction ostentatoire, que la taille de quelques unes d'entre elles rend manifeste. Il nous semble donc probable que les fibules étaient une sorte de *status symbol* et distinguaient le chef, ou l'aristocrate, en tout état de cause celui qui, en affichant cet insigne, montrait ses relations directes ou indirectes avec un monde lointain et prestigieux. La présence de plusieurs de ces objets dans les cours de rivières ou de fleuves ne fait que confirmer le caractère valorisant de ces fibules, vouées de la sorte, comme parfois les épées ou les bijoux, à une divinité des eaux ou des gués. Quant aux rasoirs et à la mode dont ils témoignent,[18] leur rôle de prestige n'est sans doute pas moindre: le visage 'glabre' acquiert alors une dimension culturelle et sans doute sociale.

Que les deux fragments de casques de type villanovien provenant de Bernières d'Ailly soient, comme la chose nous semble possible, des objets d'importation ou, comme l'estiment certains auteurs,[19] des fabrications locales, importe finalement assez peu. La seconde hypothèse suppose en effet la connaissance et donc l'existence locale de modèles italiens perdus mais assurément chargés d'une valeur plus ostentatoire que militaire. Nous sommes donc en face de véritables usages culturels, de signes sociaux, directement empruntés au monde de l'Italie villanovienne, et qui ne peuvent l'avoir été qu'à travers des contacts directs ou indirects.

Il nous semble possible de suggérer que ces objets de prestige venus d'Italie, assez nombreux pour témoigner d'un usage répandu et assez prestigieux pour avoir engendré des imitations, témoignent de contacts dont le signe majeur est l'échange de dons, de cadeaux, signe de relations plus que de commerce au sens propre. Nous sommes ici dans le cadre du δῶρον et de l'ἀντιδῶρον chers au monde homérique et hésiodique. Les objets ne sont pas à notre sens l'objet d'un commerce, mais ils peuvent en être le signe.

Mais ces relations sont géographiquement suffisamment précises pour qu'on se pose de sérieuses questions sur les causes de cette localisation.

L'explication la plus courante, la plus répandue et peut-être la plus paresseuse, est née au siècle dernier et repose exclusivement sur l'hypothèse d'un commerce de l'étain.[20] La production de l'étain dans les gisements situés au nord de l'embouchure de la Loire (zone d'Abbaretz-Nozay) et ceux de la pointe de Bretagne (région des Abers) suffirait à justifier la présence d'objets méditerranéens à St Jean Trolimon et dans la région nantaise. Mais il faudrait imaginer que la concentration d'objets en baie de Somme et dans la baie du Mont St Michel témoignerait de relations maritimes avec les Iles Britanniques dont l'étain de Cornouaille serait la marchandise majeure. Il n'est pas facile de suivre une semblable hypothèse qui suppose un trafic multiple et relativement important. Il est enfin difficile d'expliquer de la sorte la présence d'objets italiques sur le parcours de la Garonne.

On a récemment proposé de donner à l'or un rôle moteur dans ces échanges du 8ième au 6ième siècle.[21] Il est clair en effet qu'à cet égard l'âge du bronze ancien, moyen et final et le premier âge du fer sont des périodes de forte production. Mais si les gisements et les dépôts alluvionnaires aussi bien que les trouvailles d'or travaillé sont nombreux dans le massif armoricain et dans les zones du Contentin et du pays nantais, la baie de Somme, encore une fois, semble complètement extérieure à ce type d'échanges et les contacts avec cette région doivent nécessairement avoir une autre origine.

Il est facile enfin d'évoquer les denrées périssables qui ne peuvent laisser aucune trace, en particulier le miel, les fourrures, éventuellement les produits strictement agricoles. On imagine aussi la vente ou la prestation de main d'oeuvre, y compris sous forme de soldats mercenaires.[22]

Mais au nombre de ces productions périssables il en est une qui a été jusqu'à présent complètement negligée mais dont l'importance est manifeste, nous voulons parler du sel. L'importance de cette denrée sous forme de gisement explique le développement de Hallstatt; le sel peut avoir joué un rôle un peu comparable pour les régions côtières où il était extrait dans des fours durant la période de la Tène et au moment de la conquête romaine. Divers indices receuillis par de jeunes chercheurs[23] permettent de penser que, sur le littoral atlantique, les fours à augets fonctionnaient dès le bronze final. Un commerce, à moyenne ou même à courte distance, justifiait seul l'importance de ces installations. Aussi, ce que nous avons décrit comme étant des contacts vers des 'terminaux' côtiers, toujours sur des côtes à forte salinité et faible profondeur, correspondrait assez bien à des exploitations et des trafics de sel.

La carte des importations les plus archaïques pourrait être interpretée comme celle des points extrêmes de réseaux commerciaux complexes dont les échanges à courte et moyenne distance (sur le sel) se confondraient partiellement avec des relations à longue distance où les métaux joueraient un rôle plus important. Par relais successifs, les dons et contre-dons venus de Méditerranée, tout chargés de leur prestige exotique, arriveraient ainsi entre les mains de l'aristocratie locale dont ils deviendraient les insignes et engendreraient localement les imitations qui témoignent de leur usage.

Les statuettes votives. Le mobilier de luxe. (Carte 2)

Il convient de superposer à la carte précédente celle des petits bronzes à caractère votif datant de la fin du 7ième siècle. Les trois figures humaines d'offrants, provenant probablement de Volterra, trouvées à Thorigné en Charnie (Nord-est de la Mayenne), les figures bovines de ce même site et celles de St Grégoire (seuil entre la vallée de la Vilaine et celle de la Rance: axe fluvial sud-nord de la Bretagne), n'ont certainement pas la même fonction que les fibules, mais les unes et les autres se retrouvent sur les routes qui conduisent de la Loire moyenne ou de la basse Loire à la baie du Mont St Michel. Un offrant armé semblable provient de Château-Chinon, un autre de Vézelay et un autre encore d'un site reculé de Serbie (Smederevo). On a suggéré[24] que ces figures témoignaient d'un culture propre à des mercenaires itinérants. Même si on ne suit pas cette hypothèse jusque dans cette précision probablement excessive, il est clair que la présence de ces bronzes votifs évoque un culte qui ne peut être très différent de ceux du monde étrusco-italique. Il faut donc se demander si l'influence culturelle, observée à propos des fibules, n'a pas, dans quelques cas exceptionnels, atteint le niveau religieux. La statuette de Vézelay semble bien provenir du cours de la Cure:[25] serait-elle liée au culte des eaux? Le caractère relativement homogène de la trouvaille de Thorigné serait de nature de suggérer un culte qui, topogragaphiquement, se situe clairement sur une voie conduisant de la Loire à la baie du Mont St Michel.

Enfin, le protome de griffon de Ste Gemmes montre clairement que, dans le courant du 6ième siècle, les échanges de dons ne se limitaient plus à de simples objets de faible valeur: ils portaient également sur le mobilier de luxe et singulièrement sur ces objets de grand prestige qui ornent les palais de Chypre ou les tombes de Préneste, qui font la fierté du sanctuaire d'Olympie ou de Delphes.

Le roitelet qui contrôle le confluent de la Loire et de la Mayenne a reçu: *un bassin qui n'est jamais allé au feu, un beau bassin d'une contenance de quatre mesures...*,[26] qui non seulement est un objet de luxe, mais lui aussi un véritable *status symbol*, impliquant comme chez les princes celtes d'Allemagne du sud, la pratique aristocratique du banquet. Tout celà ne peut que plaider en faveur de l'existence d'échanges nourris et fructueux. Mais il n'est pas nécessaire pour autant de songer à un commerce organisé; des contacts complexes, avec de nombreux relais venant de Méditerranée, et cette fois peut-être de Marseille via la vallée du Cher et Bourges, ou celle de la Vienne où les trouvailles de fibules sont loin d'être négligeables, peuvent parfaitement rendre compte du phénomène.

Vers le milieu du 6ième siècle, les documents disparaissent et tout se passe comme si les contacts étaient rompus. Pourtant les textes, qu'il s'agisse d'Avienus[27] ou d'Hérodote,[28] semblent laisser croire que des relations existent entre méditerranée et occident celtique et que ces relations tournent autour du commerce de la cassitérite. Le silence de l'archéologie doit-il être considéré comme une lacune de documentation ou comme un indice de plus graves bouleversements de l'époque de Hallstatt final et de la difficile mise en place de nouveaux réseaux de relations dominés par les influences italo-celtiques?

Une statuette de Koré de fabrication étrusco-italique et du type 'dépôt du Lapis Niger' (milieu et seconde moitié du 6ième siècle) vient d'entrer dans les collections du Musée archéologique de Nantes. Elle a été trouvé avec un contexte du plus haut intérêt sur un site de la basse vallée de la Vilaine au point le plus intérieur atteint par la marée, et dans des conditions qui ne laissent aucun doute sur le caractère antique du dépôt. Cette statuette, dont S. Haynes et E. Richardson m'ont très courtoisement confirmé l'identification, fera l'objet d'une étude détaillée de S. Santrot, conservateur du Musée archéologique de Nantes et de moi-même. Cette trouvaille me semble de nature à justifier un certain nombre d'hypothèses évoquées dans cet article.

Les échanges du 4ième au 2ième siècle (Carte 3)

D'emblée, le problème se dessine avec clarté. D'une part les objets qui nous semblent italiques, les statuettes, les poignées de chaudron, les armes, les casques, les produits que nous serions tentés de rapprocher des productions de l'Etrurie hellénistique ou en cours de romanisation, nous apparaissent comme nettement 'celtisés'. D'autre part, à l'exception de la pointe de Bretagne, les zones côtières semblent ne pas être concernées tandis que les objets les plus nombreux se regroupent dans des foyers intérieurs dont les activités paraissent ne rien devoir à la mer.

Les statuettes qui sont diffusées sur la plus grande partie des sites sont en réalité de petits Hercules (Jublains, Montevrault, St Hilaire, St Florent sur la Loire, St Just sur Dives, près de Saumur, Le Mans, et sur trois sites finistériens) dont les formes approximatives et l'anatomie sommaire plaide tantôt en faveur d'une fabrication locale, tantôt en faveur d'un importation de la plaine du Pô. De la même manière, les guerriers retrouvés sur trois sites de la pointe de Bretagne, les chevaux trop épais, les boeufs pesants, appartiennent à un répertoire connu en Italie du Nord. Ils pourraient éventuellement en provenir, mais il se peut que ce ne soient que des imitations. Les modèles en sont, certes, italiens, mais ils proviennent de cette zone étrusco-celtique qui voit alors se développer une culture mixte. Tout se passe comme si les relations méditerranéennes s'établissaient surtout à ce moment par l'intermédiaire de la Gaule padane.

Peut-être l'exemple le plus frappant est-il cette anse de chaudron trouvée dans un dépôt proche de la confluence de la Maine et de la Loire. Ce lieu, assez proche de celui où fut retrouvé le protome de griffon, semble garder son importance de voie de passage, et l'aristocratie locale semble, comme celle qui l'a précédée, se conformer aux modes luxueuses venues de l'Etrurie. Mais le guerrier de l'anse, qui ressemble beaucoup à celui d'une anse du British Museum,[29] n'est que le résultat d'un surmoulage assez grossier, maladroitement repris au burin par un ouvrier médiocre qui se sent plus à l'aise dans le polissage d'une palmette que dans la finition d'une figure humaine. Les yeux sont à peine ésquissés, la cuirasse est molle, la musculature des bras inexistante. L'objet de luxe des ateliers arétins n'est plus ici qu'une imitation médiocre clairement déstiné à la clientèle étrangère et sans doute fabriqué expressément dans ce but, comme l'était aussi probablement celui de Vienne.[30]

Tandis que les épées à antennes italiennes se transforment progressivement pour devenir localement des glaives ornés de petites sphères et bientôt de figurines humaines, les casques de type italo-celtiques se retrouvent à partir du milieu du 4ième siècle dans l'ensemble de l'espace interne que nous avons défini. Le casque d'Amfreville,[31] celui d'Agris[32] ou celui, moins prestigieux de Tronoen[33] appartiennent au même ensemble. Comme les objets du mobilier de luxe, ils dépendent moins de l'Etrurie elle-même que de l'espace celtique de la plaine du Pô et des Marches, partiellement étrusquisé.

Il semblerait donc que les relations avec l'Italie, qui sont de nouveau attestées par des objets archéologiques vers le milieu du 4ième siècle, ne sont plus du même ordre que celle des âges archaïques. La diffusion des objets et des goûts ne paraît plus toucher ces quelques points spécifiques du littoral vers lesquels ils semblaient se diriger, mais bien des centres intérieurs plus largement répartis, comme si les importations avaient changé de nature, comme si elles étaient destinées à une autre strate de population. Tout semble se passer comme si les classes bénéficiaires de ces échanges étaient plus rurales et plus hiérarchisées. De plus, les objets qui se diffusent ainsi ne sont plus des produits de l'Italie moyenne, mais de sa frange étrusco-celtique. Les échanges semblent plus nombreux, plus étendus, plus importants et en même temps plus banals et touchent peut-être des couches plus larges de la population. Il semble qu'à cette diffusion d'objets italiens ou italianisants puisse correspondre à des commerces sur des denrées très banales, peut-être agricoles. Le réseau d'échanges qui semble se mettre en place fait déjà songer à ce que l'on observera vers la fin de l'indépendance gauloise. Enfin et surtout, les rapports semblent se dérouler dans le cadre d'une sorte de Koinè celtique dont les limites sont plus étroites que celles des contacts du premier âge du bronze, mais où les relations sont autrement plus nombreuses et plus constantes.

UN COMMERCE ETRUSQUE?

Toutes les sources fort médiocres que nous avons sollicitées nous permettent d'affirmer l'existence dès l'aube du 8ième siècle de contacts certains. Mais il est impossible de savoir si ceux-ci sont directs ou non, s'ils sont réguliers ou discontinus et les échanges qui en sont le moteur nous échappent complètement. Etain, or, sel, produits agricoles, main d'oeuvre? Nul ne peut décider d'éliminer l'une de ces explications ou de faire prévaloir une hypothèse sur les autres.

Nous ne pouvons déceler que l'existence de routes privilégiées et de points d'aboutissement. Nous ne sommes pas mieux renseignés pour la période plus tardive du 4ième au second siècle où le tissu des relations semble plus dense mais où il nous semble douteux que le point de départ soit l'Etrurie propre. A la vérité, seule la période tardo-républicaine nous apporterait des données sérieuses grâce à l'étude des amphores de transport,[34] mais il s'agit là d'une toute autre question.

Beaucoup plus qu'un commerce étrusque au sens strictement économique du terme, nous pensons qu'il faut songer ici à des contacts, à des réseaux de relais où l'aristocratie locale joue un rôle majeur, allant même jusqu'à adopter quelques insignes de dignité et quelques éléments des modes de vie méditerranéens. Dans une économie qui n'est caractérisée ni par l'importance de la production, ni par le volume des échanges, ni par la nécessité du profit, les relations marchandes apparaissent comme une sorte d'épiphénomène de relations entre aristocrates détenteurs de produits rares ou précieux. Les pauvres témoignages qui nous en sont parvenus ne permettent de s'en faire qu'une idée faussement réductrice.

NOTES

Editor's note: for non-Italian readers AA.VV. = Autori Vari (Various authors)

1. La bibliographie de la question est vaste. Une étude documentaire de base a été publiée sous la direction de R. Adam dans *Caesarodunum,* suppléments n° **57, 58, 59, 62.** Les régions qui concernent notre propos y sont étudiées par J.M. Philippe, Th. Piel et Ch. Chateigner. L'une des bases de la bibliographie est constitué par l'étude capitale de Duval *et al.* 1974. Les travaux de B. Bouloumié sur les divers vases de bronze (oinochoé, cistes, situles, stamnoi) Bouloumié 1973; 1976; 1977 et 1979, ceux de Boucher 1969; 1970; 1973 et principalement, sont sur ces points d'une importance capitale. Un aperçu rapide mais très récent se trouve sous diverses signatures; AA.VV. 1992.

2. La seule exception serait une lampe 'ionienne' à vernis noir, draguée dans la Loire à Cordemais en 1901: nous ne l'avons pas retrouvée.

3. Toutes les trouvailles que nous utiliserons proviennent de trouvailles ou de fouilles de la fin du siècle dernier ou des débuts du nôtre: c'est, dire leur caractère, peu scientifique! Les recherches récentes ne nous apportent guère de données. Faut-il pour autant conclure de cette disproportion entre les résultats actuels et les données transmises que ces dernières sont fausses?

4. *Etrusques* 1992, 180; Gran Aymerich, voir ce volume.

5. Adam 1992, *passim.*

6. Duval *et al.* 1974.

7. Bernières d'Ailly: Duval *et al.* 1974, 61-2.

8. Les objets de ce Musée sont inventoriés sur un cahier d'entrée indiquant le legs, le don ou l'achat: ces fibules n'y sont pas inscrites, ce qui permet d'imaginer qu'elle ne proviennent pas d'un don mais d'une acquisition locale. L'aspect de leur patine suggère une trouvaille en milieu humide, peut-être dans les sables de la Loire ou dans le voisinage immédiat du fleuve comme grand nombre d'autre objets de bronze, en particulier d'épées 'armoricaines'. Santrot 1993, 9.

9. Cl. Rolley a montré la présence de certains de ces objets dans le cours de la Cure (Guerrier ithyphallique de Vézelay).

10. Le Chanoine Pigeon. Cf. Friedin 1982, 736.

11. Trois des fibules de la collection Pigeon sont génériquement indiquées comme provenant 'de l'avranchin' mais quatre autres sont en revanche nettement localisées et ont été retrouvées l'une à St Senier sous Avranches, l'autre aux Genets, et les deux dernières à ND de Livoye, de plus cette dernière provenance est décrite comme étant un dépôt.

12. Sur ce point en dernier lieu Rioufret et Lambert 1978.

13. Entre autres statuettes de Blandford, cf. communication de Rigby et Swaddling.

14. Baudry 1872. Texte repris par Terouanne et Boissel 1966, 187 *et seq.*

15. Ces fibules sont très différentes de celles du littoral languedocien où aboutit la route, et sensiblement postérieures!

16. Sensiblement postérieure et de fabrication vulcienne: Jannot 1992. Cette fibule avait sans doute une soeur identique, qui fut exposée avec elle, et probablement trouvée dans des conditions comparables.
17. Peroni 1966. Cf. Duval *et al.* 1974, 44.
18. La mode du visage imberbe a été signalée par Briard 1979, 138.
19. Duval *et al.* 1974, 46, référant à Hencken 1971.
20. Sur ce point cf. Jannot 1972.
21. Cf. *Préhistoire,* **14**, 1980, cité par Bouloumié 1992, 14.
22. Nous en reparlerons un peu plus loin à propos des statuettes votives.
23. En particulier une de nos étudiantes, S. Cornu, dont les travaux paraîtront sous peu.
24. Cristofani 1985, no. 13.
25. *Caesarodunum* **57** (1987), 30.
26. *Iliade,* 23, 267.
27. In *Ora Maritima* cf. Ramin 1965, 115.
28. *Iliade,* 115.
29. Walters 1899, n° 674. Haynes 1985, 301,153, avec bibl. Boucher 1986, 107-9.
30. Maule 1977, 499.
31. Musée de St Germain.
32. Angoulème, Musée archéologique de la Charente.
33. St Jean Trolimon, Collection DuChatellier, Musée de St Germain. Schaff 1977.
34. On se reportera en particulier aux travaux de P. Galliou et E. Deniau.
35. Deux trouvailles très récentes (1955) n'ont pu être portées sur cette carte: une korè sud étrusque (vers 550) vers l'embouchure de la Vilaine (Nivillac) et un guerrier de type vulcien (vers 580) sur la côte nord de l'embouchure de la Garonne (La Réole).
36. Deux nouvelles trouvailles récentes (1994) d'Hercule combattant (3ième siècle) doivent être ajoutées sur la vallée de la Loire un peu en amont d'Angers. Elles n'ont pu être portées sur cette carte.

BIBLIOGRAPHIE

AA.VV. 1992. Les Etrusques. *Les Dossiers d'Archéologie* **175**, 4-41

AA.VV. 1987. Répertoire des importations etrusco-italiques en Gaule. *Caesarodunum, Bulletin de l'Institut d'Etudes latines et du Centre de recherches A. Piganiol*, Supplément 57, 1-129

AA.VV. 1989. Répertoire des importations etrusco-italiques en Gaule. *Caesarodunum, Bulletin de l'Institut d'Etudes latines et du Centre de recherches A. Piganiol*, Supplement 58, 1-71

AA.VV. 1990. *Répertoire des importations etrusco-italiques en Gaule.* Caesarodunum, *Bulletin de l'Institut d'Etudes latines et du Centre de recherches A. Piganiol*, Supplement 59, 1-118

Adam, R. 1992. *Répertoire des importations etrusco-italiques en Gaule. Caesarodunum, Bulletin de l'Institut d'Études latines et du Centre de recherches A. Piganiol*, Supplément 62, 1-116

Baudry, F. 1872. *Puits funéraires du Bernard.* La Roche sur Yon

Boucher, S. 1969. Une aire de culture italo-céltique aux 7ième-6ième siècles av. J.-C. *MEFRA* **81**, 37-57

Boucher, S. 1970. Importations Etrusques en Gaule à la fin du 7ième siècle av. J.-C. *Gallia* **28**, 193-206

Boucher, S. 1973. Trajets térrestres du commerce Etrusque aux 5ième et 4ième siècles av. J.-C. *RA* **1**, 79-96

Boucher, S. 1976. Recherches sur les bronzes figurés de Gaule pré-romaine et romaine. Rome

Boucher, S. 1986. Problèmes concernant une anse étrusque. In, J. Swaddling (éd.), *Italian Iron Age Artefacts,* Papers of the Sixth British Museum Classical Colloquium (1982), 107-116. Londres

Bouloumié, B. 1973. Les oenochoés en bronze du type *Schnabelkanne* en France et en Belgique. *Gallia* **31**, 1-35

Bouloumié, B. 1976. Les cistes à cordons trouvées en Gaule (Belgique, France, Suisse). *Gallia* **34**, 1-30

Bouloumié, B. 1977. Situles de bronze trouvées en Gaule (7ième-4ième siècles av. J-C.). *Gallia* **35**, 1-38

Bouloumié, B. 1979. Saint-Blaise: note sommaire sur cinq années de fouilles et de recherches (1974-1978). *Gallia* **37**, 229-36

Bouloumié, B. 1992. Le commerce des Etrusques dans le Midi. *Les dossiers d'Archéologie* **175**, 14, 10-15

Briard, J. 1979. *Protohistoire de la Bretagne.* Rennes

Cristofani, M. 1985. *I Bronzi degli Etruschi.* Novare

Duval, A., Eulère, C. et Mohen, J.P. 1974. Les fibules antérieures au 6ième siècle avant notre ère trouvées en France. *Gallia* **32**, 1-61

Etrusques 1992. *Les Etrusques et l'Europe*, Exhibition Catalogue. Paris

Freidin, N. 1982. *The Early Iron Age in the Paris Basin.* Oxford

Haynes, S. 1985. *Etruscan Bronzes.* Londres

Hencken, H. 1971. *The Earliest European Helmets.* Peabody Museum, Harvard University Bulletin **28**

Jannot, J.R. 1972. La production d'étain de la péninsule armoricaine à l'époque antique. *Actes du 97ième* congrès des sociétés savantes (Nantes), 97-109

Jannot, J.R. 1992. *Annales de Bretagne* **99**, 1-12

Maule, Q. 1977. A near-classical Sculptural Style in Italy. *AJA* **81**, 499-505

Peroni, R. 1966. Considerazioni ed Ipotesi sul Ripostiglio di Ardea. *Bolletino di Paletnologia Italiana* **12**, 175-97

Ramin, J. 1965. *Le problème des Cassitérides*. Paris

Rioufret, J. et Lambert, C. 1978. Importations italiques dans le Maine et l'Anjou, du 7ième au 2ième siècle av. J.-C.. *La Province du Maine* **25**, 1-19

Santrot, J. 1993. *Les mystères de l'Archéologie*. Catalogue. Nantes

Schaaff, U. 1977. Keltische Eisenhelme aus vorrömischer Zeit. *JRGZ* **21**, 149-204

Terouanne, P. et Boissel, R. 1966. *Annales de Bretagne* **73**, **1,** 187-92

Walters, H.B. 1899. *Catalogue of Bronzes, Greek, Roman and Etruscan in the Department of Antiquities, British Museum*. London

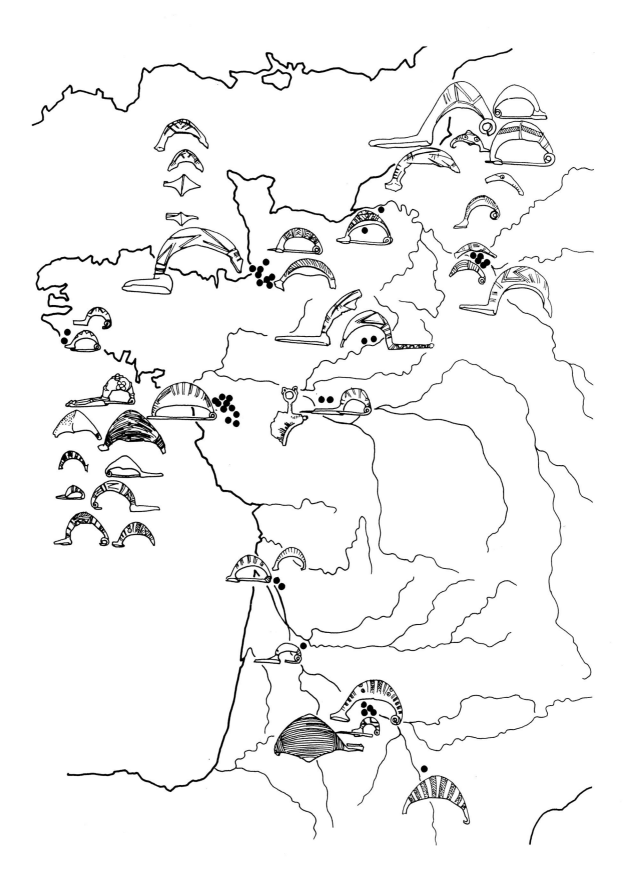

Fig. 1   Répartition des fibules et rasoirs villanoviens de probable fabrication italique, 8ième-fin 7ième siècle.

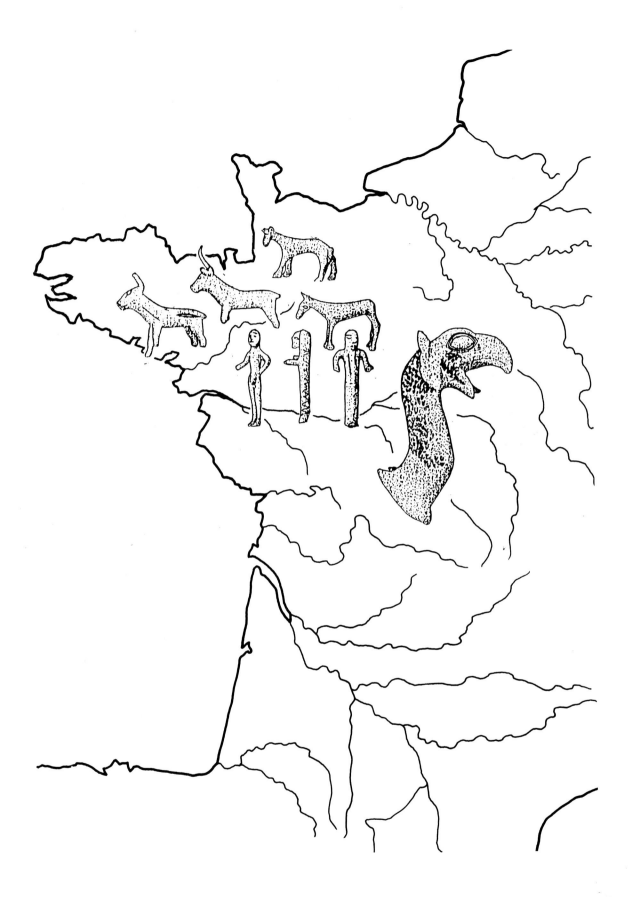

Fig. 2   Répartition des statuettes et objets mobiliers de fabrication ou importation italique, 7ième-6ième siècle.[35]

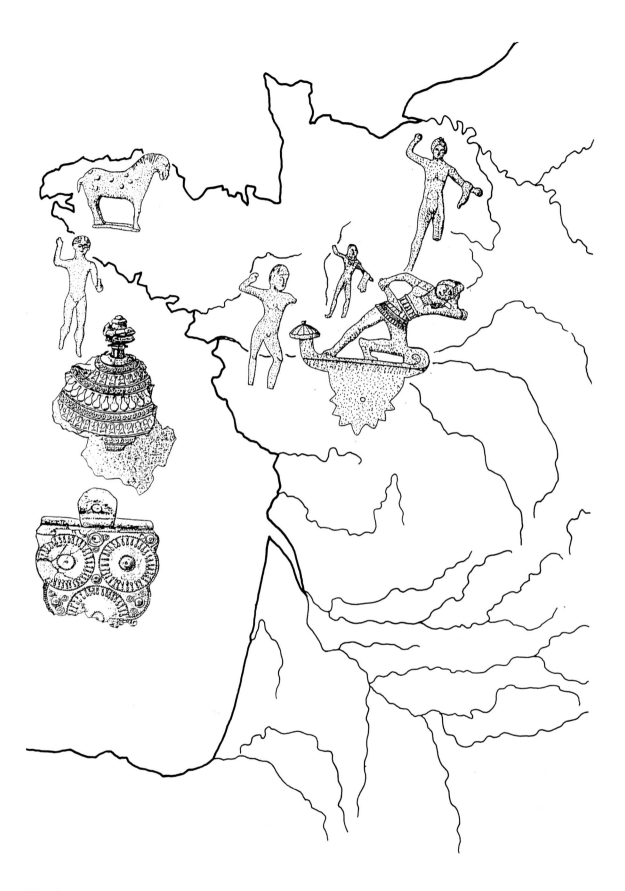

Fig. 3   Répartition des objets de fabrication étrusco-celtique, 4ième-2ième siècle.[36]

ITALIC AND ETRUSCAN IMPORTS IN THE BALTIC SEA AREA AND IN THE BRITISH ISLES DURING THE PRE-ROMAN IRON AGE: ANALOGIES, DIFFERENCES AND BACKGROUNDS

Peter F. Stary
Strandtreppe 14a, 22587 Hamburg, Germany

Contacts between northern and western parts of Europe and the cultures of the Mediterranean, which led to a mutual exchange of raw materials, artefacts and also intellectual and spiritual elements, date well back into prehistoric times. Evidence of this is seen in the spread of the Neolithic and Megalithic civilisation from the Near East and the Aegean to the Atlantic West and the North of Europe, the relationship of Mycenae with the Wessex and Nordic cultures in the Middle Bronze Age and the strong influences of East Mediterranean origin seen in the British Isles and southern Scandinavia during the Atlantic Late Bronze Age.[1]

The roots of cultural contacts in the pre-Roman Iron Age can be traced back to the first quarter of the first millennium BC, when the Phoenicians expanded to set up colonies in western parts of the Mediterranean and even beyond the Pillars of Hercules.[2] Many of the problems have not yet been studied and much research remains to be done with regard to the inter-regional relationship of the cultural groups in this very interesting period. The effects and results of the Late Bronze Age system of intercultural connections are, however, discernible in the archaeological remains, which provide evidence of material and conceptual influences on, for example, costume, arms and armour, burial customs and religion. There are several instances of the transfer of cultural elements along the Atlantic coasts to western and northern parts of Europe, and in this the Phoenicians undoubtedly played an important part as sailors, traders, and adventurers, and as the successors of the Mycenean hegemony in the Mediterranean. The economic bases for the later interdependence between these different, far distant cultures, changing in quantity and quality, origins and destinations, did not primarily consist of trade in finished goods. Herodotos points to the substance of this exchange (III, 115-116):

> About the far west of Europe I have no definite information, for I cannot accept the story of a river called by non-Greek peoples the Eridanos, which flows into the northern sea, where amber is supposed to come from; nor do I know anything of the existence of islands called the Tin Islands, whence we get our tin ... Yet it cannot be disputed that tin and amber do come to us from what one might call the ends of the earth. It is clear that it is the northern parts of Europe which are the richest in gold, but how it is produced is another mystery ... . In any case it does seem to be true that the countries which lie on the circumference of the inhabited world produce the things which we believe to be most rare and beautiful.

Thus trade in amber and non-ferrous metals seems in the Late Bronze Age to have been a most important factor in cultural exchange between Mediterranean and Atlantic parts of the continent. In this period we have considerable evidence for tin from Cornwall and Devon, and for amber from different parts of the Baltic Sea coast, being in their raw forms the main basis for trade between Britain, Scandinavia, Italy and other parts of the south; on their way from the mining and producing areas to the market regions they crossed different cultural groups in central and western Europe.[3] Italic fibulae of the ninth and eighth centuries BC are known from sporadic finds in England (Fig. 3), with analogies in France, which show their transfer from central Italy via continental trade-routes.[4] Some such fibulae are also known from northern Germany, but they are of minor importance in comparison with other evidence of Italic influence in central and northern parts of Germany, in Poland and southern Scandinavia, such as, for example, the use of miniature weapons as *pars-pro-toto* grave-goods in southern Scandinavia, with analogies in Etruria and Latium. Also to be considered is the incidence of late Villanovan and early Etruscan bronze amphorae in northern Germany, and of hut- and face-urns in many neighbouring parts of the western Baltic Sea, which seem to have been transferred via south German/east Alpine routes.

These traditions of economic and cultural contacts, generally a result of indirect relations between cultural groups, also reflect influence on the spiritual and religious aspects of life. They formed the basis of connections at the beginning of the Iron Age, which was marked and characterised by important economic changes, caused by a decrease in demand not only for copper and tin, due to the rise of Iron Age civilisations, but also for amber, due to new fashions in the Mediterranean.

In the following pre-Roman Iron Age more analogies than differences are evident in the character, quality and quantity of Italic and Etruscan imports and influences in the western and northern circumference of Europe - facts which may point to similar factors and conditions affecting the external relations of both cultural regions.[5] But the Italic and Etruscan elements did not reach the high level of cultural prominence attained in the previous period. In this phase some Italic long-footed fibulae are known from England in the west and from the Danish isles in the north. These are very rare, however, and may indicate that cultures were selecting and restricting grave-goods. Imported fibulae, for instance, occur now only as votives in Danish bogs and waters.[6] The fibulae originated in different parts of central and northern Italy: for example, an isolated, long-footed *navicella*-fibula of the seventh century from the Iller Heath in Viborg county, Jutland, and another single find of this type and period from Sengløse on the isle of Sealand, which will be published by J. Jensen of the National Museum in Copenhagen. One of the most interesting items of the sixth century was found on Tåsinge near Svendborg, south of the island of Funen: it is a bow-fibula, its foot missing, which can be compared with finds from the Adriatic coast of central Italy characterised by the foot terminating in a ram's head.[7]

Italic fibulae of the Early Iron Age are also known from England, as for example a long-footed *navicella*-fibula with knobs or antennae from Lakenheath in Suffolk (Fig. 4) and another from Hod Hill in Dorset (Fig. 5), and a long-footed serpentine-fibula from a tumulus near Castor in Cambridgeshire.[8] Several finds of this type from Britain, collected and published by D.B. Harden in 1952, seemed to be suspicious because of dubious findspots, until in 1974 A. Duval, Chr. Eluère and J.-P. Mohen published many similar fibulae from France: long-footed *navicella*- and serpentine-fibulae with and without knobs or antennae, whose main distribution in the valleys of the Rhône, Seine and Garonne seemed to mark their trade via the Gulf of Lion to northern France and across the Channel to England.[9] Several finds of such fibulae, however, are also known from Roman sites and graves in Britain and they seem to have been imported even after the Roman conquest, perhaps as amulets. Another route must be supposed for the Danish finds. Fibulae of these types found in western parts of Poland (especially Silesia and Lusitania with their close relations to cultures both north of the Baltic Sea and south of the Alps in this period) offer evidence that they were transported from Italy via the east Alpine region and the valley of the Oder to its mouth on the Baltic coast and further on by sea routes to Denmark.[10]

Similar evidence can be drawn from other groups of finds, especially bronze vessels, most of which date to the seventh and sixth centuries BC. One of the most interesting of recent finds is from the excavations of Leif Karlenberg in 1988 at a tumulus near Linköping in Östergötland, southern Sweden, and consists of parts of an ornamented water bottle, or pilgrim flask, found together with a trapezoidal bronze razor of the Hallstatt C period from Central Europe.[11] Bronze objects of this type and of central Italian origin were studied and published in 1990 by D. Marzoli.[12]

Another important find, made as long ago as 1936 in Hassle, Närke, also in southern Sweden, is a big bronze cauldron with a diameter of 40.5cm which can be compared with similar cauldrons with griffins' and lions' heads of the seventh century from Etruria and the eastern Mediterranean. The find from Hassle, together with two central European Hallstatt C swords, two cordoned italoid Hallstatt C buckets (Figs. 8, 9), (now being studied by Professor B. Stjernquist in Lund) and twelve phalerae, seems to represent part of a water-sacrifice or hoard.[13] A so-called Rhodian bronze jug (being studied by Professor B. Shefton) is known from Hillerød, north of the isle of Sealand, and is now exhibited in the Museum of Prehistory in Hamburg.[14] Other examples are a cauldron with silenus-masks, found in a cremation grave near Langå on the island of Funen (Fig. 1) and an Etruscan stamnos of the fifth century from another grave in this cemetery (Figs. 10, 11).[15]

Several bronze and clay vessels of Italic and Etruscan origin are also recorded from Britain, mainly from England, though most of them have very dubious findspots and are probably not authentic. Parts of an Etruscan so-called Rhodian bronze jug - like the one from Hillerød - were found near Minster in Kent; Etruscan oinochoai with trefoil-shaped mouths are known from the river Crouch in Essex and from Northampton, and a find of a cordoned italoid bucket - like that from Hassle - was made near Weybridge in Surrey (Fig. 7).[16]

Potentially remarkable discoveries are recorded from other parts of the British Isles, as for instance an Etruscan bronze statuette of the early Iron Age from Sligo in Ireland and another of the first half of the fifth century from Uffington in Berkshire, but their findspots are doubtful. On the other hand, in 1970 S. Boucher published some Etruscan statuettes of the seventh century from France, distributed widely from the upper Rhône basin to Normandy, which seem to mark trade-routes for such artefacts.[17] A terracotta head of about the middle of the first millennium BC is said to have been ploughed up in a field at Nutbourne in Sussex.

The types of imported bronze vessels known from southern Scandinavia and England are very frequently found in central Europe during the Hallstatt and early La Tène periods, especially in southern Germany, Bohemia, Austria, eastern France and partially also in Belgium, Holland, northern France and western Poland, where they indicate routes of transition and transport to the north and west of Europe. It is evident that most of these seventh- to fifth-century imports were traded from Italy, via the Central European Hallstatt and La Tène region, to the Atlantic and Baltic areas of the continent.

In the fourth and third centuries BC imports from the south are very rare, and Celtic finds are infrequent north and west of the Celtic world, indicating a general stagnation and decrease in contacts. A Campanian situla with palmette-ornaments was ploughed up near Keldby on the Danish island of Møn (Figs. 2, 12), and a similar one is known from the famous La Tène B grave of Waldalgesheim in the Rhineland.[18] A cauldron with mask, probably an Etrusco-Faliscan work of the third century, was found in a bog near Mosbæk in Jutland (Fig. 13), while from England there are Italic bronze jugs known from Tewkesbury in Gloucestershire with the unconfirmed provenance of 'Bath' (Fig. 6).[19] This remarkable decrease in Etruscan and other Italic imports in the fourth, third and especially the second centuries BC also occurs in the rest of the continent, including the so-called Celtic world in Central Europe. Though renewed strong contacts with western and northern parts are indicated by many Celtic imports and influences from the second half of the fourth century onwards, examples from Italy are still missing in all regions north of the Alps.

During the first century BC Italic imports start to increase again, mainly in the form of early Roman or so-called Campanian bronze vessels normally found in the context of late La Tène Celtic, Gallo-Belgic and early Germanic chieftains' graves. The various types of imported vessels have been carefully studied and described by H.J. Eggers and J. Werner.[20] One of the most important forms is a jug of the so-called Kappel-Kelheim type, with a silenus-mask at the handle, as for example from the lower Elbe area in northern Germany, from Alt-Mölln near Lauenburg and Wiebendorf near Hagenow, and with floral ornamented handles of Ornavasso-Kærumgård type from graves in

Kærumgård near Odense on the isle of Funen and from Podwiejsk near Chelmno in the lower Wistula area.

Similar jugs of the Ornavasso-Kærumgård type are also known from Gallo-Belgic graves in south east England, from grave Y in Aylesford, Kent, and from graves A and B in Welwyn, Hertfordshire (Figs. 14, 16, 18).[21] Another significant type of this period is the so-called Aylesford pan with swan-headed grip which is known from graves in Nienbüttel near Hannover, from a bog or lake near Gniewski Mlyny near Gniew in the area of the mouth of the Wistula, and again from rich graves in south east England - from grave Y in Aylesford, Kent, and grave B in Welwyn, Hertfordshire (Figs. 15, 19).

Other Italic types characteristic of this period are known either from regions south-west of the Baltic Sea or from the south-east of England.[22] There are for example situlae with dolphin, heart/leaf-shaped or trapezoidal handles from north and north east Germany, Denmark and Sweden: with dolphin handles - from graves in Banimslow near Randow, Harsefeld near Stade, Netzeband near Greifswald, Nienbüttel near Hannover and moreover from Stora Bjurum in Västergötland, southern Sweden; with heart/leaf-shaped handles - from Körchow near Hagenow, Nienbüttel near Hannover, Osterehlbeck near Lüneburg, Hoby near Maribo on Lolland, Stenløse near Frederiksborg on Sealand and from Källeråsen in Västergötland, southern Sweden, and with trapezoidal handles - from Nienbüttel near Hannover and Beldringe on Sealand.

Some types of basin with steep sides are known, from Hammoor in Stormarn, Harsefeld near Stade, Körchow near Hagenow, Nienbüttel near Hannover, Alfva on the isle of Gotland, Alguttsrum on the isle of Öland and Skeide in Moere in southern Norway; while basins with fixed handles are known from Dobbin near Güstrow, Weddel near Braunschweig and Jægerpros near Frederiksborg on the isle of Sealand.

Other characteristic imports are known from England, especially several clay amphorae from rich graves as for example at Welwyn in Hertfordshire, Mauldon Moor in Bedfordshire, Westmill in Hertfordshire and Lindsell in Essex (Fig. 17; I am grateful to V. Rigby for information regarding this material).[23]

Most current types of Italian bronze vessels are also well known from graves in parts of Europe where the custom of putting such goods into graves was customary, as for instance in the middle Rhine area, in Bohemia and the central Alpine region. Fragments of vessels have been found in Late La Tène oppida and hoards. It follows from the archaological evidence that Italic bronze vessels were widely distributed and used in the late Celtic world and also exported and traded further north and west to the cultural groups on the Atlantic and Baltic coasts. They mark the starting point of extensive later trade in Roman products into non-Roman Germany during the early centuries AD.

In considering the development of Italic and Etruscan imports during the pre-Roman Iron Age in the north and west of the continent, we see clear parallels in the origin, quality and quantity of imports, beginning with seventh- and sixth-century types of fibulae and bronze vessels in both cultural regions, a considerable number of serpentine- and *navicella*-fibulae with long foot, Etruscan cauldrons and oinochoe and other Italic types such as water bottles and cordoned buckets. In the fifth century a certain decrease is evident, though some Etruscan or Italic vessels, mainly oinochoai and stamnoi, are known. From the fourth to the second centuries BC only a few bronze vessels are so far known from Denmark and England. The imports start again about the middle of the first century BC with various types of bronze vessel of so-called Campanian or early Roman origin in southern Scandinavia and England, and also in England even amphorae, which give further evidence of the wine trade.

The distributions of Etruscan and Italic imports known from the north and west of the continent show that they were transported from Italy over the Alps, following old trade- and migration-routes, primarily along the important river-valleys of the Rhine, Rhône, Elbe, Danube, Oder and Wistula, through Central Europe and further on by sea routes in the western Baltic Sea to southern

Scandinavia and via the Straits of Dover to England. There are, of course many gaps in the evidence, mainly because of changing customs in cult and religion. For example, bronze vessels and other luxury-goods were sacrificed in lakes in southern Scandinavia and also in England during the pre-Roman Iron Age, but they were not put into graves before the first century BC. Some of the imported bronze vessels, dating from the sixth to the fourth centuries BC, are found in graves of the first century BC in Denmark, when this custom was introduced in the western Baltic Sea area.

Most of the Etruscan and Italic seventh- to fifth-century imports in the Central European Celtic area were found in the context of rich graves of high-ranking persons, a custom which after the long period of lack of evidence from the fourth to the second century BC - as in southern Scandinavia and England - recurs throughout the Celtic world during the first century BC, as for example in the Rhineland, eastern and northern France, the Balkans and the Alpine region. In the late Celtic period, however, only fragments of imports are found in settlements and sometimes in hoards. Nevertheless the distribution of imported bronze vessels shows that in this period too, trade with southern Europe crossed central European territories.

The question of reasons and circumstances for the changing quantities of imports and influences during the development of contacts with Italy cannot be answered simply by different and changing regional customs in pre-Roman Iron Age Europe, clearly shown by the archaeological record. On the contrary, there are clear indications as to reasons in political, economical and cultural developments within the Hallstatt and La Tène cultures of central Europe which were obviously the cantilever for contacts with cultures south of the Alps. Despite certain evidence for Etruscan and Italic imports and influence in the western Baltic Sea area, B. Bouloumié was right to criticise W. Szafrański's theory of the direct presence of Etruscans in the amber-producing regions controlling trade to the South.[24] Close contacts with Central Europe and the north and west which continued former Late Bronze Age relations were very intensive at the beginning of the Iron Age, as shown by many Early Hallstatt imports such as swords, bronze vessels, razors, fibulae etc. In the Late Hallstatt, a decline in contact is evident, perhaps a result of the increasing affinity of the Celtic world with the Mediterranean and the decreasing demand for tin after the introduction of iron. Baltic amber was still very much in demand, but it was traded less to Italy and more to the West Hallstatt area in south west Germany, Switzerland and eastern France. From the beginning of the fourth century onwards, only a few Etruscan and Italic imports are known from the cultures north of the Alps in the Celtic area and also in Scandinavia and Britain. It seems that the Celtic migrations of the fourth and third centuries BC to the south, south east, south west and west of the European continent interrupted the traditional trading-system.

After a certain consolidation of Celtic culture, contacts between central, northern and western Europe started again from the late fourth century onwards, but imports from Italy are still missing. Some decades before the final destruction of Celtic culture, Italic objects are found again north of the Alps, in central, northern and western Europe as well, in circumstances obviously favoured by Caesar's military campaigns in Gaul and Britain. It was now for the first time that Gaulish, Gallo-Belgic and Germanic tribes came into direct contact with the Romans and their culture, mainly in western parts of Central Europe, in the middle and lower Rhineland, central and northern France and in England. In the course of the Gallic and Gallo-Belgic wars Italic, Roman and Campanian artefacts seem to have been distributed as wages, gifts, booty or as trading goods by soldiers, traders and adventurers mainly in the Gallo-Belgic areas of northern France and England, and also in the early Germanic territories of Scandinavia, which - in contrast to the Gaulish and Gallo-Belgic tribes - could maintain their independence. We know from Caesar's records of the Gallic wars of tribes from northern parts of Europe who, driven by the desire for booty, fought in the armies of the Gauls, Gallo-Belgics and even of the Romans as mercenaries and allies. During the wars many elements of Roman culture must have been assimilated by all those tribes who took part in or were confronted by Caesar's campaigns. A substantial peaceful or warring exchange between the Romans and the 'barbarians' is evident especially around the site of the battles in the middle Rhineland and in northern France, where the frontiers between the Celtic, Gallo-Belgic and Germanic territories were situated. We know from written sources concerning Maroboduus and the Marcomanni in Bohemia, that Celtic culture at this time lost its fashion among the Germanic tribes, who from now on were much more fascinated by Roman culture. Italian imports in rich graves of the north and west point to similar tendencies in social and cultural formations and ritual behaviour among the Germanic and Gallo-Belgic tribes. We know from Caesar that the Gallo-Belgics partially traced their origins to the Celtic, Germanic and local tribes of northern France. These historical processes during Caesar's campaigns may explain how Italian goods were distributed so quickly as far as southern Scandinavia and England.

Furthermore, we have to face the problem of goods which were exchanged from the Baltic and Atlantic area of Europe to Italy. An important factor was the trade in amber to Italy from the Baltic Sea region via the Oder and Elbe, Bohemia, Bavaria and the east Alpine region in the Early Hallstatt period, and also to south western parts of Central Europe in the Late Hallstatt period, as shown by finds of amber and by recent scientific analyses of samples of amber.[25] In the Late Hallstatt period markets for amber in the west Hallstatt area obviously became much more attractive and important. The records of Herodotos which I have already mentioned point to trade in amber with the Greeks at this time. From Herodotos (III.115) and other ancient historians (eg. Pliny *Nat.Hist.* XXXVII,ii), we have evidence for amber coming by sea to the south from the Atlantic coast of Jutland and northern Germany and via the valleys of the Seine, Loire, Garonne and Rhône to the Greeks in the west, but it may not explain the important trade in Italic and Etruscan goods in exchange.

The tin-trade with the Kassiterides (perhaps the British Isles), as described by Herodotos (III.115), has already been referred to.[26] In the fourth century the Greek geographer Pytheas of Massilia visited Cornwall, named Belerion. His description of the route for the tin-trade survives in the writings of Timaios, Poseidonios, Strabo, Diodorus and Pliny. The route began (see Diodorus V.22) from Belerion to an island named Ictis, which could be reached by wagon in times of low tide. From there the tin was transported by local tribes and Gauls to the continent and from here by land-routes to the mouth of the Rhône, within thirty days. Another market is mentioned by Herodotos in Narbonne at the Gulf of Lion. Belerion can be identified with Land's End in Cornwall and the island of Ictis with St Michael's Mount off the Cornish coast. A tin ingot dredged from the Fal estuary at St Mawes, Cornwall, resembling in form the astragal-shaped tin ingots mentioned by Diodorus Siculus, may be a relic of this tin-trade. It is not clear, however, whether this Atlantic tin-trade, which seems to have had its main markets in the western Greek colonies, was of any importance for Etruscan and Italic imports in Britain, though according to the distribution of *navicella-* and serpentine-fibulae, bronze vessels and early Etruscan bronze statuettes, a greater part of the imports seems to have been transported via the west Alpine and the Rhône valley region through central parts of France to England.

On the other hand, goods such as wax, hides, skins, resin, salt, food and slaves must be regarded as potential trading items. There is no archaeological evidence, however, for such a trade and it is very doubtful therefore whether the transfer of most of these types of goods was worthwhile, considering the difficulties and dangers of long-distance transport in those times. According to contemporary evidence most of the Etruscan and Italic imports of the pre-Roman Iron Age in northern and western parts of Europe were transported through the Hallstatt and La Tène cultures, mainly through areas in central and eastern France, southern Germany, Bohemia and western Poland. The distribution of characteristic types, the increase and decrease of imports and influences and the changes in transfer-route must be seen against a background of political, economical and cultural development and the birth of the Celtic world, which was characterised by many significant changes which had consequences for the whole continent. But much work is still to be done with regard to the identification and reconstruction of the various factors and circumstances which stimulated or hindered transalpine trade and contact between Italy, central Europe, and Scandinavia and the British Isles.[27]

NOTES

1. Schauer 1983; 1984; 1985.
2. Niemeyer 1984.
3. See Adam 1990; Boucher 1970; Dehn and Frey 1962; idem. 1979; Frey 1980; idem. 1989; Kimmig 1981; idem 1983; Kromer 1986; Łuka 1959; Shefton 1979; Schaaff 1969; Stary 1991a; idem 1993. For the Baltic Sea area: Ekholm 1943; Riis 1959; for the British Isles: Harden 1952; Harbison and Laing 1974.
4. Duval *et. al.,* 1974.
5. For Mediterranean contacts with regions north of the Alps: Vienna 1992; Paris 1988; Paris 1992; Göttingen 1985.
6. Laursen 1958.
7. Laursen and Randsborg 1981.
8. *Guide* 1925, 93, fig. 93; Harden 1952, 319, fig. 3.
9. Duval *et al.,* 1974.
10. Bouloumié 1989; Szafrański 1989; Szlankówna 1937; for imports see also Antoniewicz 1947; Fogel and Makiewicz 1988.
11. Unpublished; I would like to thank U.E. Hagberg, Stockholm, for the information.
12. Marzoli 1988; idem 1989.
13. For cordoned buckets: Stjernquist 1967.
14. Unpublished; for Rhodian bronze jugs see Shefton 1979.
15. For stamnoi: Shefton 1988.
16. Harbison and Laing 1974, 4-5, no. 3; 6-8, no. 7; 8-10, no. 8; *Guide* 1925, 91, fig. 89; for oinochoé: Bouloumié 1973 (in France and Belgium).
17. Boucher 1970.
18. Riis 1959, 19, fig. 15.
19. Ekholm 1943, 108, fig. 3; *Guide* 1925, 92, fig. 90.
20. Eggers 1951; Werner 1954; idem 1978; see also Graue 1974.
21. Stary 1991b, with bibliography in the notes.
22. Eggers 1951.
23. Stary 1991b, with bibliography in the notes.
24. Bouloumié 1989; Szafrański 1989.
25. For the amber-trade and amber-routes see Bozsok-Sombathely 1983; see also Göttingen 1985, 205; Stary 1991a, 28-29, with bibliography in the notes.
26. For the tin-trade and tin-routes see Göttingen 1985, 204-205,278; see also Stary 1991a, 29, with bibliography in the notes.
27. I would like to thank Dr. Judith Swaddling for correcting and improving the manuscript.

BIBLIOGRAPHY

Adam, R. (ed.) 1990. Répertoire des importations étrusques et italiques en Gaule. *Caesarodunum, Bulletin de l'Institut d'Etudes latines et du Centre de recherches A. Piganiol*, suppl. **59**

Antoniewicz, J. 1947. Les trouvailles hallstattiennes de Bogumiłow et de Pyszków, distr. de Sieradz. *Światowit* **18**, 11-41

Boucher, D. 1970. Importations étrusques en Gaule à la fin du VIIe siècle av. J.-C. *Gallia* **28**, 193-206

Bouloumié, B. 1973. Les oenochoés en bronze du type *Schnabelkanne* en France et en Belgique. *Gallia* **31**, 1-35

Bouloumíe, B. 1989. Sur la question d'une éventuelle présence étrusque au bord de la Baltique. In, T. Malinowski (ed.), *Problemy kultury Łużyckiej na Pomorzu*, 239-52. Słupsk

Bozsok-Szombathely 1983. *Nord-Süd-Beziehungen, 1983.* Historische und kulturelle Zusammenhänge und Handelsbeziehungen die europäischen Bernsteinstraßen entlang vom 1. Jahrtausend v.u.Z. bis zum Ende der römischen Kaiserzeit. Internationales Kolloquium, Bozsok-Szombathely. *Savaria* **16**

Dehn, W. and Frey, O-H. 1962. Die absolute Chronologie der Hallstatt- und Frühlatènezeit Mitteleuropas aufgrund des Südimports. In, M. Pallottino, L. Cardini and D. Brusadin (eds.), *Atti del VIe Congresso Internazionale di Scienze Preistoriche e Protostoriche* I, 197-208, Roma

Dehn, W. and Frey O-H. 1979. Southern Imports and the Hallstatt and early La Tène Chronology of Central Europe. In, D. and F. Ridgway (eds.), *Italy before the Romans*, 489-511. London, New York, San Francisco

Duval, A., Eluère, Chr. and Mohen, J-P. 1974. Les fibules antérieures au VIe siècle avant notre ère, trouvées an France. *Gallia* **32**, 1-61

Eggers, H-J. 1951. *Der römische Import im freien Germanien.* Hamburg

Ekholm, G. 1943. Klassische Einfuhrwaren in Skandinavien. *ActaArch* **14**, 105-10

Fogel, J. and Makiewicz, T. 1988. La sconosciuta importazione etrusca in Cujavia, Polonia Centrale, e la questione della presenza degli Etruschi sul Baltico. *StEtr* **55**, 123-9

Frey, O-H. 1980. Der Westhallstattkreis im 6.Jh. v. Chr. In, D. Straub (ed.), *Die Hallstattkultur. Frühform europäischer Einheit*, Exhib. Cat. Schloss Lamberg, 80-116. Steyr

Frey, O-H. 1989. Mediterranes Importgut im Südostalpengebiet. In, M. Ullrix-Closset and M. Otte (eds.), *La Civilisation de Hallstatt*. Bilan d'une rencontre, Université de Liège (1987), 293-306

Göttingen 1985. Untersuchungen zu Handel und Verkehr der vor- und frühgeschichtlichen

Zeit in Mittel- und Nordeuropa 1. In K. Düwel, H. Jankuhn, H. Siems and D. Timpe (eds.), *Bericht über die Kolloquien der Kommission für Altertumskunde Mittel- und Nordeuropas in den Jahren 1980 bis 1983*. Abhandlungen der Akademie der Wissenschaften in Göttingen, Philologisch-Historische Klasse, 3. Folge, Nr. 143, 1985.

Graue, J. 1974. *Die Gräberfelder von Ornavasso*. Hamburg

Guide 1925. *Guide to Early Iron Age Antiquities*. British Museum, London

Harbison, P. and Laing, L.R. 1974. *Some Iron Age Imports in England*. British Archaeological Reports 5. Oxford

Harden, D.B. 1952. Italic and Etruscan finds in Britain. In, *Atti del I Congresso Internazionale di Preistoria e Protostoria Mediterranea, 1950*, 315-24. Florence, Naples and Rome

Kimmig, W. 1981. Die frühen Kelten und das Mittelmeer. In, K. Bittel, W. Kimmig and S. Schiek (eds.), *Die Kelten in Baden-Württemberg*, 248-78. Stuttgart

Kimmig, W. 1983. Die griechische Kolonisation im westlichen Mittelmeergebiet und ihre Wirkung auf die Landschaften des westlichen Mitteleuropa. *JRGZ* **30**, 5-78

Kromer, K. 1986. Das östliche Mitteleuropa in der frühen Eisenzeit (7.-5.Jh.v.Chr.), seine Beziehungen zu Steppenvölkern und antiken Hochkulturen. *JRGZ* **33**, 3-93

Laursen, J. and Randsborg, K. 1981. *Italien på Tåsinge - omkrig en fibel fra 6. årh. f. kr.* Svendborg & Omegns Museum årbog 1981, 6-11

Laursen, J. 1958. Om votivfund fra Bronzealderens slutning. *Kuml* 1958, 1-31

Łuka, L.J. 1959. Les importations de l'Italie et des Alpes orientales et leurs imitations locales chez la population de la civilisation 'Lusacienne' de la période de Hallstatt en Pologne. *Slavia Antiqua* **6**, 1-99

Marzoli, D. 1988. Doppelflasche und Waffen aus einem frühetruskischen Kriegergrab. *Jahrbuch der Staatlichen Kunstsammlungen in Baden-Württemberg* **25**, 7-15

Marzoli, D. 1989. *Bronzefeldflaschen in Italien*. Prähistorische Bronzefunde II 4. Munich

Mielczarek, M. 1989. *Ancient Greek Coins found in Central, Eastern and Northern Europe*. Wrocław

Niemeyer, H.G. 1984. Die Phönizier und die Mittelmeerwelt im Zeitalter Homers. *JRGZ* **31**, 3-94

Paris 1988. *Les princes celtes et la Méditerranee*.

Paris 1992. *Les Etrusques et l'Europe*. Exhib. Cat., Paris

Riis, J.P. 1959. The Danish bronze vessels of Greek, Early Campanian and Etruscan manufacture. *Acta Arch* **30**, 1-50

Schaaff, U. 1969. Versuch einer regionalen Gliederung frühlatènezeitlicher Fürstengräber. In, O.-H. Frey (ed.), *Marburger Beiträge zur Archäologie der Kelten. Festschrift for Wolfgang Dehn*, 187-202. Bonn

Schauer, P. 1983. Orient im spätbronze- und früheisenzeitlichen Okzident. *JRGZ* **30**, 175-94

Schauer, P. 1984. Spuren minoisch-mykenishen und orientalischen Einflusses im atlantischen Westeuropa. *JRGZ* **31**, 137-86

Schauer, P. 1985. Spuren orientalischen und ägäischen Einflusses im bronzezeitlichen Nordischen Kreis. *JRGZ* **32**, 123-95

Shefton, B.B. 1979. Die 'rhodischen' Bronzekannen. *Marburger Studien zur Vor- und Frühgeschichte* 2. Mainz

Shefton, B.B. 1988. Der Stamnos. In W. Kimmig (ed.), *Das Kleinaspergle*, 104-52. Stuttgart

Shefton, B.B. 1989. Zum Import und Einfluß mediterraner Güter in Alteuropa. *KölnJbVFrühGesch* **22**, 207-20

Stary, P.F. 1991a. Mediterrane Einfuhrgüter während der Früheisenzeit in England und Skandinavien. *RM* **98**, 1-31

Stary, P.F. 1991b. Reiche Gräber der Zeitenwende beiderseits des Ärmelkanals. *BJb* **191**, 85-123

Stary, P.F. 1993. Der Mittelgebirgsraum als Transit- und Vermittlungszone hallstatt- und latènezeitlicher Kutturelemente aus Mitteleuropa ins Westliche Ostseegebiet. *BerRGK* **74**, 535-62

Stjernquist, B. 1967. *Ciste a cordoni (Rippenzisten), Produktion-Funktion-Diffusion* 1-2. Lund

Szafrański, W. 1989. La question du séjour des Etruriens à la côte de la mer Baltique. In, T. Malinowski (ed.), *Problemy kultury Łużyckiej na Pomorzy*, 253-72. Słupsk

Szlankówna, A.A. 1937. Einige Funde altitalischer und westeuropäischer Importe in Südostpolen und der Ukraine. *Światowit* **17**, 293-306

Vienna 1992. Etrusker nördlich von Etrurien. Etruskische Präsenz in Norditalien sowie ihre Einflüsse auf die einheimischen Kulturen. In, L.A. Aigner-Foresti (ed.), *Akten des Symposiums Wien-SchloB-Neuwaldegg, 1989*. Vienna

Werner, J. 1954. Die Bronzekanne von Kelheim. *Bayerische Vorgeschichtsblätter* **20**, 43-73; see also reprint in, J. Werner (1979), Spätes Keltentum zwischen Rom und Germanien. *Gesammelte Aufsätze zur Spätlatènezeit*, L. Pauli (ed.), 68-107. München

Werner, J. 1978. Zur Bronzekanne von Kelheim. Rückblick und Ausblick. *Bayerische Vorgeschichtsblätter* **43**, 1-18; see also reprint in op.cit. 198-220

Fig. 1   Handle of the cauldron from Langå, Funen
Fig. 2   Campanian situla from Keldby, Møn

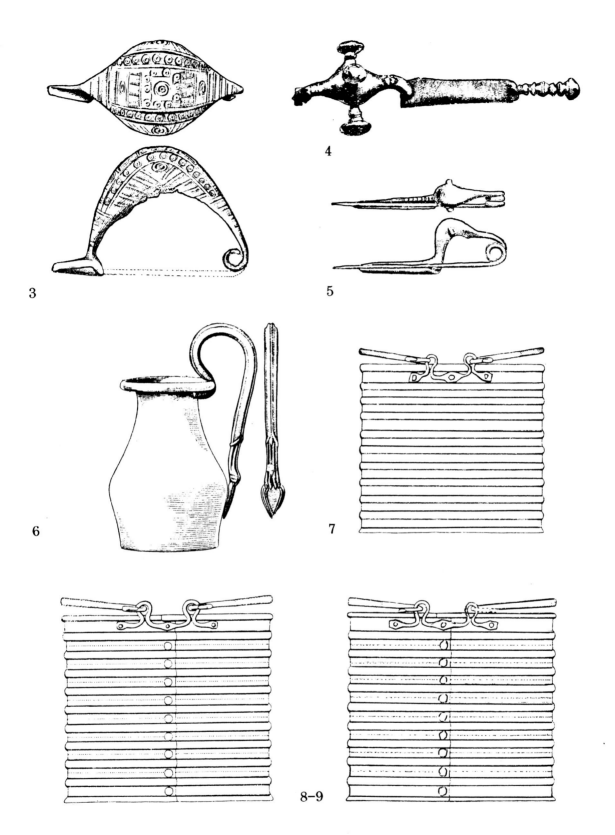

Figs. 3-9 3) Fibula from Box, Wiltshire;
4) Fibula from Lakenheath, Suffolk;
5) Fibula from Hod Hill, Dorset;
6) Jug from Tewkesbury, Gloucestershire;
7) Cordoned bucket from Weybridge, Surrey;
8-9) Cordoned buckets from Hassle, Sweden
3 = 1/2; 4-5 = 2/3; 6 = 1/3; 7-9 = 1/4

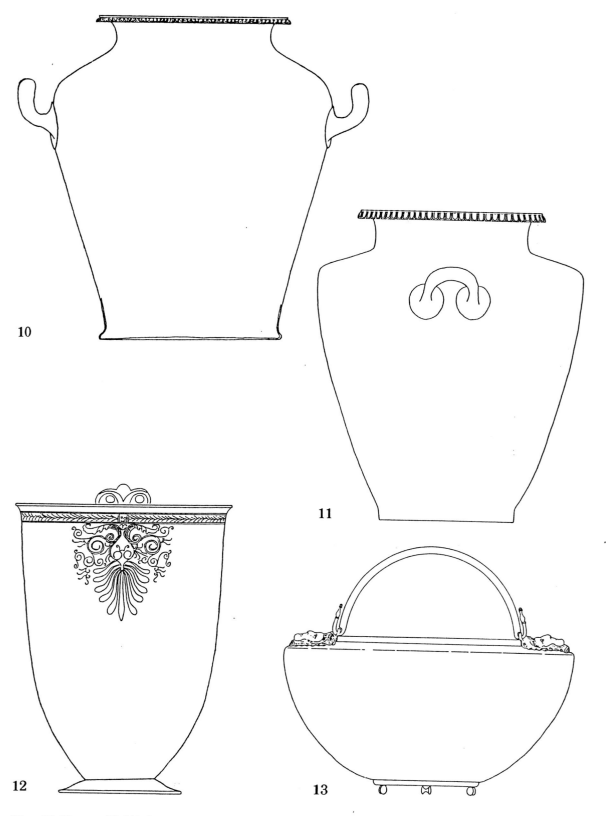

Fig. 10-13   10-11) Stamnos Langå, Funen, grave 1 (different reconstructions);
              12) Campanian situla from Keldby, Møn;
              13) Cauldron from Mosbæk, Jutland
              10-12,13 = 1/6; 12 = 1/4

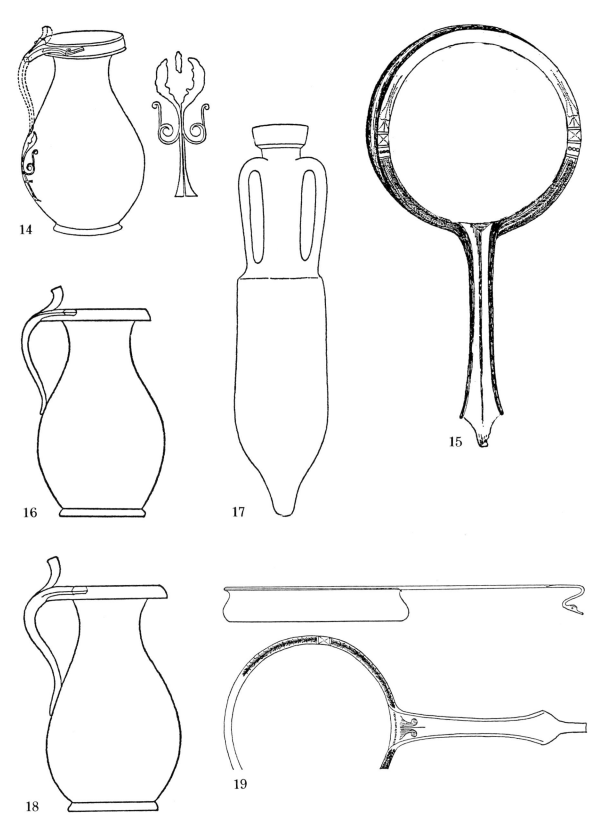

Figs. 14-19   14-15) Jug and pan from Aylesford, Kent, grave Y;
16-17) Jug and amphora from Welwyn, Herts. grave A;
18-19) Jug and pan from Welwyn, Herts. grave B
14,15,19 = 1/4; 16,18 = 1/3; 17 = 1/8

THE BLANDFORD FORUM GROUP: ARE ANY ETRUSCAN FIGURES TRUE FINDS FROM GREAT BRITAIN AND EIRE?

Val Rigby, Judith Swaddling and Mike Cowell

Respectively Department of Prehistoric and Romano-British Antiquities, Department of Greek and Roman Antiquities, and Department of Scientific Research, The British Museum, London WC1B 3DG

INTRODUCTION[1]

Since early this century claims have been made concerning the findings of various Etruscan and Italic objects in Great Britain. Now numbering about two hundred in all, they consist of bronze and ceramic objects, mainly fibulae, but also vessels and statuettes; of the last, the most impressive are the bronze Turms (Hermes) from Uffington near Oxford, the seven figures from Blandford Forum, Dorset, and a little-known spirited bronze female statuette from Lincoln's Inn, London. Although some of the 'finds' have a degree of plausibility, close investigation has revealed very little to substantiate the claims, and there appears to be a similar situation with many of the Etruscan and Italic 'finds' from France.[2]

The identification of imported artefacts is important for providing concrete evidence for contacts between cultures, to support obscure literary and epigraphic evidence and sometimes tenuous typological affinities. The Blandford bronze figures, which were acquired by the British Museum in 1923, have been published as having a genuine British provenance and described as either Iberian or Etruscan artefacts.[3] The colloquium has provided the opportunity to examine the authenticity of the individual figures, the integrity of the group and the provenance. The provenances of continental parallels are examined and Italic and Etruscan figures of other types with provenances in the British Isles are discussed.

COMPOSITION AND AUTHENTICITY OF THE BLANDFORD FORUM GROUP (Figs. 1-4)

The group now comprises seven primitive votive figures (Fig. 1, 2), one kouros (Fig. 4a-d) and two Egyptian figures (Fig. 3a,b); one figure of unknown type may be missing.[4] The Egyptian figures, which have long been rejected as evidence of ancient contacts, were examined by Carol Andrews of the Department of Egyptian Antiquities, British Museum. She reported that one is a genuine Egyptian antiquity, an Ushabti depicting Osiris, a late Ptolemaic example of the third or more probably the late second century BC (Fig. 3a). The other is a modern reproduction in metal of a figure made in antiquity only in frit (Fig. 3b). The scientific examination supports her opinion (Appendix 2, ii).

The kouros gives strong indication of being a forgery (British Museum PRB 1923.3-6.10, Fig. 4). A thick casting seam runs around the outline and has been filed flat, and where this traverses the crown of the head it constitutes what appears from the front to be a thick band of hair. A small tang such as would normally appear from the base of the feet emerges from where the legs finish, and although the tang, which is in one piece with the bronze, could have been cut at a later date, it bears much the same patination as the rest of the object. The figure appears to be derived from an Archaic kouros type of about 550-525 BC.[5] It most closely resembles several bronze kouroi statuettes found in the last century in the Roman Forum, which are perhaps of local manufacture.[6] The scientific analysis of the figure points to a modern origin (Appendix 2, ii).

It is the seven similar primitive figures, however, which are of the chief interest here.[7] The figures complete in height range between 8.6 and 9.5cm. Though they are very like each other, one has slightly sharper modelling and a dark brown patina (PRB 1923.3-6.7, Figs. 1, 2 second from right in both photographs), while the rest are greenish and discoloured with patches of iron corrosion. Scientific analysis was carried out on five of the figures and they were found to be of leaded bronze of a type consistent with analyses of Etruscan bronze statuettes, though also with those of decorative metalwork of all types and cultures (Appendix 2, i). The seven figures belong to a votive type that is well known from northern parts of Etruria and Italy, and from alleged finds north of the Alps. Balty found more than forty examples.[8] The type is a man-at-arms, wearing a triangular loincloth or *perizoma*, though in the Blandford examples there is no indication of the upper edge of this save in the case of PRB 1923.3-6.7, where the rear band of the garment can be seen on a line with the thumb (Fig. 2). The genitals appear prominent beneath the perizoma, and as Bonfante commented, it is little more than a 'phallus sheath'; the garment appears characteristic of northern Etruria.[9] The left hand rests on the hip and the right forearm is outstretched to hold a rod-like object; in some cases a spear survives (though sometimes perhaps restored), but usually the object is now missing, apart occasionally from a small section remaining in the hand, which is closed and pierced vertically to hold it (see Appendix 2, i). All the Blandford figures have this section of rod save PRB 1923.3-6.5 and 7, where the left hand is broken away. It is interesting that the feet and base of both these two figures are also missing, since it is suggested that the spear, passing through the base, may have attached the figures to a mount (Appendix 2, i). The missing parts of the figures may therefore have broken away with the spears. The arm of the slightly-differing spearman, PRB 1923.3-6.7, is bent across his rib-cage; this was presumably done subsequent to casting, otherwise, given the poor quality of the modelling, the forearm would have been cast in one with the body rather than detached from it.

Figures of the Blandford type usually have shoulder-length hair coming down to a point at the back; they have raised, almond-shaped eyes, well-defined brows, prominent, sometimes blobby, noses and often wide mouths. On some, e.g. PRB 1923.3-26.5 and 6, the details of the face are either minimal or blurred. The earliest examples of the type have been dated to the second half of the seventh century by some[10] and by others to the first half of the sixth century.[11] The basic, summary rendering of the figures makes them difficult to date, though Balty's comparison of the facial features with those of seventh-century canopic urns and bucchero figures is compelling. The spearmen's ancestors are doubtless Syrian and Lebanese warriors, and Jucker believed that the motif of the hand to the loin emphasised the votive figure's virility, intensifying a prayer for its strengthening, which would correspond to the female 'pudicitia' gesture which the Etruscans also adopted from the Near East.[12] The hand, however, does not point but simply rests on the hip in a relaxed pose, with the thumb behind the hip. If the origin of the gesture does come from the Near East then the Etruscans must have modified it.

Although the type owes something to the Greek kouros, particularly in the anatomy and hairstyle, it is essentially a north Etruscan product, and Volterra or Arezzo is usually suggested as the main source.[13] Volterra's strong political and economic association with Populonia could point to the derivation of the type from that area.[14] The costume is certainly purely Etruscan[15] though the last examples in the late sixth century dispose of the loincloth under Greek influence.[16] Conversely, the motif of hand on hip does not occur in Greek art before the beginning of the fifth century. Cristofani has suggested that the figures can be associated with a cult practised by warriors, and if the widespread alleged findspots have any validity, they could perhaps indicate groups of wandering mercenaries.[17]

The curious linking factor between Blandford-type figures is that the vast majority display extensive traces of rust.[18] This is particularly the case with PRB 1923.3-6.2, 3, and 5, which exhibit extensive rust corrosion particularly between the legs, around the arms and on the backs. Quantive analyses of the British Museum figures showed that this iron corrosion was not the result of a high iron content in the alloy. Another possibility was that the weapon or staff held in the right hand and the pin through the base of each figure were of iron and that this had contaminated the bronze. Both the weapon and pin, however, proved to be of bronze (Appendix 2, i). The most likely explanation is that the figures were originally attached to an object partly, at least, made of iron, but of which there is as yet no satisfactory identification. They perhaps could have been attached to a cult-wagon like that from Strettweg, possibly with iron axles.[19]

Another point of interest is that the Blandford type has both a female and a bovine counterpart, with which it occasionally occurs together in 'finds' (see Appendix I, The Sligo Figure). The recurrence of the combination indicates that even if the groups are not ancient imports, they are likely to have been found together originally, and then acquired as groups by modern collectors.

THE PROVENANCE OF THE BLANDFORD FORUM GROUP

The Blandford figures were donated to the British Museum in 1923 by Thomas Barnett FSA, whose four letters written between November 1922 and March 1923, and now in the British Museum archives, constitute the chief source of information about their recent history. Barnett was a collector and a generous benefactor of museums, particularly Birmingham.[20] The correspondence is one-sided because a copy of only one reply survives, the acceptance of the gift of the figures by the Keeper of British and Medieval Antiquities, which more or less ended the transaction.

With a letter dated 9 November 1922, Barnett submitted two primitive figures for identification, thinking that they resembled an Iberian figure and the Aust Figurine.[21] According to his second letter, dated 15 November, he had written to the previous owner for more information. At that time the only information which he had was that they had been 'found together with other things, in or near Blandford'. He wrote again 22 November to say that he had received no reply from the alleged owner. After a delay, he sent 'nine other figurines', 'found in or near Blandford', by registered post on 20 December. On 13 January 1923, he wrote, 'It is certainly (*sic*) the majority at least were purchased by Mr T Wilson, Church St. Christchurch from the labourer who dug them up in or near Blandford. When I saw these first only 9 were produced, later 11 were forthcoming. From the varied character of Mr W's possessions it is not unlikely that one or even more not belonging to the "find" were unintentionally included.' In fact, Wilson was a dealer, as we know from *Kelly's Directory* for 1920 and from the diary of Herbert Druitt (see below).

From the only surviving outgoing letter, dated 10 January 1923, it seems that the Department accepted the seven figures as a genuine hoard, but considered that the rest were subsequent accretions, dealers' stock-in-trade added to the group. No decision had been reached about their date or origin so all the figures were to be put into the so-called 'Suspense Account'. A letter from Barnett, dated 13 March 1923, implies that they had been identified, but since no copy of the relevant outgoing letter survives, there is no record of that identification. Some information may have passed verbally, because in earlier correspondence there is a reference to Barnett's meeting R.A. Smith, an Assistant Keeper, at a function. The Blandford find was not included in the revised British Museum Iron Age Guide published in 1925, which suggests that serious doubts about its authenticity were still held. Although the final number of figures in the correspondence is eleven, only ten could be identified in 1937, seven 'Iberian' and three 'others', which are probably the same ten that can be traced in the collection now, but since the 'others' were neither registered nor included in the original photograph, doubts remain.[22]

According to an entry in his diary, Herbert Druitt, a local antiquarian who founded the Red House Museum, Christchurch, was an interested party in the transaction. Druitt noted that Barnett had purchased the figures for 25 shillings from the dealer, Wilson, and that St George Gray and J.B. Calkin, notable local archaeologists, had tried to establish the authenticity of the find.[23] A findspot 'near Blandford' would have been both acceptable and tempting to local archaeologists and collectors at that time since it could be taken to imply, without commitment, a number of well-known sites in the vicinity. It may be significant that 'near Blandford' was used in the Durden Collection to describe the location of Hod Hill, a hill-fort and Roman camp, in the published catalogue of one of the major collections of prehistoric and Roman finds from Dorset, and would therefore have been well-known to dealers and their clients.[24]

The group of seven primitive figures was first identified and published as Iberian by Paul Jacobsthal in his paper 'An Iberian Bronze found at Sligo' with a footnote by the late Professor Hawkes, then an Assistant Keeper in the Department of British and Mediaeval Antiquities, summarising the acquisition.[25] The find could be interpreted as contaminated but essentially genuine, because of previous finds. Iberian or Iberian-type brooches had been found in the Iron Age cemetery at Harlyn Bay, Cornwall, and at Mount Batten, Plymouth, Devon, while the discovery of an Iberian figure, complete with crescent-shaped headdress, at Aust, Gloucestershire, some twenty years previously, added confirmation.[26] It was not until the major research papers by J-C Balty on figures of the Blandford and Sligo types that their Etruscan origins were demonstrated, and just over a decade later the reattribution entered the literature in Britain.[27] With their reattribution as Etruscan, any easy integration into the Iberian connection was removed, and the possibility of them being ancient imports from Etruria must be examined, the figures compared with those of the same type with continental provenances, and with other contemporary figures and Italic imports with British findspots.

Balty listed 46 examples, not including the Blandford group;[28] these included 27 in collections in Italy, 6 in France, 4 in Belgium and the rest scattered. Only two have anything approaching a precise provenance, one being from between Asquins and Vézelay[29] the other from S Ottaviano (Volterra) near the Strolla torrent, an affluent of the Era.[30] Of the rest, 36 have no provenance and 8 simply place-names.[31] Three have passed through the salerooms in the post-war period: one without provenance was sold in Basel in 1956; the second, sold in London in 1964, is the example said to be from Bologna, and the third, sold in London in 1978, had no provenance but may be the Basel figure resurfacing. Similar unsatisfactory provenances emerge from the study of all the figure-types listed by Balty and not one is well-documented. To Balty's examples Boucher[32] added those from Château-Chinon and Thorigné-en-Charnie.[33]

The figurines are of no great artistic quality and have been typical staple items in the antiquities market. A plate in a 1978 London sale catalogue includes one statuette of the Blandford type, one kouros like the Blandford example, one Umbrian figure like the one said to be from an Irish bog (see Appendix 1), and three other related types, neatly summarising the situation in the late twentieth century.[34] As a precise provenance has often been of little importance to collectors, it is not surprising that provenances of objects in private and museum collections and on the market are poor. The place-name findspot for the Blandford figures is typical of its class of artefact and no more reliable. In the absence of a body of well-recorded examples in Italy and beyond, any distribution pattern has to be treated with extreme caution, for rather than demonstrating the movement of the artefacts in antiquity, it may be distorted by the inclusion of the actual domiciles of those who collected and dealt in rather minor Italic antiquities or occasionally better ones (e.g. the Uffington Turms, below).

OTHER EARLY FIGURES IN BRITAIN

Widening the survey beyond Blandford-type figures, no authentic Iron Age statue or figure, bronze, stone or ceramic, from any source, has been found in Britain in a secure context earlier than the first century BC. Unlike Iberia and Italy, votive deposits in the British Isles do not include human or animal figures and so it seems that depiction of the complete human figure at any scale was not relevant or significant to the religion and culture of Britain in the first millennium BC. A taboo forbidding such representations may be deduced which, judging from the style of ornament used to decorate weapons and tools in Iron Age Britain (ie. from about 700 BC onwards), may even have extended to include the naturalistic portrayal of all living things, both plant and animal. In such a cultural setting, there was no need for nor any understanding of the meaning and iconography of imported figures and hence no demand for them, although outsiders could have brought them in for their own votive purposes. Six individual wooden figures and a group of five, all ranging between 16 and 148cm in height, have been recovered from wetland sites in the British Isles: they are rudimentary and totem-like in appearance, naked and apparently ithyphallic.[35] One was securely stratified in a Late Neolithic context, while the remainder are poorly documented, chance finds and only dated by C14: two date to the third millennium, one to the turn of the second and first millennia, and three to the first millennium BC.

The concept of monumental statuary, with the personification of deities and the portrayal of personages of rank and veneration, was introduced into Britain by the Romans, as was the production of small bronze figures and their deposition as votive offerings at sacred sites. Almost as a preliminary step towards the acceptance of the complete figure, human heads appear as decorative items on major artefacts such as the anthropoid sword found with an inhumation at North Grimston, North Yorkshire.[36] In southern Britain, the earliest representations in secure contexts occur in rich cremation burials of the Late Iron Age, dated to the mid-first century BC: there are three masks of unknown function in Grave B, Welwyn, Hertfordshire, and handle-mounts portraying helmeted heads on wooden buckets found at Aylesford, Kent and Baldock, Hertfordshire.[37] All are considered of British origin and are traditionally associated with the Celtic 'cult of the head'.

The earliest figure in bronze occurs somewhat later in the first century BC: an Eros and a human foot, classical in style and possibly of Italian origin, were found with boar and bull figurines in the Lexden Tumulus, a major barrow sited just outside Camulodunum, Essex, and dated *c.*17 BC.[38] Although the grave-goods are fragmentary, the burial was probably richer in these than any other British example of the same period, with other imports including fabrics, furniture and wine amphorae. There are two north Italian figures among Roman and earlier artefacts found at Mount Batten, Devon, one of which is a nude male figure probably of the fifth century BC, the other a warrior of the third or second century BC. Since they are not part of the excavated archive, and in a collection which includes accretions and fakes, their provenance remains dubious.[39] Uncertainty also exists concerning two bronze statuettes in the Corinium Museum, Cirencester, by strange coincidence of the same types and dates as the two from Mount Batten; the warrior was supposedly found at Swell, while there is no record of the discovery of the nude male figure.[40]

Perhaps the earliest votive deposit to include figures is the Hounslow Hoard. Typically it too is an old, poorly documented find, registered in two batches in 1864, and the reliability of the association is not secure.[41] The first batch included two boar figures and an elongated quadruped of indeterminate species, possibly a short-legged terrier; the second, a boar and a deer. Usually dated to the first century BC, the boar figurines may have functioned as Celtic helmet-crests or vessel-mounts, judging from the sheet metal attached to their feet; the deer is a pendant, with a suspension loop on its back, and the 'terrier' is freestanding. While the Hounslow Hoard may have been part of a votive deposit of animal figurines of the later pre-Roman Iron Age, if the boars were in fact helmet-crests, then they may be all that survives from three helmets, and so part of a weapon hoard. However, since neither association nor provenance is secure, they should not be used for any serious interpretation.

FIBULAE

Fibulae appear to be a good control group for comparison because they are the most plentiful Italic artefact of the Early Iron Age recorded in Britain. A recently published corpus lists 138 examples, a usefully-sized sample, but judging from his use of inverted commas around place-names, the editor does not seem to have found them totally convincing, and considered that some were, at best, misleading 'findspots of convenience'.[42] One fibula, only, has a detailed archaeological provenance as part of an old find of Roman antiquities excavated by Artis at Durobrivae (Castor), outside Peterborough, Cambridgeshire. In his publication of the artefacts, Artis illustrates a horned fibula and three spiral bracelets from a tumulus.[43] Even this record is not secure, for the tumulus group does not have a precise location within Durobrivae, as do all the other illustrated artefacts: there is a gap in the printed caption where the location should be. The finds from Durobrivae originally formed part of the Fitzallan collection which also included continental antiquities, and so the group may have been published as comparative material or by accident; a similar combination of objects occurs in the *corredo* of the Tomba del Guerriero in the Monterozzi cemetery at Tarquinia.[44] If the tumulus was sited near Durobrivae, then it is unique in Britain as a barrow and burial of this period, and unique, too, for its Italic grave-goods.[45]

The most reliable site provenances of the remaining 137 fibulae are those of two fairly recent finds made by reputable metal detectorists: both are unique types in the corpus, predating the British Iron Age by several centuries, and hence Bronze Age imports, if imports they were. The first, a 'violin-bow' from Avebury Down, Wiltshire, dates to around the twelfth century BC, while a two-piece type from Ide Hill, Kent, is ninth or eighth century BC in date.[46]

There is certainly one which lost its dubious provenance of 'Hungary' between the London sale of the Egger collection in 1891, where it formed part of Lot 127, and its subsequent publication as a Sussex find, along with a second Italic type.[47]

At first sight there seems no reason why fibulae should not have been imported in antiquity: they were functional and decorative, easy to make and transport over great distances and, unlike figures, not likely to be subject to any religious or cultural taboos. Perhaps the functional aspect is a problem. The archaeological evidence is that Britons dressed differently from their contemporaries in much of continental Europe and the Mediteranean world, and used other kinds of fasteners, including metal pins. The manufacture of fibulae was a comparatively late introduction in the British Iron Age, around 400 BC. This does not preclude their import in previous centuries, and certainly not the likelihood of it, as status symbols or unusual objects, perhaps attached to the garments of non-native visitors, but sound archaeological evidence is required to substantiate such theories.

There is a considerable body of 'finds' of Etruscan fibulae from France, but there, too, with the very important exception of the finds from Bourges, the vast majority lack any corroboration for the authenticity of the findspots.[48] Even if the Bourges fibulae and razor are native copies of Italic objects they remain important because if they are such, the native craftsman must have had the originals at hand.[49]

OTHER POSSIBLE IMPORTS

Other Iron Age Mediterranean artefacts recorded in Britain include a varied range of bronze vessels, lamps and pottery.[50] Again, none has a secure archaeological context, but perhaps the least implausible type of provenance is that of vessels apparently recovered from river beds. Spectacular metalwork of British manufacture has been recovered from rivers, marshes and alluvium. Such finds have been interpreted as votive deposits, part of a rite continuing from the Bronze Age, and this has been used to validate finds of vessels like the trefoil-mouthed jug perhaps made in Magna Graecia and said to be from the Crouch estuary, though the precise findspot is unspecified,[51] and the Weybridge bucket, which is of 'Kurd' type.[52] The findspots are on the south and north banks of the Thames, and are badly documented.[53] It may also be significant that their 'discovery' post-dates those of notable dredging finds like the Battersea and Witham Shields, the Waterloo Helmet, and many Roman artefacts. Given the incontestable evidence for the distribution of *Schnabelkannen* in France and Germany,[54] it would not be surprising for some at least to have reached Britain, but so far there are no attested finds.

In continental Europe, north of the Alps, the most complete and identifiable Italian Iron Age artefacts with secure archaeological provenances are in the main from 'princely tombs', *Fürstengräber*, of the 6th to 5th century BC. They are spectacular objects with very precise functions in classical life, mainly associated with the consumption of wine and food in the civilised manner, which, initially at least, were not within the repertoire of barbarian workshops.[55] There are Italic fibulae, perhaps most spectacularly those in gold in the Hochdorf burial, while a small female figure crowns the lid of the enormous crater in the Vix burial.[56] In Britain, even if there was at this time the same type of contact, the dead were disposed of in such a way that has left no comparable archaeological remains. In a wide-ranging and detailed examination of northern European Iron Age imports, it was found that the earliest definite examples of imported metalwork with secure recorded contexts are those made in the 1st century BC, and found in 'chieftain burials'.[57]

CONCLUSION

To sum up, after typological study and scientific analysis, the Blandford group proves to consist of seven authentic Etruscan figures of the seventh or early sixth century BC, one Egyptian Ushabti of the third or second century BC and two replicas, and it cannot therefore in its entirety have formed a genuine find. The provenance of Blandford cannot be substantiated, and all that is certain is that the figures were in the possession of a dealer in Christchurch in 1922. The Etruscan figures were very probably produced in northern Etruria but belong to a type which has been widely traded in the antiquities market. Three-dimensional figural representation was not part of the culture of Late Bronze or Early Iron Age Britain since no authentic ancient statue or statuette has been found in a recorded archaeological context. There are as yet no other Italian Iron Age artefacts from Great Britain or Eire providing definite data for direct contacts, regardless of the possibility or even the likelihood of such contacts. The Blandford figures themselves cannot therefore be used as reliable evidence to support theories of cultural contact, and far less trading links, with Italy in the Early Iron Age.

APPENDIX 1: OTHER ITALIC AND ETRUSCAN BRONZE 'FINDS' FROM THE BRITISH ISLES AND NORWAY

The Sligo Figure (Fig. 5)

The Sligo figure was the central topic of Jacobsthal's paper, where it was identified as an import and used to support the theory of strong Iberian trading connections with western Britain in the Iron Age, along with the enigmatic female figurine found at the foot of Aust Cliff, Gloucestershire/Avon.[58]

The figure is in fact of an Etruscan early archaic type,[59] depicting a woman wearing a head-veil with lappets, and dating to the late seventh or early sixth century BC.[60] Flat in profile and with outstretched arms, the type almost certainly derived from a north Etruscan workshop. Over half of the figures belonging to the general category are in the museums of Arezzo, Volterra and Florence, though all without firm provenance.[61] Similar figures seem to have emanated from a centre in the Veneto.[62]

The Sligo figure is part of the Sirr Collection, which contained some 400 items and was therefore considered one of the major collections of antiquities in Ireland in the nineteenth century.[63] On his death in 1841, Major Sirr's collection was bought by the Royal Irish Academy from his son and heir for £350 plus the cancellation of all arrears to the Academy, and free life membership thereafter, and ultimately formed part of the National Museum of Ireland. The collection includes material from Italy, and is badly documented, so that provenances are not necessarily reliable (information from Mary Cahill, National Museum of Ireland). It is, however, curious and worth noting that, stylistically, the type forms a female counterpart to the spearmen exemplified by the Blandford figures, Richardson going so far as to say that certain specimens of each type would appear to be by the same hand.[64] Further, a figure of the Blandford type and two figures of the Sligo type are associated together in a find from Thorigné-en-Charnie.[65] The combination of a spearman and two veiled women, all mounted on a single stone base, occurs in the Fondo Baratela, Este.[66] Both are Etruscan transformations of a Near Eastern type.

The Irish Bog Figure (Fig. 6)

This was first illustrated in the *Dublin Penny Journal* 1834, but with no other details than found in a bog in Ireland. In fact 'an Irish bog' has been offered repeatedly and genuinely as a findspot for artefacts of all types and periods. The figure is in the National Museum of Ireland at Dublin.[67] More recent illustrations, a drawing and a photograph, differ somewhat from the original depiction.[68]

Like the Picene ring reputed to be from Co. Derry (below), this figure derives from eastern central Italy, a striding warrior or Mars of the type which Colonna ascribes to southern Umbria, the 'Gruppo Foligno', dating probably to the late sixth or early fifth century BC.[69] Close parallels are in the Antikensammlung, Berlin, n. 76271[70] and in a Swiss private collection, which Richardson puts in the Late Archaic period, in the span between 520 and 450 BC.[71]

Addendum: During correspondence with Raghnall O'Floirin of the National Museum of Ireland, Dublin, concerning the provenances of Figures 5 and 6, our attention was drawn to a figure, said to be from Ireland, in Alnwick Castle. When J. Collingwood-Bruce compiled the catalogue of antiquities at Alnwick Castle, he described the figure as 'A small bronze helmeted figure, probably intended for

Mars, of rude and early workmanship. It is from the Walker collection, and is said to have been found in the County of Roscommon. It has probably been originally brought from Italy'.[72] More recently, it was listed with Roman material with questionable provenances in Ireland.[73]

A brief view of the figure as presently displayed in the museum of antiquities at Alnwick Castle confirms that it is like Figure 6, and hence a second example of Colonna's 'Gruppo Foligno'. It is the more complete of the two figures, and perhaps more nearly equates to the condition of the example featured in the *Dublin Penny Journal*. Recording and research continues.

Lincoln's Inn Figure (Fig. 7a-c)

This unpublished Etruscan bronze statuette of a woman stepping forward in spirited fashion is said to have been found at Lincoln's Inn in 1904, 16 feet (4.87 m) below ground level. This information is written on the label stuck to the base on which it was mounted, presumably early this century. There are no other records concerning the figure, but Mr David Corsellis of the Treasury at Lincoln's Inn kindly looked into the matter and found that round about 1904 there was a considerable amount of digging in progress for drainage work in the region of the court, so that the statuette could have been discovered then. There is, however, no reference to the finding of any other ancient material at the time, and the bronze may have been deposited at a period later than antiquity. The Inns of Court were attended by the offspring of noble and landed families from the sixteenth century onwards, and the possibility that the figure was acquired on the Grand Tour and brought back to London cannot be ruled out.

The figure is of Late Archaic type, probably dating to about 510-490 BC.[74] There is a good parallel for it in the Vatican, no. 12095, which has the same double row of dots punched down the front of the bodice of the dress and down each leg,[75] though the pointed cap of the Lincoln's Inn figure puts it slightly earlier. The right hand of this type occasionally holds an egg or fruit, and the left hand is open, palm down, but the Lincoln's Inn figure was designed to be empty-handed, rather like a figure of the same type but with finer detail in Boston.[76] Professor Richardson believes that this latter type is probably intended to be dancing, on account of the animated pose, emphasised by the size of the hands and feet, and the flicked-up hem of the dress and sleeve. Kouroi of the period, however, often adopt the same pose, and the intention of the craftsman may have been simply to convey motion, in contrast with the hitherto customary standing pose.[77]

The Uffington Turms (Hermes) (Fig. 8a,b)

This bronze statuette was said to have been found during the ploughing of a field at Uffington, near Oxford.[78] It is of a north Etruscan type probably made at Vulci about 475-450 BC.[79] It is an early example of a type which often represents votaries, wearing a semicircular mantle draped around the waist and over the left arm. The earliest in the series is the figure found in 1882 in the open-air sanctuary at Monteguragazza in the Apennines, along with a number of bronze statuettes of lesser quality and size. It can be dated about 480-470 BC.[80] This type of half-draped male votary was also popular in later Etruscan art and, as Brendel has noted, the image was adopted in the early days of the Roman Empire for representations of Imperial princes. The Uffington figure, from its winged boots clearly a Turms, or Hermes, now lacks the attributes which it once held.

In 1846 a drawing of the statuette was displayed at a meeting of the Royal Archaeological Institute, where it was stated to have been 'discovered in ploughing land in the neighbourhood of

Abingdon'.[81] The figure next came to light considerably later at the Ashmolean Museum, where it had been deposited on long-term loan by its then owner, an antiquarian named A.E. Preston of Abingdon. It was bequeathed to the Ashmolean on his death in 1942. Mr Preston had apparently bought it at the sale of the effects of a Mrs Beesley, and it was during its possession by Mr Beesley that a water-colour of it was painted by the artist Jesse King, with an inscription by King that it was 'Found by a labourer near Uffington, Berks'. King is known to have carefully recorded the findspots of the objects which he illustrated. The drawing was acquired by the Ashmolean along with the figure. It is perhaps the one exhibited at the Royal Archaeological Institute in 1846, but if so the inscription must have been ignored at the Institute's meeting. The confusion is perhaps understandable, bearing in mind that although Uffington, its alternative findspot, is a parish noted for its ancient White Horse and earthworks, about 15½ miles (24.8 km) from Abingdon, the figure had had two owners resident at Abingdon; inevitably, however, some uncertainty about the provenance has crept in. The figure's fine, hard patina gives little indication that it has been immersed in soil in the British climate for any length of time, and it would of course be surprising for a figure of such quality to be an isolated deposit in this country, assuming that there were no related remains.[82]

Bergen Figure (Fig. 9a-c)

This female figure, wearing a short-sleeved chiton and domed headdress, was purchased by the British Museum from a Mrs Mary Griffin in 1906.[83] According to publication, it was found with three Italic fibulae in a drawer in the shop of an antiques dealer in Bergen, who was not absolutely certain, but believed that they had been dug up recently in Bergen.[84] There is no further record of the fibulae.

The bronze is in good condition with very little corrosion, though it may have been stripped. The figure appears very worn, particularly over the face and head, perhaps as a result of continued handling, or because it was made in a rather indistinct mould. The figure has two distinct peculiarities, however, one of which is the zigzag incision going around the top of the feet, apparently representing either the lower edge of the skirt or the top edge of the boots. Etruscan bronzes often have two triangles indicating the top of the tongues of the boots, but here the zigzags continue along the sides. The other unusual feature is the heavily incised line between the legs both front and back. This is hard to equate with the motif of lifting the skirt at the side, which should draw the garment across the legs, and with the otherwise subtle rendering of detail on the figure, albeit rather worn, for example the spreading of the locks of hair at the back. These features may be due to quirks of the maker rather than indications of forgery, though the possibility of the figure's having been cast from an indistinct mould inevitably raises the question of whether it is a modern re-cast from an ancient piece, the incised line between the legs and zigzag lines around the feet then being added at this stage. It is difficult to tell from the break whether the missing right forearm ever existed. Both the stylistic and scientific analyses are unfortunately at present inconclusive. The derivation is, however, like that of the Blandford spearmen and the Sligo figure, north Etruscan,[85] and dating to about 550-525 BC.

Picene Ring (not illustrated)

Another reputed find of Italian origin from Ireland is a heavy bronze ring in the Belfast Museum, labelled 'from Co. Derry'.[86] It is of a type well known from eastern central Italy, with six biconical knobs, belonging to the sixth and fifth centuries BC.[87] Many examples are preserved without details of their original context, but where findspots are certain they are exclusively from women's graves (usually at the chest or pelvis level of the deceased) in the Picene area, making a true find in Ireland improbable. There is perhaps a connection between the ring and the Earl of Bristol, Bishop of Derry, who brought back many Italian antiquities from his travels.

Torch-holder (not illustrated)

Another uncorroborated find is an Etruscan torch-holder said to have been found in a rivulet running from a bog and obtained near Saintfield, County Down from an itinerant rag-and-bone man.[88]

APPENDIX 2: SCIENTIFIC REPORT

Mike Cowell

i) The Blandford Spearmen (PRB 1923.3-6.1-7)

INTRODUCTION

The figures are 8-10cm high and most depict a standing warrior holding a separate (now mainly lost) staff or rod-like weapon. Most are patinated with corrosion typical of copper-based alloys but there are also extensive deposits in some cases of iron oxides. Some of the figures have been examined previously to determine their approximate composition, by non-destructive analysis, and also to identify the mineralogy of the patination. All of those analysed were found to be leaded tin bronzes with traces of arsenic and other metals. The patination, which included malachite and hydrated ferric oxide, was considered to be consistent with that of ancient metalwork and the iron oxide deposits were thought to have derived from association with corroding iron.

The aims of the present investigation were:

1. To confirm that the copper alloy is low in iron and could not have contributed to the iron oxide deposits.
2. To investigate the composition and form of the weapon carried and of the pin penetrating the base of some of the figures, now present only as fragments.

BODY COMPOSITION

Samples were drilled from five of the figures and analysed by X-ray fluorescence (XRF). The following results were obtained:

Reg. PRB BMRL	1923.3-6.1 20772T	1923.3-6.2 20773R	1923.3-6.3 20774P	1923.3-6.4 20775Y	1923.3-6.6 20777U
Copper	90	95	94	93	95
Zinc	<0.3	<0.2	<0.2	<0.2	<0.2
Lead	4	3	3	3.5	2.5
Tin	6	2	2	2	1.5
Nickel	<0.2	0.1	0.1	0.1	0.1
Arsenic	<0.5	0.3	0.3	0.3	<0.2
Iron	0.3	0.2	0.5	0.9	0.1
Antimony	0.2	<0.2	0.2	<0.2	0.2
Silver	<0.1	0.1	0.1	0.1	0.1
Bismuth	<0.1	<0.1	0.2	0.1	0.2

The precisions of the above analyses are $\pm$1-2% for copper, $\pm$ 5-10% for tin and lead and $\pm$20-50% for the remaining metals. The accuracies will be similar and an improvement over the previous non-destructive surface analyses.

In all cases iron is a relatively minor constituent of the alloy, typical of the traces often found in bronzes, and it is not present in sufficient amounts to account for the surface deposits of iron oxide observed. It is notable that all of the figures analysed are made of similar alloys, in fact the close similarity of PRB 1923.3-6.2 with 3, 4 and 6 suggests a common origin.

REMAINS OF WEAPON HELD AND PINS THROUGH BASE

The remains of the staff or spear held in the right hand and the pin through the base of each figure were analysed by XRF and also examined using optical microscopy. The XRF analysis was intended to compare its composition with that of the body of the figure. In practice, because of the small size of the remains of the weapons, it was not possible to analyse them uniquely without also including some of the body metal of the figure. It would therefore be misleading to quote individual analyses. However, the compositions of the weapons seem in general to be bronze with lower amounts of tin and lead than in the corresponding figure. This would be consistent with a component requiring working rather than simple casting for manufacture.

The cross-sections of the weapon preserved in the hand and the pin preserved in the base were examined to determine their consistency in size and form. In all six figures examined which have sufficient remains (PRB 1923.3-6.1-6), the weapon seems to be round in section and, where it is present in the hand and the base, of consistent size and shape. It seems possible that the same piece continued from the hand to the base although this cannot be conclusively proven.[89]

ii) The other Blandford Figures, Lincoln's Inn and Bergen Figures

ANALYSIS

These five figures were analysed by X-ray fluorescence (XRF) and some patination and internal corrosion examination was also carried out.

The Lincoln's Inn and Bergen figures could not be sampled and these were analysed non-destructively on unprepared but unpatinated surfaces. Since XRF is a surface analysis method and the surface of even unpatinated metalwork may not be representative of the bulk composition, the results are approximate and are therefore not quoted here in full. Both figures are made of leaded tin bronze with traces of iron, nickel and arsenic.

The other three figures, all said to be from Blandford, Dorset, could be sampled by drilling and these were also analysed by XRF. The accuracies of these analyses will be better than those above because the samples are of the interior metal and not subject to the effects of inhomogeneity present at the surface.

Table of quantitative XRF analyses of drilled samples

	Description	%Cu	%Sn	%Pb	%Zn	%Fe	%Ni	%As	%Sb	%Ag
43625U	Osiris, PRB 1923.3-6.8	82	7	9	<0.1	<0.03	0.05	0.9	1.0	0.1
43626S	'Egyptian' figure, PRB 1923.3-6.9	83	2	7	5	0.6	0.2	1.0	0.4	0.1
43627Q	'Kouros', PRB 1923.3-6.10	70	4	6	20	0.6	0.1	0.5	0.3	0.1

Precision: ±1-2% relative for copper, ±10-20% for tin and lead, and zinc, ±20-50% for remainder. The accuracy is similar to the precision.

EXAMINATION

Blandford Osiris, PRB 1923.3-6.8

This figure is covered with a uniform dark green patina containing a basic copper chloride which seems to have been coated with a waxy material. There is soil trapped in the recesses. The patination is firmly attached, it was not removed by organic solvents and resists probing with a scalpel. There is an underlying layer of cuprite. A taper section was prepared on the base of the figure and examination of this in a scanning electron microscope revealed extensive internal corrosion.

The XRF analysis (see Table) shows it to be made of leaded tin bronze with large traces of arsenic and antimony. This composition is not inconsistent with Egyptian cast statuary metalwork,[90] although examples with antimony contents up to 1% are infrequent. The metallographic examination indicates that it is of some antiquity and thus the evidence is in favour of this figure being ancient and possibly Egyptian.

Blandford 'Egyptian' Figure, PRB 1923.3-6.9

This figure has a thin, dark patina covering the front, face and part of the back. There are traces of a bright green deposit not identified mineralogically in some of the recesses on the back. The latter is very superficial and this, and the dark patina, were easily removed with a scalpel to reveal bright metal beneath.

The XRF analysis (Table) shows it to be made of a leaded gunmetal (leaded bronze containing zinc) with traces of arsenic and antimony. This composition is not consistent with Egyptian statuary metalwork. The presence of significant amounts of zinc in Egyptian metalwork in general is very unusual. Reiderer[91] reports only five statuettes out of 500 examined with 5% zinc or more and Cowell[92] finds only one from almost 300 artefacts examined containing over 1%. The evidence is therefore against this figure being ancient Egyptian.

Blandford 'Kouros', PRB 1923.3-6.10

This figure has a superficial, patchy light green patina. In many areas bright, uncorroded metal is visible. The patina is only loosely attached and is easily removed with a scalpel. There is no cuprite layer between the green patina and the metal.

The XRF analysis (Table) shows the composition to be a high zinc brass with tin and lead and traces of some other metals. This composition is not fully consistent with cast Greek or Etruscan statuary metalwork[93] which is usually leaded tin bronze. Reliable examples of brass in Etruscan metalwork are extremely unusual and, in any case, have lower amounts of zinc. The evidence, therefore, suggests that this figure is not ancient.

Figures from Lincoln's Inn (Private Collection) and Bergen, GR 1906.3-13.3

Neither of these figures have any surface corrosion products or patina. Both may have been chemically stripped. They were analysed semi-quantitatively by XRF and both are leaded bronzes with some trace elements. This is not inconsistent with Etruscan metalwork[94] which, as noted above, is usually leaded tin bronze. However, this alloy is certainly not specific to Etruscan metalwork. It has been commonly used for cast metalwork over the last two millennia. Hence the analytical evidence can only be said not to contradict the typological attribution of the figurines.

CONCLUSIONS

In summary, therefore, two of the Blandford figures, the 'Egyptian' figure and the 'kouros', are probably not ancient whereas the third, the Osiris, could be Egyptian. The two female figures are not inconsistent with their attribution but in their case the technical evidence is not completely conclusive.

NOTES

1.   *Acknowledgements:* We are grateful to Catherine Johns, Ellen Macnamara, Ian Stead and Susan Walker for reading the text and providing constructive criticism, and to Sybille Haynes and Emeline Richardson for helpful comments. Special thanks are also due to the Benchers of the Honourable Society of Lincoln's Inn, represented by Sir George Engle and Dr. David Corsellis, for making their Etruscan bronze figure available to us for study; and to Richard Warner at the Ulster Museum, Belfast, and Mary Cahill and Raghnall O'Floirin, National Museum of Ireland, Dublin, for providing significant information concerning the provenance of the Irish figures.

2.   Cf. Adam *et al.* 1992, 182, 186; Ridgway 1992, 188; Boucher 1976; also Gran Aymerich, Jannot and Stary in this volume.

3.   As Iberian: Jacobsthal 1938; as Etruscan: Richardson 1983, 73-6.

4.   Jacobsthal 1938.

5.   Cf. Richardson 1983, Middle Archaic kouroi Series A, Group 1, 109 ff; Galestin 1987, 37, VI no. 38.

6.   Cristofani 1985, 76-7, 246-7.

7.   Richardson 1983, 73-6.

8.   Balty 1961, with additions, 1966.

9.   Bonfante 1975, 24.

10. e.g. Cristofani 1985, 129 no. 13; Jucker 1970, 203 and Balty 1961, 10, 39 ff.

11. e.g. Richardson 1983, 225; and Galestin 1987, 26.

12. Cf. Richardson 1983, 65, Boucher 1970, 196; Seeden 1980 pl. 1 ff. and 133 ff. for discussion of type. For gesture, Jucker 1970, 203.

13. 7 examples are now in collections at Volterra and 9 at Arezzo; for other locations, see p. 110.

14. Jucker 1970, 203; Cateni 1985, 229.

15. Bonfante 1975, 24; Balty 1961, 6, n. 1.

16. e.g. Ashmolean Museum, Oxford, Fortnum B22: Haynes 1985, 258 no. 38, illustrated 145.

17. Cristofani 1985, 129.

18. Balty 1961, 20, 28 ff.; Boucher 1970, 200.

19. See conjectures on the purpose of the figures by Balty 1961, 20,26-7. Strettweg: Megaw 1970, 59, fig. 38; cf. also an example from Lezoux, Freidin 1980, 320-27.

20. Information kindly provided by Mr David Symons, Birmingham Museum and Art Gallery.

21. Smith 1905, figs. 63, 124.

22. Jacobsthal 1938.

23. Information and photocopies of diary entry, Tuesday 25 September 1923, kindly provided by Christine Taylor, Hampshire Museum Service.

24. Payne 1891.

25. Jacobsthal 1938, and see Appendix 1 here for the Sligo figure.

26. For a discussion of the Aust Figurine see Rigby in preparation; Bullen 1912; Cunliffe 1988.

27. Balty 1961, 1966; Harbison and Laing 1974.

28. Balty 1961, 1966.

29. Balty 1966, 6 no. 21.

30. Balty 1966, 7 no. 8.

31. One each from Volterra, Bologna, Porto San Giorgio, the environs of Chiusi, Montaulin, Menthon and Smederevo, while one is stated simply as from Pomerania.

32. Boucher 1970.

33. Cf. also Piel 1990, 50 top left; and see Jannot in this volume.

34. Christie's Catalogue, 1978, pl. 41.

35. Coles 1990.

36. Stead 1979, fig. 22.

37. Smith 1912, pl. II; Stead 1971, pls. lxxvii and xc.

38. Foster 1986.

39. Cunliffe 1988, fig. 36, 128-9.

40. Henig and Paddock 1993, 85-6.

41. Smith 1905, fig. 123.

42. Hull and Hawkes 1987.

43. Artis 1828, pl. 31, nos 1, 2, 7, 8; Harden 1950, 319.

44. 8th century BC: Hencken 1968, 207.

45. A *sanguisuga* fibula of the 8th century BC, British Museum GR 1920.11-18.2, previously in the Guildhall Museum, London has the provenance of Reculves (Reculver, Kent?) in the Departmental register, but there is no supportive evidence for this findspot.

46. Hull and Hawkes 1987, pl. 1, no number; pl. 17, 7253.

47. Sotheby *et al* 1891, pl. XVIII, 127; *AntJ* **IV** (1924) 50-1; Hull and Hawkes 1987, pls. 12, 15.

48. See however Jannot in this volume for a possible pattern and chronological development of these proposedly ancient imports in northern and western France.

49. For the material from Bourges, see Gran Aymerich in this volume. To the other possible examples of imports into France could be added two in the British Museum, both Etruscan fibulae, of the 7th century BC, in the Department of Greek and Roman Antiquities; a *navicella* fibula GR 1851.8-13.77 from the Comarmond collection and said to be from Isère, Crémieux, and a serpentine fibula, knobbed on both sides, in two fragments, GR 1905.12-1.24 and 25, said to be from Herpes, Charente. An Italic bow fibula of the 9th or early 8th century BC, GR 1920.11-18.5, previously Guildhall Museum, is said perhaps to have been found in the Rhineland.

50. Harden 1950; Harbison and Laing 1974; Stary 1991.

51. Harbison and Laing 1974, 8-10 pl. IV; Bouloumié 1986, 65; for the type, see Weber 1983, Taf. II Type B 241-52, *c*. 550-500 BC.

52. Stead 1984, 43-4, fig. 16; Stjernquist 1967 no. 44; Thomas 1956, 134; Bouloumié 1976, 17 and especially 25 on the origin of the type. Illustrated in this volume, Stary Fig. 7.

53. Harbison and Laing 1974, 8-10, pl. IV; Stead 1984.

54. See Shefton in this volume, also Bouloumié 1985 and 1986.

55. Cf. Shefton in this volume.

56. Biel 1985, Taf. 21; Joffroy 1954, pl . XVII.

57. Stead 1984; see Rigby in this volume.

58. Jacobsthal 1938; illustrated by Raftery 1984, 11.

59. H. 8.2cm.

60. Balty 1961, 21 ff.; Richardson 1983, 52 ff. gives a somewhat later dating for the type of 550-500 BC.

61. Richardson 1983, 54.

62. Balty 1966, 11, 15.

63. Inventory no. D.387.

64. Richardson 1983, 53.

65. Piel 1990 45, $17.53.10; 17.53.01 [sic] in drawing, p. 50; Boucher 1970, 196 f.

66. Ghirardini 1888, tav. VII, 71 ff.

67. Petrie Collection Reg. no. 757.

68. H. 7.6cm. Raftery 1984, 11, fig. 3; Kelly 1993, 11, photo 4, where the provenance is given as Co. Roscommon, which is apparently incorrect.
69. Colonna 1970, 96 ff.
70. Colonna 1970, 97 no. 267, tav. LXIX.
71. Richardson 1983, 194, pl. 134 fig. 451.
72. Collingwood-Bruce 1880, 520.
73. Bateson 1971, no. 38.
74. H. 12.4cm. Unpublished.
75. Richardson 1983, 317, figs. 756-7.
76. 01.7482, Richardson 1983, 293, figs. 693-4.
77. Cf. Richardson 1983, Late Archaic kouroi, series B-C, pls. 100-106 *passim*; Cristofani 1985, 84, 2.11 fig. 249, Mus. Arch. Firenze; Galestin 1987, 75, V 76.
78. Ashmolean Museum, Oxford, inv. 1943.38, h. 22.2cm.
79. Cristofani 1985, 285 no. 102, tav. 208; Haynes 1985, 275 no. 78, illustrated 171; Richardson 1983, 359, fig. 863; Brown 1980, 62-3 and front cover.
80. Museo Civico, Bologna; Richardson 1983, 240 figs. 546-8; Cristofani 1985, 108 no. 5, 1; Brendel 1978, 295f fig. 213.
81. *Archaeological Journal* **II** (1846), 209.
82. Cf. Ridgway 1992, 188.
83. GR 1906.3-13.3; h. 7.0cm.
84. Yeames 1906.
85. Cf. Richardson 1983, Middle Archaic korai, Groups 1, 2.
86. Jope 1958.
87. Cf. Adam 1984, 135.
88. *Journal of Ulster Archaeology* **4**, 1856, 96-7; for the type see Haynes 1985 no. 107.
89. Cf. Balty 1961, 20-1, no. 5.
90. Riederer 1978.
91. Reiderer 1978.
92. Cowell 1987.
93. Craddock 1986.
94. Craddock 1986.

BIBLIOGRAPHY

Adam, A-M. 1984. *Bronze étrusques et italiques*. Paris

Adam, R., Briquel D. and Gran-Aymerich, J. 1992. Les relations transalpines; Dans l'Europe du Centre-Ouest. In, *Les Étrusques et l'Europe*, 180-7. Réunion des musées nationaux, Paris. (German edition *Die Etrusker und Europa*, Paris 1992)

Artis, E.T. 1828. *Durobrivae of Antoninus*. London

Balty, J-C. 1961. Une centre de production de bronzes figurés de l'Italie septentrionale (deuxième moitié du VIIe - première moitié du VIe siècle avant J.-C.) Volterra ou Arezzo? *Bulletin de l'Institut historique belge de Rome* **XXXIII**, 5-38

Balty, J-C. 1966. Une centre de production de bronzes figurés de l'Etrurie septentrionale. Note additionnelle. *Bulletin de l'Institut historique belge de Rome* **XXXVII**, 5-16

Bateson, J.D. 1971. Roman material from Ireland: a reconsideration. *Proceedings of the Royal Irish Academy* **71**, 21-97

Biel, J. 1985. *Der Keltenfürst von Hochdorf.* Stuttgart

Bonfante, L. 1975. *Etruscan Dress.* Baltimore and London

Boucher, S. 1970. Importations étrusques en Gaule à la fin du VIIᵉ siècle avant J.-C. *Gallia* **XXVIII**, 193-206

Boucher, S. 1976. *Recherches sur les bronzes figurés de Gaule pré-romaine et romaine.* Bibliothèque des Ecoles Françaises d'Athènes et de Rome, 28. Rome

Bouloumié, B. 1976. Cistes à cordons trouvés en Gaule. *Gallia* **XXXIV**, 1-30

Bouloumié, B. 1985. Les vases de bronze étrusques et leur diffusion hors d'Italie. In, M. Bellisario (ed.), *Il commercio etrusco arcaico*, Atti dell'Incontro di studio 5-7 dicembre 1983, 167-78. CNRS, Rome (*Quaderni del Centro di Studio per l'Archeologia Etrusco-Italica*, **9**)

Bouloumié, B. 1986. Vases de bronze étrusques du service du vin. In, J. Swaddling (ed.), *Italian Iron Age Artefacts in the British Museum, Papers of the Sixth British Museum Classical Colloquium* (1982), 63-75. London

Brendel, O. 1978. *Etruscan Art.* Penguin

Brown, A. 1980. *Ancient Italy before the Romans.* Ashmolean Museum Oxford

Bullen, R.A. 1912. *Harlyn Bay.* Padstow

Cateni, G. 1985. sv. Populonia. In, M. Cristofani (ed.) *Dizionario della Civiltà Etrusca*, 229-32. Florence

Coles, B. 1990. Anthropomorphic wooden figures from Britain and Ireland. *PPS* **56**, 315-33

Colonna, G. 1970. *Bronzi votivi umbro-sabellici a figura umana, I Periodo 'arcaico'.* Studi e materiali di etruscologia e antichità italiche VII. Università di Roma

Collingwood-Bruce, J. 1880. *A Catalogue of Antiquities at Alnwick Castle.* Newcastle

Cowell, M.R. 1987. Chemical analysis. In, W.V. Davies, *Catalogue of Egyptian Antiquities in the British Museum (Axes)*, 96-118. London

Craddock, P.T. 1986. The metallurgy and composition of Etruscan bronzes. *Studi Etruschi* **52**, 211-71

Cristofani, M. 1985. *I Bronzi degli Etruschi.* Novara

Cunliffe, B. 1988. *Mount Batten, Plymouth.* Oxford University Committee for Archaeology Monograph **26**. Oxford

Foster, J. 1986. *The Lexden Tumulus.* British Archaeological Reports **156**. Oxford

Freidin, N. 1980. A bronze cult-wagon from Lezoux (Puy-de-Dôme) in the Ashmolean Museum, Oxford. *AntJ* **LX**, 320-7

Galestin, M. 1987. *Etruscan and Italic Bronze Statuettes.* Warfhuizen (Rijksuniversiteit Groningen)

Ghirardini, G. 1888. Intorno alle antichità scoperte nel fondo Baratela. *NSc* 1888, 71-127.

Harbison, P. and Laing, L.R. 1974. *Some Mediterranean Imports in England.* British Archaeological Reports **5**. Oxford

Harden, D.B. 1950. Italic and Etruscan Finds in Britain. *Atti del I Congresso di Preistoria e Protostoria Mediterranea*, 315-24. Florence

Haynes, S. 1985. *Etruscan Bronzes.* London and New York

Hencken, H. 1968. *Tarquinia, Villanovans and Early Etruscans.* Cambridge, Massachusetts

Henig, M. and Paddock, J.M. 1993. Metal figurines in the Corinium Museum, Cirencester. *Trans. Bristol and Gloucestershire Archaeological Society*, **CXI**, 85-6

Hull, M.R. and Hawkes, C.F.C. 1987. *Corpus of Ancient Brooches in Britain.* British Archaeological Reports **168**. Oxford

Jacobsthal, P. 1938. An Iberian bronze found at Sligo. *Journal of the Royal Society of Antiquaries of Ireland* **LXVII**, I, 51-4

Joffroy, R. 1954. *Le Trésor de Vix (Côte d'Or).* Paris

Jope, E.M. 1958. A heavy bronze ring of Italian type from Co. Derry. *Ulster Journal of Archaeology* **21**, 14-16

Jucker, H. 1970. Etruscan votive bronzes of Populonia. In, S. Doeringer, D.G. Mitten and A. Steinberg (eds.), *Art and Technology. A Symposium on Classical Bronzes*, 195-219. Cambridge, Massachusetts and London

Kelly, E. 1993. *Early Celtic Art in Ireland.* Dublin

Megaw, J.V.S. 1970. *Art of the European Iron Age*, New York and Evanston

Payne, G. 1891. *Catalogue of the Museum of Antiquities collected by Mr Henry Durden.* Lewes

Piel, T. 1990. Répertoire des importations étrusques et italiques en Gaule, 17: Pays de Loire. *Caesarodunum III. Bulletin de l'Institut d'Etudes latines et du Centre de recherches A. Piganiol.* Supplement no. **59**, 39-50

Raftery, B. 1984. *La Tène in Ireland.* Veröffentlichung des Vorgeschichten Seminars Marburg. Sd. 2. Marburg

Reiderer, J. 1978. Die naturwissenschaftliche Untersuchung der Bronzen des Ägyptischen Museums. *Berliner Beiträge zur Archäometrie* **3**, 3-42

Richardson, E. 1983. *Etruscan Votive Bronzes.* Mainz am Rhein

Ridgway, D. 1992. Les relations transalpines: En Angleterre. In, *Les Étrusques et l'Europe,* 188. Réunion des musées nationaux, Paris. (German edition *Die Etrusker und Europa,* Paris 1992)

Riis, P.J. 1946. The bronze statuette from Uffington, Berkshire. *Journal of Roman Studies* **XXVI**, 43-7

Seeden, H. 1980. *The Standing Armed Figurines in the Levant. Prähistorische Bronzefunde.* Abteilung I, Bd. 1. Munich

Smith, R.A. 1905. *British Museum Guide to the Antiquities of the Early Iron Age.* London

Smith, R.A. 1912. On late-Celtic antiquities discovered at Welwyn, Herts. *Archaeologia* **63**, 1-30

Sotheby *et al* 1891. *Catalogue of Bronze Arms and Implements of Dr S Egger*

Stary P. 1991. Mediterrane Einfuhrgüter während der Früheisenzeit in England und Skandinavien. *MdI* **98**, 1-31

Stead, I.M. 1971. The reconstruction of Iron Age buckets from Aylesford and Baldock. *BMQ* **XXXV**, 1-4, 250-82

Stead, I.M. 1979. *The Arras Culture.* York

Stead, I.M. 1984. Some notes on imported metalwork. In, S. Macready and F.H. Thompson (eds.), *Cross Channel Trade between Gaul and Britain in the Pre-Roman Iron Age.* Society of Antiquaries of London Occasional Paper (New Series) **IV**, 43-66

Stjernquist, B. 1967. *Ciste a cordoni.* Bonn

Thomas, E.B. 1956. *Archäologische Funde in Ungarn.* Budapest

Weber, T. 1983. *Bronzekannen: Studien zu ausgew. archaischen u. Klass. Oinochoenformen aus Metall in Griechenland u. Etrurien.* Frankfurt am Main/Bern (Archäologischen Studien, Bd. 5)

Yeames, A.H.S. 1906. A statuette from Norway. *JHS* **XXVI**, 281-5

1

2

Figs. 1,2   Etruscan bronze spearmen, said to be from Blandford Forum, Dorset.
British Museum, left to right: PRB 1923.3-6. 3, 6, 2, 5, 1, 7, 4

127

Fig. 3a,b   Etruscan bronze figures, said to be from Blandford Forum, Dorset. British Museum,
                a, Egyptian Osiris, PRB 1923.3-6.8;   b, 'Egyptian' figure, PRB 1923.3-6.9

Fig. 4a-d   Bronze 'kouros', said to be from Blandford Forum, Dorset. British Museum,
                PRB 1923.3-6.10

7a   7b   7c

Fig. 5   Etruscan female figure, said to be from Sligo, Ireland. Dublin, National Museum of Ireland. Photo: Trustees of the National Museum of Ireland

Fig. 6   Etruscan/Umbrian bronze figure, said to be from an Irish bog. Dublin, National Museum of Ireland. Photo: Trustees of the National Museum of Ireland

Fig. 7a-c   Etruscan bronze female figure, said to be from Lincoln's Inn. London, Lincoln's Inn

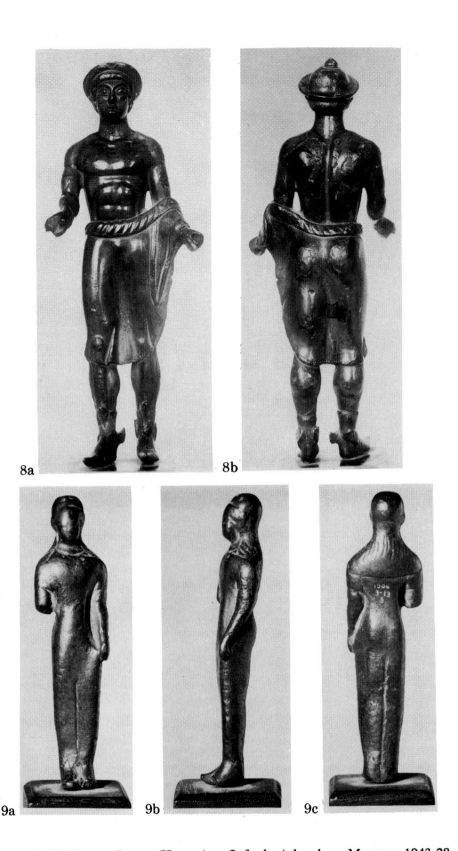

Fig. 8a,b   The Uffington Turms (Hermes).   Oxford, Ashmolean Museum 1943.28.   Photos: Ashmolean Museum

Fig. 9a-c   Etruscan(?) bronze kore, said to have been found at Bergen, Norway.   British Museum, GR 1906.3-13.3

ETRUSCAN ROUTES OUT OF ITALY

NOVITÀ SUL COMMERCIO ETRUSCO ARCAICO: DAL RELITTO DEL GIGLIO AL CONTRATTO DI PECH MAHO

Mauro Cristofani

Consiglio Nazionale delle Ricerche, Istituto per l'archeologia etrusco-italica,
Viale di Villa Massimo 29 - 00161 Roma

Nonostante un decennio fitto di studi, che si impernia sugli Atti del Convegno 'Il commercio etrusco arcaico' organizzato dal CNR nel 1983, pubblicato due anni dopo, e sulla monografia di Michel Gras apparsa sempre nel 1985 dedicata ai *Trafics tyrrhéniens archaïques*, può accadere che un tema sul quale si è lavorato intensamente rischi di perdere il suo interesse e di divenire una sorta di accumulo di luoghi comuni, come dimostra la banalizzazione cui è andata incontro la sezione, dal titolo deviante 'La vocation maritime des Etrusques', della esposizione 'Les Etrusques et l'Europe' del Grand Palais di Parigi che chiude in questi giorni.[1] Alcune scoperte rese note in quest'ultimo quinquennio consentono invece di affinare il quadro finora delineato, passando da una fase quantitativa dell'approccio alle evidenze a una qualitativa, che permette di riaprire una discussione solo apparentemente esaurita.

La pubblicazione del relitto scoperto nella rada di Campese, all'isola del Giglio, nell'arcipelago toscano, per quanto preliminare, costituisce un punto fermo non solo per la dinamica dei traffici alto-arcaici nel Tirreno, ma anche per la storia del commercio greco arcaico. Nonostante manchi la pubblicazione definitiva,[2] che permetta di riferire i materiali rinvenuti alle rispettive giaciture, può essere proposta una lettura delle evidenze utile a ricostruire la fisionomia del *naukleros*.[3]

La nave, del tipo 'cucito', aveva funzioni essenzialmente onerarie: il carico, per quanto possiamo evincere, a differenza delle navi naufragate lungo le coste della Provenza, a Cap d'Antibes, Bon Porté, Esteù dou Mieù e Pointe du Dattier, che sembrano 'specializzate' nel trasporto di anfore vinarie e vasellame da mensa, si presentava composito. Il naufragio avvenne dopo una sosta effettuata in Etruria, dal momento che la percentuale maggiore di anfore da trasporto (circa 130) è etrusca e che esse conservavano resina, pinoli e olive, mentre le poche altre rimanenti riflettono lo spettro 'internazionale' dei traffici mediterranei dell'epoca: sei anfore samie di piccola misura, forse destinate all'olio, alcune di tipo greco-orientale, probabilmente clazomenie, e pochi altri frammenti appartengono a contenitori corinzi e laconici. In una prospettiva 'greca' della dinamica del carico le anfore da trasporto non etrusche rappresentano contenitori residuali, data la notevole percentuale di anfore da trasporto greche rinvenute nelle tombe e negli scarichi cittadini di Caere. La novità sostanziale è offerta dai prodotti contenuti nelle anfore: non solo vino, ma anche olive e resina che rappresentano, pertanto, un surplus derivato da conifere e da una coltura intensiva di cui si poteva presagire, da altri indizi, l'alta antichità in Etruria. La mercanzia includeva anche olii profumati: 28 aryballoi corinzi arcaici, del tipo orange-quarter, quatrefoil e con figurazioni inseribili nel Warrior Group, 16 aryballoi laconici, una lekythos samia, una pisside lenticolare in bucchero greco-orientale e un aryballos etrusco-corinzio che quasi conferma la tappa del naviglio sulle coste etrusche. Il cospicuo numero di coppe ioniche di tipo A 2, circa 80, induce a ritenere che anch'esse facessero parte, come vasellame da mensa, delle merci sottoposte allo scambio, assieme ai kantharoi di bucchero, peraltro scarsi numericamente rispetto ad altri relitti dell'epoca.

Oltre a prodotti alimentari pregiati e profumi il carico comprendeva anche metalli: si sono recuperati quattro pani di rame del peso di 40 kg ciascuno, 9 lingotti di piombo del peso di 8,40-11,70 kg, muniti pure di contrassegno alfabetico, e ferro ridotto in spiedi (che poteva essere incluso nelle ricchezze personali del *naukleros*). L'ambra non lavorata, infine, faceva parte delle merci di lusso

131

certamente reperite in Etruria, utilizzata non a caso come offerta votiva nel deposito dell'Artemision di Efeso.

Alcune evidenze possono in qualche modo fornirci la fisionomia del *naukleros*. L'elmo, che appartiene alla seconda fase dei tipi corinzi ed è fornito di una decorazione incisa che costituirà il modello per gli elmi apulo-corinzi, fa parte di una panoplia da parata; il servizio scrittorio in legno, un dittico e uno stilo, indica che il personaggio è letterato. La *kline* lignea intarsiata, un servizio potorio coerentemente acquisito dal Ceramico di Corinto, composto da un cratere con 'padded dancers' della fine dell'EC, quattro oinochoai dell'inizio del MC, un kothon e quindi gli auloi in avorio e in legno di bosso rinviano a un modello di vita 'aristocratico' che si conserva anche a bordo. Nel quadro della vita di bordo possono inserirsi oltre allo strumentario per la pesca, le lucerne e la ceramica d'uso che sembrano greco-orientali, probabilmente samie, e, forse, i meno pregiati bicchieri laconici, rarissimi in Sicilia, del tutto assenti in Etruria.

La combinazione dei vari elementi presenti nel carico, comporta che il naufragio è avvenuto nel decennio 590-80 a.C., stando soprattutto alla cronologia degli inizi del Corinzio medio e del'aryballos etrusco-corinzio inseribile nel Ciclo dei Galli Affrontati.

La provenienza greco-orientale, forse samia, assicurata dal vasellame comune e dalle lucerne, non esclude una tappa del naviglio a Corinto: nel Trader's Complex, che dovremo identificare come una sorta di *emporikòs oîkos*, riprendendo la terminologia da Stesicoro, la ceramica rinvenuta include un cratere corinzio di passaggio dall'EC al MC, un bicchiere laconico, una coppa ionica del tipo A2, un calice chiota e un kantharos di bucchero del tipo Rasmussen 3e.[4] L'ulteriore tappa, prima del naufragio, include scali tirrenici, controllati da Caere e dal Vulci, come indicano frammenti di impasti ceretani e l'aryballos etrusco-corinzio. L'ulteriore destinazione del naviglio, che doveva utilizzare la baia di Campese come punto di appoggio nella navigazione tirrenica, poteva essere la Gallia meridionale, come conferma lo spettro di ceramiche rinvenute negli insediamenti costieri, in particolare a Marsiglia, che vedono prevalere le anfore etrusche e dove non mancano anche le ceramiche greche del genere trasportato dall'*holkas* naufragata presso l'isola del Giglio.[5]

La fisionomia del *naukleros* che emerge dalla nostra lettura evoca l'immagine di un mercante-aristocratico che esercita l'*emporia* sulla propria nave da carico, portando un *phorton idion* composto, in cui si individuano i residui di un carico smerciato presso gli Etruschi e beni acquisiti in Etruria. Il modello sembra quasi quello descritto da Dionigi a proposito di Demarato (III, 46, 3), quale che sia la fonte da cui lo storico di Alicarnasso l'ha derivato, ma la compagine storica da cui egli proviene appare piuttosto quella dei *naukleroi* greco-orientali ai quali, come insegnano le evidenze di Graviscá, a partire dalla fine del VII secolo a.C., le aristocrazie etrusche concedono luoghi e spazi di accoglienza.[6]

La seconda scoperta, avvenuta a Pech-Maho, un oppidum iberico sulla costa dell'attuale Linguadoca occupata in antico dagli Elysici ricordati da Erodoto (VII, 165), rende conto, invece, dell'avvenuto passaggio delle forme di scambio nelle mani di *phortegoi*. Si tratta di una lamina di piombo sulla quale è inciso un testo di transazione commerciale in dialetto ionico datato al secondo quarto del V secolo a.C. che riutilizza una superficie già impiegata per un documento scritto in etrusco.[7] Nel testo etrusco vengono nominati due individui, designati col solo nome personale (*Venel* etrusco e *Utavu* di probabile origine latina) impegnati in un'operazione che comporta un conteggio (*kisnee* per kisnei* 'nel terzo') che avviene a Massalia (*Mataliai* 'a Massalia'), operazione che ha bisogno di una *graphé* (designata col corrispondente lessema etrusco *zik*).[8] I dati ricavabili dal testo etrusco presentano motivi di interesse se confrontati con il testo greco, il cui contenuto registra l'acquisto di un'imbarcazione compiuto a Emporion da due mercanti, Kyprios, nominato nel testo, e Heron di Ios, il cui nome è scritto nel *verso*. La compartecipazione del secondo si è svolta effettuando il pagamento della metà, un terzo della quale ricevuta come caparra in un luogo specifico, un non meglio identificato fiume, dove erano ormeggiate altre barche, il resto in contanti. Le operazioni si sono svolte alla presenza di testimoni diversi, tutti dai nomi iberici.[9] Colpiscono alcune analogie nei due testi: il nome della località in cui è avvenuto l'acquisto (Massalia da un lato, Emporion dall'altro), le modalità del pagamento che prevedono un 'terzo' (la caparra è *trite* in greco, in etrusco troviamo *kisne*), la presenza di più personaggi, etruschi e latini nel primo caso (Venel, Utave) greci (Kyprios, Heron) e iberi (Basigerros, Bleruas, Golo.biur,.avaras, Nalbe..n) nel secondo.

La riutilizzazione della superficie scrittoria può indicare, ma non necessariamente, che il contenuto del testo etrusco non avesse più valore e che il mercante focese avesse impiegato la lamina come promemoria per un affare personale: certamente se n'era impossessato in un luogo della costa provenzale, forse nella stessa Marsiglia. L'estensore del testo etrusco aveva a sua volta impiegato una scrittura i cui caratteri rinviano inequivocabilmente alle poche iscrizioni etrusche di Aleria della prima metà del V secolo a.C., in particolare a due graffiti incisi su due kylikes attiche a figure rosse con i nomi personali *Klavtie* e *Kaile*. Il sistema di scrittura permette dunque di ravvisare nei personaggi nominati nella lamina di Pech-Maho etruschi in contatto con l'ambiente di Aleria: ciò consente di riconsiderare, sotto questa luce, il ruolo svolto da un centro esterno all'Etruria propria, nel quale si è creata, a partire dagli inizi del V secolo a.C., una cultura 'coloniale' che doveva comportare la conservazione di un sistema scrittorio proprio dell'epoca dei 'fondatori' e i cui titolari, a questo punto, sembrano proiettati in un mondo di traffici diretto non solo verso la madrepatria, ma anche verso i centri liguri, verso Marsiglia con gli scali greci che punteggiavano le coste della Francia meridionale, e verso centri come Pech-Maho, presumibilmente in mano dei nativi Iberi.

Stando a Eforo di Cuma, fonte di Diodoro Siculo, le città fondate dagli Etruschi in Corsica dopo la battaglia del Mar Sardo ricevevano come tributi dai nativi resina e prodotti dell'apicoltura, ma utilizzavano i Corsi anche come schiavi (Diod. Sic. 5,13, 1-14, 2). Una di queste città, non espressamente identificabile nel testo di Diodoro, doveva essere Aleria. L'archeologia degli anni '70, dominata da un lato dalla ricerca di conferme alle notizie delle fonti letterarie, dall'altro dall'analisi filologica dei rinvenimenti effettuati nella necropoli (l'ampia messe di ceramica figurata, greca ed etrusca, entrava nel dibattito sui circuiti distributivi del Tirreno), ha prestato un'attenzione poco più che modesta all'ambiente scelto per l'insediamento dai Focesi e poi rioccupato dagli Etruschi o alla stessa composizione dei corredi funerari, rivelatrice, invece, dello status sociale dei sepolti. La scelta del sito effettuata dai Focesi, poi sostituiti dai dominatori Etruschi, si configura, come 'nicchia' ecologicamente ottimale nei confronti del resto dell'isola, che già le fonti di Strabone (Posidonio o Artemidoro) definiscono in gran parte inaccessibile (Str. 5,2, 7). La pianura alluvionale attraversata dal Tavignano era idonea per coltivazioni cerealicole per un' estensione di oltre 15 kmq; non mancavano le sorgenti; l'entroterra forniva resine e legname, oltre che i minerali, e poteva accogliere il bestiame per il pascolo estivo; la costa lagunosa, già allora caratterizzata dagli stagni, favoriva pesca e forme di allevamento. La condizione ecologica era quella propria di una colonia di popolamento con un territorio agricolo sufficientemente esteso e con buone risorse nell'entroterra. Dell'abitato più antico si sono recuperate una serie di evidenze riferibili alla fase più antica dello stanziamento e alla produzione del ferro,[10] al punto che i dati appaiono di grande interesse per la storia del medio Tirreno, nel quale Aleria sembra porsi, dopo le nuove scoperte, assieme all'Elba e a Populonia, in quella sorta di circuito metallurgico che permette la fioritura economica di tutto il distretto marittimo proprio fra V e IV secolo a.C.[11] Una ricerca svolta complementarmente sulle fotografie aeree e sul terreno ha rivelato, come in un palinsesto, segni di sistemi di divisione riferibili a diverse epoche. Uno di questi sistemi, apparentemente il più antico, si rintraccia su un asse che collega il più meridionale Stagno d'Urbino con l'antico insediamento, un asse sul quale si colloca l'unica strada acciottolata finora scoperta, larga circa 2,50 m, lungo la quale sono disposte le tombe a camera messe in luce negli anni '60, nella località Casabianda. Lungo questo asse, spostato di 15 gradi verso Est rispetto all'orientamento astronomico Nord-Sud, si distinguono diversi incroci: su di essi si organizzano un allineamento di tombe della necropoli, quasi perpendicolare alla strada sepolcrale e, nell'insediamento, anche il bastione difensivo che circonda il pianoro.[12] Questi segni di una delimitazione del suolo, che rivelano anche la sua appropriazione, ben si attagliano a un'operazione di tipo 'coloniale' che, attraverso forme di modellamento e di divisione della campagna, sfrutta le risorse del territorio. Attribuire agli Etruschi tale tipo di operazione sembra quasi ovvio: si ricorderà, fra l'altro, come interventi di questo genere, esito di una scienza agrimensoria avanzata, che segna profondamente il paesaggio rurale e urbano, vengono applicati sia a Marzabotto sia a Capua agli inizi del V secolo a.C.[13]

Anche le scoperte avvenute nella necropoli con le tombe a camera, fornite di corridoio, i cui ingressi si allineano perpendicolarmente alla via sepolcrale tracciata secondo l'asse principale di divisione del territorio, pertinenti a 'guerrieri' con armamenti compositi (armi etrusche, italiche e ornamenti iberici)[14] pienamente inseriti nella cultura simposiaca dell'epoca, si rivelano come quelle di capi-militari designati da *simplicia nomina*, quali Klavtie e Kaile, non diversamente dai titolari della *graphé* di Pech-Maho. I proprietari delle due kylikes iscritte sono senza dubbio i titolari delle rispettive tombe che si affiancano lungo la strada sepolcrale, due 'capi' militari appartenenti al vertice gerarchico di quanti parteciparono al popolamento della 'colonia', sepolti con un rituale che li omologa al rango degli aristocratici della madrepatria di qualche decennio prima, oppure due partecipanti al rito funerario in onore di esponenti di spicco della comunità.

A questo ambiente di 'coloni' che protegge militarmente i territori conquistati vanno dunque attribuite anche forme di commercio organizzato che ci fanno intravvedere una rete di traffici innestata su rotte già percorse dalla navigazione focese, i cui partners frequentano le coste del Mar Ligure, in particolare Genova, e gli insediamenti collegati con Massalia, nel quadro di un'intensa attività mercantile che caratterizza il Tirreno settentrionale anche dopo la battaglia di Cuma[15]: in questo contesto si spiega il piombo di Pech-Maho, il cui contenuto, al pari di quello successivo in greco, atteneva a transazioni mercantili correnti in un mondo di traffici caratterizzato da una mobilità di personaggi etnicamente differenziati e più perfezionato nelle sue procedure di quanto avremmo potuto credere finora.

NOTE

1. *Etrusques,* 44-52.
2. Dopo le prime relazioni preliminari (cfr. Bound et Vallintine 1983) si vedano Bound 1985; Bound 1991; Bound 1991a; Bound 1991b. Quanto alla tecnica di costruzione dello scafo cfr. Bound 1985b.
3. Per un'analisi approfondita del carico rinvio a Cristofani (in stampa).
4. Williams *et al.* 1974.
5. Cfr. Py 1985. Sulla ceramica greca cfr. ad es. i livelli de La Liquière Py 1967 e Saint-Blaise Bouloumié 1982, 173.
6. Sul problema: Ogilvie 1970², 141; Bravo 1984; Musti 1987, in particolare pp.140, 142; Martinez Pinna 1989, in particolare pp.130, 142-4. Sul commercio aristocratico cfr. Mele 1979, 96-107; il panorama emerge chiaramente dalle dediche del santuario greco di Gravisca (Torelli 1982).
7. Edizione principale dei testi: Lejeune *et al.* 1990. Si veda anche Pouilloux 1990.
   Per un primo esame del testo etrusco, di cui M. Lejeune mi fornì cortesemente un apografo e con il quale ebbi una corrispondenza al proposito: Cristofani 1990, 123-6; Cristofani 1992 nonché la lettura proposta da Rix dopo una visione diretta del pezzo: Rix 1991, 332, Na 01.
   Per un commento al testo, che ha raggiunto del tutto autonomamente risultati analoghi ai miei

per quanto concerne il riferimento alle iscrizioni di Aleria (da cui una collocazione 'periferica' del testo) e il riconoscimento del nome di Massalia: Colonna 1990.

8. Sulle questioni sono intervenuto diffusamente in Cristofani 1993, cui rinvio per l'approfondimento delle questioni qui trattate.
9. Sul contenuto del testo greco sono intervenuti successivamente: Chadwick 1990; van Effenterre et Yelissaropolous-Karakostas 1991; Lejeune 1991; Ampolo e Caruso 1990-91.
10. Sulle scoperte nell'insediamento: Jehasse 1981-82; 1982; 1985; Lenoir et Rebuffat 1983-84, 83, (couches 14-16), 91 (couche 4); Jehasse 1985-86.
11. Cristofani e Martelli 1981-82.
12. Charre 1983-84. Si veda *ibidem* 113, il commento di J. e L. Jehasse. Sulla strada vedi già Jehasse 1974.
13. Per quanto concerne Marzabotto cfr. la sintesi recente di Malnati in Malnati e Manfredi 1991, 187ss. La ristrutturazione dell'abitato di Capua, orientato anch'esso NS, (Frederiksen 1984, tav. 6), dovrebbe risalire agli inizi del V secolo a.C.: si veda Allegro 1984, ripreso da Colonna 1991, 61.
14. I corredi sono pubblicati in Jehasse 1973, in particolare le tombe da considerare sono le nn. 93, 92, 102, 91, 90, 89, 87, 85, 98, allineate lungo la strada N-S della necropoli. Di alcune di queste tombe sono pubblicate le rispettive planimetrie: tavv. 8-12, 14.
15. Sul problema Cristofani 1987, 70-3, 124-6; Milanese 1987; Maggiani 1990.

BIBLIOGRAFIA

Allegro, N. 1984. Scavi e scoperte. *StEtr* **52**, 514-517

Ampolo, C. e Caruso, T. 1990-1991. I Greci e gli altri nel Mediterraneo occidentale. Le iscrizioni greca ed etrusca di Pech-Maho: circolazione di beni, di uomini, di istituti. *Opus* **IX-X**, 29-56

Bouloumié, B. 1982. *Recherches stratigraphiques sur l'oppidum de Saint-Blaise.* Avignon

Bound, M. and Vallintine, R. 1983. A wreck of possible Etruscan origin. *JNArch* **12, 2**, 113-22

Bound, M. 1985. Una nave mercantile di età arcaica all'Isola del Giglio. In, CNR (ed.), Il commercio etrusco arcaico. *QAEI* **9**, 65-70

Bound, M. 1985b. *Sewn Plank Boats.* BAR International Series **276**, 49-65

Bound, M. 1991. The pre-classical wreck at Campese Bay, first season report. *Studi e materiali, Scienza dell'antichità in Toscana* **VI**, 181-98

Bound, M. 1991a. The pre-classical wreck at Campese Bay, second interim report. *Studi e materiali, Scienza dell'antichita in Toscana* **VI**, 199-244

Bound, M. 1991b. *The Giglio wreck.* Enalia suppl. **1**. Athens

Bravo, B. 1984. Commerce et noblesse en Grèce archaïque. *DHA* **10**, 122-32

Chadwick, J. 1990. The Pech-Maho Lead. *ZPE* **82**, 161-66

Charre, R. 1983-84. Les cadastres antiques d'Aléria. *ArchCorsa* **8-9**, 103-8

Colonna, G. 1990. L'iscrizione etrusca del piombo di Linguadoca. *Scienze dell'Antichità* **2**, (1988) 547-55

Colonna, G. 1991. Le civiltà anelleniche. In, G. Pugliese Carratelli (ed.), *Storia e civiltà della Campania. L'evo antico*, 25-67. Napoli

Cristofani, M. 1987. *Saggi di storia etrusca arcaica.* Roma

Cristofani, M. 1990. Etruschi e genti dell'Italia preromana: alcuni esempi di mobilità in età arcaica. In, E. Campanile (ed.), *Rapporti linguistici e culturali fra i popoli dell'Italia antica, Atti del Convegno Pisa 1989*, 111-28. Pisa

Cristofani, M. 1992. Rivista di epigrafia etrusca. *StEtr* **57**, 1991 (1992), 285-7

Cristofani, M. 1993. Il testo di Pech Maho, Aleria e i traffici del V secolo a.C. *MEFRA* **105,** 833-45

Cristofani, M. (in stampa) Un *naukleros* greco-orientale nel Tirreno. Per un'interpretazione del relitto del Giglio. *ASAIA* (1995), 68-9

Cristofani, M. et Martelli, M. 1981-82. Aléria et l'Etrurie à travers les nouvelles fouilles de Populonia. *ArchCorsa* **6-7**, 5-10

van Effenterre H. et Yelissaropoulos-Karakostas, J. 1991. Un affaire d'affrètement. A propos du 'plomb de Pech Maho'. *RevHistDroitFrance* **2**, 217-26

Etrusques 1992. *Les Etrusques et l'Europe.* Milano e Parigi

Frederiksen, M. 1984. *Campania.* Hertford

Jehasse, J. 1974. Conscription de Corse. *Gallia* **32**, 529-33

Jehasse, J. et L. 1973. *La nécropole préromaine d'Aléria (1960-68).* Gallia **XXV**ᵉ supplément. Paris

Jehasse, J. et L. 1981-82. L'âge du fer et le début de l'urbanisation en Corse. *ArchCorsa* **6-7**, 13-18

Jehasse, J. et L. 1982. Alalia/Aléria après la 'victoire à la cadmeénne'. *ParPass* **37**, 247-55

Jehasse, J. et L. 1985. Aléria et la metallurgie du fer. In, CNR (ed.), Il commercio etrusco arcaico. *QAEI* **9,** 95-101

Jehasse, M.-J. 1985-86. Un four à fer d'Aléria préromaine. *ArchCorsa* **10-11**, 65-75

Lejeune, M. 1991. Ambiguités du texte de Pech-Maho. *REG* **104**, 311-29

Cristofani

Lejeune, M., Pouilloux, J., et Solier, Y. 1990. Etrusque et ionien archaïques sur un plomb de Pech Maho (Aude). *RANarb* **21**, (1988) 19-59

Lenoir E. et Rebuffat, R. 1983-83. Le rempart romain d'Aleria. *ArchCorsa* **8-9**, 73-95

Maggiani, A. 1990. La situazione archeologica dell'Etruria settentrionale. In, Ecole française de Rome (ed.), *Crise et transformation des sociétés archaïques de l'Italie antique au Ve siècle av. J.-C.*, *Actes de la table ronde 1987*, 37-43. Roma

Malnati L. e Manfredi V. 1991. *Gli Etruschi in Val Padana.* Milano

Martinez Pinna, J. 1989. El origen de Tarquinio Prisco. In, Istituto di Studi Etruschi (ed.), *Atti Secondo Congresso Internazionale Etrusco* II, 129-45. Roma

Mele, A. 1979. *Il commercio greco arcaico. Prexis ed emporie.* Napoli

Milanese, M. 1987. *Scavi nell'oppidum preromano di Genova.* Roma

Musti, D. 1987. Etruria e Lazio arcaico nella tradizione (Demarato, Tarquinio, Mezenzio). In, M. Cristofani (ed.), Etruria e Lazio arcaico. *QAEI* **13**, 139-42

Ogilvie, R.M. 1970². *A Commentary on Livy. Books 1-5.* Oxford

Pouilloux, J. 1990. Un texte commercial ionien trouvé en Languedoc et la colonisation ionienne, *Scienze dell'Antichità* **2**, (1988) 535-46

Py, F. 1967. La céramique corinthienne. *RivStLig* **33**, 277-87

Py, M. 1985. Les amphores étrusques de la Gaule méridionale. In, CNR (ed.), *Il commercio etrusco arcaico*, *QAEI* **9**, 74-83

Rix, H. 1991. *Etruskische Texte, Editio minor.* Tübingen

Torelli, M. 1982. Per una definizione del commercio greco orientale: il caso di Graviscia. *ParPass* **37**, 320-5

Williams, C.K. (II), MacIntosh, J., and Fisher, J.E. 1974. Excavations at Corinth 1973. *Hesperia* **42**, 14-32

SU UN BRONZETTO NURAGICO PROVENIENTE DA LANUVIO

Fritzi Jurgeit
Via Castiglione del Lago 14, I-00191 Roma

Nella sala XXXI del Museo di Villa Giulia, dedicata al materiale proveniente dal Latium vetus, una 'vecchia' (Figs. 1a,b) - secondo la descrizione no. 42.190 dell'inventario - rimaneva nell'ombra fino ad oggi, mai riconosciuta come d'origine sarda. Insieme ad altro materiale fittile (terracotte votive no. 42.181-42.188) e bronzeo (testa maschile (?), no. 42.189) fu donata al Museo dalla Contessa di Santa Fiore, verso il 1916, con la provenienza 'Civita Lavinia'.[1]

Il bronzetto a pieno fuso (alt. cm. 11.5) è un po' ammaccato nella parte superiore e mal conservato nella superficie. Questa, nelle parti conservate, è nerastra e liscia; dove si è staccata le parti sono molto ruvide con formazione di pustole e con efflorescenze verdi brillanti. Mancano l'avambraccio destro, quello sinistro dal polso in giù, i due piedi ed inoltre gran parte del capotto. Il sottoveste è staccato nella zona tra i piedi.

La figura femminile è vestita d'una 'tunica' stretta sopra un sottoveste lungo e d'una pellegrina fino alla vita come la conosciamo dai gruppi 'madre e figlio' - adulto o bambino. I capelli spioventi - in gran parte smarriti - finiscono nella nuca in un bozzetto non ben spiegabile.[2] Gli occhi tondi accerchiati ed il mento a punta dominano il viso ovoidale. Con questi dettagli il bronzetto da Lanuvio si aggancia ad un paio di pastori (Fig. 2), recentemente acquistato dalla Prähistorische Staatssammlung a Monaco.[3] Questi da parte loro si avvicinano molto alle statue da Monti Prama, statue arenarie che 'monumentalizzano' i bronzetti.[4] In seguito ai ritrovamenti scarsi dagli scavi di Monti Prama si potrebbero inserire anche le statuette nel VII sec. a.C.[5]

I rapporti bilaterali tra la Sardegna e l'Etruria sono stati studiati ripetutamente.[6] La navicella da Porto si conosceva, fino ad oggi, come l'unica prova per il contatto (sul campo dei vincoli familiari?) del Lazio con la Sardegna.[7] Gli ormai rari ritrovamenti archeologici a Lanuvio attestano un insediamento stabile sul luogo nei Colli Albani già nel IX sec. a.C.[8]

Vorrei attirare l'attenzione anche su un bronzetto sardo raffigurante un pastore nella collezione del Campo Santo Teutonico a Roma.[9] Il pezzo fu trovato probabilmente fuori Sardegna (nel Lazio?).

RINGRAZIAMENTI

Ringrazio il Soprintendente per l'Etruria Meridionale, G. Schichilone, e la Direttrice del Museo Nazionale di Villa Giulia, F. Boitani, per il permesso di pubblicazione e la cessione della foto; inoltre ringrazio M. Cocchieri per i suoi aiuti tecnici. Sono riconoscente a A. Weiland del suo prezioso aiuto nello studio del bronzetto nel Campo Santo.

NOTE

1. Il bronzetto è menzionato come proveniente dalla stipe del tempio di Giunone Sospita da Moretti 1962, 231-2.
2. Per i vestiti della figura: Lilliu 1966, nos. 63.123.124. Per l'abbigliamento sardo in genere: Jurgeit 1983. Capelli della figura: cfr. Lilliu 1966, nos. 69.70.123.
3. Thimme 1980, no. 120.121; Thimme 1983, no. 26.27; Zahlhaas 1991, fig. 13. Si deve riflettere sul giudizio di Lilliu 1981, 251 'non pochi esemplari d'una collezione privata svizzera ... assolutamente inautentici ...'.

4.   Tronchetti 1986, spec. 47-8.
5.   Per i problemi della datazione dei bronzetti sardi: Thimme 1980, 109-17; Lilliu 1981, 230-40;
       Ferrarese Ceruti 1985; Bernardini 1985; Gras 1985, 137-42; Serra Ridgway 1986, 92-3;
       Tronchetti 1988, 71.
6.   Gras 1980; Nicosia 1980; Gras 1985, 113-252; Tronchetti 1988.
7.   Jurgeit 1980, no.190; Colonna 1981. La provenienza della navicella nella coll. Este Milani
       di Busto Arsizio (Lilliu 1966, no. 314) è indicata genericamente come 'Lazio'.
8.   Quilici 1990.
9.   Cfr. Lilliu 1966, no. 57; Kuhn 1962, no. 274 (D 23).

BIBLIOGRAFIA

Bernardini, P. 1985. Osservazioni sulla bronzistica figurata sarda. *BASard* **2**, 119-66

Colonna, G. 1981. La barchetta nuragica di Porto ritrovata. In, *Gli etruschi e Roma. Atti dell'incontro di studio in onore di M. Pallottino (1979)*, 171-2. Roma

Ferrarese Ceruti, M.L. 1985. Un bronzetto nuragico da Ossi (Sassari). In, G. Sotgiu (ed.), *Studi in onore di Giovanni Lilliu per il suo settantesimo compleanno*, 51-62. Cagliari

Gras, M. 1980. In, *KKS*, 126-33

Gras, M. 1985. Trafics tyrrhéniens archaiques. *BEFAR* **258.** Rome

Ichnussa 1981. (AAVV) *La Sardegna dalle origini all'età classica*. Milano

Jurgeit, F. 1980. In, *KKS*, 406 no.190

Jurgeit, F. 1983. Beobachtungen zu einigen sardischen Gewändern. In, *Antidoron. Festschrift für J. Thimme zum 65. Geburtstag am 26. Sept. 1982*, 119-124. Karlsruhe

KKS 1980. J. Thimme (ed.), *Kunst und Kultur Sardiniens vom Neolithikum bis zum Ende der Nuraghenzeit*. Catalogo della mostra. Karlsruhe / Berlin

Kuhn W. 1962. In, *Frühchristliche Kunst aus Rom,* Catalogo della mostra Villa Hügel, no. 274 (D 23). Essen

Lilliu, G. 1966. *Sculture della Sardegna nuragica*. Cagliari

Lilliu, G. 1981. In, *Ichnussa*, 177-251

Moretti, M. 1962. *Il Museo Nazionale di Villa Giulia*. Roma

Nicosia, F. 1980. In, *KKS*, 200-11

Quilici, L. 1990. Lanuvium. In, *La grande Roma dei Tarquini.* Catalogo della mostra, 196-7. Roma

Serra Ridgway, F.R. 1986. Nuragic Bronzes in the British Museum. In, M.S. Balmuth (ed.), *Studies in Sardinian Archaeology* 2, 84-101. AnnArbor

Thimme, J. 1980. In, *KKS*, 99-120

Thimme, J. 1983. *Kunst der Sarden bis zum Ende der Nuraghenzeit, Slg. E. Borowski.* Catalogo della mostra. München

Tronchetti, C. 1986. Nuragic Statuary from Monte Prama. In, M.S. Balmuth (ed.), *Studies in Sardinian Archaeology* 2, 40-59. AnnArbor

Tronchetti, C. 1988. La Sardegna e gli Etruschi. *Mediterranean Archaeology* 1, 66-82

Zahlhaas, G. 1991. Zwei sardische Statuetten. *MüJb* **42,** 181-3

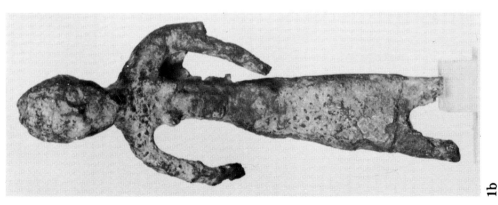

2

1b

1a

Figs. 1a,b   Bronzetto Sardo. Roma, Museo di Villa Giulia n.42.190. Foto Soprintendenza Archeologica per l'Etruria Meridionale n.43166 e autrice
Fig. 2   Due bronzetti Sardi. Foto D. Widmer, Basilea. Già coll. Borowski. n. Bor.1280

143

EXCHANGE NORTHWARDS FROM PENINSULAR ITALY IN THE FIRST MILLENNIUM BC: THE WESTERN PO PLAIN AND THE ALPINE PASSES

Mark Pearce

Dipartimento di Scienze dell'Antichità - Archeologia, University of Pavia,
Strada Nuova 65, 27100 Pavia, Italy

(Abbreviations used in this paper: AL Alessandria; GE Genova; MN Mantova; NO Novara; PC Piacenza; PV Pavia; VA Varese)

The subject of this brief paper is the western Po Plain which, although it is now culturally and politically part of Italy, has in many periods been more closely linked to Central Europe than to the Italian peninsula.[1] For most of the first millennium BC the western Po Plain represents the first non-Etruscan territory crossed by exchange northwards.

There are of course a number of reasons for this 'Central European vocation', but perhaps the major explanation is to be sought in the nature of the mountain ranges which surround the Po Plain.[2]

The classical authors present us with a *topos* on the frighteningly impassable Alps; for example, Livy (V, 34, 6) and Pliny the Elder (*Nat. Hist.* XII, 5) maintained that they had in the past been insurmountable, and Horace (*Odes* IV, 14, 12) calls them *tremendae*, and paints a picture of the savage nature of the environment and of the Alpine tribes:

> *... milite nam tuo*
> *Drusus Genaunos, implacidum genus,*
> *Breunosque veloces et arces*
> *Alpibus impositas tremendis*
>
> *deiecit acer plus vice simplici;*
> *maior Neronum mox grave proelium*
> *commisit immanisque Raetos*
> *auspiciis pepulit secundis*

10

15

However, this *topos* is just that, a commonplace, and is misleading. The high and snow-capped Alps were indeed an unfamiliar environment for peninsular Romans, but the range had long been permeable.[3] The passes are high but are numerous and relatively easy compared to the Apennines which, despite being a comparatively low range, have very few passes and crossing them involves negotiating narrow and difficult defiles.[4] We may therefore say that the Apennines are less permeable than the Alps.

A demonstration of the ease with which the Alps could be crossed has, paradoxically perhaps, been recently provided by the discovery of the Similaun ice-man, whose resting place, close to passes over 3000m above sea-level, would seem to suggest that even the higher, secondary Alpine passes were negotiated by the late neolithic Alpine populations.[5]

The distribution of Luco A type beakers in the East-Central Alps in the twelfth and eleventh centuries BC is further confirmation of the permeability of the Alpine range. Their widespread distribution in the valleys of the Adige, the Inn, and the Upper Rhine presupposes the use of mountain passes between these valleys, most of which are over 2000m above sea-level.[6]

In the western Po Plain too, transalpine connections were strong. The Late Bronze Age Canegrate culture seems to be closely connected to Northern Switzerland and Northern Savoy,[7] and

145

many aspects of the ensuing Protogolasecca (Final Bronze Age) and Golasecca (Early Iron Age) cultures can best be understood in the light of the Western Hallstatt region.[8]

The altitude of the passes across the Alps was, in sum, not a major limitation on movement or contact.

EXCHANGE ROUTES

Transalpine exchange (Fig. 1)

A number of models exist to explain the presence of Etruscan and other southern imports and behaviour patterns (such as the symposium) in northern Europe, and the routes that these may have taken across the Alps.[9]

In a number of papers on the Golasecca culture and its role as a mediator for transalpine exchange relations Raffaele De Marinis has emphasised the use of the Central Alpine passes, the Saint Gotthard and the Val Levantina, the San Bernardino and the Val Mesolcina, the Spluga and the Val Chiavenna, primarily on the basis of findspots in the valleys leading to these passes (Fig. 1, B).[10]

On the other hand Ludwig Pauli has preferred to emphasise the route via the Vallée d'Aoste - the Great Saint Bernard pass - Martigny and the Rhône valley - the Col des Mosses - the Saane valley and then Châtillon sur Glâne, the settlement where the Glâne becomes navigable, and where black-figure Attic pottery has been found (Fig. 1, A).[11]

Donati cautions against the use of distribution maps and modern alpine geography for reconstructing ancient routes; he emphasises that the present-day passes often owe their existence to political and economic expedients rather than to their actual ease of passage[12] and maintains that it is impossible to know which passes were in fact used in the Iron Age.[13]

Since, as we have seen, the geography of the Alpine range does not constrain exchange routes, I should like to argue that attempts to identify the passes used in this exchange must also be based on the examination of the distribution of these exotic goods in the western Po Plain, the first non-Etruscan territories crossed by such exchange.

Transapennine exchange (Fig. 1)

Although the Alps may be described as archaeologically permeable, the geography of the Apennines constrains routes across them.[14] Three major transapennine routes towards the western Po Plain may be identified:

a)   a western route, the Scrivia valley, leading from the Giovi pass above Genoa (Fig. 1, G);

b)   a central route which, from the passes above Chiavari, follows the Aveto and then the Trebbia valleys (Fig. 1, H);

c)   an eastern route, the Reno valley leading from *Etruria interna* via Marzabotto to *Etruria padana* at Bologna, and connecting with the western Po Plain via the Po (Fig. 1, J).

THE WESTERN ROUTE (Fig. 2)

This is documented by sixth-century bucchero along the Scrivia valley, at Libarna and Serravalle Scrivia, and along its affluent the Val Curone at Monleale (AL) and Ponte Nizza (PV) - loc. Guardamonte (di Gremiasco):[15]

Serravalle Scrivia (AL), four fragments of bucchero made at Chiusi with plastic human-head decoration, datable to the second half of the sixth century BC;[16]

Serravalle Scrivia (AL) - loc. Libarna, a trilobate oinochoe made at Chiusi from the site of the later Roman city of *Libarna*, datable to the second half of the sixth century BC; and two sherds of bucchero from the same locality, datable to the sixth century BC;[17]

Monleale (AL), a miniature kyathos in bucchero;[18]

Ponte Nizza (PV) - loc. Guardamonte (di Gremiasco), bucchero, including kantharos sherds, from the fortified *castelliere* on the ridge between the Val Curone and the Val Staffora.[19]

Indeed, bucchero *pesante* is absent at Bologna, and this sixth-century material probably implies that the foundation of the Etruscan emporium at Genoa, which took place in the early years of the fifth century as a result of political changes brought about by the Battle of Alalia in *c.* 540 BC,[20] was a result of transapennine exchange northwards, and not the stimulus for such a pattern (as has been maintained, for example, by Venturino Gambari[21]):

THE CENTRAL ROUTE (Fig. 2)

Final Bronze Age metals exchange along the transapennine Trebbia route was hypothesised by Tizzoni,[22] and I have recently examined the pattern and the possible mechanism of this exchange; continuity of this route in the eighth and seventh centuries BC seems to be documented by Chiavari type armrings.[23] That the route continued to maintain a role in trade from the Etruscan-controlled Tyrrhenian Sea has recently been confirmed by surface-collection finds at a sixth- to fifth-century site at Rivergaro (PC) - loc. Monte Dinavolo,[24] between the Trebbia and Nure valleys (Fig. 2), with numerous sherds of Etruscan pottery and a sherd of Attic pottery; indeed the presence of Golasecca material in the valley would tend to confirm this view, even though Catarsi and Dall'Aglio, who publish the Rivergaro (PC) - loc. Monte Dinavolo material, prefer to explain it as the result of a '*penetrazione etrusca*' westwards from the Bologna area.[25]

THE EASTERN ROUTE

Bologna, situated at the mouth of the Reno valley, seems to have been the major mediator of Etruscan exchange with northern Italy and towards Central Europe.[26]

Exchange across the western Po Plain

At this stage in the discussion it may be useful to make a series of considerations about the western Lombard plain (Figs. 1, 2). Although the eastern, Venetian plain is marshy and subject to the uncertain regimes of the rivers that cross it, the western plain is largely dry,[27] and the height of the river terraces puts the plain out of the reach of even severe flooding. Thus land as well as river exchange routes would have been practicable, although waterborne transport, much cheaper in the classical world,[28] was probably also more convenient in the early first millennium.

The Po was navigable in antiquity at least as far as its confluence with the Tanaro (according to Polybius II, 16, 10) or perhaps even as far as Turin (according to Pliny the Elder (*Nat. Hist.* III, 17, 123)) and with flat-bottomed boats the Ticino could easily be navigated as far as the rapids at Golasecca, at the mouth of Lake Maggiore. The Po was still navigable with small boats as far as Turin in the eighteenth century.[29]

Indeed, it seems that in the seventh and sixth centuries the main route for exchange from Bologna towards northern and Central Europe followed the Po and Ticino corridor towards the Golasecca heartland[30] at the southern end of Lake Maggiore, centred around Golasecca (VA), Sesto Calende (VA) and Castelletto sopra Ticino (NO), and indeed it is striking how Golasecca II material concentrates along this corridor in the provinces of Pavia and Milan.[31]

Over the past ten years our knowledge of the Golasecca culture, and particularly of its last phase, GIIIA, corresponding to the fifth century, has increased dramatically with stratigraphic excavations at Bergamo,[32] Brescia,[33] and Como.[34] The results of these investigations have led De Marinis[35] to suggest that the foundation of the Etruscan colonies around Mantua in the late sixth century led to a new exchange route (Fig. 1, C), which went up the Mincio from Bagnolo San Vito (MN) - loc. Forcello[36] to Lake Garda, and then cut across the foot of the prealpine piedmont to Como (fifth-century Como, the major Golasecca IIIA centre, may have covered as much as 150ha) via the fifth-century centres at Bergamo and Brescia. This new route completely bypassed the Lake Maggiore western heartland of the Golasecca culture, which went into a rapid decline; from Como, De Marinis' route crossed the Sotto Ceneri range in Canton Ticino to the Upper Ticino valley, and then on up the Val Levantina to the Saint Gotthard pass and more particularly up the Val Mesolcina towards the San Bernardino pass.[37]

It is my contention that this model is in part flawed. It pays little attention to the geographical difficulties of the posited piedmontane route, and indeed the Alpine rivers have cut deep valleys in the upper plain. River travel would surely have been easier in all periods of antiquity than cross-country travel. The model also overlooks the great concentration of Golasecca IIIA, fifth-century, sites around *Laus Pompeia* - Lodi Vecchio,[38] to the south of Milan, first identified by Castelfranco in 1883,[39] and the recently discovered fifth-century, GIIIA, settlement at Milan.[40] These sites suggest that a fluvial route along the Po and then the Lambro might have in fact now been important (Fig. 1, E). Indeed the great size of fifth-century Milan, perhaps 700 x 260m, can best be explained by a role in such an exchange pattern towards Como and the north, a role that is supported by the presence of bucchero and Attic sherds:

via Santa Maria Segreta, two sixth-century kantharoi in bucchero;[41]

recent excavations at the Ambrosian Library, a sherd of a red-figure Attic kylix, attributed to Vienna painter 155 and therefore datable to after the first half of the fourth century;[42]

recent excavations in via Moneta, a sherd from a 'St Valentin' type kantharos, datable to the end of the sixth or the beginning of the fifth century.[43]

Although our major problem in testing Pauli's Great Saint Bernard pass route to the Rhône valley and western Switzerland is the lack of archaeological information for the Early Iron Age in Piedmont and the Vallée d'Aoste, evidence from western Lombardy and in particular from Pavia province may document an exchange route of long duration.

I have recently drawn attention to a sixth-century cross-country route in the western Po Plain which is later followed by the Roman *Ticinum-Galliae* Itinerary (Fig. 1, F; Fig. 2).[44] Indeed Etruscan sixth- to fifth-century imports have been found in two centres which were later *stationes* along this major Roman route towards France.[45] An olpe in bronze (Fig. 3), probably made at Vulci, datable to the mid-sixth to mid-fifth century BC from Dorno, later a *mutatio*,[46] and Etruscan buccheroid vessels[47] (Figs. 4-6) at Lomello, later a *mansio*,[48] suggest the beginning of a long-term, cross-country trade route that may have led towards the Vallée d'Aoste and the Great Saint Bernard pass. Moreover at Alessandria (AL) - loc. Villa del Foro, a *forum* on the Turin to Tortona *via Fulvia*, there is bucchero at a sixth- to fifth-century settlement site,[49] and evidence from Emilia suggests that the later Roman *via Aemilia* had already become an exchange route.[50]

Thus just as many of the fifth-century Golasecca IIIA centres of Lombardy - Brescia, Bergamo, Como, Milan, Lodi - became Celtic *oppida* and later Roman *municipia*, so the fundamental pattern of land routes may also have been set up at this time.

Other exchange from the south

As a final reflection, and contribution to the study of exchange northwards from peninsular Italy, I should like to draw attention to a series of seven Daunian and Enotrian pots in the Voghera (PV) town library archaeological collection, recently completely published by Elena Calandra.[51] They date from between the seventh and the fourth centuries, and Stenico[52] believed that they could best be explained by Roman antiquarianism, whereas Calandra prefers transapennine exchange from the Tyrrhenian[53] (though there is little evidence for such material along the northeastern coast of Italy) and as an alternative suggests that they could have been brought back to the Voghera area by Gallic mercenaries, documented in Daunia between 400 and 380 BC.[54]

I prefer to see them as documenting the continuing use of the Po corridor in the GIIIA period, in a minor exchange pattern westwards from the Adriatic.[55] They are indeed best understood in the light of the well-documented connections between the Adriatic Picene cultures and Golasecca,[56] and it may be remembered that a Messapic trozzella has recently been found at the mouth of the Po.[57] This explanation, first suggested by Frova,[58] is also clearly supported by the extensive evidence presented in this paper for traffic along the Po in the first millennium BC.

NOTES

1.   This paper was submitted in July 1993, and no further bibliographical information has been added since that date. Pearce 1991a, XVI-XVII.
2.   Chevallier 1988, 106-7.
3.   Gabba 1975, 97. In this paper I shall use the concept of 'permeability' to describe the degree of contact that can take place across a geographical barrier.
4.   Chevallier 1988, 106-7.
5.   Höpfel *et al.* (eds.) 1992.
6.   De Marinis 1988a, 105, tav. I.
7.   Pauli 1984, 22.
8.   Frey 1989; De Marinis 1988b, 197-200.
9.   e.g. Wells 1980; 1984.
10.   De Marinis 1986; 1988b, 167, 190, 219, tav. II.
11.   Pauli 1984, 197-9; 1987, 24.
12.   Donati 1989, 63, 67, 73.
13.   Ibid. 63.

14. Pearce 1991b.
15. Arslan 1984, 114-15; Pearce 1991a, XXIV.
16. Lo Porto 1956, 204, fig. 5; Donati 1968, 330-43; 1969, 458; Venturino Gambari 1987, 18.
17. Lo Porto 1956, 204-6, fig. 5; Venturino Gambari 1987, 18.
18. Finocchi 1976; Venturino Gambari 1987, 18.
19. Lo Porto 1954; 1957; De Marinis 1986, 60.
20. Milanese and Mannoni 1986, 145; Milanese 1987; 1989.
21. Venturino Gambari 1987, 17.
22. Tizzoni 1976.
23. Pearce 1991b.
24. Catarsi and Dall'Aglio 1987, 407-8, fig. 3.
25. Ibid., 407.
26. De Marinis 1988b, 195-7, 213.
27. Cf. Pearce 1987, 189-91.
28. Brunt 1971, 179.
29. Castignoli and Fiorina 1984, 26.
30. De Marinis 1986, 52-9, 68-9, 71.
31. Pearce 1991a, XXIII-XXIV.
32. Poggiani Keller 1986.
33. Ongaro 1987.
34. *Como* 1986.
35. De Marinis 1986, 71.
36. De Marinis (ed.) 1986, 140-299.
37. De Marinis 1986, 71; 1988b, 190, 213-14.
38. Cf. De Marinis 1990, 17.
39. Cf. De Marinis 1981.
40. De Marinis 1988b, 214-15; Jorio 1988; Ceresa Mori *et al.* 1988; Ceresa Mori 1991.
41. De Marinis 1981, 167; 1984, 31, fig. 19; 1986, 60, 84.
42. Pagani and White 1991, 175; Ceresa Mori 1991.
43. Ceresa Mori *et al.* 1988; De Marinis 1990, 22, 31, note 42; White 1991, 182.
44. Pearce 1991a, XXIV.
45. Tozzi 1984, 168-9.
46. Ponte 1964, 183, tav. VI, no. 4; Arslan 1984, 111; Gatti 1986; Pearce 1991a, 142, tav. LXXI, no. 315.
47. Pearce 1991a, 140-1, tav. LXX, nos. 312-14; perhaps datable to the fifth century - Arslan 1984, 111.
48. Blake and Maccabruni 1985; 1987; Maccabruni and Blake 1992.
49. Gambari and Venturino Gambari 1982a; 1982b; 1983, 110; 1985, 425, fig. 39, nos. 16-21; Venturino Gambari 1984.
50. Cremaschi *et al.* 1988, 17, 32, tav. 3.
51. Calandra 1992a; 1992b.
52. Stenico 1951.
53. Calandra 1992b, 17.
54. Calandra 1992a, 61; 1992b, 17.
55. Pearce 1991a, XXIII-XXIV.
56. Cf. De Marinis 1988b, 195.
57. Visser Travagli 1975-76.
58. Frova 1953.

BIBLIOGRAPHY

Abbreviations in addition to those in *Archäologischer Anzeiger*:

AMediev	*Archeologia medievale*
BAnnMusFerr	*Bollettino annuale. Musei ferraresi*
BPréhistAlp	*Bulletin d'Etudes Préhistoriques Alpines*
BSPSP	*Bollettino della Società pavese di Storia patria*
NotALomb	*Notiziario. Soprintendenza archeologica della Lombardia*
QuadAPiem	*Quaderni della Soprintendenza archeologica del Piemonte*
RAComo	*Rivista archeologica dell'antica provincia e diocesi di Como*
StDocA	*Studi e documenti di archeologia*

Arslan, E.A. 1984. Le culture nel territorio di Pavia durante l'età del ferro fino alla romanizzazione. In, E. Gabba (ed.), *Storia di Pavia*, vol. I, 107-46. Pavia

Blake, H. and Maccabruni, C. 1985. Lo scavo a Villa Maria di Lomello (Pavia), 1984. *AMediev* **12**, 189-212

Blake, H. and Maccabruni, C. 1987. Dallo scavo a Villa Maria di Lomello (Pavia), 1984: la buca tardo-antica 203. *AMediev* **14**, 157-87

Brunt, P.A. 1971. *Italian Manpower 225 BC - AD 14*. Oxford

Calandra, E. 1992a. Ceramiche indigene daunie ed enotrie in provincia di Pavia. In, M. Pearce (ed.), *Nuove ricerche archeologiche in provincia di Pavia, Atti del II° Convegno di Casteggio, 14 ottobre 1990*, 53-64. Casteggio

Calandra, E. 1992b. *Archeologia a Voghera. La raccolta archeologica della Civica Biblioteca Ricottiana*. Voghera

Castignoli, P. and Fiorina, U. 1984. Età Medievale. In, *Vie viaggi e viaggiatori nel pavese dai romani ai giorni nostri,* 25-8. Pavia

Catarsi, M. and Dall'Aglio, P.L. 1987. Il territorio piacentino dall'età del Bronzo alla romanizzazione. Ipotesi sulla formazione dell'ethnos ligure. In, D. Vitali (ed.), *Celti ed Etruschi nell'Italia centro-settentrionale dal V° sec. a.C. alla romanizzazione. Atti del Colloquio Internazionale, Bologna 12-14 aprile 1985*, 405-14. Bologna and Imola

Ceresa Mori, A. 1991. Milano, indagini nell'area del foro. I materiali. *NotALomb* 1990, 179

Ceresa Mori, A., Owes, B., Pagani, C. and White, N. 1988. Milano, Via Moneta. *NotALomb* 1987, 137-41

Chevallier, R. 1988. *Geografia, archeologia e storia della Gallia Cisalpina. 1: Il quadro geografico*. Turin

Como 1986. *Como fra Etruschi e Celti.* Como

Cremaschi, M., Marchetti, G. and Dall'Aglio, P.L. 1988. Il settore emiliano. *StDocA* **4**, 13-44

De Marinis, R. 1981. Il periodo Golasecca III A in Lombardia. *Studi Archeologici* **I**, 41-284. Bergamo

De Marinis, R. 1984. Protostoria degli insediamenti urbani in Lombardia. In, *Archeologia Urbana in Lombardia*, 22-33. Modena

De Marinis, R. 1986. I commerci dell'Etruria con i paesi a nord del Po dal IX al VI secolo a.C. In, R. De Marinis (ed.), *Gli Etruschi a nord del Po*, vol. I, 52-80. Mantua

De Marinis, R. (ed.) 1986. *Gli Etruschi a nord del Po*, vol. I. Mantua

De Marinis, R. 1988a. Le popolazioni alpine di stirpe retica. In, G. Pugliese Carratelli (ed.), *Italia omnium terrarum alumna*, 99-155. Milan

De Marinis, R. 1988b. Liguri e Celto-liguri. In, G. Pugliese Carratelli (ed.), *Italia omnium terrarum alumna*, 157-259. Milan

De Marinis, R. 1990. La preistoria e protostoria. Dal neolitico all'età del ferro. In, *Lodi. La Storia*, vol. I, 7-32. Lodi

Donati, L. 1968. Vasi di bucchero decorati con teste plastiche umane (zona di Orvieto). Notiziario, *StEtr* **36** (serie 2), 319-55

Donati, L. 1969. Vasi di bucchero decorati con teste plastiche umane (zona di Orvieto). Notiziario, *StEtr* **37** (serie 2), 441-62

Donati, P.A. 1989. Il problema dei passi alpini (tra Etruschi e Celti). *RAComo* **171**, 63-75

Finocchi, S. 1976. Monleale (Alessandria). Notiziario, *StEtr* **44**, 461

Frey, O.H. 1989. Como fra Etruschi e Celti: rapporti con il mondo transalpino. *RAComo* **171**, 5-26

Frova, A. 1953. Ceramica greca e preistoria lombarda. *RAComo* **135**, 5-21

Gabba, E. 1975. Il sistema degli insediamenti cittadini in rapporto al territorio nell'ambito delle zone subalpina ed alpina in età romana. In, *Le Alpi e l'Europa*, 2. *Uomini e territorio*, 87-108. Bari

Gambari, F.M. and Venturino Gambari, M. 1982a. Alessandria, fraz. Villa del Foro. Abitato e necropoli dell'età del Ferro. Notiziario, *QuadAPiem* **1**, 144-5

Gambari, F.M. and Venturino Gambari, M. 1982b. Villa del Foro (Com. di Alessandria). Notiziario, *StEtr* **50**, 533

Gambari, F.M and Venturino Gambari, M. 1983. Rapporti tra le culture preistoriche piemontesi e le aree transalpine: nuovi dati e proposte interpretative. *BPréhistAlp* **15**, 99-124

Gambari, F.M. and Venturino Gambari, M. 1985. Villa del Foro (Com. di Alessandria). Notiziario, *StEtr* **53**, 421-5

Gatti, E. 1986. Dorno (PV). In, R. De Marinis (ed.), *Gli Etruschi a nord del Po*, vol. I, 88-9. Mantua

Höpfel, P., Platzer, W. and Spindler, K. (eds.) 1992. *Der Mann im Eis*. Band I. *Bericht über das Internationale Symposium 1992 in Innsbruck*. Veröffentlichungen der Universität Innsbruck 187.

Jorio, S. 1988. Milano, Palazzo Reale. Scavo nell'angolo S-W del cortile principale. *NotALomb* 1987, 132-7

Lo Porto, F.G. 1954. Una stazione dell'età del ferro nel Tortonese. *RivStLig* **20**, 154-204

Lo Porto, F.G. 1956. Documenti di vita preromana in Piemonte. *RivStLig* **22**, 199-210

Lo Porto, F.G. 1957. Gremiasco (Tortona) - Il castelliere ligure del Guardamonte. *NSc* fasc. **7-12**, 212-27

Maccabruni, C. and Blake H. 1992. Scavi di Lomello 1990. In, M. Pearce (ed.), *Nuove ricerche archeologiche in provincia di Pavia, Atti del II° Convegno di Casteggio, 14 ottobre 1990*, 73-8. Casteggio

Milanese, M. and Mannoni, T. 1986. Gli Etruschi a Genova e il commercio mediterraneo. *StEtr* **52**, 117-46

Milanese, M. 1987. *Scavi nell'oppidum preromano di Genova (Genova - S. Silvestro)*. Studia Archeologica **48**. Rome

Milanese, M. 1989. Gli scavi nell'oppidum preromano e la presenza etrusca a Genova. In, E. Benedini (ed.), *Gli Etruschi a nord del Po, Atti del Convegno, Mantova 4-5 ottobre 1986*, 227-35. Mantua

Ongaro, G. 1987. Brescia preromana. In, R. De Marinis (ed.), *Gli Etruschi a nord del Po*, vol. II, 36-8. Mantua

Pagani, C. and White, N. 1991. Milano, indagini nell'area del foro. Periodi I-VI. *NotALomb* 1990, 175-9

Pauli, L. 1984. *The Alps. Archaeology and Early History*. London

Pauli, L. 1987. La società transalpina nel V secolo a.C. In, R. De Marinis (ed.), *Gli Etruschi a nord del Po*, vol.II, 18-30. Mantua

Pearce, M. 1987. Aspetti diacronici del territorio del comune di Lomello (PV): indagine di superficie 1985. *AMediev* **14**, 189-98

Pearce, M. 1991a. *Materiali preistorici.* Cataloghi dei Civici Musei di Pavia, 1. Milan

Pearce, M. 1991b. Indices of exchange: the western Apennine passes in the early first millennium BC. In, E. Herring, R. Whitehouse and J. Wilkins (eds.), *Papers of the Fourth Conference of Italian Archaeology, 2, The Archaeology of Power*, Part 2, 89-99. London

Poggiani Keller, R. 1986. Bergamo pre-protostorica. Le presenze preistoriche e l'insediamento protostorico di Bergamo. In, R. Poggiani Keller (ed.), *Bergamo dalle origini all'altomedioevo - Documenti per un'archeologia urbana*, 61-4. Modena

Ponte, G. 1964. Notizie sulle antichità lomelline conservate nel civico Museo pavese di storia patria. *BSPSP* **64**, n.s. 16, 173-90

Stenico, A. 1951. Ceramica Geometrica Apula rinvenuta nel territorio di Voghera. *Ultrapadum. Bollettino della Società di Storia, Arte e Scienze dell'Oltrepò* **5**, nos. 5-6, 34-41

Tizzoni, M. 1976. Il ripostiglio del Bronzo Finale di Zerba (Piacenza). In, *Atti della XIX Riunione Scientifica, Istituto Italiano di Preistoria e Protostoria*, 311-26. Florence

Tozzi, P. 1984. Il territorio di Ticinum romana. In, E. Gabba (ed.), *Storia di Pavia*, vol. I, 151-82. Pavia

Venturino Gambari, M. 1984. Alessandria, fraz. Villa del Foro. Abitato e necropoli della prima età del Ferro. *QuadAPiem* **3**, 249

Venturino Gambari, M. 1987. Alle origini di Libarna. Insediamenti protostorici e vie commerciali in Valle Scrivia. In, S. Finocchi (ed.), *Libarna*, 16-26. Alessandria

Visser Travagli, A.M. 1975-76. Una trozzella messapica di provenienza locale nel Museo Schifanoia di Ferrara. *BAnnMusFerr* **5-6**, 203-7

Wells, P.S. 1980. *Culture contact and culture change: Early Iron Age central Europe and the Mediterranean world.* Cambridge

Wells, P.S. 1984. *Farms, Villages, and Cities: Commerce and Urban Origins in Late Prehistoric Europe.* Ithaca and London

White, N. 1991. Milano, indagini nell'area del foro. Via Moneta. *NotALomb* 1990, 181-4

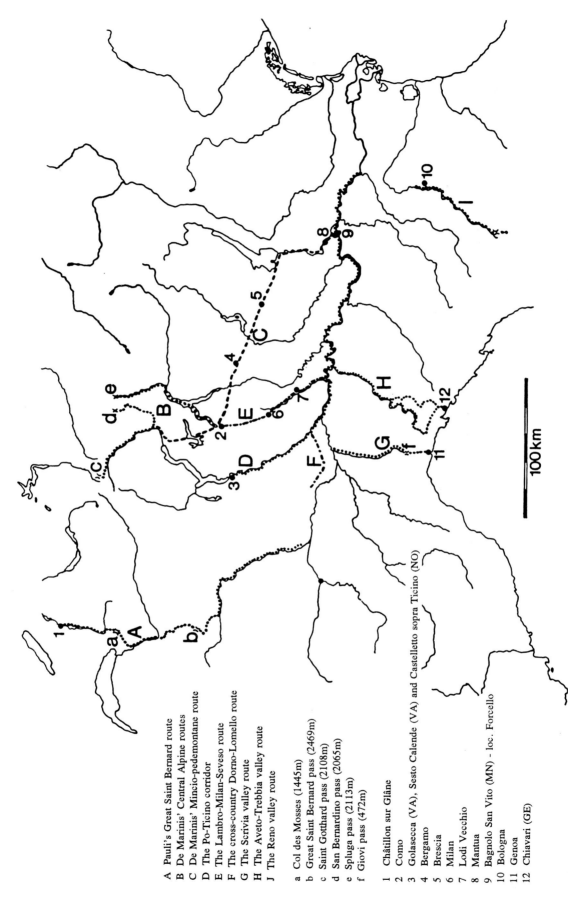

A Pauli's Great Saint Bernard route
B De Marinis' Central Alpine routes
C De Marinis' Mincio-pedemontane route
D The Po-Ticino corridor
E The Lambro-Milan-Seveso route
F The cross-country Dorno-Lomello route
G The Scrivia valley route
H The Aveto-Trebbia valley route
J The Reno valley route

a Col des Mosses (1445m)
b Great Saint Bernard pass (2469m)
c Saint Gotthard pass (2108m)
d San Bernardino pass (2065m)
e Spluga pass (2113m)
f Giovi pass (472m)

1 Châtillon sur Glâne
2 Como
3 Golasecca (VA), Sesto Calende (VA) and Castelletto sopra Ticino (NO)
4 Bergamo
5 Brescia
6 Milan
7 Lodi Vecchio
8 Mantua
9 Bagnolo San Vito (MN) - loc. Forcello
10 Bologna
11 Genoa
12 Chiavari (GE)

Fig. 1   Northwest Italian exchange routes

155

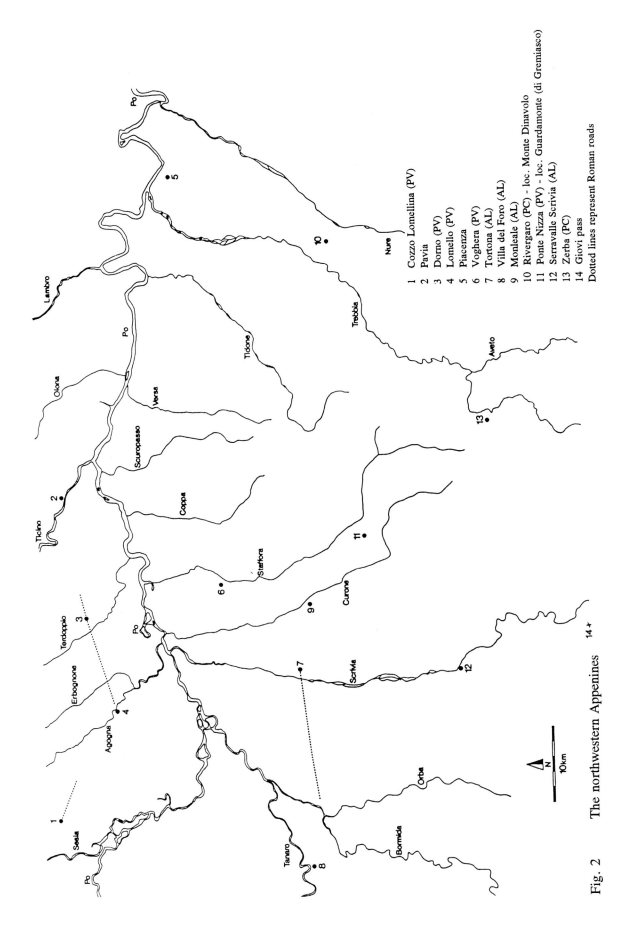

1 Cozzo Lomellina (PV)
2 Pavia
3 Dorno (PV)
4 Lomello (PV)
5 Piacenza
6 Voghera (PV)
7 Tortona (AL)
8 Villa del Foro (AL)
9 Monleale (AL)
10 Rivergaro (PC) - loc. Monte Dinavolo
11 Ponte Nizza (PV) - loc. Guardamonte (di Gremiasco)
12 Serravalle Scrivia (AL)
13 Zerba (PC)
14 Giovi pass

Dotted lines represent Roman roads

Fig. 2   The northwestern Appenines

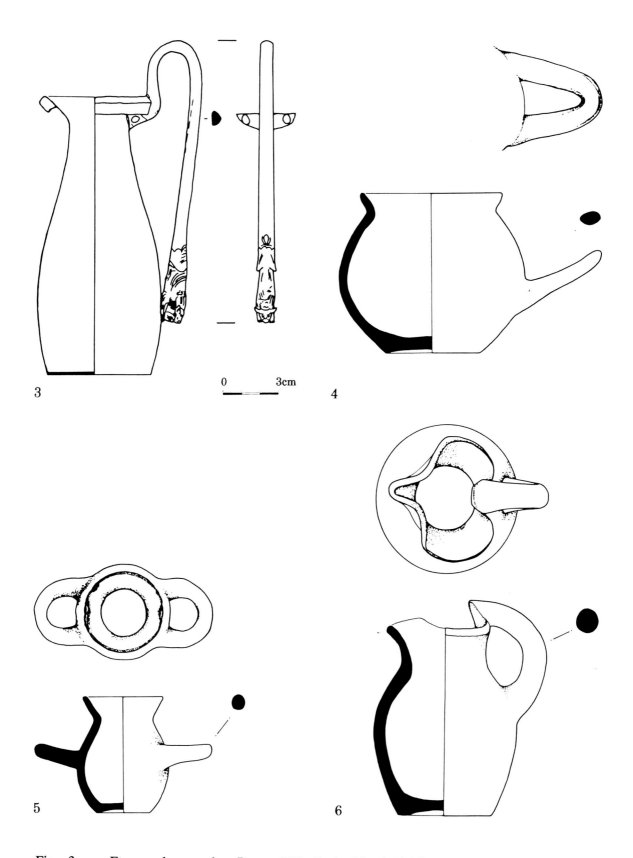

3

0   3cm

4

5

6

Fig. 3   Etruscan bronze olpe, Dorno (PV), Pavia, Musei Civici A171
Figs. 4-6   Etruscan buccheroid pottery, Lomello (PV), Pavia, Musei Civici 4: A158; 5: A111;
            6: A159. Drawings by D. Argese

ETRUSCAN CRAFTSMANSHIP IN ITALY

ETRURIA AND SITULA ART:
THE CERTOSA SITULA - NEW PERSPECTIVES

Gilda Bartoloni* and Cristiana Morigi Govi**

*Università di Roma, Instituto di Etruscologia e Antichità Italiche, Piazzale Aldo Moro 5, 00185 Roma. **Museo Civico Archeologico di Bologna, Via Musei 8, 40124 Bologna

'Fu allora che colla più alta ammirazione mi arrestai dinnanzi al grave e solenne monumento!'
(A. Zannoni, *Scavi della Certosa*, p.101)

The recent discoveries of Etruscan remains to the north of the Apennines have provoked much discussion about the role of Bologna in the expansion of Etruscan influence in northern Italy and have shed new light on one of the most representative pieces of the area, the Certosa situla, known as the 'queen' of situlae (Figs. 1a,b, 2).

Current restoration of this famous bronze work has brought about the re-evaluation of certain themes that have not always been treated in sufficient depth in the relevant literature.[1] In this paper the aim is to present some of the problems that have emerged during the comprehensive re-editing of the evidence concerning situlae, a process that can be completed only when the restoration is complete. It would seem, therefore, an opportune moment to make some observations on the following problems: form and technique, chronology, iconography.

FORM AND TECHNIQUE

The typological differences between the Certosa situla and other more or less contemporary bronze vessels have been noted since its discovery[2] and were discussed in the first works on the topic (Ghirardini; Grenier; Ducati, etc.)[3]. Giuliani Pomes, in a classification of situlae discovered in Etruria, assigns the vase from Bologna to the very heterogeneous A3 type; morphologically she sets it alongside the Etruscan vases from Populonia, Marsiliana and in particular Orvieto.[4] To these should be added the examples discovered in the Picene areas[5] and at Golasecca,[6] which are generally considered Etruscan. The same type (consistently undecorated) has also been documented at Este (the Este Ricovero type ovoid situla[7]) found in a context dating to the close of the seventh century BC (Este III B2: 625-575 BC). A particularly close comparison can be made with the Ricovero situla, recovered from tomb I in 1962.[8]

In fact, the rounded shoulders, surmounted by a small folded collar, distinguish the Certosa situla (Fig. 3) from all other figured situlae. From a technical point of view it can be maintained that the craftsman executed the embossing of the four decorative registers on a thin trapezoidal sheet of bronze, while it was still flat. He then formed the shoulder by hammering it, and folded the trimming over a core of copper-alloy. Next he overlapped the ends of the sheet and fixed them together with ten rivets. Finally, he decorated the shoulder with bands of lines and pendant hatched triangles and, again with embossing technique, obtained the two symmetrical volutes of the attachments. The mounting of the base was achieved by attaching a smooth band to the bottom of the situla, into which the concave base was inserted, with the edges then folded back on to themselves.

The situla originally had a movable handle, probably removed along with the attachments when the situla was to be used as an ossuary, and which was not deposited in the tomb. Evidence for such a ritual is offered by finds in the Golasecca area where, according to de Marinis, situlae used as urns for ashes are always found without handles.[9]

The handle-attachments, of which only the holes for insertion remain, one on each side, probably consisted of a simple ring linked to a plate fixed from the inside.[10] The structural simplicity of the attachments is compensated by the elaborate rendering of the embossed double volutes, which constitute a decorative finishing touch for an object of a high level of artistry.

The result is a vase of rounded profile (Fig. 3) and no neck, a form which draws this example within the series of situla-stamnoi of the sixth century BC.[11] Morphological comparisons therefore place this type of situla squarely in the sixth century BC, with precedents in the late seventh century BC.

CHRONOLOGY

The situla comes from cremation tomb no. 68 of the Certosa cemetery[12] where it served as an ossuary. The well-preserved skeletal remains have now been analysed[13] for the first time, and the results leave no doubt that the deceased was female.[14] The grave-goods, which included an Attic black-figured lekythos, a yellowish bowl and two Certosa-type bronze fibulae 'con arco a gomito', date the burial to the beginning of the fifth century BC. For a long time the grave context made it necessary to accept a date for the situla between the late sixth and the early fifth centuries BC.

Thus Lucke,[15] assuming the burial date to be almost contemporary with the production of the situla, proposed a distinct series of figured situlae, including examples from Magdalenska Gora and from Vače, which are attributed to a single craftsman of the first half of the sixth century BC., that from Providence (mid-sixth century) and that from the Certosa cemetery of Bologna, dated to the late sixth century on the basis of the grave-goods (above). Lucke justified the attribution of a more recent date to the Certosa situla, especially in comparison with that of the Providence situla, by assuming the continuity of a figurative tradition that would have enabled the 'Master' artist of the bronze situla from Bologna to have received and utilised Etruscan motifs that were by then no longer in evidence in Etruria. Frey[16] has recently hypothesised a long period of development for the figurative language of situla art which continued up until the second half of the sixth century BC.

However, Ducati had already recognised the date of manufacture of the situla to be about twenty years earlier than the date of the burial (480-475 BC). He saw it as 'one of the first local art products of Etruscan Felsina with strong influences from the preceding Umbrian culture', i.e., of Bologna's Villanovan culture. In fact, Ducati cites comparisons from the Bologna area, including the proto-Felsinian stelae, and from Etruria, including the amphora from the Cannicella necropolis of Orvieto, which date, at the latest, to the last decades of the seventh century BC.

In recent publications the date of the grave is no longer considered binding and the dating of the situla has been put back to the first half of the sixth century.[17] Moreover, recent discoveries reveal the presence of grave-goods, especially those in bronze and therefore of some prestige, which pre-date the burial, in some cases by up to five generations.[18]

In our opinion, the basis for an earlier dating of the situla, and consequently for identifying the area of production, depends on its relationship with the tintinnabulum from the Arsenale Militare of Bologna (Fig. 4a,b).[19]

The iconographic comparison to the tintinnabulum of objects from northern Etruria, especially from the inland regions of Chiusi and Volterra (as shown by G. Colonna), may also be applied to the

Certosa situla, though it was probably made at least a generation later. The Etruscan objects that are cited (small bronzes from Volterra-Montalcino, thrones from Chiusi, ivory pyxides and silver plates from Chiusi and terracottas from Murlo) are classified as products from the late Orientalising and Archaic period.[20] Already in 1972 Bianchi Bandinelli noticed a common feeling between the acroteria statues from Murlo and the tintinnabulum from the Arsenale, attributing it to that *primitiva* vein of imagination and improvisation, '*a quella inventività dell'artigianato estroso, che si compiaceva raffigurare la realtà con fantasia*'.[21]

With regard to the Poggio Civitate complex (dated, as is well known, to the second quarter of the sixth century BC),[22] a notable similarity can be found, not only in the men wearing broad-brimmed hats, but also between the figures on the friezes from Murlo and the figures in the procession on the second register of the situla (Fig. 2). Among the small bronze statuettes from northern Etruria a parallel is found, for example, with the figurines from Montalcino (in the territory of Chiusi), now at the Leiden Museum, dated to the second half of the seventh century BC.[23] All these comparisons indicate the Chiusi district as the centre of diffusion of figurative motifs. Presumably, many arrived in the Po Valley via objects, but more important still were the craftsmen employed by rich purchasers who were open to outside influences and who saw Etruria as the model to imitate.

Unfortunately, the late Orientalising and Archaic period in Bologna is so very poorly documented that for a long time it was common to talk of a cultural hiatus, but that interpretation depended essentially on the circumstances of the documentation. The necropoleis that concern this period (Arsenale and Arnoaldi) were badly excavated in the nineteenth century, and subsequently insufficient attention was paid to the sites, with no systematic exploration of the areas before urban expansion rendered them inaccessible. Only in the western zone were some portions of the cemeteries saved, in the areas of the Ippodromo Zappoli, Arnoaldi and Via Zucchi.[24] Recently, by chance, twin sandstone monuments were discovered in Via Fondazza in the eastern zone.[25]

The lack of documentation does not permit the reconstruction of a chronological scheme and thus does not allow the precise insertion into the local sequence of a few, but very significant, tombs; these include the Arsenale tomb with its tintinnabulum, the Melenzani tomb with its small inscribed amphora and the Arnoaldi tomb with its decorated axe.[26] The case of the Aureli tomb no. 11 is significant among the others. It is still dated to the seventh century,[27] but is probably more recent, given the presence of fibulae *a sanguisuga* with lengthened catches which are documented, for example, in tomb no. 1 in the Giardini Margherita[28] and which date to the middle of the sixth century BC. A further point of similarity is offered by the burial of the deceased in a large dolium, a ritual widely documented in the Arnoaldi necropolis. The stela from Via Augusto Righi[29] is also significant: its iconography of cavalrymen places it fully in the sixth century and strongly suggests the continued use of proto-Felsinian stelae in this century.[30] The only usable contexts come from the Giardini Margherita necropolis (Gualandi's excavations of 1962) and date to the middle of the sixth century or shortly afterwards before the explosion of the Certosa phase. They demonstrate a community that was open to outside influences: in tomb no. 6 was found the well-known *bacile* with small lions, for which a south Etruscan origin (perhaps Orvieto) was hypothesised; from tomb no. 1 came the oinochoai with trefoil mouth and decorative attachments, and ivory objects which are undoubtedly of Etruscan origin.[31] Imported Greek pottery is also present (e.g. fragments of Little Master kylikes in tombs no. 2 and no. 8), and is presumed to have arrived via southern Italy and Etruria, though it could also have come by way of Adria.[32]

Contacts with Este were highlighted by Carancini in his research on Bologna's Villanovan 'Period IV',[33] especially through an analysis of the fibulae a *drago con dischetti* and fibulae *con arco rivestito*, all of the same period. There seems to be no reason therefore for supposing that Bologna's role as a focal point of distribution of goods (and craftsmen), well documented in preceding[34] and subsequent periods, should have been interrupted at this point.

ICONOGRAPHY

Narrative style seems to have been a feature peculiar to the craftsmanship, especially of prestigious goods, made for the communities in Emilia and Romagna, and is evident from the second half of the seventh century BC (for example, the Bologna tintinnabulum, Verucchio thrones, etc.). In Etruria proper there was a predilection for heroic or ceremonial themes (Fig. 5) that exalted the *gentes*, the owners of the various objects; on the other side of the Apennines, however, scenes from real life were preferred, naturally scenes from the life of the *aristoi*. Thus in the decorations of the Palazzo di Murlo, the patrons are likened to divinities, while on the Certosa situla the different powers of the lord (in war, in peace and in the sacred sphere) are expressed in scenes from real life (first register: parade of warriors; second register: sacred procession; third register: life in the palace and in the fields). Thus, we have in the Certosa situla (in the Providence situla, and also that from Bologna) an image of what life must have been like in the princely residences such as those of Murlo and Acquarossa.

The feminine counterpart of the narrative on the Certosa situla would appear to be the tintinnabulum from the Arsenale Militare: just as war represents the highest expression of male activity, so spinning and weaving represent that of the female. 'Working with wool is the symbol of woman in the same way that working with weapons is the symbol of man', both of these activities being the gifts of Minerva.[35]

Even though the celebratory intent of the situla decoration is clear, the interpretation of the individual scenes is much more difficult: it is unclear whether a single narrative or one divided by registers was intended.[36] For what kind of occasion was such a work of art designed? Was it to celebrate the funeral ceremony or another important event?

There are reasons for choosing to interpret the scene as a single narrative in which the military parade, the preparation for the sacrifice and banquet and the musical *agon* were all portrayed: i.e. triumph, sacrifice, *agon*.[37] The focal point of the narrative is the scene of the two musicians playing the lyre and the syrinx while seated on a rich *kline*: they are most likely depicted indoors (in the house of the lord), as the situla hanging above the heads of the musicians suggests.[38] Not only does this zone prove to be in a central position within the decorative scheme; its importance is further highlighted by the richly decorative ornamentation of the volute placed exactly above it.

In our opinion the intended distinction between outdoor and indoor activities is further demonstrated by the hunting and ploughing scenes. Hunting is an activity emblematic of the aristocracy, while the ploughing of the fields is surely a reference to the importance of landed property and of the cultivation of the vast expanses of land owned by the prince, on which a large part of the population was employed.[39] These two episodes are shown at opposite ends of the third register and do not seem to be included in the sequence of the long procession; rather they are two autonomous scenes which take place on another plane of perspective. In fact, the ploughman and the hunter are the only figures that do not follow the flow of the other figures.

The participants in the long procession snake towards the house of the lord (Fig. 6, reconstruction in front); portrayed to the left of the musical performance is the scene of the libation, probably with the figure of the *dominus* himself, followed by the victim to be sacrificed and eaten at the banquet.[40] Then embossed in the second register follow members of the lord's family, *clientes* (or followers) and servants with all the necessary ingredients for the banquet.[41] At the end comes the parade of the military contingent, composed of five formations, one of cavalrymen[42] and four of infantrymen.[43] With regard to the portrayal of parades in Tyrrhenian Etruria, it has been supposed that scenes of military processions or *pompae* are to be recognized as private triumphs, referring to the practice of maintaining private armies and the military exploits of the noble clans.[44] These distinct and heterogeneous troops would evidently be contingents of a private army: therefore it would seem that, before the establishment of the organised state, certain military activities were still the prerogative of family groups.[45]

It seems an obvious step to make comparisons with the exploits of the different rulers shown in the Assyrian palace reliefs; there are some interesting similarities that may be observed in the carriers of baskets and bundles of wood.[46]

It would seem that the occasion for which this splendid situla was created was a particular event, very probably the feast for the return of a military expedition. However, as has been recently pointed out with reference to the scenes depicted on the roofs of aristocratic palaces in Etruria,[47] the narrative can also be interpreted in a funerary sense.[48] The guiding theme of this iconography is a celebration of the prince's deeds. However, the scenes could also be interpreted as the portrayal of the funeral of a *dominus* whose ashes were enclosed in the similar situla depicted hanging above the *kline* and apparently framed by the two boxers.[49] In our opinion this does not change the unitary character of the story.

Factors which undermine the funerary interpretation, however, are the circumstances in which the situla was discovered, the much later grave and the female gender of the deceased. It seems likely from the iconography that the vase had a male association, even if situlae were used predominantly as containers of the ashes of dead women.[50] The comparison with the Providence situla,[51] the purpose of which is explained in its inscription[52] defines this artefact as an exceptionally prestigious gift and, as such, worthy of being treasured and passed on from one eminent person to another for generations.[53]

NOTES

1. Essential bibliography on the situla: Zannoni 1876-84, Ghirardini 1900; Grenier 1912; Ducati 1923; *Arte delle Situle* 1961; Lucke and Frey 1968; Mansuelli 1965; Frey 1969; Frey 1986; De Fogolari 1992, 200-5; Kruta 1992, 264-70.
2. Zannoni 1876-84.
3. Ghirardini 1893, 64; Grenier 1912, 371; Ducati 1923.
4. Giuliani Pomes 1954, 184.
5. Sgubini Moretti 1987.
6. De Marinis 1987, 58.
7. Peroni *et al.*, 1975, 239.
8. Chieco Bianchi and Calzavara Capuis 1985, 217, 2.
9. De Marinis 1974, 77.
10. This may only be confirmed by checking the inside of the situla, which is at present sealed with a layer of plaster.
11. De Marinis 1987, 57.
12. Sassatelli 1984, 255-6.
13. We should like to thank Maria Antonietta Fugazzola Delpino, Superintendent of the L. Pigorini Museum of Prehistory and Ethnography, for her willing co-operation and kind permission in allowing us use of the facilities. The analyses were performed by Loredana Salvadei, to whom we give special thanks.
14. The osteological analysis, the results of which will be published in the complete edition, provided the following data:
    i   sex as determined from the morphology of the femur: female;
    ii   age determined on the base of the macroscopic morphology of the cortical section of the femur: 30-40 years;

iii age from the microscopic section of the cortical bone tissue from the femur: 33 years.

15. Lucke and Frey 1968, 44.

16. Frey 1992, 100-1.

17. Cristofani 1984, 79; Bartoloni 1985, 101; Cristofani 1986, 92; Sassatelli 1989, 63; Kruta 1992, 264; Malnati 1993, fig. 25.

18. Baglione 1986, 141.

19. A review of the problem of the development of situla art following the publication of the tintinnabulum may be found in Colonna 1980.

20. Colonna 1980, 186-7. Further documentation of the analogy with the northern Etruscan area: from the Orientalising period also come the princely grave-goods of the Castelnuovo Berardenga tomb, very recently published by E. Mangani. Especially noteworthy is the bronze jewel-box with embossed animals (Mangani 1991).

21. Bianchi Bandinelli 1972, 246-7; 'to that inventiveness of the inspired craftsman who rejoiced in portraying reality with imagination'.

22. Philips 1993, with bibliography.

23. Richardson 1983, 45-7: Early Etruscan Types: The Ladies, Series B. Group 1.

24. Contu 1953, 213-31 (Ippodromo Zappoli); Mansuelli 1954, 357-82; Macellari 1988, 57-65 (Arnoaldi); Gentili 1970, 122-41 (Via Zucchi).

25. Ortalli and Bermond Montanari 1988.

26. Morigi Govi 1971 (Arsenale); Morigi Govi and Colonna 1981 (Melenzani); Pincelli 1975 (Arnoaldi).

27. Martelli 1987, 274-5.

28. Macellari 1987, 50 (colour photograph).

29. Guida Bologna 1988, 262.

30. In opposition to Kruta Poppi 1977, 81; Cerchiai 1988, 228.

31. Gualandi 1969, 61-5; Macellari 1987, 47-54, figs. 27-30.

32. Gualandi 1969, 65; Colonna 1974, 20, no. 80; Martelli 1985, 98.

33. Carancini 1969, 295-6.

34. Bartoloni 1986.

35. Maurin 1983, 139. A revealing comparison is offered by the identical positions of the distaff and the spear, placed alongside the deceased in many cemeteries, so that some of the elements from one or the other, e.g. bronze points, have often been erroneously transposed (Bartoloni 1988).

36. Jackson Fund 1975, 96. The same problem also arises in connection with the interpretation of the Providence situla.

37. Comparison with the situla from Plikásná (Martelli 1973) and, through this object, with the series of cauldrons and Cypriot gold-plated silver paterae decorated with analogous scenes (Bernardini, Regolini Galassi: Canciani-von Hase 1979).

38. Naturally, one should not exclude the possibility of it being an outdoor scene with the musicians either covered by a kind of *velarium* or in a true tent, as documented in several different painted tombs found in Etruria proper: Kruta 1992, 270: '*le lit centrale évoque la tranquillité du foyer retrouvé*'.

39. Torelli 1993, 61.

40. It is well known that meat was considered a food to be eaten only occasionally by the greater part of the population, and that in literary sources (especially those regarding Ancient Greece) the rituals of eating meat and of offering a sacrifice were confused and were entirely identified with the elementary forms of society. In the same way in which the spoils of war were divided, so too was meat divided among warriors. In some complex civilisations of the Near

East or in ancient Indo-Iranian society it seems that meat was consumed at sacrificial meals, though the (prohibited) consumption of meat by warriors on other occasions was not unheard of (Bartoloni 1988).

41.   An example is offered by the last figure on the right who is carrying a large spit and not a sword as it is usually described.

42.   It is interesting to note how in Etruscan figurative art cavalrymen are often depicted in pairs (see for example the ossuary (?) covers from Pitigliano: Martelli 1973).

43.   On the different types of panoplies, see the latest work by Pascucci, 1990. We cannot accept the proposal to recognise the last group of infantry as a formation of craftsmen, identified as 'true and authentic blacksmiths, according to the model documented at Rome under Servius Tullius' (Malnati 1993, 151). Besides the fact that their weapons are the same as those of the cavalrymen, the axe or hatchet seems to have been peculiar to the armament of Bologna from the Villanovan period (Morigi Govi and Tovoli 1994).

44.   Jannot 1985.

45.   As in the centres of southern Etruria, so it seems that also in the Etruscan settlement of the Po Valley the process of urban formation was concluded by the last years of the sixth century BC.

46.   Nimrud. For example Mallowan 1966, 446-7, no. 371, panel a.

47.   Torelli 1993, 249-74.

48.   An example referring to the voyage in the Afterworld is the scene portrayed in the fourth zone of the Pania situla from Chiusi.

49.   Thuillier does not consider them to be ornamental objects, but small boxers (Thuillier 1985, 226-7).

50.   Capuis 1993, 159.

51.   Probably it came originally from one of the Bologna necropoleis.

52.   Olzscha in Lucke and Frey 1968, 85-6; Tibiletti Bruno 1978, 241; Colonna 1980, 182-3. It is probable that the inscription was written by a foreigner, the author of the situla working in Bologna, who did not know the Etruscan language well. We should like to thank Carlo De Simone for his encouragement in proposing this hypothesis.

53.   *DArch* 2, I (1980), 144: *Il.* XXIV, 228; *Od.* IV, 587.

BIBLIOGRAPHY

Arte delle situle dal Po al Danubio 1961. Padua

Baglione, M.P. 1986. Il Tevere e i Falisci. *Archeologia laziale* **VII, 2**, 124-42

Bartoloni, G. 1985. Dalla Stanza delle Antichità al Museo Civico. Bologna. *Bollettino d'Arte* **30**, 107-11

Bartoloni, G. 1986. Relazioni interregionali nell' VIII secolo a.C.: Bologna - Etruria mineraria - Valle Tiberina. *Studi e documenti di archeologia* II, 45-56

Bartoloni, G. 1988. A Few Comments on the Social Position of Women in the Protohistoric Coastal Area of Western Italy Made on the Basis of a Study of Funerary Goods. International

Symposium of Physical-Anthropology and Prehistoric Archaeology 1987. *Supplemento della Rivista di Antroplogia* **LXVI**, 317-35

Bartoloni, G. 1989. *La civiltà villanoviana*. Rome

Bianchi Bandinelli, R. 1972. Qualche osservazione sulle statue acroteriali di Poggio Civitate (Murlo). *DArch* **VI, 2-3**, 236-47

Canciani F. and von Hase F-W. 1979. *La Tomba Bernardini di Palestrina*. CNR Rome

Capuis, L. 1993. *I Veneti. Società e cultura di un popolo dell'Italia preromana*. Milan

Carancini, G. 1969. Osservazioni sulla cronologia del Villanoviano IV a Bologna. *Bullettino di Paletnologia Italiana* **78**, 277-97

Cerchiai, L. 1988. Le stele villanoviane. AION *ArchStANt* **X**, 227-38

Chieco Bianchi, A.M. and Calzavara Capuis, L. 1985. Este I. Le necropoli Casa Muletti Prosdocimi, Casa Alfonsi. *MonAnt* **51**

Colonna, G. 1974. I Greci di Adria. *Rivista storica dell'antichità* **IV**, 1-21

Colonna, G. 1980. Rapporti artistici tra il mondo paleoveneto e il mondo mediterraneo. *Este e la civiltà paleoveneta a cento anni dalle prime scoperte. Atti XI Convegno di StEtr Este - Padova 1976*, 179-90

Contu, E. 1953. Il sepolcreto villanoviano dell'Ippodromo Zappoli. *StEtr* **XXII**, 213-31

Cristofani, M. 1984. Agricoltura e allevamento. In, M. Cristofani (ed.), *Gli Etruschi. Una nuova immagine*, 74-83. Florence

Cristofani, M. 1986. Economia e società. In *Rasenna. Storia e civiltà degli Etruschi*, 79-156. Milan

De Marinis, R. 1974. La situla di Trezzo. *Varia Archaeologica. Posavsky Muzej Brezice* **I**, 67-86

De Marinis, R. 1987. I commerci dell'Etruria con i paesi a nord del Po dal IX al VI sec. a.C. In, R. De Marinis (ed.), *Gli Etruschi a nord del Po*, 52-80. Mantua

Ducati, P. 1923. La situla della Certosa. *Mem. Acc. Scienze di Bologna*, s.II, tomi **V-VII** (1920-1923), 3-74. Bologna

Fogolari, G. 1992. L'arte delle situle. Prima esperienza figurativa europea. In, *Gli Etruschi e l'Europa*, 200-5. Paris and Milan

Frey, O.H. 1969. Die Entstehung der Situlenkunst. *RGF* **31**

Frey, O.H. 1986. Les fêtes dans l'art des situles. *Ktema* **11**, 199-209

Frey, O.H. 1992. Beziehungen der Situlenkunst zum Kunstschaffen Etruriens. In, L. Aigner Foresti (ed.), *Etrusker Nordlich von Etrurien. Akten des Symposions von Wien ott. 1989*, 93-101. Vienna

Gentili, G.V. 1970. Bologna (Via Zucchi): scoperta di tombe villanoviane. *NSc* **95**, 122-41

Ghirardini, G. 1900. La situla italica studiata specialmente ad Este. *MonAnt* **X,** 134-231

Giuliani Pomes, M.V. 1957. Cronologia delle situle rinvenute in Etruria. *StEtr* **XXIV** (1954), 149-94

Grenier, A. 1912. *Bologne villanovienne et étrusque*. Paris

Gualandi, G. 1969. Problemi urbanistici e cronologici alla luce degli scavi dei Giardini Margherita e della Facoltà di Ingegneria. *Atti e Memorie della Deputazione di Storia patria per le province di Romagna*, 47-67

Jackson Fund, M.B. 1975. Situla. Classical Bronzes. *Museum of Art Rhode Island School of Design*. 90-100. Providence Rhode Island

Jannot, J.P. 1985. Les cités étrusques et la guerre. *Ktema* **10**, 127-41

Kruta, V. 1992. *L' Europe des origines*. Paris

Kruta Poppi, L. 1977. Una nuova stele protofelsinea da Casalecchio di Reno. Contributo ai problemi dell' Orientalizzante bolognese. *StEtr* **XLV**, 63-83

Lucke, W. and Frey, O.H. 1968. Die Situla in Providence (Rhode Island). Ein Beitrag zur Situlenkunst des Osthalstattkreises. *Römanisch-germanische Forschungen* **26**

Macellari, R. 1987. Giardini Margherita. In, G. Bermond Montanari (ed.), *La formazione della città in Emilia Romagna*, 47-54. Bologna

Macellari, R. 1988. Il sepolcreto Arnoaldi. In, *Atti e Memorie della Deputazione di Storia patria per le province di Romagna*, n.s. **XXXV** (1986), 56-65

Mallowan, M.E. 1966. *Nimrud and its Remains*. London

Malnati, L. 1993. Le istituzioni politiche e religiose a Spina e nell'Etruria Padana. Spina. In, F. Berti, P. Guzzo (eds.), *Storia di una città fra Greci ed Etruschi*, 146-77. Ferrara

Mangani, E. 1991. Castelnuovo Berardenga. L'orientalizzante recente in Etruria settentrionale: tomba A della necropoli principesca del Poggione 1980. *NSc* **XLII-XLIII**, 5-84

Mansuelli, G.A. 1957. Una stele felsinea di tradizione villanoviana. *RIA* **V-VI**, 5-28

Mansuelli, G A 1965. The East, the Adriatic, Etruria, and Situla Art. In, J. Kastelic, K. Kromer, and G.A. Mansuelli (eds.), *Situla Art* 27-33. Belgrade

Mansuelli, G.A. 1967. L'arte delle situle fra Mediterraneo ed Europa. *Primo Simposio di Preistoria e Protostoria, Orvieto 21-24 settrembre 1967*, 115-17

Martelli, M. 1973. Documenti di arte orientalizzante di Chiusi. *StEtr* **XLI,** 97-120

Martelli, M. 1985. Bologna: la tomba Aureli. In, M. Cristofani, M. Martelli (eds.), *Bibliografia topografica della colonizzazione greca in Italia e nelle isole tirreniche* IV, 90

Martelli, M. 1987. Bologna: la tomba Aureli. In, *L'oro degli Etruschi*, 274-5. Milan

Morigi Govi, C. 1971. Il tintinnabulo della 'Tomba degli ori' dell'Arsenale Militare di Bologna. *ArchCl* **23**, 211-35

Morigi Govi, C. and Colonna, G. 1981. L'anforetta con iscrizione etrusca da Bologna. *StEtr* **49**, 67-93

Morigi Govi, C. and Tovoli, S. 1994. Due piccoli scudi di bronzo e il problema dell'armamento nella società villanoviana bolognese. *Arch Cl* **XLV,1** (1993), 1-54

Olzscha, K. 1968. Die Inschrift auf der Situla Providence. In, Lucke and Frey 1968, 85-6.

Ortalli, J. and Bermond Montanari, G. 1988. Il complesso monumentale protofelsineo di Via Fondazza a Bologna. *StEtr* **54**, 15-45

Pascucci, P. 1990. I depositi votivi paleoveneti. Per un'archeologia del culto. *Archeologia veneta* **XIII**

Peroni, R. *et al.* 1975. *Studi sulla cronologia delle civiltà di Este e Golasecca.* Florence

Philips, K.M. 1993. *In the Hills of Tuscany.* Philadelphia

Pincelli, R. 1975. Un nuovo documento dell'orientalizzante settentrionale. *Emilia Preromana* **7**, 131-47

Richardson, E. 1983. *Etruscan Votive Bronzes. Geometric, Orientalizing, Archaic.* Mainz

Sassatelli, G. 1984. Sepolcreto della Certosa. Tomba 68. In, C. Morigi Govi, G. Sassatelli (eds.), *Dalla Stanza delle Antichità al Museo Civico*, 255-6. Bologna

Sassatelli, G. 1989. Ancora sui rapporti tra Etruria Padana e Italia Settentrionale. Qualche esemplificazione. In *Gli Etruschi a Nord del Po. Atti del Convegno, Mantova 1986*, 49-81.

Sgubini Moretti, A.M. 1992. Pitino. Necropoli di Monte Penna: tomba 11. In, *La civiltà picena nelle Marche. Studi in onore di G Annibaldi 1988,* 178-203. Ripatransone

Thuillier, J.P. 1985. *Les jeux athletiques dans la civilisation étrusque.* Rome

Tibiletti Bruno, M.G. 1978. Camuno, retico e pararetico. In, A. Prosdocimi (ed.), *Popoli dell'Italia antica,* VI, 208-56

Torelli, M. 1993. I fregi figurati delle *regiae* latine ed etrusche. Immaginario del potere arcaico. *Ostraka* 2 (1993), 259-74

Zannoni, A. 1876-1884. *Gli scavi della Certosa di Bologna.* Bologna

1a

1b

Fig. 1a,b   Certosa situla, Bologna.   Bologna Museo Civico Archeologico

171

172

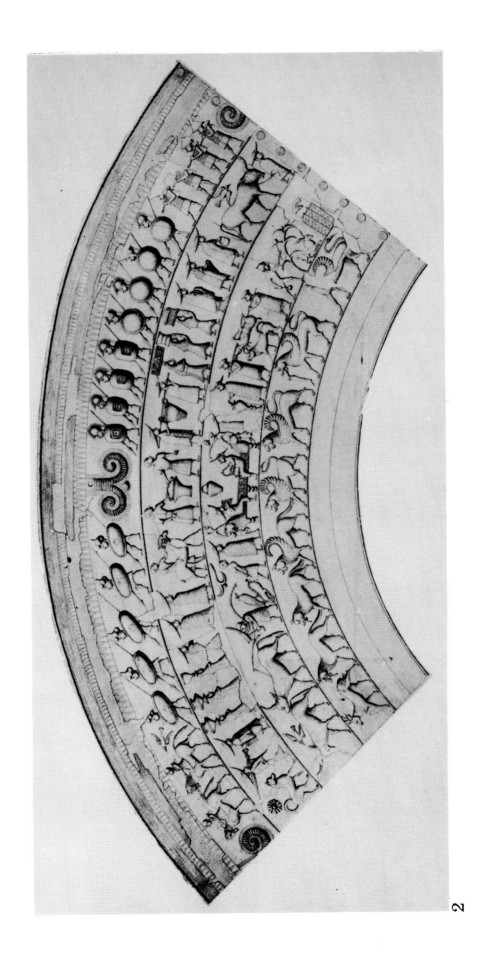

2

Fig. 2   Certosa situla: decoration

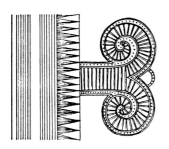

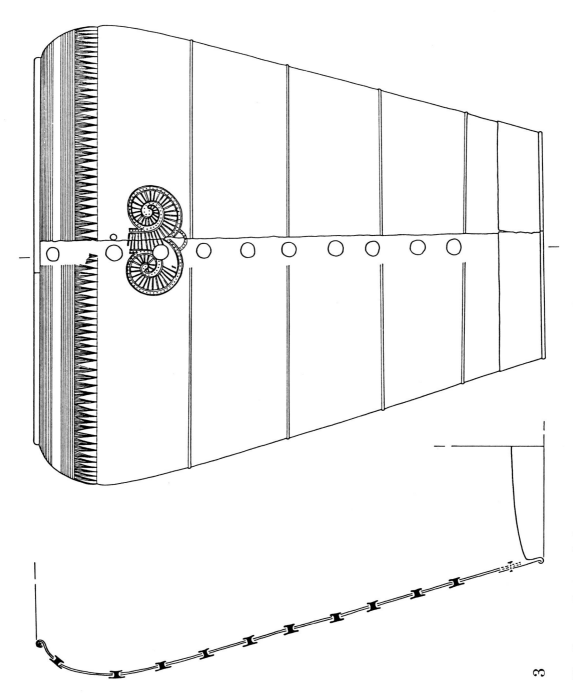

3 Fig. 3 Certosa situla

173

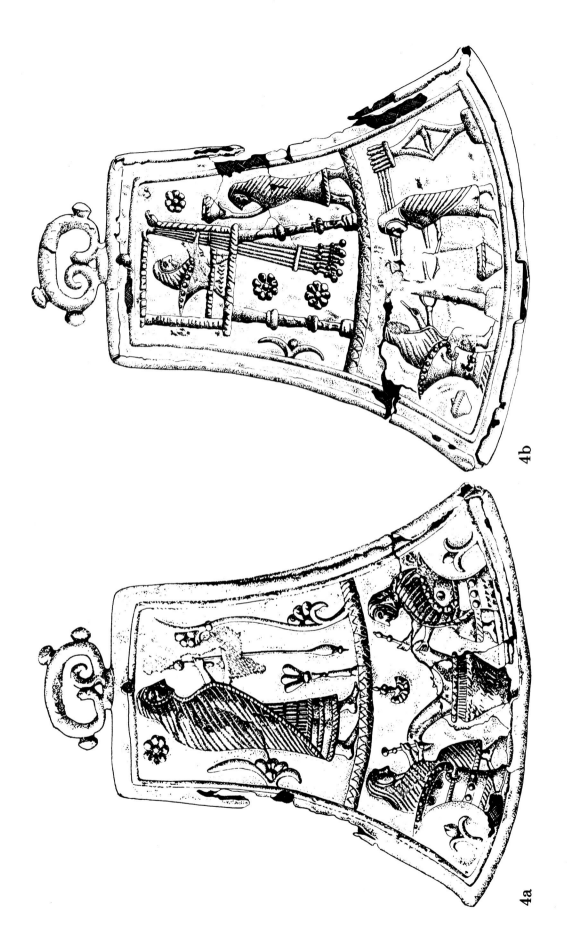

4b

4a

Fig. 4a,b   Tintinnabulum from Arsenale Militare, Bologna.   Bologna Museo Civico Archeologico

174

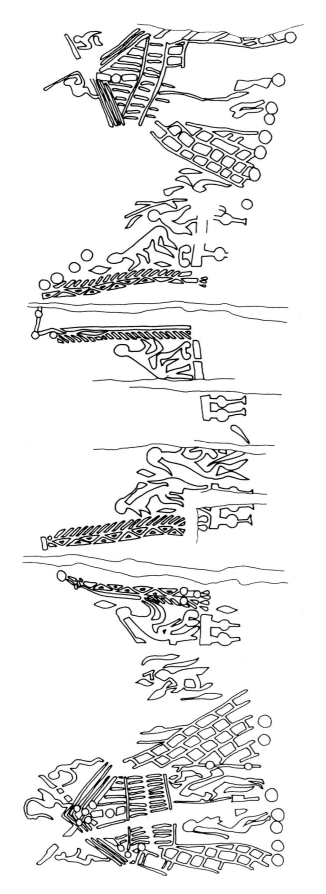
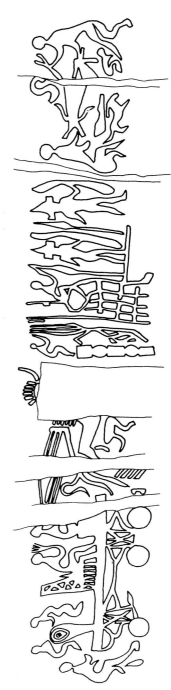

Fig. 5   Throne from Verucchio: detail of decoration.   Bologna Museo Civico Archeologico

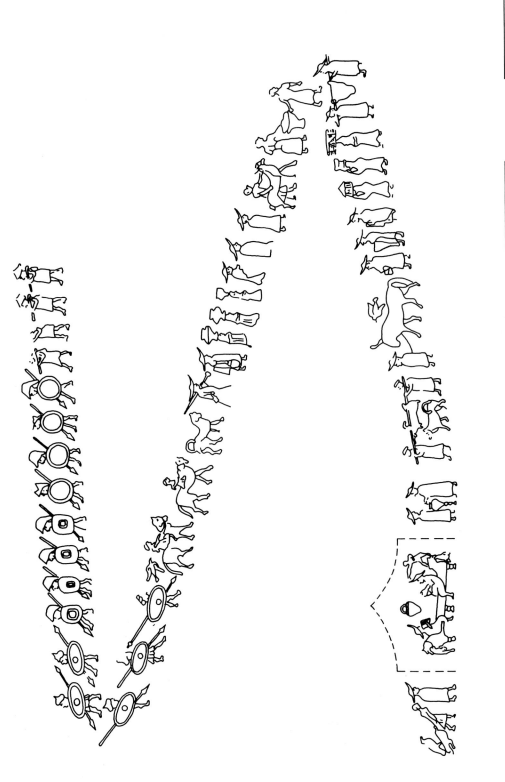

Fig. 6   Certosa situla: reconstruction of the procession

THE BRONZE HEAD-VASE FROM GABII IN THE LOUVRE: ITS HISTORY AND ECHOES

Sybille Haynes
Flat 17, Murray Court, 80 Banbury Road, Oxford OX2 6LQ

To Denys Haynes[†] for his eightieth birthday on 15 February 1993

The fine bronze jug in the Louvre in the form of the head of a youth (Fig. 1a-c) is said to have been excavated at Gabii by Prince Aldobrandini. It was first published by de Ridder and although it has since been discussed by various scholars[1] its origin and subsequent history have not previously been investigated.

In my first publication of the life-sized bronze head in the British Museum of a young man from Lake Bolsena (Fig. 2), I associated this important sculpture, which was in all probability made in Orvieto-Volsinii, with the Gabii head-vase on stylistic grounds and compared it with the related bronze head-vase in Munich and with the 'Mars' from Todi in the Vatican.[2] The 'Mars' has since convincingly been claimed by Roncalli[3] as the product of a master working with the artists who created the large-scale terracotta figures from the Temple of the Belvedere at Orvieto; and Orvieto is now recognised as one of the most significant cities in Central Etruria for the reception and interpretation of models of Athenian sculpture of the Classical period.[4]

To the evidence of a close stylistic relationship - in terms of facial features and treatment of the hair - between the head-vase in the Louvre and the most notable bronze sculptures of Orvietan origin can now be added further arguments for the claim that the vase was made in the same town, arguments based on its decoration and shape. The trefoil mouth of the head-vase has an overhanging rim ornamented with ovolos along the edge and a row of beading above. The two re-entrant angles of the rim flanking the spout are each adorned with a small modelled shell (Fig. 1c). The shell is a comparatively rare decorative motif on bronze vessels but occurs on the handle-attachments of a number of bronze situlae, two of them found in the Tomba del Guerriero at Settecamini near Orvieto (Fig. 3a,b), one in the necropolis of S. Raffaele at Todi,[5] the others at Spina and Valle Pega near Comacchio. In a recent publication of the bronze situla from Offida in the British Museum[6] I have attempted to show that this group of vessels with shell ornament was made in an Orvietan workshop. The shape of the Louvre head-vase, particularly its slim neck with a band at the bottom, its flaring trefoil mouth rimmed with ovolos and beading and its high curved band-handle decorated with three parallel beaded ridges and ending below in an oval attachment-plate with a pendent plastic palmette of nine leaves, is extremely closely related to a bronze jug (Fig. 4a-c) excavated from the same Tomba del Guerriero at Settecamini.[7] Adembri has drawn attention to the fact that this oenochoe belongs to a small group of such jugs found predominantly in inner Central Etruria. Two of them come from a chamber-tomb of fourth-/third-century date at Bolsena, one from Chiusi, one from Talamone , while a further example in Florence is without provenance.[8] This pattern of distribution of provenances supports the assumption that all six oenochoai were made in a Central Etruscan workshop. As we have seen, three of them were excavated in close proximity to Orvieto (two at Bolsena and one at Settecamini), which suggests that this workshop was located at Orvieto itself.

Adembri dated the bronze situlae and the jug from the Tomba del Guerriero to the third quarter of the fourth century, whereas the related situlae with shell-ornament from Tomb 136 A in Valle Pega near Comacchio and the pair from Tomb 58 C of Spina have been dated from the late fifth to the second quarter of the fourth century on the strength of the associated material[9] . It is quite possible that the manufacture of such vessels extended over a considerable period. But the remarkable similarity in style between the bronze head from Bolsena in the British Museum, dated by both myself and Cristofani to 375-350 BC,[10] and the head-vase from Gabii in the Louvre, leads to the conclusion that both bronzes were made during the second quarter of the fourth century at Orvieto. Such a date and origin for the head-vase would accord well with that of the related bronze jug and situlae from the Tomba del Guerriero at Settecamini near Orvieto discussed above. All the fine vessels from this tomb were destined for use during banquets.

The head-vase from Gabii, too, was a banqueting vessel. Cristofani has identified the youthful head of the jug in the Louvre with its bulla-shaped pendant above the forehead as that of a free-born cup-bearer, a subject also found in Etruscan tomb-painting and sculpture of the fourth century; further, he compares with it similar youthful heads embossed in profile on Etruscan gold bullae, which he dates to the beginning of the fourth century. While bullae are frequently shown suspended from a necklace or a bracelet, they are rarely represented as pendants on a hairband or diadem. It is therefore interesting to find bullae so worn by no less than three figures on an incised Praenestine cista in Berlin (Misc.3238), namely the two young boys riding the outer horses of the quadriga and the man behind the table laden with paterae. According to R.Adam, all three are members of the same family, who have not yet assumed the *toga virilis*. Adam suggests that the subject of the complex representation on the cista is a Praenestine *gens* of Etruscan extraction with marriage links with the Volsinii, and he dates the cista to 340-330 BC.[11] Cristofani's own comparisons support the date of 375-350 BC suggested by me above, rather than that of 425-400 BC proposed by himself for the head-vase in the Louvre. Although he assumes it to be an Etruscan bronze, derived from Attic prototypes in pottery of the fifth century, Cristofani does not speculate on the head-vase's place of manufacture. Regarding its provenance from Gabii, he conjectures that it may have come from a votive deposit in the sanctuary of Juno there, which received offerings from the Archaic period onwards.

Gabii was an important city of ancient Latium, situated about 18 km east of Rome on the Via Praenestina in a strategic position controlling not only old routes of transhumance between the Central Italian Apennine and the coastal lowlands of the Tyrrhenian, but also the north-south transit route from Umbria and Etruria to Campania that followed the natural connections offered by the river-valleys of the Paglia, Tiber, Sacco and Liri.[12] According to tradition, the city was founded by Siculi (Solin. II, 10) and became a colony of Alba Longa (Virgil, *Aeneid* VI. 773). In early times Gabii outshone Rome and was regarded as a centre of diffusion of Greek civilisation in Latium. As boys, Romulus and Remus are said to have been sent there to be educated in writing, music and the use of Greek arms (Dion.Hal.I, 84,5).[13] In the sixth century, during the reign in Rome of the Etruscan dynasty of the Tarquins, Gabii fell by a ruse into the hands of Sextus Tarquinius, the son of Superbus, who was made its ruler by his father (Livy, I, 53f., 60; Dion.Hal.IV, 54ff.; Ovid, *Fasti* II, 690). These traditional stories illustrate the close political and cultural involvement of Gabii both with Rome and with Etruscan civilisation. The city's decline began in the fifth century BC with the ascendancy of hostile Rome and as a result of the eventual shifting away of the profitable trade-routes onto newly constructed Roman roads, such as the Via Appia. By the second century Gabii was almost deserted and the area of the city served mainly as a quarry for the *saxum gabinum*, a prized building stone of volcanic extraction used in Rome (Strabo, V, 238; Tac. *Annals* XV, 43). Only the main road of Gabii, the Via Praenestina, with inns and some buildings probably connected with the renowned Temple of Juno, seems to have continued in use (Dion.Hal. IV, 53). Evidence of a recovery of the city in imperial times came to light when in 1792 the Scottish painter Gavin Hamilton excavated in the area E of the great temple and found a large open space, surrounded by porticoes and public buildings with inscribed statues of magistrates of the city, as well as imperial portraits and other sculptures.[14] The whole territory was then owned by the Borghese family (the depression south of Gabii is still known as Pantano Borghese) and the antiquities discovered by Gavin Hamilton passed into the possession of

Prince Marcantonio Borghese, who installed them in his newly created Museo Gabino of the Villa Borghese.[15]

The ruins of a great temple, reconstructed in the second century BC and thought to be that of Juno Gabina, survive at Gabii on the southeast side of the former crater lake (Lago di Castiglione) which was drained at the end of the nineteenth century.[16] In 1976/7 foundations of another sanctuary were discovered outside the ancient city, towards Tivoli, with votive offerings dating from the seventh to the second century BC.[17] At the same time three chamber-tombs were excavated east of Fosso S.Giuliano, one unplundered and containing material from the end of the fourth century BC.[18] An important recent find made at Gabii is that of a late Archaic bronze statuette of a draped man holding an augur's staff.[19]

Brief and lacunary as this outline of Gabii's history is, it does make clear how an Etruscan bronze could have come to be found in this Latin city. We have noted its close cultural connections with Etruria which were favoured by natural lines of communication. The bronze head-vase could easily have travelled from Orvieto, its presumed place of manufacture, by a route following the valleys of the Paglia, the Tiber and the Aniene. It may have been an offering, buried in a votive deposit of one of Gabii's temples or, being a banqueting-vessel, it may have been a prized personal possession that accompanied its owner into his tomb. As we have seen, chamber-tombs containing grave-goods of fourth-century BC date have been excavated at Fosso S. Giuliano.

Unfortunately, we know nothing about the circumstances and date of the discovery of the head-vase. We have, however, two clues which enable us to narrow the period during which it might have been found. Firstly, the records of the Louvre state that the vase came to light in excavations carried out by Prince Aldobrandini at Gabii,[20] and secondly, we possess in the Royal Collection at Windsor Castle a drawing (Inv. No. 11174), contained in one of the Cassiano Dal Pozzo albums entitled *Disegni Varie Antichi-Nettuno* (Vol. A 31) which was acquired as part of the Dal Pozzo collection for George III in 1762.[21] I firmly believe this drawing to represent the head-vase (Fig. 5).

Even though it is somewhat wooden and artless, nevertheless the drawing faithfully reproduces all the details of the head-vase: the moulded base, the eyes with the strongly marked iris and pupil, the wavy hair ending in snail-curls on the temples and nape, the plaited cord circling the head with its bulla-shaped pendant, the high, ribbed handle, the trefoil mouth; even the small plastic shells decorating the re-entrant angles of the spout are hinted at. Unfortunately, the caption written beneath the drawing gives us no information on the head-vase's provenance; it merely states in curious Italian 'vaso che servia neli sagrifiti antichi'. However, what the drawing does provide indirectly is the information that the bronze must have been discovered in the seventeenth century when Dal Pozzo had the antiquities then available in Rome drawn for his *Museo Cartaceo*.

We must now turn our attention to the Aldobrandini family (and I am most grateful to Donna Livia Aldobrandini Pediconi for guiding me through the complexities of their history).[22]

The first Prince Aldobrandini, Gianfrancesco, was born in 1545 and died in 1601. He had come from Florence to Rome and made his fortune under Pope Clement VIII, whose niece Olimpia he married. From this marriage sprang twelve children, all of whom died young, unmarried or without leaving male heirs. Gianfrancesco's second son, Giangiorgio (1591-1637), was the second Prince Aldobrandini. His only daughter, a second Olimpia (1623-1681), inherited all the accumulated wealth of the family through her uncle, Cardinal Ippolito Aldobrandini (1592-1638). Olimpia married first Prince Paolo Borghese (1624-1646) in 1638 and bore him five children. After his premature death she married Prince Camillo Pamphili (1622-1666) with whom she had another five children. When Olimpia died in 1681, most of the Aldobrandini fortune went to her eldest son by the second marriage, Gian Battista Pamphili; but at the extinction of the Pamphili family in 1760, the Aldobrandini inheritance reverted to the Borghese descendants of Olimpia's first marriage. Though the Aldobrandini family had died out, the title had lived on and the family was revived by a new legitimate male line in 1839, when Camillo Borghese (1816-1902), second son of Prince Francesco Borghese, assumed the name of Aldobrandini in accordance with his father's testamentary wish. It seems thus that the most likely Aldobrandini Prince to have excavated the head-vase from Gabii, drawn for Cassiano Dal Pozzo during the first half of the seventeenth century, was either the first Prince, Gianfrancesco, or the second, Giangiorgio, but we cannot be sure which. As we have seen, the Aldobrandini properties, which will have included Gabii, passed to the Borghese, whose name is still attached to the area neighbouring the ancient city - the Pantano Borghese. We must assume that the head-vase formed part of the Aldobrandini inheritance which the Borghese had acquired and that it remained in the family, probably to be incorporated into the ancient sculpture collection of the Casino Borghese known as the *Museo Gabino*, which was created by Marcantonio Borghese IV (1730-1800). The catalogue of the *Museo Gabino*, compiled by the archaeologist Ennio Quirino Visconti in 1797,[23] describes only the marbles recently discovered at Gabii; the bronze head-vase is therefore not to be found in it.

It remains to trace the subsequent fate of the head-vase. We know from the records of the Louvre that at the beginning of the nineteenth century the vase became part of the collection that the Empress Josephine had assembled at her residence Malmaison near Paris. The inventory of Josephine's possessions was drawn up between 8 June 1814 and 25 March 1815 at the request of the heirs, her children by Beauharnais, Eugène and Hortense. The head-vase is listed on p.177 as no.1333: 'Item autre vase en bronze à anses, en forme d'aiguiere représentant une tête de femme portant une fibule au dessus du front; antiquité provenant d'Herculaneum'. It is interesting to note that the head is here described as that of a woman and that the vase is said to have come from Herculaneum. A number of the antiquities assembled by Josephine between 1799 and 1814 at Malmaison had been a gift to her and Napoleon from Ferdinand IV of the Two Sicilies and Maria Carolina of Austria and consisted of objects from Herculaneum; the cataloguer must have mistakenly thought that the head-vase formed part of that gift. We do not know exactly how the information, recorded by de Ridder (1915: no.2955), that the head-vase was found at Gabii in excavations by Prince Aldobrandini, was handed on. It is probable that Eugène, who had inherited Malmaison and most of its contents, was aware that the vase had come from the Borghese collection and thus ultimately from the Aldobrandini.[24] In a sale in Paris on 23 March 1819 Eugene Beauharnais anonymously sold some of his antiquities, which must have included the head-vase, whose pedigree will have been communicated to the buyer, Edmé Durand, from whose collection it was acquired by the Louvre in 1825.[25]

The head-vase's passage from the Borghese collections to Malmaison finds its explanation in Napoleon's habit of marrying off members of his family for political ends and his passion for amassing works of art from countries conquered by him. Pauline Bonaparte, Napoleon's favourite sister, was first given in marriage in 1797 to one of his generals, Victor Emanuel Leclerc, who died of yellow fever in San Domingo in 1802. Early in 1803 the young widow returned to France and, after much manoeuvring, was married to Prince Camillo Borghese (1775-1832) later that year. His father, Marcantonio Borghese, the creator of the Museo Gabino, had died in 1800. Camillo was a francophile who came to Paris in 1803, attracted by Napoleon's fame and the brilliant life at the court. At first, Camillo was a somewhat reluctant suitor of Pauline's, but the marriage took place later in 1803; it was to turn out to the satisfaction of neither. The couple moved to Rome, where Pauline felt restless, homesick and disappointed in her new husband, while he suffered from his wife's reckless extravagance and her unwillingness to share his Roman life. Before her marriage Pauline had bought the Palais de Charost in the rue du Faubourg St Honoré (now the British Embassy) which she enlarged and furnished at vast expense. She longed to return to this home and to the more amusing atmosphere of Paris and soon succeeded in doing so, with Camillo an increasingly unwelcome and barely tolerated visitor there. Napoleon disapproved of Pauline's behaviour and, in 1805, entrusted Camillo with military and, later on, administrative tasks. By 1806, the cuckolded husband had returned to Rome, while Pauline took a succession of lovers.[26] It seems that by now Camillo was in serious financial difficulties, partly caused by the cost of keeping his spendthrift wife and partly by the forced monetary contributions which his father had had to make between 1796-99. Camillo considered selling the Borghese antiquities, possibly to an English buyer.[27] The archaeologist Ennio Quirino Visconti, author of the catalogue of the Borghese collections, had come to Paris in 1799 and was appointed director of the Louvre by Napoleon at the end of that year. He may originally have suggested the purchase to Napoleon, or it may have been Camillo himself, who was anxious to put his financial affairs on a sounder basis.[28] On 14 May 1807 the Emperor wrote: '*Je désire que M. Daru très secrètement et en demandant le plus grand secret à M. Denon et à M. Visconti, fasse une évaluation de tous les chefs d'oeuvres de la Maison Borghese; combien puis-je en donner en supposant que le Prince veuille les vendre?*' Denon, the influential director of the Musée Napoléon, estimated that the value of the Borghese collection was five million francs, but added that double that figure would not be too much. Visconti drew up a list of the objects which comprised 523 items: 159 statues and groups, 160 busts and herms, 170 bas-reliefs, vases, altars, sarcophagi, sphinxes etc., 30 columns and 4 tables of precious marble. Although the final evaluation submitted by Denon and Visconti came to almost eight million francs, the sum had risen to thirteen million by the time the decree of purchase was signed on 27 September 1807. Camillo Borghese must have been extremely satisfied with the generous settlement by his brother-in-law; and it is perhaps not surprising that he did not succeed in reclaiming the antiquities after Napoleon's final defeat in 1815.

We must assume that the bronze head-vase was included among the Borghese vases that appear in unspecified numbers in Visconti's list. The unusual form of the jug and its delicate finish may have particularly appealed to Napoleon, who probably decided to retain it for the decoration of Malmaison, where he and Josephine had assembled a large number of antiquities and other works of art.[29] When, in 1810, the Emperor had his first marriage nullified in order to wed the Austrian Princess Marie Louise, Malmaison remained Josephine's home and it is from here that, after her death in 1814, the head-vase was sold to the Durand collection and, in 1825, to the Louvre.[30]

Even if I have not succeeded in documenting every single step in the long and complex journey of the head-vase from Gabii to the Louvre, enough new facts have emerged to make the course of events as just sketched plausible and, I hope, convincing. But we have not reached the end of the story, for the head-vase exercised its fascination on others before it came into the possession of Napoleon and Josephine.

Sometime while it was in the Borghese collection, the head-vase must have been moulded in plaster, because the British Museum possesses a copy of it in bronze (GR 1824.4-89.87; ht. 29cm. Fig. 6a-c) which must have been cast in a five-piece-mould taken from the original or from a plaster cast. Faint traces of the mould-webs are visible on the neck and head of the bronze copy, which reproduces the original faithfully; only some small details that could not be moulded easily were omitted, such as the little shells in the angles of the trefoil mouth, the ovolo and beading on its rim, the beading on the three ribs of the strap-handle and the hatching on the plaited cord circling the youth's hair.

The bronze copy came to the Department of Greek and Roman Antiquities in 1824 as part of the bequest of the collection of Richard Payne Knight (1751-1824) who, in 1780, had become a member of the Society of Dilettanti and in 1814 a Trustee of the British Museum.[31] A wealthy, self-taught classical scholar, traveller, avid collector and opinionated connoisseur of art and antiquities, Knight had first gone on a tour of France and Italy in 1772-3 and again visited Italy and Sicily in 1776-7. During these journeys he must have acquired the bronze copy of the head-vase, most probably in Rome, under the mistaken impression that it was an ancient piece.[32] In the register of the Department of Greek and Roman Antiquities for 1824 it appears listed among the genuinely ancient objects from the Payne Knight collection left to the British Museum.

It is likely that either this bronze copy of the head-vase from Gabii once in the possession of Knight, or a plaster cast of it, served as model for a 'bronzed' version of it made in Josiah

Wedgwood's 'Etruria' factory from his famous Black Basalt Ware and originally gilded (Fig. 7). Now preserved in the Department of Medieval and Later Antiquities in the British Museum,[33] this copy shows the same omission of minor details already noted above in the bronze copy from the Payne Knight collection. In addition, the modeller of the Wedgwood head-vase has left out the plastic pendent palmette under the handle-attachment, the incised wavy lines on the individual strands of hair and the hatching of the cord of the bulla; but he has prettified the bulla by turning it into a piece of jewellery with a frame of small globes and by adding a tied bow to the hairband above it. This turned the head into an altogether more feminine-looking piece, which may have been thought by Wedgwood's to have greater appeal for eighteenth- and nineteenth-century buyers.[34]

We do not know precisely when the head-vase was first modelled for Wedgwood. The unglazed black stoneware which he later named Basaltes was invented by him in about 1768 and he used it for the six so-called First Day Vases, potted by himself on the inauguration of 'Etruria', his new factory for ornamental vases in Staffordshire, on 13 June 1769. A mould for the head-vase, which appears to be of eighteenth-century date, is still preserved in the Wedgwood Museum at Barlaston, Stoke-on-Trent.[35] Only one further specimen of the Wedgwood 'bronzed' head-vase is known at present; it is in the Metropolitan Museum in New York.[36] The fact that both the surviving examples are of 'bronzed' (that is to say, gilded) Black Basalt Ware, makes it clear that the manufacturers knew the original model to have been of bronze. It is reasonable to assume that this was the supposedly ancient bronze copy of the Gabii head-vase in Payne Knight's collection which was accessible in England, rather than the ancient bronze original in the Borghese collection. We have no knowledge of any personal meeting between Knight and Josiah Wedgwood, but they could have been in contact through a number of people,[37] one of the most likely being Sir William Hamilton, through whose good offices Wedgwood had in 1786 been enabled to copy the Portland Vase.[38] Hamilton and Knight had met in Naples during Sir William's period as envoy there and later on in England they were fellow members of the Society of Dilettanti. Hamilton must have known the bronzes in Knight's collection and may well have been instrumental in making the bronze head-vase available to his friend Wedgwood as a model for his 'bronzed' Black Basalt version of it.[39]

There is, however, another possibility, though a less likely one: from letters of Wedgwood to Sir William Hamilton and to the Rt. Hon. William Eden[40] we know that between 1787 and 1789 Wedgwood employed several modellers in Rome and one of them may have had the chance of copying the original head-vase in the Borghese collection or a plaster cast of it.

Thus the shape of an unusual and beautiful Etruscan banqueting vessel, originally made at Orvieto-Volsinii in the fourth century BC, can be seen to have captivated and inspired in the course of more than 2000 years a succession of owners, among them princes, artists, collectors and even an emperor.

NOTES

1.   de Ridder, 1915: no. 2955, ht. 32cm. Subsequent discussions: Sieveking 1919, 49 ff.; Messerschmidt 1928, 163, pl. 20; Pallottino and Jucker 1955, pl. 99; Haynes 1965, 524, pl. 125a; Cristofani 1975, 71, n. 2; Hus 1975, 110, pl. 46; Dohrn 1982, 49 ff., 64, pls. 38, 40.2, and Haynes 1985, 300, no. 149, and Cristofani 1985, 291, no. 115.

2.   Head from Lake Bolsena: *BMCatBronzes* 1692 (GR 1824.4-70.6): Haynes 1965, 524 ff. Munich vase: Antikensammenlungen inv. 2573. Todi 'Mars': Museo Gregoriano Etrusco, inv. 693.

3.   Roncalli 1973, 103 f.

4. Orvieto: Roncalli 1973, 106 f.; Dohrn 1982, 64; Haynes 1985, 94 f. and nos. 149, 150; Cristofani 1985, 292, no. 116.

5. Shell motif at Settecamini: Adembri 1982, 80 f., nos. 5,6. I am most grateful to Dottoressa A. Romualdi for providing me with photographs of the banqueting vessels from this tomb, kept in the Museo Archeologico of Florence: situla, inv. 70521; situla, inv. 70522; oinochoe, inv. 70523. pls. 5-9. Todi: Giuliani-Pomes 1957, 48, fig. 28.

6. *BMCat Bronzes* 650 (GR 1853.11-12.1): Haynes 1991, 134 f.

7. Adembri 1982, 82 f., no. 7.

8. Oenochoai from Bolsena: Vatican, Museo Gregoriano Etrusco, inv. nos. 12715 and 12802; from Chiusi: Chiusi Museo Archeologico, inv. no. 2074; from Talamone: Florence, Museo Archeologico, inv. no. 70581; provenance unknown: Florence Museo Archeologico, inv. no. 1488.

9. Arias 1955, 152, figs. 91, 94, 160; Massei 1978, 261 f., pl. LXII, 2; Hostetter 1989, 90.

10. Haynes 1985, no. 150; Cristofani 1985, 224 f., no. 118.

11. Cristofani 1985, 291, no. 115; Adam 1989, 629 f.

12. For Gabii see *RE* **VII**,I, 420-422; Pinza 1903; Quilici Gigli 1970; Quilici 1974, 32; 1990 Zaccagni 1978; Guaitoli 1977; 1981a; 1981b; Almagro-Gorbea 1982; Cristofani 1990, 159 ff., 7.3

13. It is interesting to note in this context that in the exemplary excavation of the Iron Age cemetery of Osteria dell'Osa near Gabii (Bietti Sestieri 1992, 686f., figs. 3a. 269, 270), there appears a one-handled impasto flask from Tomb 482, a female cremation burial, with incised Greek letters on it. This is the earliest (*c.* 775 BC) Greek inscription so far known in the West. It has been read as Eulin = εὔλινος, a good spinner (Ridgway forthcoming).

14. Smith 1901.

15. Visconti 1797.

16. Zaccagni 1978, 42.

17. Guaitoli and Zaccagni 1977; Guaitoli 1981a, 161 ff.

18. Guaitoli and Zaccagni 1977, 435 f.; Guaitoli 1981a, 171 f.

19. Cristofani 1985, 287 ff., 10.33; 1990, colour pl. XI.

20. I am most grateful to Françoise Gaultier of the Département des Antiquités Grecques, Etrusques et Romaines for information and photographs, Fig. 1a-c.

21. In recent years there has been renewed interest in Cassiano Dal Pozzo's *Paper Museum* and the bibliography has increased accordingly. The publication project, managed by the Royal Library at Windsor Castle, has produced a series of *Quaderni Puteani*, published by Olivetti, which have appeared in advance of the eventual catalogue of all the drawings traceable to the *Paper Museum*. The bibliography published with each *Quaderno* represents the latest updated list of studies on the subject. The most recent *Quaderno* is *Quaderno* **4**, 1993. On the later history of the *Paper Museum* and its transmission to this country through its purchase for George III see Fleming 1958.

Mrs Henrietta Ryan, Deputy Curator of the Print Room, and Miss Gwyneth Campling of the Photographic Services of the Royal Collection, have been most helpful in providing the photograph from which Fig. 10 is reproduced by gracious permission of Her Majesty the Queen.

Dr Ian Jenkins of the Department of Greek and Roman Antiquities, British Museum has generously provided me with information on the Dal Pozzo drawings after the antique.

22. See the biographies of the Aldobrandini in *Diz.Biog.It*; D'Onofrio 1963, with earlier literature, especially the works by R. Lefevre.

23. See note 15.

24. I am most grateful to Dr André Morel for drawing my attention to Grandjean 1964. For the vase's findspot: de Ridder 1915, no. 2955.

25. Françoise Gaultier has recently kindly informed me that in Durand's handwritten catalogue of 1824, compiled before the sale of his first collection and now in the Louvre, the notice that the vase's provenance was Gabii is first recorded. Eugène died in 1824 and his widow sold further antiquities on 19 July 1829 at Malmaison, some of which were also bought by E. Durand.

26. For the life of Pauline see Dixon 1964.

27. Haskell and Penny 1981, 113.

28. The following account is based on Boyer 1970, 197-202.

29. See the inventory mentioned in note 24.

30. See note 25.

31. For a biography of R.P. Knight see Clarke and Penny 1982.

32. For pieces in his collection which he mistakenly believed to be ancient see Clarke and Penny 1982, 68, n. 21.26

33. MLA 1909.12-1.106; ht. 28.8cm. The vase was presented to the British Museum in 1909 by Mr and Mrs Isaac Falke. I am most grateful to Ms Aileen Dawson of the Department of Medieval and Later Antiquities, British Museum, for her generous help with information on the Wedgwood head-vase and for the photograph (Fig. 7). The vase has been published by Grant 1910, pl. VIII,1; Tait 1963, 36, pl. 5; Dawson 1984, 42, fig. 29; Reilly 1990, 473, fig. 681.

34. See the description in *Leeds*, cat. no. 2487: 'Wedgwood black basalt Rhyton in the form of a female head, trefoil lip' and in *Wedgwood*, 76, no. 378: 'Vase, basalt, formed of a female head and in the shape of a classic Rhyton etc.'. For a similar mistake about the sex of the bronze head-vase from Gabii, made by the cataloguer of the contents of Malmaison, see above.

35. Letter of 23 October 1991 from Mrs Lynn Miller, Information Officer of the Wedgwood Museum, Barlaston, Stoke-on-Trent, England ST12 9ES, to Ms A. Dawson. The mould has been renumbered 106-1 and is located in cupboard 5a.

36. Department of European Sculpture and Decorative Arts, inv. 32,95.14. Exhibited: *Metropolitan*, no. 66; illustrated: Buten 1980, 121, fig. 102; *Etrusques*, no. 450; *Etrusker*, no. 450.

37. I am most grateful to Nicholas Penny for this information.

38. Haynes 1975, 11; Painter and Whitehouse 1990, 47-54.

39. The copies in bronze and black basalt of the head-vase from Gabii have been published by the author in *Etrusques*, 313, nos. 450, 451 and *Etrusker,* 313, 394 f. nos.450, 451; most recently, Haynes 1994.

40. Fisher and Savage 1965, 307 and 317.

BIBLIOGRAPHY

Abbreviations in addition to those in *Archäologischer Anzeiger*:

Diz.Biog.It   *Dizionario Biografico degli Italiani*. Vol. 2, 1960. Rome
QuadIstTopAnt   *Quaderni dell'Istituto di topografia antica dell'Università di Roma*

Adembri, B. 1982. *Pittura Etrusca a Orvieto*. Orvieto

Almagro-Gorbea, M. 1982. *El santuario de Juno en Gabii: excavaciones 1956-1969*. Rome

Arias, P.E. 1955. *RIA* **4**, 152-160

Bietti Sestieri A.M. (ed.) 1992. *La necropoli laziale di Osteria dell'Osa*. Rome

BMCatBronzes 1899. H.B. Walters, *Catalogue of Bronzes, Greek, Roman and Etruscan in the Department of Antiquities, British Museum*. London

Boyer, F. 1970. *Le monde des arts en Italie et la France de la Révolution et de l'Empire*. Turin

Buten, D. 1980. *18th Century Wedgwood*. New York

Clarke M. and N. Penny (eds.) 1982. *The Arrogant Connoisseur: Richard Payne Knight, 1751-1824*, Exhibition Catalogue, Whitworth Art Gallery. Manchester

Cristofani, M. 1975. *Statue cinerario chiusine di età classica*. Rome

Cristofani, M. (ed.) 1985. *Civiltà degli Etruschi*. Milan

Cristofani, M. (ed.) 1990. *La Grande Roma dei Tarquinii*, Exhibition Catalogue. Rome

Dawson, A. 1984. *Masterpieces of Wedgwood in the British Museum*. London

Dixon, P. 1964. *Pauline, Napoleon's favourite Sister*. London

Dohrn, T. 1982. *Die etruskische Kunst im Zeitalter der griechischen Klassik. Die Interimsperiode*. Mainz

D'Onofrio, C. 1963. *La Villa Aldobrandini di Frascati*. Rome

Etrusker 1993. *Die Etrusker und Europa*. Exhib. Cat., Berlin

Etrusques 1992. *Les Etrusques et l'Europe*. Exhib. Cat., Paris

Fisher A. and G. Savage (eds.) 1965. *The Selected Letters of Josiah Wedgwood*. London

Fleming J. 1958. Cardinal Albani's drawings at Windsor: their purchase by James Adam for George III. *Connoisseur* **CXLII**, 164-9

Giuliani-Pomes, M.V. 1957. Cronologia delle situle rinvenute in Etruria, Parte II. *StEtr* **25**, 39-85

Grandjean, S. 1964. *Inventaire après décès de l'Impératrice Joséphine à Malmaison*. Paris

Grant, M.H. 1967. *The Makers of Black Basaltes*, pl. VIII,1. (1910, reprinted 1967) London

Guaitoli, M. 1977. Considerazioni su alcune città ed insediamenti del Lazio in età protostorica ed arcaica. *RM* **74**, 5-25

Guaitoli, M. 1981a. Gabii. *PP* **36**, 152-73

Guaitoli, M. 1981b. Gabii, osservazioni sulle fasi di sviluppo del abitato. *QuadIstTopAnt* **9**, 23-54

Guaitoli, M. and Zaccagni, P. 1977. Gabii. *StEtr* **45**, 434-6

Haskell F. and Penny, N. 1981. *Taste and the Antique*. London

Haynes, D.E.L. 1975. *The Portland Vase*. London

Haynes, S. 1965. Ein etruskischer Bronzekopf vom Bolsenasee. *StEtr* **33**, 523-5

Haynes, S. 1985. *Etruscan Bronzes*. London

Haynes, S. 1991. Die Situla aus Offida. *RM* **98**, 131-40

Haynes S. 1994. Ein einsamer Etrusker in Josiah Wedgwood's Etruria. *Antike Welt*, **25**, **2**, 140-51

Hostetter, E. 1989. A bronze banqueting service from tomb 58C Valle Pega. *Dionysos, Mito e Mistero. Atti del Convegno Internazionale, Commacchio 3-5 Novembre 1989*, 89-106

Hus, A. 1975. *Les bronzes étrusques*. Brussels

Leeds 1868. The catalogue of the *National Exhibition of Works of Art at Leeds*. Leeds

Massei, L. 1978. *Gli askoi a figure rosse nei corredi funerari delle necropoli di Spina*. Milan

Messerschmidt, F. 1928. Untersuchungen zum Mars von Todi. *RM* **43**, 147-64

Metropolitan 1979. *Treasures from the Metropolitan Museum of Art*. Ethnike Pinakotheke, Athens

Painter K. and Whitehouse D. 1990. The History of the Portland Vase. *Journal of Glass Studies* **32**, 24-84

Pallottino, M., Jucker, H. and I. 1955. *Etruskische Kunst.* Zürich

Pinza, G. 1903. Gabii e i suoi monumenti. *BullCom* **XXI**, 23-54.

Quilici Gigli, S. 1970. La valle del Sacco nel quadro delle communicazioni tra Etruria e Magna Graecia. *StEtr* **38**, 364-6

Quilici, L. 1974. *Collatia.* Rome

Reilly, R. 1990. *Wedgwood.* London

de Ridder, A. 1915. *Les bronzes antiques du Louvre* II. *Les Instruments.* Paris

Ridgway D. forthcoming. Greek Letters at Osteria dell'Osa. *Opuscula Romana* **XX**

Roncalli, F. 1973. Il 'Marte' di Todi. Bronzistica etrusca ed ispirazione classica. *MemPontAcc* **XI**, **II**, 1-141.

Sieveking, J. 1919. Constantius Chlorus. *MüJb* **11**, 49-50

Smith, A. H. 1901. Gavin Hamilton's letters to Charles Townley. *JHS* **21**, 306-21

Tait, H. 1963. The Wedgwood Collection in the British Museum, Part II, Basalt and Jasper-Wares. *Proceedings of the Wedgwood Society* **5**

Visconti, E.Q. 1797. *Monumenti Gabini della Villa Pinciana descritta.* Rome

Wedgwood 1885. Old Wedgwood Ware, Handbook to the Collection formed by Richard and George Tangye. London

Zaccagni, P. 1978. Gabii - la città antica ed il territorio. *Quaderni del Centro di Studio per l'Archeologia Etrusco-Italica*, Archeologia Laziale I, 42-6

Illustration Credits

Figs. 1-3	Musée du Louvre
Figs. 4, 11-14	British Museum
Figs. 5-9	Soprintendenza alle Antichità d'Etruria, Gabinetto Fotografico, nos.3511, 3511/3, 35112/1.3.5
Fig. 10	Her Majesty the Queen

1a   1b

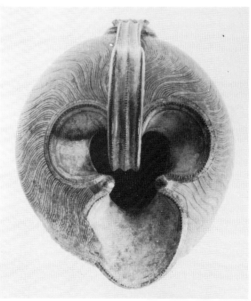

1c

Fig. 1a-c   Bronze jug from Gabii. Louvre, Br. 2955

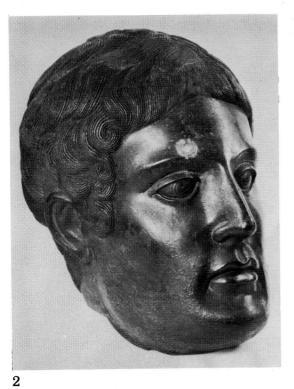

2

3a

3b

Fig. 2   Bronze head from Lake Bolsena. British Museum GR 1824 4-70.6
Fig. 3a,b   Bronze situla from Settecamini. Florence, Museo Archeologico

4a

4b

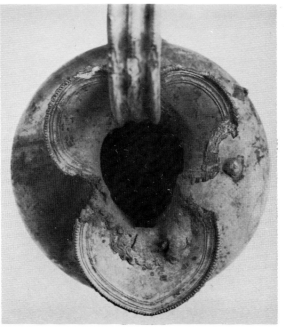

4c

Fig. 4a-c   Bronze jug from Settecamini. Florence, Museo Archeologico

5 *Vaso che serviva neli sagrifici antichi*

Fig. 5 Bronze jug: Cassiano Dal Pozzo album, Inv. no. 11174. Windsor Castle 1991
Figs. 6a-c Bronze jug, copy after ancient original. British Museum GR 1824. 4-89.87

Fig. 7   Wedgwood copy of a bronze jug. British Museum MLA 1909.12-1.106

RATTLING AMONG THE ETRUSCANS AND GREEKS

Tom Rasmussen

History of Art Department, The University, Manchester M13 9PL

In the early 1970s when I was a graduate student making a study of Etruscan pottery, I picked up a bucchero cup from Veii in the old Museo Preistorico in Rome and drew it.[1] As I handled it it spoke to me, that is to say it rattled when I shook it. As the museum was on the point of moving its location there was little more I could do at the time; all the material was immediately taken to the new Museo Pigorini at the Esposizione Universale di Roma where it remained packed away in boxes for many years.

A year before that encounter the first Greek rattling cups were published. Several are now known in Athenian black-gloss pottery, and the series begins in the first half of the fifth century BC. Among the earliest is a Type C in Oslo. All these fifth-century cups have a hollow groove inside the foot around which clay pellets move freely, and in the case of incomplete cups the groove may be the sole indicator.[2]

Fourth-century Greek rattlers are deeper cup-kantharoi with a thick hollow lip for the pellets. The greatest ancient authority on different types of cup is Athenaeus, and it was Brian Shefton who, in studying the Athenaeus passages, spotted that rattling cups are mentioned there, described by the comic poet Euboulos as *psephoperibombetrios* - 'pebble-rattling'.[3] So this somewhat rare and bizarre phenomenon has its place in the literary record. Euboulos was writing in the fourth century, and it is presumably the cup-kantharoi that he has in mind.

To return to the cup from Veii (Fig. 1), it is of an unusual form with notched carination and central omphalos. There is only one other example similar, from Cerveteri,[4] and that one is totally silent however hard you shake it. Both are from tombs and their contexts are early, much earlier than the Greek cups: later seventh or early sixth century. Recently I obtained X-ray photographs of the Veii cup (Figs. 2, 3) for which I have to thank Elisabetta Mangani of the Pigorini Museum, who also supplied a new drawing (Fig. 4). There are only two or three pellets and they do not move around the circumference of the lip or foot as in the Greek examples but are contained in a void at the top of the stem and omphalos.

When I was taking the photograph of Fig. 1 one of the assistants in the Pigorini storeroom handed me another mesomphalic cup from a different shelf and that too rattled (Fig. 5). This also is of an unusual form and with its inward-leaning lip is not unlike a Greek lekanis, apart from the small stemmed foot. Of a refined grey impasto, it is unpublished and the inventory states merely that it was acquired at Chiusi.[5] The X-ray (Fig. 6) shows up more and smaller pellets this time, moving about in a larger void similarly positioned. On the underside of the foot there is a small hole, presumably a vent-hole to assist in firing, a feature which some of the Greek cups have, including the one in Oslo. With no close parallels and without any context the date is far less certain here, but I imagine from the stemmed foot that the cup belongs to the late sixth or fifth century.

What are we to make of these vessels? Is the rattling phenomenon the result of an exchange of ideas between Etruscans and Greeks, akin to others that occurred later in the trading of pottery and metalware?[6] Who is borrowing from whom?

To make the cup sound you have to move it. The best-known context in which cups were moved at speed is the game of kottabos; here a finger is placed through the horizontal U-handle and, by a flick of the wrist, dregs of wine are ejected at a target across the room. Commonly depicted on Athenian pottery it has been aptly described as a game 'beloved of rich young Athenian louts', but its appeal was pan-Hellenic and Athenaeus, writing *c*. AD 200 - for whom it was of antiquarian interest, a pastime enjoyed by men of old (*hoi palaioi*) - tells us at least three times that it was the Sicilians who invented it, while according to a fragment of Alcaeus by the early sixth century it had already reached Ionia.[7]

Certainly the game was popular in the Greek west, and from here come some of the most memorable depictions of it, mainly on fourth-century South Italian vase-scenes such as Python's actors, but beginning in the previous century with the Tomb of the Diver at Paestum. Rattling cups were made here too, and Vickers mentions a South Italian skyphos in Lyon with pellets in the hollow lip (on the authority of D. von Bothmer). But representations in Etruscan art take us back to the later sixth century, and the image in the Cardarelli Tomb at Tarquinia is among the earliest of all.[8] Is it from here that the Greeks took the ideas of kottabos and the rattling cup?

It is tempting to link the rattling cup with the drinking game for they both span very much the same period of time: from *c.* 600 BC into the fourth century. But the connection will always be beyond proof, and where the two Etruscan cups are concerned there is a feature which they share that makes a link with kottabos less likely. In a fit of early experimental archaeology Hayley[9] apparently attempted to recreate the game using rough-and-ready modern equipment; it would be more informative to use the ancient cups, though it might be difficult to find a willing museum curator. However, I suspect that the omphalos would prove fatal to any accurate throw, for instead of the dregs being collected neatly at the bottom of the cup they would be dispersed. (Vickers[10] would also see an obstacle in the offset lip, though in fact lipped cups and skyphoi are frequently represented in kottabos scenes). Omphaloi are extremely rare on Etruscan cups; they essentially belong to another shape altogether, the phiale, of eastern origins, which in the Etruscan and Greek worlds is primarily a vessel for making libations.

Etruscan metal phialai had a wide reputation in antiquity, and are the one Etruscan vessel - the phiale of beaten gold (*chrysotypos*) - specifically mentioned in Greek literature.[11] Greek metal rattling phialai are also known from the late Archaic period, in the form of a matching silver mesomphalic pair in New York with miniature hollow Persian heads on the exterior in which bronze pellets had been inserted.[12]

Is it possible then that the omphalos denotes a votive use for the Etruscan cups? This is the use which Vickers suggests for the Greek rattlers, noting that the context of the Euboulus passage is one of reverence to Zeus Soter. But there are a number of arguments against. First, in pouring a libation there is no cause to move the vessel sufficiently to make it sound. Then the fixed notion of the phiale as solely a vessel of libation is insecure, as in a number of banquet scenes in both Etruscan and Greek art it is used as if it were any handled cup (though in representations it is impossible to know whether it is mesomphalic or not). Seeberg[13] reminds us that the Euboulus fragment is from a comedy, and the description of making a solemn dedication with a 'pebble-rattling' cup may have been to raise a laugh. One could also argue that the rattling phialai in New York were themselves made as a joke, with their conceit of human heads rattling like empty vessels, a very costly joke at the Persians' expense.

Cups are not the only things that were made to rattle in early Italy. Simple pottery (impasto) rattles serving as toys or musical instruments are also known; in Early Iron Age Latium they have been found at Osteria dell'Osa in both child and adult graves, and it is conceivable that rattling cups may owe their origin to artefacts such as these. Also from Latium are the rattling vessels from Ficana of the second half of the seventh century BC, where clay balls sounded in the hollow knob of the lid. These are lidded pyxides, but in the context of the banqueting set with which they were found it is likely they were used as containers for food.[14]

At Ficana the pyxides were found in a domestic context. The bucchero cup from Veii is from a tomb-group, and among the other contents are three more bucchero cups (of Greek shapes), seven bucchero kantharoi, an impasto chalice and two jugs (one bucchero, one painted). It looks very much as if the deceased's drinking set was included. If the two New York rattling phialai are indeed from a 255-piece hoard recovered from four tombs near Sardis, as has been claimed,[15] then the nature of the associated pieces - kyathoi, strainers, oinochoai - suggests that they too formed part of drinking services, only here on a luxury scale. (The phialai are the only metal rattling vessels so far known, but one wonders whether the rattling phenomenon did not originate in metalware; for one thing, you would get a louder rattle.) The only other archaeological context for a rattling vessel is votive: a black-gloss cup comes from the recent excavations at the Aphaia sanctuary on Aegina, its foot broken and the pellets found separately. But the inscription mentioning Apollo on the rattling foot of a Greek cup in a private collection appears not to be a conventional dedication.[16]

The finds from Ficana show that rattling vases in the ancient Mediterranean are not confined to drinking vessels, but in most cases where the archaeological context is known there does seem to be a strong link with drinking and banqueting. The solution to the use of such vases may be that they did not figure prominently during the banqueting so much as afterwards when, in the Greek and Etruscan worlds, drinking was often followed by energetic dancing (the Greek *komos*).[17] It may seem strange to us today that the dancers frequently carried pots as they cavorted, but anyone who has seen the antics of dancers swinging and balancing pots and bottles at festive occasions in Arab countries of the Mediterranean would feel less surprise. At any rate Greek, especially Athenian, vase-paintings are full of drunken dancers clutching pots of all sorts, usually cups but also other shapes[18] such as kraters and jugs, in fact almost any vessel that came to hand. Doing silly things with vases is also featured in a number of dancing scenes in Tarquinian painted tombs: a cup is carried above the dancer's head in the Tomba della Fustigazione; another is prominent in the Tomb of the Leopards;[19] while on the back wall of the Tomb of the Lionesses a frenzied dancer rushes forward with a jug.[20] The archaeological record tells us that most of these vessels would have made no sound, but I suggest that a few potters did on occasion adapt their pots with this particular use in mind, so that in the vase-dance the interior pellets would add percussion to any rhythmic shaking.

There may not of course be a single solution to the use of these vases, and it is always possible that some of them may have been intended for purposes of which we have no idea, others for dancing, others again for kottabos. However, the visual excitement generated by the kottabos game would surely have been sufficient in itself; an additional aural element seems superfluous. There are, moreover, no indications that the introduction of kottabos antedates the adoption of eastern-style banqueting couches in Greece, for which there is no visual evidence before the end of the seventh century BC.[21] But the rattling vases from Veii and Ficana may well belong in the era of the earlier style of seated banquet which also originated in the Near East, and which in its Greek form with Greek-style cups and wine containers was later introduced into Central Italy,[22] the idea of banqueting couches arriving here (from Greece) later still in the first half of the sixth century BC. This new-fangled Greek banqueting equipment may already have included rattling vases for the vase-dance, of which a few craftsmen in Etruria and Latium took sufficient note to copy the idea for themselves.

NOTES

1. Excavated at the Picazzano cemetery in 1889 (Palm 1952: Tomb 20, pl. 7.16); drawing in Rasmussen 1979, 121, fig. 235.
2. First publication of rattling cups: Shefton 1970; Vickers 1970. Type C: Seeberg 1972. Incomplete examples: Vickers 1973.
3. Fourth century examples: Shefton 1970. 'Pebble-rattling': Athenaeus 471d.
4. Rasmussen 1979, fig. 234.

5.   Inv. 24929. 'Chiusi, acquisto Giovanni Brogi 1882.' Max. ht. 6.3cm. Max. diam. 12.00cm. There are traces of four horizontal lines on the lower bowl in dark paint.

6.   Rasmussen 1985.

7.   Kottabos: Hayley 1894; Sparkes 1960. Athenian louts: Spivey and Stoddart 1990, 149. Alcaeus: in Athenaeus 481a.

8.   Python: Trendall 1989: fig. 372; Lyon skyphos: Vickers 1970. Tarquinia: Sprenger and Bartoloni 1983, pl. 94. Later Etruscan kottabos scenes, see Steingräber 1984, 343 (Tomba Querciola 1, back wall); Beazley 1947, 114, pl. 27.9 (red-figure cup tondo).

9.   Hayley 1894.

10. Vickers 1970, 200.

11. Critias, in Athenaeus 28b.

12. Bothmer 1984, 6, 24, nos. 16, 17.

13. Seeberg 1972.

14. Osteria dell'Osa: Bietti Sestieri 1992, 131; Ficana: Rathje 1983, 16, fig. 5k. (I am grateful to Annette Rathje for a full-scale drawing.)

15. Kaylan 1987.

16. Aegina example: pers. comm. Dyfri Williams; Apollo inscription: Vickers and Jeffery 1974.

17. On the banquet/symposium komos in Greece, see Ghiron-Bistagne 1976, 231 ff.

18. One of the many examples is the Euergides Painter's cup in Paris: Lissarague 1987, fig. 16.

19. Tomba della Fustigazione, Tomb of the Leopards: Steingräber 1984, pls. 73, 106. Other Tarquinian painted tombs with dancers wielding cups: T. Citharode, T. Inscriptions, T. del Morto, T. Painted Vases, T. 5591 (Steingräber 1984, 307, 319, 330, 358, 374).

20. Steingräber 1984, pl. 100.

21. Dentzer 1982, 56.

22. Rathje 1990.

BIBLIOGRAPHY

Beazley, J.D. 1947. *Etruscan Vase Painting*. Oxford

Bietti Sestieri, A.M. 1992. *The Iron Age Community of Osteria dell' Osa*. Cambridge

Bothmer, D. von 1984. A Greek and Roman Treasury. *BMetrMus* (summer 1984), 5-72

Dentzer, J-M. 1982. *Le Motif du banquet couché dans le Proche-Orient et le mond grec du VII au IV siècle avant J.-C.* Paris

Ghiron-Bistagne, P. 1976. *Recherches sur les acteurs dans la Grèce antique*. Paris

Hayley, H.W. 1894. The kottabos kataktos. *HarvSt* **5**, 73-82

Kaylan, M. 1987. Who stole the Lydian hoard? *Connoisseur* (July), 66-73

Lissarague, F. 1987. *The Aesthetics of the Greek Banquet*. Princeton

Palm, J. 1952. Veian tomb-groups in the Museo Preistorico, Rome. *OpArch* **7**, 50-86

Rasmussen

Rasmussen, T. 1979. *Bucchero Pottery from Southern Etruria.* Cambridge

Rasmussen, T. 1985. Etruscan shapes in Attic pottery. *AntK* **28**, 33-9

Rathje, A. 1983. A banquet service from the Latin city of Ficana. *AnalRom* **12**, 7-29

Rathje, A. 1990. The adoption of the Homeric banquet in Central Italy in the Orientalizing period. In, O. Murray (ed.), *Sympotica*, 279-88. Oxford

Seeberg, A. 1972. Musical drinking-cups. *JHS* **92**, 183-4

Shefton, B.B. 1970. The Greek Museum, University of Newcastle-upon-Tyne. *AR* (for 1969-70), 52-62

Sparkes, B. 1960. Kottabos. An Athenian after-dinner game. *Archaeology* **13**, 202-7

Spivey, N. and Stoddart, S. 1990. *Etruscan Italy.* London

Sprenger, M. and Bartoloni, G. 1983. *The Etruscans: Their History, Art and Architecture.* New York

Steingräber, S. (ed.) 1984. *Catalogo ragionato della pittura etrusca.* Milan

Trendall, A.D. 1989. *Red Figure Vases of South Italy and Sicily.* London

Vickers, M. 1970. A note on a rattling black glaze cup in Dublin. *JHS* **90**, 199-201

Vickers, M. 1973. An ex-rattling cup in Oxford. *AJA* **77**, 196-7

Vickers, M. and Jeffery, L.H. 1974. Two more rattling cups? *AJA* **78**, 429-31

Illustration credits

Figs. 1, 5   T. Rasmussen
Figs. 2, 3, 6   Photograph Istituto Centrale del Restauro, Rome
Fig. 4   Drawing G. Calandra

1

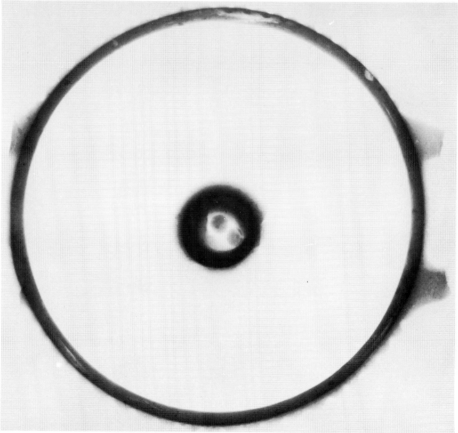

2

Fig. 1   Bucchero cup from Veii (Picazzano), diagonal view from above, Museo Pigorini (Rome, EUR) inv. 70823

Fig. 2   Bucchero cup from Veii, (Picazzano), X-ray from above, Museo Pigorini (Rome, EUR) inv. 70823. Photo Istituto Centrale del Restauro, Rome

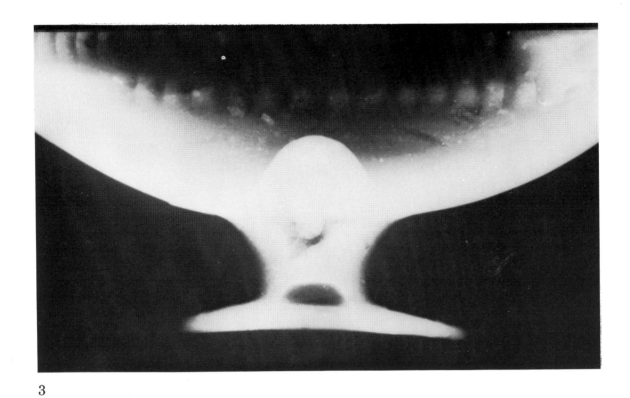

3

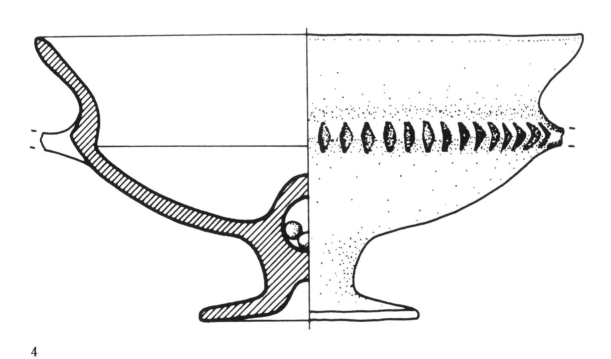

4

Fig. 3   Bucchero cup from Veii (Picazzano) X-ray from side, Museo Pigorini (Rome, EUR)
          inv. 70823. Photo Istituto Centrale del Restauro, Rome
Fig. 4   Drawing of bucchero cup from Veii (Picazzano). Drawing G. Calandra

5

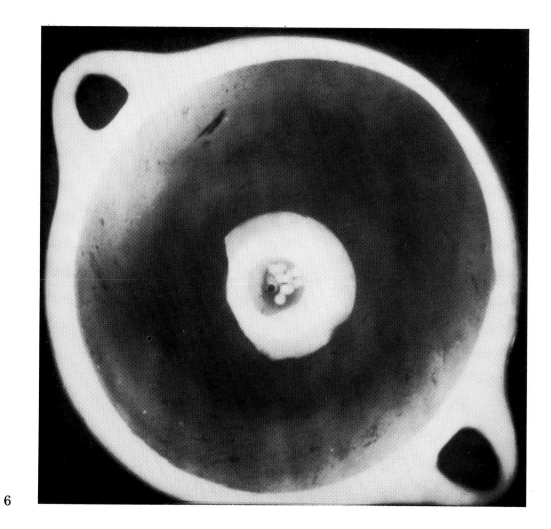

6

Fig. 5   Impasto cup from Chiusi, view from side, Museo Pigorini (Rome, EUR) inv. 24929
Fig. 6   Impasto cup from Chiusi, X-ray from above, Museo Pigorini (Rome, EUR) inv. 24929.
        Photo Istituto Centrale del Restauro, Rome

THE ROMANS

THE EFFECTS OF ROMANISATION IN ITALY

THE ECONOMIC IMPACT OF THE ROMAN PRESENCE IN DAUNIA

Emmanuele Curti

Department of History, University College, London

> Lucerini ac Samnites ad internecionem caesi; eoque ira processit ut Romae quoque, cum de colonis mittendis Luceriam consuleretur senatus, multi delendam urbem censerent. Praeter odium, quod execrabile in bis captos erat, longinquitas quoque abhorrere a relegandis tam procul ab domo civibus inter tam infestas gentes cogebat. Vicit tamen sententia ut mitterentur coloni. Duomilia et quingenti missi. (Liv. IX 26, 2 ff.)

The text of Livy concerning the foundation of Luceria gives us a good idea of how very distant the land of Daunia seemed to the Romans. In 315 BC the Senate decided to create a Latin colony in the northern part of Daunia; the groups of people from Rome who had to move there did so but reluctantly. For how could they imagine or prepare for life at such a great distance from their area, surrounded by dangerous (*infesta*) people?[1]

The military activity of Rome in the last quarter of the fourth century BC represented a great step in the opening up of the unknown world of the indigenous peoples of Southern Italy, those people on the east side of the Apennine mountains (Fig.1). The main reason for the undertaking was to restrain and to reduce the dangerous southward expansion of the Samnites, who were to assume 'mythical' proportions as the enemies of Rome. To achieve this, Rome needed to control areas such as Daunia that were in very close geographical contact with Samnium. At the same time, this activity signalled a vital moment in the development of foreign policy at Rome. It became necessary to create a completely new system for 'international' relationships, to invent formulae for the conduct and control of these new frontiers.

Livy is our most important source for this period; however, a great amount of information concerning the activity of the Roman army from 326 BC onwards is not easily intelligible because of continuous changes and transformations in the relationship between Rome and the local inhabitants of Daunia. During this period we see firm allies becoming enemies, and enemies becoming allies. The evaluation of events was probably very difficult for Livy too. He attempts to clarify the situation by making generalisations about the Daunian people as a whole, calling them Apulians. But much of the confusion probably stems from the existence of several different treaties between Rome and the individual towns of Daunia (Arpi, Canosa, Teano, etc.).[2]

The only point on which we can be more confident is that the foundation of Venusia in 291 represents the last act in the conquest of the region after more than thirty years of continuous fighting. The creation of a second Latin colony signifies complete control of the area, as well as the solution of the Samnite problem.

The Romans had now to begin to organise their presence in the region. They were challenged by a situation that was completely new for them, the novelty heightened by the singularity of the Daunian world they had entered. In recent years the archaeological investigation of Daunia has intensified, and today we know a considerable amount about this peculiar region: peculiar in itself, but also because of the particular relationship it maintained with the rest of the Mediterranean world up until the fourth century BC. Despite the closeness of the rich Greek colonies of Magna Graecia - and the Greek regions on the other side of the Adriatic sea - the Daunian region preserved its own character, accepting the influence of the dominant culture of the period - namely Greek culture - less easily than the other neighbouring indigenous regions.

The Daunians continued for example to produce their own pottery, with little influence from the Greeks; they maintained their form of living in settlements organised into small villages and necropoleis spread over restricted areas, without circuits of walls; their funerary custom of burying people in the foetal position was still in use during the initial period of the Roman presence. Unfortunately there is no space here to describe the various different aspects of their culture. We now have some evidence of their material culture, but any understanding we may derive from this evidence concerning the complex systems and strategies underpinning the society awaits a more extensive analysis.[3]

It was only in the fourth century BC that Daunia - now drawn more deeply within the Hellenic cultural sphere, probably through closer economic relationships with the Greek regions or colonies (such as Taranto) - appeared to accept more eagerly new models coming from elsewhere, as the monumental tombs at Canosa, Arpi and Teano testify. The high artistic quality of these structures (Fig.2) - the plans, the architectural and fresco decorations - suggests the presence of artists and architects from outside the region. It seems that the aristocracy of Daunia had begun to participate in the Hellenising cultural dialogue, adopting expressions typical of high society in contemporary neighbouring cultures.[4]

Evidence of this transformation can also be seen in the increasing popularity of mythical stories about Diomedes. In Greek literary tradition of the fourth century BC, we discover that the hero is suddenly described as the founder of Arpi, whereas according to the archaic tradition his presence was limited to a peripheral position such as the *Diomedeia* (modern Tremiti) islands: having been an offshore spectator, the Greek Diomedes moved inland, into the heart of Daunia.[5] The locals were searching for a sacred guarantee of their status; and this guarantee had to be rooted in Greek tradition, because Greek culture had become the social currency of the times. In this manner, Daunia opened the door to external influence. Yet, at the same time, the region maintained its own customs and traditions, with a degree of conservatism often difficult to understand alongside innovations such as the monumental tombs.

For example, the custom of living in centres that have no open spaces suitable for large public gatherings indicates the continuity of a political system still presumably operated by small clans operating from small villages, one close to the other. (This is with regard to the centres we know; unfortunately we still do not have enough data on the main towns, such as Arpi and Canosa, which appear to have been more open to Greek influence.) In the matter of religious life, sacred structures may have been found: in Ascoli Satriano and Teano two similar rectangular buildings have been excavated. Their appearance suggests that these may well be Daunian temples, dating from the fourth century BC (Figs. 3, 4; the other hypothesis is that they are 'aristocratic' houses).[6]

This, in short, was the world that the Romans encountered when they arrived in Daunia. The Latin literature does not in any manner convey the nature of this different culture. Hence, the impact of Roman culture can be estimated only through analysis of the archaeological record. Prior to discussing the foundation of the two Latin colonies, we should identify possible transformations taking place in other Daunian centres.

There is very little that we can say about the richest settlements at Canosa and Arpi. Continuous occupation in the first case, and the destruction of the latter by the Romans immediately after the Second Punic War, together with the looting of graves in modern times, has obscured the record, and with it our understanding of the situation. However, some important elements do survive.

At Canosa, immediately after the arrival of the Romans, a large temple was built on the hill (S. Leucio) overlooking the city and the main road going from north Daunia towards the south of Apulia.[7] The form of the temple is of considerable interest (Fig. 5); the rich decoration of this impressive building (e.g. Fig. 6) has striking analogies with the products of the workshops of nearby Taranto, the main centre of artistic production of the Apulian region. But of more interest is the fact that, in contrast to the sacred structures of the Greek world, the temple was built on a large podium, so incorporating an element of Roman tradition. There appears to have been a conscious intention here to celebrate the birth of a new relationship between the Romans and the local aristocracy, a willingness to create a symbol of the new bond, bridging geographical and cultural distances.

At the same moment, we find throughout southern Daunia - an area more affected by Samnite infiltration - the sudden appearance of pottery produced in the Canosan workshops. The small centres surrounding Canosa, such as Località Toppicelli, disappear and the area of Forentum, on the southwestern border, appears completely transformed, with the abandonment of previously important settlements and cemetery areas, and the creation of a new privileged funerary area, where the new tombs contain only material coming from Canosa.[8] It seems therefore that the presence of the Romans helped the aristocracy of Canosa greatly to increase and secure their economic control of the area. Rome aimed to bring order to the new territory, establishing a social equilibrium that required a strong focal point - strong groups of families bound together by mutual interest - and brought this about through the strengthening of the local aristocracy. In Arpi - as in Canosa - this phenomenon can also be seen in the continuity of use of aristocratic monumental tombs. By contrast, the necropoleis of the lower levels of society completely disappeared. The aristocrats maintained the symbols of their power, imposing their tradition, their past, as the unassailable guarantee of their superiority. Similarly, we may consider the interesting cultural messages conveyed by some vases of Arpan production (Fig.7), which had previously made use of the traditional motif of mythical fighting between Greeks and Barbarians.[9] The new and significant development is that the Greeks were now represented as Romans, and the Barbarians as Samnites. Here too we can see the Hellenised upper classes affirming the new reality, creating the cultural conditions whereby they could accept the presence of the new 'Greeks', the Romans. Contemporaneously, new variations appeared in the mythical story of Diomedes, where the hero became a vehicle for pro-Roman propaganda. All of this material is useful in recreating the atmosphere of Daunia during the early years of the Roman presence. Indeed, without taking all these different elements into account it would be impossible to estimate how strong the impact of Rome must have been.

Going back to archaeological evidence, this sense of impact can be felt even more strongly when considering the material transformation of the region. At practically the same time as the construction of the big temple of Canosa, mentioned above, the two Daunian sanctuaries of Ascoli and Teano were completely abandoned and destroyed. It is evident that the local people had been forced to leave their religious centres and to abandon some of their traditional practices.

One of the clearest records of urban transformation comes from the best-known archaeological site in Daunia, Herdonia, excavated by the Belgian School under the direction of Joseph Mertens. Herdonia had continuity of occupation stretching from the eighth century BC through to medieval times. Until the fourth century BC, the living space was organised into clusters of small villages - with enclosed necropoleis - spread across a huge plateau overlooking the Carapelle valley. Suddenly, at the beginning of the third century BC we find the construction of a circuit of walls built of mud-brick, which encloses only a part of the same plateau. All the surrounding small villages disappeared, and settlement was restricted within the walls. The necropoleis which had been situated adjacent to the earlier huts - or buildings - were now located outside the walls, according to the 'new' urban norm.[10]

In the middle of the third century, it becomes possible to identify spatial remodelling within the town. A large empty space appears, with tabernae constructed alongside it. Here, we have the first phase in the development of the forum at Herdonia. On the same side of the open space as the tabernae development is located a large underground chamber. From its form this appears to be a huge storehouse. There is sufficient evidence here to argue that, in a few decades, the people of

Herdonia had been compelled to alter completely their way of life, their traditions and customs - the transition encompassing everything from an alteration in funerary practice through to a change in economic strategy, as evidenced by the presence of the tabernae and underground storehouse. It is clear that during this period Herdonia was reacting to unprecedented political and economic pressures; the people were compelled, by their new situation, to accept social models underwritten by the presence of Rome. At the period when these transformations of Daunian centres were taking place, the Romans founded the two colonies of Luceria and Venusia, in 315 and 291 BC respectively. To the former, as we have seen already, 2500 colonists were sent. In respect of the latter, we have the text of Dionysius of Halicarnassos (Dion. Hal. XVII-XVIII, 5), who reports the impressive number of 20,000 colonists: there is no space here to discuss this data but I think that, instead of correcting the text as has always been done, it might be possible that within this number were counted the indigenous local people of Venusia, to underline the enterprise of the foundation of a big town.

However, it is essential to take into account the fact that a large number of colonists had moved into the region, building their cities according to Roman rules and practices. Orthogonal spaces (Figs. 8-9), fora, sanctuaries - in both colonies there have been found Latian votive terracottas dating to the beginning of the third century BC - and necropoleis:[11] the Daunians were surely not accustomed to live in these conditions. Further, a Latin colony does not just comprise a city structure, but also brings organisation to territory, to the land that will become the lifeblood of the colony.

Centuriation - found in the territory of Luceria, but not yet in that of Venusia - is a grid superimposed on the land, that carries with it a particular conception of agrarian order.[12] Unfortunately, we do not have any information concerning the earlier territorial organisation of the Daunians; nevertheless, considering the nature of their settlements, the traditional agrarian system was most probably very different from that of the Romans. The question is: could two different agrarian systems live together, side by side? Even if we do not have elements to prove that, it is very likely that the imposition of the centuriation system must have led to a reaction in neighbouring territories; either the indigenous population had to continue with their traditionally self-sufficient land practice or, more likely, slowly but surely, they were compelled to adapt their own practices round the new system, as was clear by the second century BC, when centuriation is found in the indigenous territories.

The Romans became the leaders, the reference point of the new economic strategy, and, in obtaining that status, they were also able to utilise other important Roman innovations in the region, such as the consular roads - the via Appia, dating to the middle of the third century BC, and the via Minucia, dating to the end of the third quarter of the same century.[13] The Romans, no longer needing to resort to military activity, had, through the violent impact of their social systems, effectively destroyed traditional Daunian society, its customs and practices, at nearly every level.

One of the few characteristics that may not have been changed was the political administration of the Daunian centres; the local aristocracy, with the guidance of Rome - as we have seen above with the control of Canosa in the west Daunian area - probably continued to control their own communities. The impression is that Rome preferred to establish a general policy of *laissez-faire*, while maintaining a stabilising presence in the area, promoting equilibrium in the relationships between the indigenous towns. The consequences of the strategy are further illuminated by subsequent events. Daunia was to become one of the most important scenes of clashes during the Hannibalic War; the towns of northern Daunia allied themselves with the Carthaginians, while Canosa remained an ally of Rome. In my opinion, this may have its explanation in the new commercial organisation of the region; if we consider the geographical location of the Roman roads, we see that the northern part of Daunia was cut off from the new economic causeways. Arpi and Salapia were probably the first victims of this reorganisation; and considered from this aspect, their subsequent alliance with Hannibal is more understandable.

The Romans, present in Daunia and throughout Apulia, must at this period have begun to think about destinations overseas. The already large production of grain and salt - the main products of Daunia together with wool - probably increased in the third century BC. Modern studies have always underlined the importance of the Italic peoples in mediating the first relationship with Greece and, more generally, with the Mediterranean world. But I think, bearing in mind the Apulian situation, that such an expansive commercial development could only have been carried out through there being a real policy of investment by the *gentes* of Rome. Without considering all the different links between the Romans and the Greek peoples on the other side of the Adriatic, it is important to remember that routes overseas were insecure, and that Rome in 229 BC deployed something in the order of 200 ships, 20,000 soldiers and 2000 horsemen in ridding the sea of Illyrian piracy which was endangering trade.[14] It is less relevant to discuss to whom ships captured by the pirates belonged; evidently, Rome wanted to eliminate the problem and was prepared to do so at some cost, because it greatly inconvenienced her interests. Rome had her eyes on the Greek world, and was laying down foundations - consciously or unconsciously - for the future conquest of the eastern market.

In the short space available, I have tried to convey an impression of the great transformations that the land of Daunia underwent in a period of only one hundred years. The absence of the text of Livy for this period contributes to the sense that this is a 'dark age'. Hence, the third century BC has tended to be undervalued in studies of Romanisation, and the presence of Rome among the native population considered significant only from the period immediately following the Second Punic War. But the Romans had already long been present in Daunia, leaving their strong and violent mark: it is impossible to evaluate the complex situation of the second century without understanding the deep and lasting transformation of the third.

NOTES

1. This paper is a very brief summary of my Tesi di Dottorato, (Curti forthcoming). In the following notes I have mentioned only the most recent bibliography.
2. Cf. Grelle in press.
3. The bibliography is very rich, but there is no one general work on the evolution of Daunian culture; however cf., as the best and most recent work on the subject, *Principi*.
4. For the monumental tombs of Canosa: *Principi, passim*; for Arpi: Mazzei 1990; 1992.
5. Musti 1988.
6. Mazzei *et al.* 1990.
7. Pensabene 1990; *1992*.
8. Bottini *et al.* 1991.
9. Mazzei 1987; 1992.
10. All the data can be found in Mertens 1988.
11. Luceria: Mazzei *et al.* 1990, 181 f.; Venusia: Salvatore 1990.
12. For the centuriation in the Latin colonies and, in general, in Daunia, see Volpe 1990.
13. Cf. Wiseman 1987; Coarelli 1988.
14. Polybius II. 11, 1 and 7.

BIBLIOGRAPHY

Basilicata 1990. AA.VV. Basilicata. L'espansionismo romano nel sud-est d'Italia. Il quadro archeologico. *Atti del Convegno, Venosa 1987.* Venosa

Bottini, A., Fresa, M.G. and Tagliente, M. 1991. *Forentum* II. *L'acropoli in età classica.* Venosa

Coarelli, F. 1988. Colonizzazione romana e viabilità. *DialArch* n.s. **VI**, 35-48

Curti, E. forthcoming. Il fenomeno della romanizzazione della Daunia. IV-I sec. a.C. (Tesi di Dottorato 1992) Perugia

Grelle, F. (in press). La Daunia e Canosa nell'età della romanizzazione. In, AA.VV., *L'età annibalica e la Puglia, Atti del II Convegno di studi sulla Puglia romana, Mesagne 1988.*

Italici 1990. AA.VV. *Italici in Magna Grecia, Lingua, insediamenti e strutture, Atti Convegno Acquasparta 1986.* Venosa

Mazzei, M. 1987. Note su un gruppo di vasi policromi decorati con scene di combattimento da Arpi. *AION* **IX**, 167-88

Mazzei, M. 1990. Arpi. In, *Italici,* 57-64

Mazzei, M. 1992. Arpi. In, *Principi,* 587-90

Mazzei, M., Mertens J. and Volpe, G. 1990. Aspetti della romanizzazione della Daunia. In, *Basilicata,* 177-225, figs. 2-6

Mertens, J. 1988. Ordona 1978-86. *Ordona* **VIII,** 7-67.

Musti, D. 1988. Il processo di formazione e diffusione delle tradizioni greche sui Dauni e su Diomede. In, D. Musti, *Strabone e la Magna Grecia,* 173-95. Padua

Pensabene, P. 1990. Il tempio ellenistico di S. Leucio a Canosa. In, *Italici,* 269-337

Pensabene, P. 1992. Il tempio italico sotto S.Leucio. In, *Principi,* 620-54

Principi 1992. Cassano R.(ed.), *Principi imperatori vescovi. Duemila anni di storia a Canosa.* Venice

Salvatore, M.R. 1990. Venosa. In, *Basilicata,* 11-15

Volpe, G. 1990. *La Daunia nell'età della romanizzazione. Paesaggio agrario, produzione, scambi.* Bari

Wiseman, T.P. 1987. Roman Republican Road-Building. In, *idem, Roman Studies,* 144-53. Liverpool

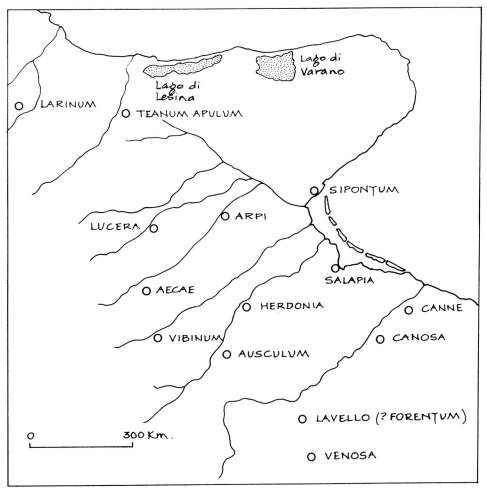

1

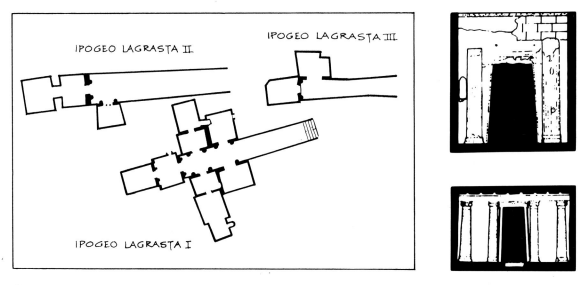

2

Fig. 1   Plan of Daunia
Fig. 2   The Ipogei Lagrasta at Canusium

213

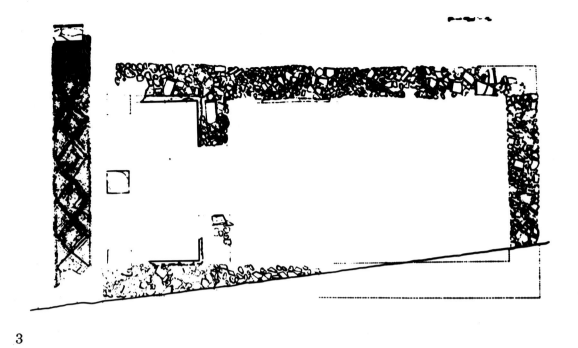

3

4

Fig. 3   The 'sanctuary' of Teanum
Fig. 4   The 'sanctuary' of Ascoli

214

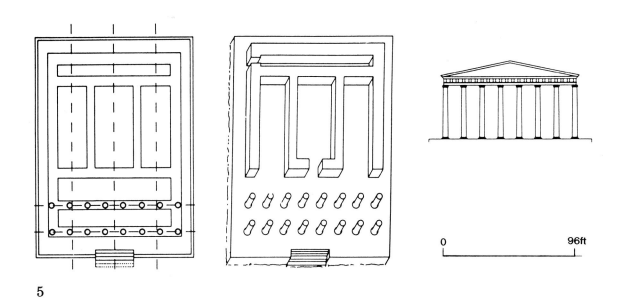

5

6

7

Fig. 5   The plan of the temple of S. Leucio
Fig. 6   One of the capitals of the temple of S. Leucio
Fig. 7   The Arpan vases with Romans fighting against Samnites

215

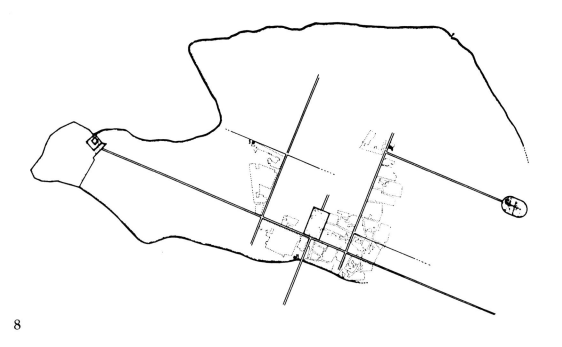

8

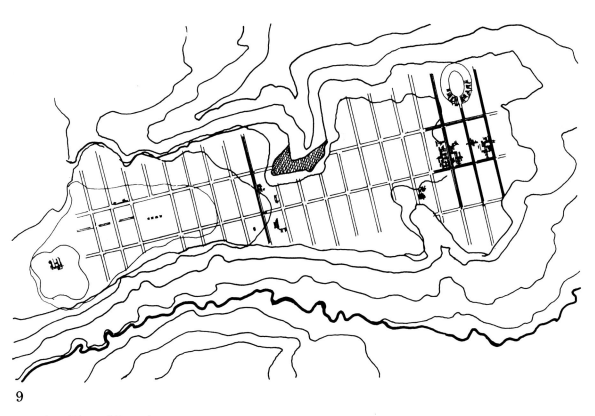

9

Fig. 8   Plan of Luceria
Fig. 9   Plan of Venusia

216

L'ANTICA HATRIA PICENA E L'USO DEL SUO PORTO NELL'ANTICHITÀ

Oliva Menozzi
Via San Domenico 37, 64302 Atri(TE), Italy

Antichissime sono le origini di Hatria e soprattutto discusse ed avvolte nella leggenda. Molti studiosi ritengono che la fondazione di *Hatria* sia stata opera dei Siculi, popolazione illirica che, secondo la testimonianza di Plinio, giunse in Abruzzo e si stanziò in questo territorio.[1] La maggior parte delle fonti fa risalire proprio ai Siculi il toponimo *Hatria/Hadria*, ma varie e controverse sono le etimologie.

Licofrone riferisce che ci sono due tesi sulla fondazione di questa cittadina, che sarebbe opera del re illirico Adrio oppure di Dionisio il Vecchio, tiranno di Siracusa.[2] Questa opinione è condivisa anche da altri autori antichi, come Aurelio Vittore,[3] Paolo Diacono[4] e Dionigi Periegete.[5] Una lieve variante di tale tesi è riportata da Eudosso che riferisce che Messapo, figlio di Adrio, avrebbe fondato la città, chiamandola poi *Hadria* in omaggio al padre.[6] Secondo il Sorricchio,[7] uno studioso locale, il nome di questa antica cittadina è legato al nome del dio della guerra *Hadranus* o *Hatranus*, al quale i Siculi intitolarono anche altre città da loro fondate. Secondo lo studioso i legami con questa divinità non si limiterebbero alla sola somiglianza del nome, ma la presenza sull'asse fuso della zecca di *Hatria* di una testa barbata sul dritto, da molti interpretata come *Hadranus*, e di un cane, animale sacro al dio, sul rovescio, sarebbero una ulteriore prova di essi. Legata al nome di *Hadria* è la notizia che il Mare Adriatico abbia preso il nome da questa cittadina; ma anche un'altra città, la colonia etrusca Adria nel Veneto, rivendica la paternità di questo nome. Le numerose fonti antiche che riguardano l'etimologia del nome del *Mar Hadriaticus* non chiariscono l'equivoco e spesso confondono esse stesse *Hatria Picena* ed Adria Veneta.[8] Affascinante si rivela la tesi avanzata dal Brandestein, secondo cui tutti questi nomi potrebbero derivare da una stessa antica radice illirica *ADU* = acqua, per cui le due città avrebbero preso il nome dal mare su cui fiorirono i loro commerci.[9] Risulta comunque difficile datare lo stanziamento illirico-siculo nel territorio di Atri non supportato da alcun rinvenimento archeologico. La tradizione popolare vuole che i Siculi fossero stati cacciati da altre popolazioni che ne presero il posto, come ad esempio il mitico popolo dei Pelasgi, la cui presenza però non è confermata da testimonianze archeologiche.

Ad un periodo che possiamo definire 'storico' invece, poiché più ampiamente documentato sia dalle fonti storiche che archeologiche, si deve far risalire l'immigrazione in *Hatria* e nell'*ager* dei Piceni. La tradizione storica riportata dalle fonti letterarie vuole che questa popolazione, di origine Sabina, fosse migrata e si fosse stanziata in area adriatica in seguito ad un *Ver Sacrum*.[10] Sulla causa di queste migrazioni le fonti stesse ci informano. Plinio ad esempio narra che alcuni componenti delle varie tribù venivano *'sacrati'* sin da piccoli a celebrare tale rito religioso, secondo il quale i prescelti dovevano partire sotto le insegne di un dio, in genere Marte, e fondare altrove nuove città. Così il nome dei Piceni deriverebbe dal picchio - *picus* - uccello sacro a Marte, sotto le cui insegne essi erano partiti per le sacre migrazioni, come ci attestano Strabone e Festo.[11] Nella tradizione letteraria, attraverso una visione leggendaria di queste popolazioni Italiche nate a seguito di Primavere Sacre, si possono intravedere anche realtà storiche, quali ad esempio la derivazione diretta di tali popolazioni da stirpe Sabina. L'emigrazione in altri territori poteva essere dettata da desideri espansionistici e da esigenze demografiche. Alcuni studiosi hanno anche avanzato l'ipotesi che il *Ver Sacrum* potesse essere connesso in origine con migrazioni dettate dalle leggi della transumanza.[12]

Le testimonianze archeologiche più importanti della cultura picena in Atri sono le due necropoli del Colle della Giustizia e della Pretara, che hanno restituito circa una cinquantina di tombe.[13] Dai corredi funebri, constituiti soprattutto da armi ed ornamenti personali in ferro e bronzo (Fig. 1), le necropoli sono state datate ai primi tre quarti del VI sec. a.C.[14] Con i Piceni *Hatria* raggiunse un alto grado di sviluppo economico, agricolo ed artistico e divenne un ricco ed affermato centro dell'Adriatico, come testimonia anche Ecateo, autore che scrive proprio alla fine VI inizio del V sec. a.C.[15]

I primi rapporti con Roma avvennero con le guerre Sannitiche, soprattutto durante l'ultima nel 290 a.C., quando *Hatria* si alleò con l'esercito Romano, capeggiato da Curio Dentato, che conquistò buona parte del Piceno. Certamente la posizione strategica e le possibilità economiche che la città offriva dovettero indurre i Romani ad interessarsi di *Hatria*, che rappresentava anche una roccaforte da cui controllare sia le coste adriatiche che le popolazione limitrofe. Così *Hatria* fu dedotta come colonia latina già nel 289 a.C., come ci testimonia lo stesso Livio.[16] Il patto che legava questa colonia a Roma era quello della Confederazione Latina, che prevedeva alleanza difensiva ed offensiva e pace tra Romani e Latini. Dal momento della deduzione a colonia di *Hatria* la storia di questa città è legata alla storia di Roma, al fianco della quale si trova a combattere, proprio come colonia in base al patto della confederazione latina, prima nelle Guerre Tarentine (280-277 a.C.), poi contro gli stessi Piceni ribellatisi ai Romani (269 a.C.). Durante le Guerre Puniche *Hatria* prese parte ai combattimenti, tanto che Livio la loda per l'aiuto ed il sostegno dato a Roma nel conflitto contro Cartagine.[17] Livio e Polibio riferiscono che proprio durante la seconda Guerra Punica, nel 216 a.C., il territorio atriano fu devastato dalle truppe di Annibale.[18] La fedeltà di *Hatria* per Roma rimase tale anche quando, durante il proseguimento della guerra, nel 209 a.C., molte colonie latine si ribellarono, ed il Senato, riferisce Livio, le rese pubblico onore insieme alle altre colonie rimaste fedeli.[19] Alla fine della Guerra Sociale e con la promulgazione della *Lex Iulia* e la *Lex Papiria*, che estendevano la cittadinanza romana a Latini ed Italici, *Hatria* divenne un *Municipium Civium Romanorum*. Fu dedotta a colonia romana, secondo alcuni studiosi con Silla o con Cesare, con il nome di *Colonia Veneria*, mentre secondo altri la nuova deduzione avvene con Augusto.[20] La conferma della deduzione a colonia romana è data prima di tutto dal fatto che Plinio la annovera tra le colonie romane esistenti al tempo di Augusto,[21] ed inoltre dal rinvenimento nell'*ager Hatrianus*, e precisamente a Monte Giove, di una epigrafe che menziona la colonia ed il suo patrono.[22]

Sino al II sec. d.C. non si hanno più notizie storiche dalle fonti su *Hatria*, che riacquista una certa importanza durante l'impero di Adriano, in quanto patria dei suoi genitori. Sparziano infatti ci informa che i genitori del futuro imperatore erano originari di questa cittadina, e che Adriano stesso tra le sue cariche fu quinquennale sia di Italica, la cittadina spagnola in cui nacque, sia di *Hatria*.[23] Aurelio Vittore invece asserisce che l'imperatore sarebbe addirittura nato ad *Hatria*,[24] il che è certamente errato, ma al tempo stesso è una ulteriore prova dell'interesse di Adriano per *Hatria* e del fastigio che la città aveva raggiunto durante il suo impero, tanto da venire denominata *Colonia Aelia*. Infatti, un'iscrizione rinvenuta in Atri, forse base di una statua, dopo la dedica ad Antonino Pio, si chiude specificando *Colonia Aelia Hadria (publico) voto*.[25] Da questo momento in poi per *Hatria* comincia una lenta decadenza e sempre più rare sono le fonti su questa cittadina. Tra il 367 e il 375 d.C., con gli imperatori Valentiniano, Valente e Graziano, nell'ambito di una ristrutturazione delle vie di communicazione romane, vengono ampliate e ristrutturate le strade dell'*ager Hatrianus*, come attesta un miliario rinvenuto a Castilenti con dedica a questi imperatori.[26]

Ben presto le invasioni barbariche sconvolgono l'assetto politico dell'*ager*. Cassiodoro riferisce che nel 476 Atri è completamente in mano ai Goti.[27] Nel 555 con Giustiniano, imperatore d'Oriente, che vince i Barbari, Atri viene a far parte di un ducato con Fermo capitale. Con i Longobardi, nel 726, Atri viene a far parte del ducato di Spoleto e Paolo Diacono la descrive ormai '*vetustate consumpta*'.[28]

Archeologicamente l'*ager Hatrianus* si presenta una zona molto interessante. Confini dell'*ager* sono il fiume Vomano a Nord, il fiume Saline a Sud e la valle del Mavone ad Ovest (Fig. 2). Morfologicamente la zona è formata da colline, crinali e valli poco profonde, caratterizzati da una ricca rete idrografica e fertili terreni argillosi. Le favorevoli condizioni geografiche e climatiche hanno favorito nell'antichità numerosi insediamenti a carattere agricolo-pastorale. Le prime tracce archeologiche risalgono all'età Neolitica ed alcuni siti presentano una notevole continuità storica. In un recente lavoro di ricognizione sul territorio, cui hanno partecipato, oltre alla sottoscritta altri studiosi,[29] si è giunti alla compilazione di una carta archeologica dell'*ager Hatrianus* con la computerizzazione di circa duecento siti databili dal Neolitico al Medioevo. Il numero dei siti inoltre potrebbe ulteriormente salire con ricognizioni a tappeto di tutto l'*ager*. I grafici (Fig. 3) illustrano le tipologie d'insediamento riscontrate nell'*ager Hatrianus*. Alla struttura paganico-vicana di età preromana, fa riscontro nell'*ager* una organizzazione territoriale di età romana basata sullo sfruttamento agricolo ed economico del territorio.

Il centro storico dell'antica *Hatria Picena*, odierna Atri, è stato invece studiato e pubblicato di recente.[30] La cittadina sorge su una collina a 500m, posta a circa 7km dal mare. L'attuale centro storico si presenta nell'assetto urbano di età medievale, che oblitera quasi completamente i resti d'età precedente, ma che ricalca nei tracciati viari gli assi principali di età romana. Resti romani di notevole interesse sono le terme romane sotto la Cattedrale, di cui si conservano le interessanti cisterne ed i mosaici pavimentali con scene marine, vari complessi edilizi, ed un teatro romano, la cui presenza è stata confermata da fotografie aeree e da saggi di accertamento, e di cui a breve termine verra iniziato lo scavo.[31] L'importanza storica di tale cittadina è comprovata anche dalla ricca rete viaria che percorreva il suo ager in età romana, ricalcando percorsi naturali già sfruttati in età preromana (Fig.2).

L'esistenza di un approdo portuale invece ci è innanzi tutto testimoniato dalle fonti. Strabone infatti ci parla dell'esistenza di un porto alle foci di un fiume definito *Matrinus*, che scorreva direttamente da *Hatria*.[32] Differenti sono sempre stati i tentativi di identificazione di tale fiume. Secondo gli studiosi locali tale fiume era da identificare con il Vomano, che sfocia a circa 12km a nord di *Hatria*, o con il Piomba o il Saline, che sfociano a 10km più a sud.[33] Tali ipotesi sembravano contraddire la testimonianza di Strabone, che citava un fiume che scorresse direttamente dalla cittadina, mentre tutti e tre i fiumi presi in considerazione nascevano ai confini del suo *ager* e non toccavano la cittadina con il loro corso, per cui gli studiosi locali hanno dichiarato in parte erronea tale testimonianza letteraria.

Probabilmente un approdo naturale di *Hatria* era in funzione come piccolo scalo commerciale già in età preromana, come sembra si possa leggere dalla testimonianza di Ecateo, se effettivamente egli si riferisce ad *Hadria Picena* e non ad Adria Veneta.[34] Ma la costruzione di un porto vero e proprio, che rafforzasse l'insenatura naturale, si deve attribuire a tempi posteriori, certamente in epoca romana. Secondo studi recenti il porto di Hatria era stato definito da Strabone come 'ἐπίνειον', e non come λιμήν, poiché si trattava di un porto commerciale di una città non marittima, come anche il porto di Ostia ed il Pireo, rispettivamente porti di Roma ed Atene, e non di un porto direttamente connesso con una città sul mare, quale si intende con λιμήν.[35] L'attività marinara della città è ampiamente documentata anche da fonti indirette, quali l'esportazione di prodotti locali e i simboli marini presenti nella monetazione della zecca locale, come la conchiglia, l'ancora, la raggia, il delfino. Il porto ebbe in età romana grande importanza per l'economia locale, ma decadde con la fine dell'impero e solo con il Medio Evo, i Papi Innocenzo IV ed Alessandro IV fecero ricostruire un porto per Atria divenuta sede vescovile nel 1251.

Con le nuove scoperte di archeologia subacquea sembra attualmente farsi strada un'altra ipotesi di localizzazione dell'antico porto di *Hatria* secondo cui il fiume *Matrinus* in realtà non esisterebbe più come tale oggigiorno, ma che un tempo scorresse da Hatria al mare, proprio come voleva Strabone, e sfociasse a 5km dalla cittadina in località attualmente denominata Torre di Cerrano, ove era situato il porto. In tale località infatti nel Luglio 1982, durante una immersione, il Prof. P. Data, direttore della Scuola di Specializzazione di Medicina Subacquea ed Iperbarica di Chieti, insieme ad altri suacquei volontari ed a studenti del suo corso, effettuarono una prima esplorazione subacquea e rinvennero varie strutture.[36] La torre di Cerrano, fatta costruire nel XVI sec. a scopo di difesa e di avvistamento per eventuali attacchi dal mare sui resti di un più antica struttura difensiva, era stata acquistata dalla locale Amministrazione Provinciale, per restaurarla e transformarla in un attrezzato Centro di Ricerche di Biologia Marina. Fu proprio durante la progettazione di tale centro che furono notate in mare ampie e regolari ombreggiature tra i chiari fondali sabbiosi, visibili, se il mare è tranquillo, anche dall'alto della Torre (Fig. 4). Alla prima immersione seguirono delle altre durante tutta l'estate, alla quale presero parte vari subacquei volontari ed un archeologo della Soprintendenza Archeologica d'Abruzzo, il Dott. G. Angeletti. Le ricerche effettuate permisero di evidenziare nel tratto di mare antistante la Torre di Cerrano una vasta area archeologica subacquea, su fondali fra i 4 e gli 11m di profondità. L'area più ricca di lacerti è proprio quella antistante la Torre, ove sono visibili strutture ascrivibili ad un molo nord, formato da grandi blocchi (2 x 4 x 6 m, o 2 x 4 x 4 m) in pietra d'Istria, posti regolarmente con pianta ad L rovesciata, con l'apice del lato lungo tangente alla costa (Fig. 5). Vicino al molo sono visibili diverse strutture murarie, identificabili con magazzini inerenti alla vita commerciale del porto. Tra questi resti numerose sono le strutture in *opus quadratum* ed in *opus latericium* (Figs. 6, 7). In un buono stato di conservazione sone state rinvenute anche strutture murarie caratterizzate dall' alternanza di pietre squadrate e mattoni (Fig. 8). Accanto a queste strutture, durante le varie immersioni, si rinvennero numerosi altri reperti, come ad esempio lastre di rivestimento modanate, rocchi di colonne, tratti di basolato, resti di canalette in pietra (Fig. 10). Tra le strutture rinvenute una in particolare desta molte perplessità. Si tratta di tre gradoni concentrici in pietra, degradanti verso l'alto, di cui sembra difficile rintracciare la funzione. Si potrebbe ipotizzare che si tratti di una base di un piccolo faro o di un monumento (Fig. 9). Lo stato di insabbiamento delle strutture non ha permesso nel 1982 di effettuare sondaggi precisi, per cui appare difficoltoso datare con precisione le strutture. In base ad i materiali fittili rinventi durante le immersioni del 1982, alcuni dei quali incastrati nelle strutture, si può ipotizzare che una delle fasi di vita di questo porto è ascrivibile al periodo tra I e II sec. d.C. I materiali rinvenuti consisterebbero in anfore ed altri frammenti fittili di uso comune.[37]

Una recente pubblicazione su questo porto ripropone l'ipotesi che il porto romano di *Hatria* non fosse questo rinvenuto a Cerrano, ma fosse da situare alla foce del Vomano, secondo le vecchie ipotesi, negando di nuovo la testimonianza di Strabone e proponendo per le strutture rinvenute una datazione a dopo il XIII sec. Si nega però in tal modo non solo la testimonianza storica delle fonti letterarie ma anche l'evidenza dei vari rinvenimenti. Ci sono infatti notizie di rinvenimenti in passato di anfore romane in tale tratto di mare.[38] Oltre ai dati pubblicati, numerosi reperti, ripescati nelle acque di questa zona da pescatori locali si trovano in collezioni private e tra essi figurano numerose anfore Lamboglia 2/ Dressel 6. Si è avuta anche notizia, che però non ho potuto verificare personalmente, che durante recenti lavori edilizi nella zona retrostante la Torre di Cerrano sarebbero stati rinvenuti numerosi frammenti di anfore, ceramica comune e monete romane ora in collezioni private, a testimonianza, se veritiera, che la zona era praticata in questo periodo.

Non si può negare, inoltre, l'evidenza che se a Cerrano sono state rinvenute numerose strutture e parte di un molo, alla foce del Vomano, invece, nulla è stato segnalato se non resti di muri in località Scerne,[39] visibili all'inizio del secolo ma ora completamente obliterati dall'edilizia moderna, che allo stato attuale delle conoscenze potrebbero essere attribuiti a qualsiasi tipo di struttura.

Per ora gli unici dati conosciuti sono quelli emersi dai rinvenimenti archeologici effettuati a Cerrano che sembrano rivestire un notevole interesse e che solo con futuri scavi ed analisi delle strutture potranno essere confermati o smentiti.

RINGRAZIAMENTI

Si ringrazia in tale sede il prof. P. Data, che gentilmente mi ha fornito informazioni e fotografie delle immersioni subacquee a Torre di Cerrano.

NOTE   (La bibliografia si trova alla fine del articolo di G. Martella.)

1.   Plinio, *Nat. hist.*, III, 122.
2.   Licofrone, in *Tze Tze*, sez.II.
3.   Aurelio Vittore, *Epitome de Caesaribus*, XIV, I.
4.   Paolo Diacono, *Historia Longobardorum*, II, 19.
5.   Diogini Periegete, in Eustachio, *Descriptio Terrarum*, s.v. Italia.
6.   Eudosso, *Etymologum Magnum*, s.v. Hatria.
7.   Sorricchio 1911, 9.
8.   Plinio, *Nat. Hist.*, III, 18; Pomponio Mela, *Chorographia*, II, 17; Ecateo, in *Hecatei Milesii Fragmenta*, a cura di G. Neci (Firenze 1954), fr. 58, 61, 69; Tolomeo, V, 1, 25; Tacito, *Le Storie*, III, 42.
9.   In RE, *Picenum*, XX, s.v. Hatria.
10.   Plinio, *Nat. hist.*, III, 13, 110.
11.   Strabone, *Geographia*, 5, 4, 2; Festo, 255 L.
12.   Puglisi 1959, 29-44; Landolfi 1988, 357.
13.   Brizio 1901, 190-3; Brizio 1902a, 229-57.
14.   Giove e Baldelli 1982, 633-51.
15.   Ecateo, in Stefano Bizantino, *Viaggio intorno al Mondo*, s.v. Hatria.
16.   Livio, *Periochae*, XI.
17.   Livio, *Storie di Roma*, LVIII, 107.
18.   Livio, *Storie di Roma*, XXII, 9.4; Polibio, *Storie*, III, 88, 3.
19.   Livio, *Storie di Roma*, XXVII, 10, 7-9.
20.   Azzena 1987, 21.
21.   Plinio, *Nat. hist.*, III, 110.
22.   Testo dell'epigrafe: PAULLO FABIO MAXI
              COS PONTIF PATRON
                  COLONIAE
23.   Sparziano, *Scriptores Historia Augusta*, 19, 1.
24.   Aurelio Vittore, *Epitome de Caesaribus*, XIV.
25.   L'iscrizione è conservata attualmente a Palazzo Acquaviva in Atri.
26.   Ephemeris Epigraphica, 1-2.
27.   Cassiodoro, *Variae*, I, 19.
28.   Paolo Diacono, *Historiae Longobardorum*, II.
29.   Per il lavoro 'Studio e Progetto di Massima, Recupero e Valorizzazione Aree Archeologiche e Centri Storici', patrocinato dalla Comunità Montana di Cermignano, attualmente in fase di stampa, hanno preso parte alla compilazione della Carta Archeologica: Dott. G. Martella, Dott. F. Grue, Dott. R. Calanca, Dott. C. Antonelli.
30.   Azzena 1987.
31.   Azzena 1987, 24-64.
32.   Strabone, *Geographia*, V, 4, 214.

33. Sorricchio 1911, 47; Nissen 1883-1902, 34.
34. Ecateo, cfr. nota 15.
35. D'Emilio e Mattucci 1991, 7-10, 25-35.
36. Data e Angeletti 1983, 117-23, fig. 1-6.
37. Data e Angeletti 1983, 120.
38. Cherubini 1882, 419.
39. Sorricchio 1911, 47.

L'AGER HATRIANUS: SFRUTTAMENTO ECONOMICO DEL TERRITORIO, CONTATTI E SCAMBI COMMERCIALI

G. Martella
Via Finocchi 68, 64032 Atri(TE), Italy

L'Ager Hatrianus è un territorio caratterizzato da ampi terrazzi fluviali e da una cospicua abbondanza di acqua che ha favorito lo stanziamento di popoli fin dalla preistoria, testimoniato da moltissimi rinvenimenti lungo tutto il corso del fiume Vomano e che ha avuto una sua continuità anche in periodo romano. La scelta del luogo da occupare è sempre stata subordinata alla presenza di acqua ed alla possibilità di difesa del territorio occupato, per questo la civiltà romana ha lasciato vestigia in tutto l'*Ager*, sebbene i romani fossero in grado di sopperire alla mancanza di acqua nelle immediate vicinanze con l'utilizzo di acquedotti o fonti, impostati su preesistenti sistemi cunicolari naturali.

L'esistenza di un tracciato viario, favoriva ulteriormente la fondazione di abitati, nei pressi di crocevie, di grandi arterie o tratturi, utilizzati per il passaggio di uomini, di bestiame, di merci e di idee.

Il territorio dell'*Ager Hatrianus* appare articolato in una serie di *pagi* ruotanti intorno a centri maggiori quali Atri, l'antica *Hatria Picena,* e Basciano, località nella quale è stato individuato il *Vicus* di S.Rustico posto alla confluenza dei fiumi Vomano e Mavone ed attraversato da una strada di età imperiale.[1] Iscrizioni rinvenute *in loco* attestano la presenza di *magistri vici* qui ed anche a Cellino Attanasio.[2]

Principali attività della zona sono sempre state l'agricoltura e la pastorizia, praticate secondo usi propri e con notevoli profitti. Per quanto concerne l'agricoltura, essa era organizzata secondo una parcellizzazione del territorio che ha permesso il costituirsi di una serie notevole di ville rustiche nelle quali si provvedeva sia alla produzione sia alla vendita dei prodotti. È possibile notare ciò osservando il grafico che dimostra come le strutture riferibili a ville costituiscano la maggioranza dei rinvenimenti (Fig. 3). I prodotti piu coltivati erano il grano, l'ulivo e la vite, ed è proprio la vite che ha fatto conoscere questa zona d'Abruzzo nel bacino del Mediterraneo.

Il vino prodotto nell'*Ager Hatrianus* era piuttosto famoso nell'antichità, tanto che ne parlano i più autorevoli storici e medici di età repubblicana ed imperiale.

Plinio tramanda la notizia secondo la quale la produzione del vino in Italia ha origini antiche, ma che viene apprezzata solo a partire dal 154 a.C circa, in un periodo in cui l'Italia prende coscienza della propria ricchezza e comincia a sviluppare il senso della conservazione e del suo uso abituale.[3] Per l'*Ager Hatrianus* abbiamo però un informazione precedente tramandataci da Polibio che riporta la notizia secondo la quale Annibale, dopo aver distrutto questa zona, lavò i suoi cavalli con il vino prodotto nella regione per curare la scabbia che li aveva colpiti.[4] Quindi deduciamo che il vino nell'*Ager Hatrianus* fosse già prodotto con successo alla fine del III sec. a.C. e la fama crebbe sempre di più. Le sue virtù terapeutiche erano conosciute anche da Dioscoride di Anazarbo, che lo ritiene poco astringente e tale da non infestare i nervi, e da Galeno di Pergamo che dice come fosse salutare per i vecchi, astringente, austero e nobile.[5] All'opinione di Galeno si associa anche Ateneo, il quale aggiunge che sono migliori i vini invecchiati di qualche anno.[6]

La zona è nota anche oggi per la sua produzione di buon vino, ed oggi come allora, la produzione è affidata alle 'ville rustiche', ai contadini che in parte lo vendono ad aziende maggiori, ed in parte lo conservano per sè. Vari rinvenimenti archeologici attestano l'antica parcellizzazione del territorio che risale, all'incirca, agli anni seguenti la guerra sociale, ed anche le antiche case coloniche e fattorie. Per ciò che riguarda la zona settentrionale dell' Ager si deve al Dr A.R. Staffa l'aver eseguito una attenta ricognizione sul territorio che ha permesso di dare concretezza alle fonti aggiungendo nuovi elementi.[7] Una particolarità che ha caratterizzato l'area è la mancanza di sinecismo in età augustea. Il territorio continuò ad essere diviso in *vici* e *pagi* senza che singoli membri si riunissero in un unico nucleo; come si è già detto, sono identificabili almeno due *vici* nella zona, escludendo la colonia latina di *Hatria*, Basciano-Vico S.Rustico e Cellino Attanasio, attestati da fonti epigrafiche.

Questa divisione può spiegare perchè solo il vino ha varcato i confini nazionali, mentre altri prodotti per cui la zona era famosa si sono mossi solo in ambito nazionale. Ricordiamo, ad esempio, le olive esportate a Roma e Pompei, il grano prodotto in abbondanza, tanto da permettere ad uno dei maggiori centri produttivi di derivarne il nome, infatti, sembra che Cermignano derivi il suo toponimo da Cerere, la dea delle produzioni cerearicole, appunto per la grande produzione locale.[8]

Altro prodotto molto apprezzato, secondo Plinio, era l'olio, nè dobbiamo dimenticare le galline e le pecore anch'esse note nell'antichità.[9] Ecateo, ripreso da Stefano Bizantino e Plinio, racconta che le galline e le pecore erano molto feconde, tantoché queste ultime partorivano due volte l'anno; Plinio ci parla ancora delle galline notando che erano piccolissime, mentre Aristotele aggiunge che erano talmente feroci da uccidere i propri figli.[10]

Abbiamo parlato dell'esportazione del vino, ma dove e come avveniva? Plinio ci dice che il vino di Atri era molto apprezzato ad Atene ed Alessandria, ed infatti entusiasti ne erano gli Egizi ancora nel III sec. d.C. secondo tre frammenti dei papiri di Ossirinco che ci riferiscono come questo vino fosse ritenuto migliore degli altri; si fa anche menzione di anfore definite Adrianas nelle quali, probabilmente, il vino veniva trasportato.[11]

Le indagini archeologiche nella valle del Vomano non hanno ancora portato a scavi di un livello tale da poter portare in luce delle fornaci e quindi dare corpo alle varie ipotesi che sono state formulate, si parla di Atri, di Cellino, ma nulla di concreto e tangibile è stato ancora rivelato. Con certezza si può affermare che per lo più fossero le ville rustiche a produrre contenitori fittili per uso proprio, come una villa rinvenuta a Guardia Vomano che ha restituito resti di una fornace che doveva produrre sia ceramica che laterizi, e tanti altri insediamenti rustici nella zona di Cellino Attanasio.

Ci sono varie ipotesi anche sul tipo di anfore che venivano prodotte ed utilizzate per il commercio del vino. L'ipotesi più probabile è quella secondo la quale il vino di Atri fosse esportato in anfore del tipo Lamboglia 2 e che fossero prodotte nella colonia latina (Fig.11). Dobbiamo tenere presenti le fonti antiche sempre perchè offrono notizie per noi importanti, ed anche per la produzione anforaria abbiamo testimonianze 'd'epoca'. Antiphilo di Bisanzio e Antipatro di Tessalonica accennano al vino atriano contenuto in anfore di Adria.[12] Queste sono ritenute solidissime da Plinio, Esichio le accomuna a quelle corcirane e la loro fama giunge fino al III sec. d.C.[13]

Tchernia ritiene che le Lamboglia 2 fossero prodotte ad Atri e non ad Adria nel Veneto perchè proprio le fonti indicano l'agro atriano a Sud del Piceno come grande produttore di vino.[14] Anche Silio Italico menziona questo territorio come ricco di vigneti.[15]

La collocazione cronologica di questo tipo di anfora è alla fine dell'età repubblicana ed è tipico delle regioni adriatiche. Come già accennato, la località in cui veniva prodotto, non è ancora stata individuata, ma Tchernia ritiene probabile che sia proprio Atri, facendo riferimento ad una informazione contenuta nelle Notizie degli Scavi del 1882 in cui si legge che nei pressi della suddetta città si rinvenne un tappo d'anfora con le lettere arcaiche HAT, non raro a trovarsi e per lo studioso questa è una prova che una produzione di anfore ci sia stata già dal II sec. a.C.[16] Di bolli su anfore in città ne sono stati ritrovati tanti, i più recenti appartengono agli scavi effettuati nell'area a SE della Cattedrale e riportati dal Dr Azzena nella carta archeologica della città, nonchè i rinvenimento del Cherubini ed, infine, i punzoni bronzei rinvenuti nel territorio.[17]

Aggiunge sicurezza a questa ipotesi la produzione fittile decorativa e cultuale nonchè la produzione di laterizi bollati HP per la construzione di edifici di pubblica utilità.

Dati archeologici che attestano la frequenza di anfore Lamboglia 2 ve ne sono, si tratta soprattutto di rinvenimenti effettuati durante ricognizioni sul territorio ed interessano tutto l'agro atriano, dalle ville rustiche di Guardia Vomano, all'area di Colle Morino fino alla foce del Vomano, in località Antiche Scerne.

Un nuovo elemento è aggiunto dalla studiosa M.B. Carre che pubblica la notizia del rinvenimento di una fornace per Lamboglia 2 (di tipo C secondo la divisione tipologica fatta da Peacock, infatti i puntali delle anfore rinvenute in questa fornace sono a bottone) a Cologna Spiaggia a circa 28km da Atri.[18]

Indice di contatti con altri paesi sono degli oggetti particolari venuti alla luce in varie epoche ed in varie località.

Ad Atri nel 1902, in località La Pretara, si rinvenne un sepolcreto dell'età del ferro di una cinquantina di tombe a fossa con corredo in una delle quali era contenuto uno scarebeo in pasta vitrea bianca con l'incisione di uno sparviero, una penna di struzzo e un vasetto a forma di cratere. Si tratta di un oggetto particolare che aveva significato solo per gli Egizi, all'epoca, rappresentando per loro il moto del sole e della luna; da notare che un simile esemplare è stato rinvenuto anche nella necropoli di Campovalano.

Un particolare rilievo meritano nove tombe rinvenute nel 1974 a Penna Sant'Andrea dalla Dr.ssa Scrinari, all'epoca Soprintendente archeologo di Chieti.

Le nove sepolture ad inumazione, tutte femminili, presentano un corredo piuttosto singolare; non vi compaiono, infatti, oggetti di uso comune, quali pesi da telaio o fuseruole, ma solo oggetti ornamentali e da toletta, come fibule, anelli digitali, netta-unghie.

La particolarità che, tuttavia, contraddistingue una delle tombe classificata come N.8, di incerta datazione, è la presenza di due testine fenice barbate in pasta vitrea, delle quali la più grande ornava la fronte della defunta, grazie ad una acconciatura rituale formata da una cuffia trattenuta da perle vitree, dischetti ossei e bulle in bronzo disposti a festoni sul capo (Figg. 12-13).[19]

Il Dr D'Ercole ha ipoteticamente supposto che le sepolture siano appartenute a sacerdotesse di un collegio religioso o a persone di una casta particolare, ricordando che vicino alla necropoli, in località Monte Giove, era situato un tempio.[20]

Questo tipo di testine fenice è stato rinvenuto a Cartagine, in Sardegna, in Sicilia, in Etruria ed anche in Abruzzo, a Montebello di Bertona.[21]

Le testine, in genere, rappresentano divinità puniche quali Baal-Hammon o Astarte-Tanit; proprio con quest'ultima è possibile collegare la pratica della prostituzione sacra che, in ambito locale, è testimoniata in età posteriore in relazione al culto di Cerere, come rivela una stele rinvenuta a Rapino nella quale viene approvata per il popolo marrucino una *lex publica* per l'istituzione della *hierodouleia* nel santuario di Giove Padre dell'Arce Tarincria. Secondo la legge, le schiave ancelle del santuario dovevano prostituirsi in onore di Cerere ed il denaro ricavato poteva essere utilizzato per il proprio affrancamento.[22]

Questa iscrizione è stata oggetto di una conferenza tenuta dal Dr Adriano La Regina presso la Facoltà di Lettere e Filosofia dell'Università di Chieti, nell'ambito della quale il Dr D'Ercole è intervenuto ricordando che la singolarità dei corredi femminili di Penna S.Andrea indurrebbe a suggerire l'appartenenza delle donne ad un collegio religioso forse dedito alla prostituzione sacra.[23]

Ciò spiegherebbe l'acconciatura della defunta nella tomba n.8 e non escluderebbe l'introduzione di credenze religiose straniere accanto agli oggetti di importazione fenicia quali le testine.

La stele di Rapino è un documento distante sia cronologicamente (è più recente di almeno un secolo) che geograficamente da Penna S.Andrea, tuttavia, non si può non soffermarsi sul fatto che il tempio, prossimo alle sepolture, si trova nel comune di Cermignano, il cui toponimo è collegabile con la dea Cerere, in onore della quale si praticava la prostituzuione sacra, e che la località dove sorgeva il tempio è denominata Monte Giove.

È utile ricordare che rapporti locali con il popolo fenicio non dovevano essere rari, se in un tesoretto monetario, rinvenuto a Tortoreto, è compresa una moneta fenicia e se navi puniche sono rappresentate su tre stele provenienti da Novilara rappresentanti battaglie navali.[24]

Sempre a Penna S.Andrea, nella stessa zona della necropoli, sono state rinvenute tre stele funerarie riproducenti a rilievo nella parte superiore volti barbati, terminanti probabilmente con un copricapo realizzato separatamente. Queste stele, dalla forma allungata e stretta, recano nella parte anteriore iscrizioni italiche con andamento bustrofedico. Solo due di esse conservano a rilievo il volto barbato del defunto.

Le tre stele sono state datate al V sec. a.C. e rappresentano una sorta di evoluzione rispetto alla statua del famoso Guerriero di Capestrano databile al VI sec. a.C.

Adriano La Regina ne ha fatto un' analisi approfondita', evincendo particolari salienti. Il primo dato importante è che dalle tre stele emerge una pertinenza etnica espressa nel modo seguente: *safinus, safinum, safinas, safina*.[25]

Tale pertinenza etnica individua i Sabini come popolo abitante la zona, come è naturale, dal momento che i Piceni, così come i Sanniti, erano di stirpe sabina, staccatisi dal ceppo originario per un *Ver sacrum* sotto le insegne del *Picus*. Anche la forma etnica identificante i piceni, rintracciabile nel termine *pupun*, è presente nelle stele provenienti dalla zona centro settentrionale del Piceno, da Magliano, Loro Piceno, Catignano, S. Omero.[26]

Le tre stele riportano, inoltre, la più antica testimonianza della *touta*, cioè della *res publica*, già diffusa ad esempio fra i Marrucini, come conferma la stele di Rapino, mentre la fase regia è attestata dal Guerriero di Capestrano.

È quindi importante che le testimonianze esistenti per il VI-V sec. a.C. siano unitarie e cioè abbiano potuto dar vita al paleosabellico che, dal III sec. a.C., prenderà differenziazioni dialettali, a seconda delle aree e dei singoli gruppi etnici: Piceni, Peligni, Marrucini, Vestini, Pretuzi, ecc.

Si colloca in un quadro di contatti con l'Illiria un pettorale bronzeo proveniente dalla necropoli di S.Giovanni al Mavone, nel comune di Basciano, probabilmente di ispirazione illirica (Figg. 14-15).

Il pettorale è in bronzo ed in origine doveva essere composto da due lastre di cui una trapezoidale ed una a navicella con le cime ornate da protomi ornitomorfe. L'esemplare di cui si parla conserva solo la piastra trapezoidale spessa cm 0,1, larga min. cm 0,27 max. cm 0,88, lunga cm 0,58, decorata sulla superficie superiore da disegni geometrici che ne delineano i contorni. Questo tipo di pendaglio trova confronti con le culture liburnica, dauna e picena.

È ormai accertato che la civiltà picena abbia assorbito molti degli usi e costumi dei Liburni a partire dalla tarda età del bronzo fino alla fine dell'età del ferro, quando cioè il popolo liburnico perde la sua importanza ed il suo predominio sull'Adriatico.

È Plinio a dare informazioni circa il passaggio di alcune stirpi illiriche che dalle loro sedi mossero verso la Grecia e verso l'Italia centro-meridionale, in particolare, ricorda la venuta dei Liburni nel Piceno.[27]

Tre furono le ondate migratorie pannonico balcaniche: la prima alla fine del XIII sec. a.C., la seconda alla fine del XII sec. a.C. e la terza alla fine del X sec. a.C. La stirpe liburnica è presente nel Piceno dalla terza migrazione dopo la quale si diffonde in Italia centrale e meridionale e questa presenza coincide con l'inizio dell'età del ferro. Lo sviluppo si interrompe dal VI-V sec. a.C. in poi, secoli nei quali assistiamo alla dominazione greco-etrusca e poi all'espansione romana che provoca l'impoverimento dello sviluppo autonomo.

È comprensibile la posizione dominante del gruppo liburnico sull'Adriatico fino al V sec. a.C., poichè la sua forza si basava sulla navigazione e sul commercio, e ciò ha loro permesso di colonizzare l'Adriatico, ma non il Mediterraneo, poichè in tal modo avrebbero intaccato gli interessi dei Greci.

Il pendaglio rinvenuto a Basciano rientra in questo quadro di corrispondenze liburnico-picene, essendo, forse, nato come modello in area liburnica ed è poi passato in Daunia dove cambia completamente la forma originaria.

Dai confronti con esemplari rinvenuti nelle necropoli picene[28] e conservati nei musei di Ancona,[29] Ascoli Piceno,[30] Villa Giulia[31] e nelle necropoli di Novilara-Servici[32] emerge che il pettorale preso in considerazione presenta elementi di maggiore antichità dal momento che è molto più schematico, ha un numero minore di catenelle ed è meno elegante, ma proprio per questo più rispondente al modello originale. Ad esso si avvicinano due esemplari da Porto S.Elpidio confrontabili con il tipo da Zaton e Nin.[33] Altri confronti in area illirica si possono fare con pendagli rinvenuti a Zaton tomba 6, Nin tomba 13, Komplje tomba 263 e di altri rinvenuti nelle stesse zone, segnalati da Batovic, Lo Schiavo e Stipcevic.[34]

Molto diversi sono gli esemplari rinvenuti nel territorio melfese ed in Daunia, ma sempre collegabili con oggetti già esistenti in Illiria. Si confrontino i pendagli di Ascoli Satriano,[35] Lavello,[36] Monte Saraceno,[37] confrontabili con oggetti simili provenienti da Zaton, Prozor e Nin.[38] Il Dumitrescu segnala l'esistenza di pettorali di tipo piceno anche nella cultura di Halstatt e nelle regioni di Perugia, Norcia, etc.[39]

Riguardo alla datazione del pettorale di Basciano, non sembra inopportuna una collocazione all'VIII sec. a.C., tenendo anche conto della datazione della Lollini per gli esemplari di Porto S.Elpidio che maggiormente si avvicinano a quello di Basciano.

Un elemento caratterizzante la colonia latina di *Hatria* è l'esistenza di una serie monetale fusa che dà lustro alla città e pone dei problemi di datazione sui quali si dibattono da sempre gli studiosi (Fig. 16). Infatti, le tesi più discusse vertono sulla collocazione temporale delle monete, poiché una datazione alta supporrebbe un nucleo abitativo di un certo livello ed uno sviluppo tale da necessitare il conio di una propria moneta; invece, la datazione bassa ridimensionerebbe il tutto riportando il conio delle monete ad una zecca romana.

Questo problema di datazione nasce dal fatto che le monete di Atri seguono l'unità librale italica-orientale dal peso di g 379 e non quella romana di g 327 e dal fatto che le monete hanno una divisione decimale della libbra e non duodecimale come accade nella libbra romana. I maggiori studiosi di numismatica si sono espressi per questo problema. Delfico, Sambon, Pansa, Sorrichio ed Hackens propendono per una cronologia alta precedente al 289 a.C., data della deduzione di *Hatria* a colonia latina.[40] In questo caso, si supporrebbe un' area di gravititazione commerciale in Adriatico con contatti con Siracusa, da cui deriverebbe l'*aes grave* romano dagli italici orientali che avrebbero tratto i loro tipi da modelli magno-greci.

Mommsen, Head, Thomsen, Panvini Rosati, Cianfarani seguono la teoria della datazione bassa notando come la zecca di Roma abbia influenzato la monetazione atriana ad esempio con il segno del valore caratteristico delle monete romane repubblicane; in questo caso il commercio sarebbe stato interno e per l'estero avrebbero usato monete della zecca romana.[41]

Sulla moneta di *Hatria* usata per scambi commerciali, ha esposto una sua teoria il Crawford proprio in occasione del presente Convegno. Egli ritiene che le monete atriane siano romane, coniate intorno al 270 a.C., forse emesse durante la guerra pirrica o la I guerra punica e che la legenda sia in latino. La loro durata copre circa un decennio e pare che non siano indice di commercio, bensì potrebbe trattarsi di una monetazione militare a circolazione limitata. In ogni caso è bene ricordare che sono state rinvenute anche nel territorie riminese.

La serie di queste monete comprende undici pezzi di sette valori e solo due sono le serie complete conservate nella Collezione Sorricchio e nella Collezione di Lord Narvik a Londra.

Degni di nota, anche se non sono indici di commercio, sono degli oggetti di fattura etrusca conservati presso il British Museum di Londra che pare vengano da Atri, ma la notizia è piuttosto dubbia.

Si tratta di una collana, un paio di orecchini, un anello ed uno specchio facenti parte della Collezione Hamilton e passati in seguito al British Museum nel 1772.[42] Nel manoscritto del catalogo della suddetta Collezione è indicata la provenienza come Viterbo, poi corretta in Atri ed inoltre non si menziona lo specchio.

Atri ed il suo territorio hanno avuto un glorioso passato che in qualche modo li ha portati a contatto con altri popoli che ne hanno potuto apprezzare le qualità. La speranza è che vi siano degli scavi in futuro che possano dissipare le ombre che ancora avvolgono la storia di questo territorio.

NOTE

1.   Messineo e Pellegrino 1986, 136-66.
2.   Staffa e Moscetta 1986, 194.
3.   Plinio, *Nat. hist*, XIV, 11 (13), 87; XIV, 14 (16), 97.
4.   Polibio, *Historiae*, III, 88,3.
5.   Dioscoride di Anazarbo, *Rerum medicarum*, V, 10; Galeno di Pergamo, *Meth.medem.*, p. 7; c7; 1,12, c4; *De arte curativa*, 1.2, c.2; Class.7;2,1,5c.5.
6.   Ateneo, *I deipnosofisti a banchetto*, I, 30.
7.   Staffa e Moscetta 1986, 167-217; Staffa 1986a; 1986b.
8.   Marziale, XIII, 36; IV, 46,13.
9.   Plinio, *Nat. hist.*, XV, 16.
10. Ecateo, *Viaggio intorno al mondo*, v. Italia (in Stefano Bizantino); Plinio, *Nat. hist.*, X, 53; Dionigi Periegete, *Descrizione della terra,* Italia (in Eustachio); Aristotele, *Storia degli animali*, VI, 1.
11. Rathbone 1983, 81-98.
12. *Antologia greca*, VI, 257,2 (Antiphilo di Bisanzio); IX, 232, 1 (Antipatro di Tessalonica).
13. Plinio, *Nat. hist.*, XXXV, 12; Esichio, *Raccolta in ordine alfabetico di tutte le voci*, s.v. Ceramiche.
14. Tchernia 1986, 168.
15. Silio Italico, XV, vv. 568-569; VIII, vv. 433-439.
16. Cherubini 1882, 149.
17. Azzena 1987, 104-6; Cherubini 1877, 14-15; *CIL* IX, Signacula, 14, 42, 55, 91, 95, 143, 148.
18. Carre 1989, 80-5.
19. D'Ercole 1986, 134, nota 5.
20. *Idem, ibidem*, 131.
21. Il materiale di Montebello, inedito, è attualmente oggetto di studio in una tesi di laurea della Dr P. Riccitelli.
22. Vetter 1983, 218.
23. La Conferenza 'Lex Marrucinorum de sacro meretricio' è stata tenuta il 13/05/1991.
24. de Petra 1896; Dumitrescu 1929, 13-20.
25. La Regina 1986, 125-30; *idem* 1981, 129-37.
26. *Idem, ibidem*, 129.
27. Plinio, *Nat. hist.*, III, 110,112. Si veda anche Festo, *De verb.sign.*, 1913, 248.
28. Dumitrescu 1929, indica le necropoli di Novilara-Molaroni, Novilara-Sevici, Cupramarittima, Belmonte, Montegiorgio, Monteroberto, Acquaviva Picena, Monteprandone.
29. Dall'Osso 1915, 164.
30. Randall-McIver 1927, 729, pls. 27-28.

31.   Scapaticci 1980, tav. XXII, c.

32.   Brizio 1902b, tav. VIII, 34-43.

33.   Porto S. Elpidio: scavi eseguiti nel 1917, zona A, tomba 6, ancora inediti nel 1976; Lo Schiavo 1970, 466, tav. XXXV, 8-17; un esemplare compare anche in Lollini 1972, tav. III, 20, p. 124.

34.   Batovic 1965, tav. VIII, 15, 1; *idem* 1968a; *idem* 1968a, pl. III,1; Lo Schiavo 1970, tav. III, 2-3; Stipcevic 1963, 56.

35.   AA.VV. *La Daunia antica* (Milano 1984), figg. 203-206, p. 165.

36.   Adamesteanu 1974, 461-74, tav. CVI, tomba 104.

37.   De Juliis 1984; Batovic 1975, tav. 104, p. 405.

38.   Batovic 1975, tav. 104, nn. 3, 4, 5, 6, 7, 8, 9, p. 405.

39.   Dumitrescu 1929, p. 137, note nn. 1-11, p. 137, 1-2, p. 138.

40.   Azzena 1987, 10, nota n. 2.

41.   *Idem, ibidem*, 11, nota n. 3.

42.   Fabbricotti 1982-83, 272-7, con indicazioni bibliografiche.

BIBLIOGRAFIA per O. Menozzi e G. Martella

Adamesteanu, D. 1974. *La Basilicata antica, storia e monumenti.* Cava dei Tirreni

Adamesteanu, D. 1974. Metaponto. *Atti del XII Convegno di Studi sulla Magna Grecia.* Napoli

Azzena, G. 1987. *Atri.* Rome

AA.VV. 1984. *La Daunia Antica.* Milan

Batovic, S. 1965. Die Eisenzeit auf dem Gebiet des Illyrischen Stammes der Liburnen. *Archeologia Jugoslavica* **6**

Batovic, S. 1968a. *Nin in Prehistory.* Zadar

Batovic, S. 1968b. *Nin, Problems of Archaeological Excavation.* Zadar

Batovic, S. 1975. L'Età del ferro in Dalmazia. In, *Civiltà preistoriche e protostoriche della Daunia.* Florence

Brizio, E. 1901. La necropoli del colle della Giustizia. *NSc*, 190-3

Brizio, E. 1902a. La necropoli della Pretara. *NSc*, 229-57

Brizio, E. 1902b. La necropoli di Novilara-Servici. *MonAnt* **V**, 34-43

Carre, M.B. e Cipriano, M.T. 1989. Production et typologie des amphores sur la côte adriatique de l'Italie. In, *Amphorae romanes et histoire economique*, Collection de l'Ecole Française de Rome, 67-104.

Cherubini, G. 1882. Rinvenimenti di anfore. *NSc* **7**, 149, 419

Cherubini, G. 1877. Cunicoli e recinto emisferico a occidente della città. *NSc* **2**, 14-15, 125-6, 144-5, 217

Dall'Osso, I. 1915. *Guida illustrata del Museo Nazionale di Ancona*, 164. Ancona

Data, P. e Angeletti, G. 1983. *Cerrano ieri e oggi.* S. Atto

D'Emilio, L. e Mattucci, L. 1991. *Il porto di Atri: un invito alla ricerca.* Teramo

D'Ercole, V. 1986. Penna S.Andrea, Necropoli e santuario. In, *La valle del medio e basso Vomano*, 131-6. Rome

De Juliis, E.M. 1984. Magna Grecia, Epiro e Macedonia. *Atti Taranto XXIV*

Dumitrescu, V. 1929. *L'età del ferro nel Piceno.* Bucarest

Fabbricotti, E. 1982-83. Segnalazioni. *Quaderni dell'Instituto di Archeologia e Storia Antica.* Università di Chieti, 3. Chieti

Giove, M e Baldelli, G. 1982. Necropoli dell'Età del ferro in Atri. In, *Studi in onore di Ferranti Rittatore Vonwiller*, 633-51. Como

Landolfi, M. 1988. I Piceni. In, *Italia omnium terrarum alumna,* 315-72. Rome

La Regina, A. 1981. Appunti su entità etniche e strutture istituzionali nel Sannio antico. *AION*, 129-37

La Regina, A. 1986. Penna S. Andrea. Le stele paleosabelliche. In, *La valle del medio e basso Vomano*. Rome

Lollini, D.G. 1976. *Sintesi della civiltà picena. Jadranska Obala u protostorji*, 117-52. Zagreb

Lo Schiavo, F. 1970. Il gruppo liburnico iapodico. *MemLinc*, s. VIII, vol. **XIV**, fasc. **6**, 466.

Messineo, G. e Pellegrino, A. 1986. Il Vicus di S.Rustico. In, *La valle del medio e basso Vomano*, 136-58. Rome

Nissen, H. 1883-1902. *Italische Landeskunde.* Berlin

Peacock, D.P.S. e Williams, D.F. 1986. *Amphorae and the Roman Economy.* London

de Petra G. 1896. Tortoreto - Ripostiglio di monete fuse e battute. *NSC,* 366-8

Puglisi, S.M. 1959. La civiltà del Piceno dalla preistoria alla protostoria alla luce delle più recenti scoperte. In, I Piceni e la civiltà etrusco-italica, *Atti del Convegno Studi Etruschi* II, 29-44

Randall-MacIver, D. 1927. *The Iron Age in Italy.* Oxford

Rathbone, D.W. 1983. Italian Wines in Roman Egypt. *Opus* **II**, 81-98

Scapaticci, M.G. 1980. Bronzi inediti al Museo Nazionale di Villa Guilia. *StEtr* XLVIII, 70-2

Sorricchio, L. 1911. *Hatria-Atri* I. Rome

Staffa, A.R. e Moscetta, M.P. 1986. Contributo per una carta archeologica della media e bassa valle del Vomano. In, *La valle del medio e basso Vomano*, 167-217. Rome

Staffa, A.R. 1986a. Note preliminari sulle produzione ceramiche comuni fra la tarda repubblica e l'età imperiale. In, *La valle del medio e basso Vomano*, 224-43. Rome

Staffa, A.R. 1986b. Economia ed insediamenti fra l'età repubblicana e la prima età imperiale: le produzioni vinarie. In, *La valle del medio e basso Vomano*, 244-51. Rome

Stipcevic, A. 1963. *Arte degli Illiri*. Milan

Tchernia, A. 1986. Le vin de l'Italie romaine. *BEFAR* **261**, 51-7, 167-8, 259-61, 348-9

Vetter, E. 1983. *Handbuch der italischen Dialecte*. Heidelberg

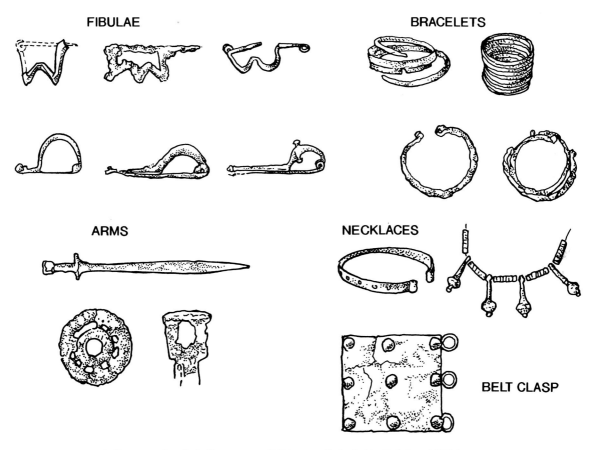

FIBULAE

BRACELETS

ARMS

NECKLACES

BELT CLASP

Fig. 1   Materiali provenienti delle necropoli Picene di Atri (da Brizio, 1902a)

Fig. 2   L'Ager Hatrianus ed i suoi confini:

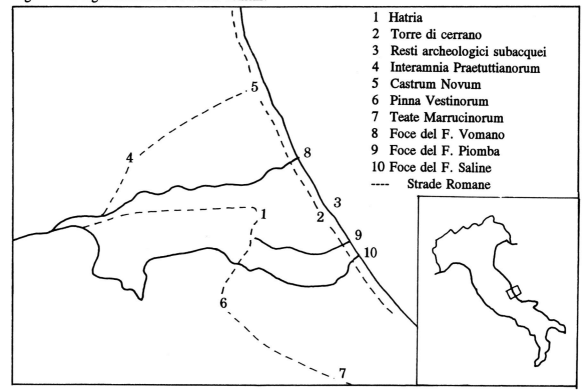

1   Hatria
2   Torre di cerrano
3   Resti archeologici subacquei
4   Interamnia Praetuttianorum
5   Castrum Novum
6   Pinna Vestinorum
7   Teate Marrucinorum
8   Foce del F. Vomano
9   Foce del F. Piomba
10 Foce del F. Saline
----   Strade Romane

233

CRONOLOGIA DEGLI INSEDIAMENTI

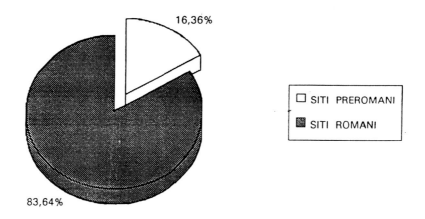

16,36%

83,64%

☐ SITI PREROMANI

▨ SITI ROMANI

TIPOLOGIA DEGLI INSEDIAMENTI PER IL PERIODO PREROMANO

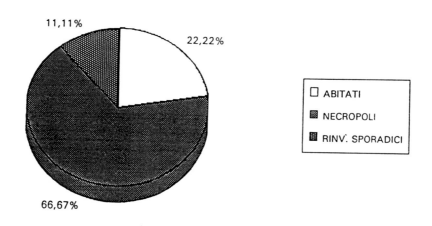

11,11%

22,22%

66,67%

☐ ABITATI

▨ NECROPOLI

▨ RINV. SPORADICI

TIPOLOGIA DEGLI INSEDIAMENTI PER IL PERIODO ROMANO

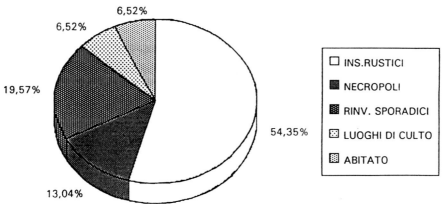

6,52%

6,52%

19,57%

54,35%

13,04%

☐ INS.RUSTICI

▨ NECROPOLI

▨ RINV. SPORADICI

▨ LUOGHI DI CULTO

▨ ABITATO

Fig. 3   Dati statistici sulla cronologia e la tipoligia dei siti archeologici dell'Ager Hatrianus

4

5

Fig. 4 Tracce dei resti archeologici subacquei visibili da ricognizione aerea
Fig. 5 Resti del molo

235

6

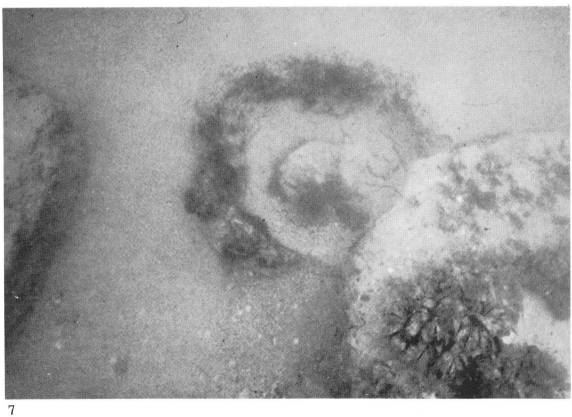

7

Figs. 6,7   Resti delle strutture murarie ed elementi architettonici

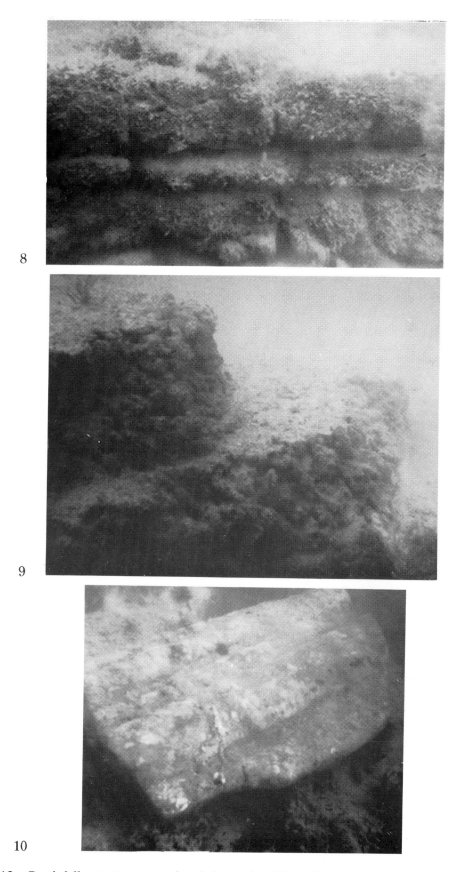

8

9

10

Figs. 8-10   Resti delle strutture murarie ed elementi architettonici

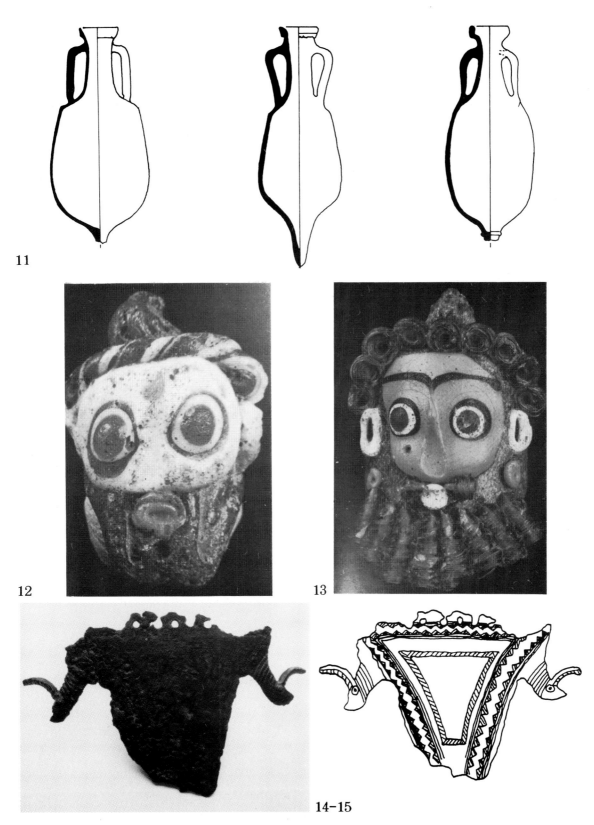

11

12   13

14-15

Fig. 11   Tipologia delle anfore Lamboglia 2 (Peacock and Williams 1986)
Figs. 12-13   Testine barbate finice in pasta vitrea da una necropoli di Penna S. Andrea (D'Ercole
                 1986)
Figs. 14-15   Rappresentazioni del pendaglio proveniente da Basciano-S. Giovanni al Mavone

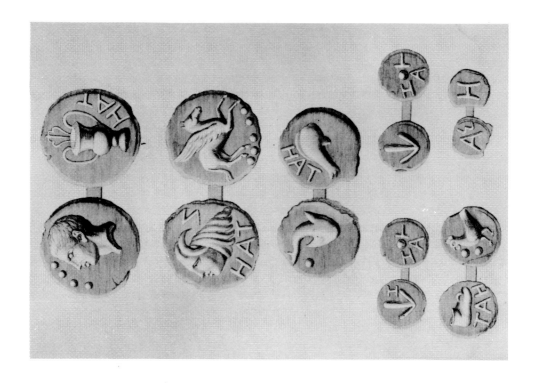

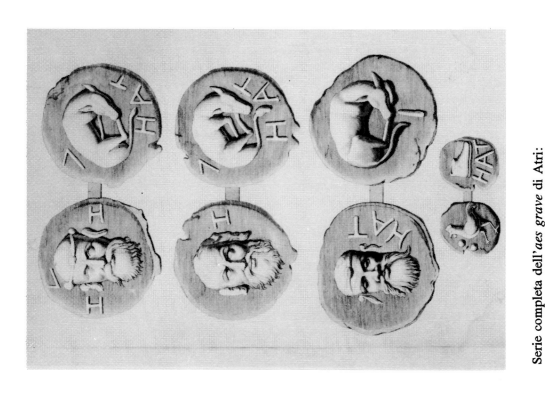

Fig. 16   Serie completa dell'*aes grave* di Atri:

1-3 Asse: D/testa barbata senile di fronte; iscrizione HAT. R/ cane accovacciato   4 Sestante: D/Calzatura a destra; iscrizione HAT. R/ gallo a sinistra   5 Triente: D/testa giovanile imberbe a sn; R/ Kantharos; iscrizione HAT   6 Quincuncia: D/testa sporgente da un *murex*; iscrizione HAT. R/Pegaso a ds.   7 Quadrante: D/delfino a sn.; iscrizione HAT. pesce raia   8-11 Oncia

ROMAN EXPORTS TO THE NORTH
WINE IN THE WEST: A VIEW FROM CAMPANIA

Paul Arthur

Dipartimento di Beni Culturali, Università degli Studi di Lecce, Via D. Birago 64, LECCE, Italy

The significance of Campania has often been underestimated by classical archaeologists, probably because of a lack of published fieldwork. Even so, this may occasion a certain amount of surprise given the rich textual and epigraphic evidence not only for its own direct role in the Roman economy as an area of agrarian surplus production, but also for its role as middleman between Rome and the provinces.[1] In this paper I shall explore Campania's position over the period running roughly from the Second Punic War, when the area began truly to participate in a Mediterranean-wide Roman economy, to the beginning of Imperial times, when it apparently started to lose its grip as it came to terms with provincial interests.

Quite the most abundant material evidence for Campania's economic relations is provided by pottery, pride of place among which should go to commercial amphorae, indicators of the movement of organic goods - principally foodstuffs such as wine and olive oil. It has long been asserted that Campania provided a large quota of the wine exported from Italy, both east and west, in an attempt by the Roman government and *mercatores* to forge political links and exploit the budding markets of developing provinces and other areas of economic interest. Indeed, Campania has at times assumed an undue share of the credit, which is now being rectified through our increasing capabilities in analysing ceramic fabrics and typologies. Its wine exportation was flanked by that from Etruria and Latium, from Calabria, Puglia and Sicily, and eventually from provincial areas such as Cisalpine Gaul, southern France and Spain, and even from Hellenic territories such as the Rhodian Pereia. Even so, there is no doubt that Campania was one of the foremost lands of surplus wine production from at least as early as the beginning of the second century BC.

What effects did this somewhat privileged position in agrarian surplus production have on the region and on Roman policy in general? The rather extraordinary role of the area has been examined by scholars from standpoints of family interests or of urban and architectural development. This paper will examine ceramic evidence for Campania's exceptional economic position, taking the view that most wine in later Republican times was marketed in amphorae, and that direct trade-corridors or routes are usually marked by distinct distributions and fall-offs of other ceramic vessels that travelled piggy-back as makeweight cargoes. The pattern provided by the ceramic evidence will then be compared with known settlement patterns in the principal areas of Campanian wine production, to see if there are any apparent connections.

The exportation of Campanian ceramic products is eminently attested by a wide distribution, both to the east and to the west, of Graeco-Italic and later amphorae, of dolia, of the fine tablewares, known as Black Glaze A and its red-slipped successors (local sigillata wares) as well as of certain coarse wares, particular among which are mortaria, jugs of form Camulodunum 139, the precocious non-stick 'Pompeian red ware' pans, various other lid-seated pans and flat roofing-tiles.[2] However, it is the distribution of Campanian amphorae, simply as containers, that is the clearest indicator of the shipment of noted wines, upon which much of the economy of Roman Campania was based.

It is still not certain when Campanian amphorae were first exported, though the earliest recognisable wine amphorae seem to date from the second half of the third century BC.[3] Despite a certain amount of petrological analysis conducted in recent years it is still not clear if vessels from sites such as the oppidum of Pech-Maho, in southern France, which has yielded later third-century Graeco-Italic amphorae, or from Ampurias in Spain, effectively came from Campania or from Sicily. Nonetheless, after the Second Punic War Gaul became one of the largest if not, indeed, the largest export market for Italian wine which served as an exchange commodity chiefly for the slaves needed to work the Italian estates, and much of this came from Campania. Through the first half of the second century the problem of acquiring slaves was largely resolved through Roman conquest, the pace of which slackened during the latter part of the century.

In Gaul massive importation of wine took place following the conquest of southern France in 125 BC. Indeed, by 100 BC finds from the site of Nages indicate an Italian monopoly on wine.[4] The Gallic wars, however, broke the Italian monopoly. In the post-Caesarian period quantities of Italian amphorae in France drop markedly, and Spanish and Gaulish products start to dominate the markets.[5] It may be suggested that the disruption provoked by the Gallic conquest led primarily to a difficulty in obtaining slaves at favourable prices, although in the immediate aftermath of the wars many reached Italy as booty. Subsequently the newly opened-up territories saw an expansion of provincial vineyards. Though this presumably created competition for Campania, some Italians themselves would have invested directly in Gallic viticulture, testified perhaps by the establishment of Dressel 1 kiln sites in the Rhône valley during the second half of the first century BC, thus underwriting the costs of importing common wine from central and southern Italy.[6]

Data from Italy, where a slave cost from HS600 upwards and an amphora of *vin ordinaire* cost about HS8 to HS12, seems realistic.[7] The late Republican ships of Albenga and the Madrague de Giens may each have held 10,000 standard wine amphorae.[8] According to Cato a vineyard of 100 *iugera* needed a staff of 30 people excluding the *vilici*, while an olive orchard of 250 *iugera* needed only 24.[9] Ignoring overheads, a shipload of amphorae could, on Italian prices, theoretically equal enough slaves to cultivate over 550 *iugera* of vineyards, especially as slaves would have cost less and wine more in Gaul. Diodorus gives a value of one to one for a wine amphora and a slave on the Gallic market. Though these are very approximate anecdotal figures, they serve the purpose of indicating that the exchange rate for slaves in Gaul was extremely favourable for those who could export enormous quantities of wine, and that substantial profits could be had.[10] Thus, for those who continued to hold the large *fundi* in Italy, if the new economic pattern after the conquest of Gaul did not represent potential economic disaster, at the very least it could have brought about substantial financial loss. We may take a possible example. On archaeological evidence, Gaul appears to have been the major market of the wine production of the family of the Sestii. The production was based in the agricultural hinterland of the town of Cosa, and comprised Dressel 1A wine amphorae bearing stamps of the family and dating from the last years of the second century BC to just after 50 BC, on present dating of the ceramic type. They may be shown to have had a wide distribution in France, following both the Rhône valley route and the Narbo/Toulouse-Garonne (?) route.[11] On present dating, the amphora manufacture of the family, and thus presumably their wine exportation, was arrested abruptly shortly after the mid-first century BC, coinciding with the Gallic wars.[12] It may have been this very event that signalled the demise of rich villas such as Settefinestre, in the *ager Cosanus*, quite possibly a property of the Sestii themselves.

Though the Republican state itself was not seen as actively involved in wine production and relative exchange, various members of the senate and their friends and partisans were actively involved and this, if nothing else, must have created a lobby that influenced government policy in favour of their financial interests. Caesar himself and many of his friends had vested interests in the wine market. Research in the rich lands around the ager Falernus, where many prime vineyards were sited, has yielded names of many of these late Republican landed proprietors, including Caesar and various other contemporary notables such as Lepta, Macula and L. Quinctius.[13] Other names certainly escape us. All the evidence suggests that the northern Campanian property market was lively from Sullan to Caesarian times. The land in and around the ager Falernus was intensively farmed by slave-run villas at this time, and the main produce appears to have been wine. This is shown both by the large number of villas and farms or peripheral sites in existence (Figs. 1, 2), and by the veritable industrial production of wine amphorae along the coast, close to points of overseas shipment.

A good proportion of later Republican wine amphorae found in the provinces are clearly of Campanian origin.[14] There is no doubt regarding vessels in Pompeian 'black sand' fabric, including those with L. EVMACHI stamps, or certain vessels from around the ager Falernus with recognised stamps: L.M., MAESCELS, IESO, ΓΑΓΑ, ΓI, II, VARS, RODO/CALLI and some anepigraphic examples.[15] It is to the former part of this period that we may also assign the Spargi shipwreck, transporting wine and other goods, including Calenian Black Glaze pottery, probably from one or more Campanian estates.[16]

In the period closely following the Gallic wars, the settlement pattern in the ager Falernus remained basically the same, though with a marked increase in the number of kiln sites producing amphorae, and with investment in a small number of exceedingly wealthy maritime villas. The new kiln sites produced Dressel 2-4s, and are also found for the first time at Teanum and Cales, in inland Campania, and even in the Melfa area of the Middle Liri valley.[17] The progressive shift of amphora kilns to inland areas may have represented the attempt to relocate amphora production onto the estates, cutting down on the middlemen who had probably owned and managed the 'industrial' potteries along the coast.

Thus in northern Campania and elsewhere, despite the Gallic wars, commercial agricultural activity appears to have remained healthy if not distinctly buoyant, though of course the increase in number of kiln sites does not necessarily indicate that there had been an increase in the quantities of amphorae produced. This pattern continued into the Principate, though already by the mid-first century AD much of this land had passed under Imperial control, and by the second century a number of sites had become deserted.

If much of the Gallic market was lost to the Italian *fundi*, alternative markets had to be cornered so that they could remain economically viable. Where could alternative markets be found? It is suggested that for a brief time free Britain may have represented one of these alternatives and that various Italian, and especially Campanian, *fundi* geared to producing immense surpluses may have actively targeted Britain as a market.

Peripheral Britain had received Italian wine during the late pre-Roman Iron Age. The Hengistbury Head finds, dating to the second century BC, might suggest exchange for various metals, as Barry Cunliffe has proposed, as well as slaves, and seem to presage the analogous Mediterranean-British trade evidenced by Byzantine amphorae found at Tintagel.[18] It is likely that wine reached Britain largely as a prestigious commodity though through regular exchange and not predominantly, as has recently been suggested, through a system of down-the-line kinship ties and gift exchange, though the Lexden Tumulus with its Augustan medallion does hint at diplomatic overtones shortly before the conquest.[19]

On the export side, some evidence seems to indicate that Britain had become one of the alternative markets to Gaul for Italian and Campanian wine in the period ranging from 50 BC to AD 50.

A number of Dressel 2-4 vessels from Britain are in the typical Pompeian area 'black sand' fabric, including an example stamped MAR OF, from Stanmore, Middlesex. Almost half of the forty-four examples from Sheepen are certainly Italian: eight are apparently from the Pompeii region, while seven others are not provenanced.[20] The majority of Dressel 2-4s from Skeleton Green, against one Dressel 1, are probably Italian, and one is almost certainly Campanian.[21] A Dressel 2-4 amphora from Colchester bears the *titulus pictus* FAL/LOLL, and is very likely to have been imported after the conquest of AD 43.[22] Now while there is no evidence that the Lolli possessed holdings in the *ager Falernus* proper, recent excavations have proved them to have produced wine amphorae and other ceramics at inland Cales, also in northern Campania.[23]

Towards the end of the pre-Roman Iron Age the Italian vessels in Britain were complemented by wine amphorae from both southern and northeastern Spain, naturally enough as these expanding production areas were closer to the British markets.[24] Nonetheless, Italian amphorae continued to arrive, if in lesser quantities than before. At Colchester Sheepen, for example, Dressel 2-4s are commoner than Dressel 1Bs.[25] Perhaps Italian amphorae continued to reach areas of pre-conquest Britain in a persisting trade in slaves, by means of an Atlantic route that had been rather attenuated during the Gallic wars, and later through Romanised Gaul with its own budding surplus production.

Quantities of imported amphorae increased with the conquest of Britain, both as military supplies and as market commodities towards a Roman way of life. What is of particular note is that irrefutable pre-conquest vessels are almost exclusively Italian, though whether Campanian or not is still hard to tell, while with the conquest other types, from the Rhodian Pereia, Cos and elsewhere, make an appearance, perhaps suggesting the breaking of earlier trade monopolies based on exchange of slaves, metals and other commodities and their supplanting by an open market with less favourable rates of exchange.[26] However, despite all these finds, the overall impression is that Italian wine imported into Britain in the century preceding the conquest was but a fraction of that imported into Gaul in the preceding century. Admittedly part of the Italian wine industry may have collapsed in post-Caesarian times, if we may judge from the example of the Sestius amphorae, and overall Italian output may have shrunk. The Campanian productive sector, however, seems to have continued at a fairly healthy rate for a number of decades and, while the British market may have satisfied part of the demand, it cannot have consumed the total output released from the Gaulish market. So, leaving aside a steady or marginally increasing market of Rome, other alternatives need to be located.

The location of the wine-exporting *fundus* of Maesianus Celsus lets us identify stamped Dressel 2-4s and variants from Carthage and Oberaden as having come from Campania.[27] The German campaigns of Augustus certainly took a quota of Campanian wine. Many of the amphorae from Vidy, Avenches and Augst, predominantly of Dressel 2-4 form, are of this period and, though many are still not provenanced, identified examples have been shown to be largely Campanian.[28] However, the greatest quantities seem to have gone south and east.

Carthage itself seems to have taken a large share of Campanian wine. The proportion of stamped to unstamped amphorae is low, though Carthage has yielded thirty amphora stamps of the Maesiani Celsi and forty of L. Eumachius.[29] There is also some evidence from both Sabratha and Benghazi that Italian Dressel 2-4s were commoner than Dressel 1s.[30]

Many Campanian amphorae reached Alexandria (> 20 L. Eumachius stamps) and some were even re-exported through the Red Sea ports to the Far East. The now famous amphorae from Arikamedu and other Indian sites include Campanian Dressel 2-4s, though these were probably exchanged for exotica far more appealing than slaves.[31] Alexandria, however, was an important centre for the slave trade as is indicated by the literary sources.[32]

Central Europe was another area for potential commercial expansion, especially after the annexation of Pannonia in 11 BC. Strabo indicates the important role of Aquileia for slaves coming over the Alps. The slave-trade seems to have reached Romania, if we may so interpret the massive presence of Republican denarii there mainly in the last century BC.[33] The distribution is not yet matched by amphorae but it is difficult to say whether this is because of a lack of published evidence or, indeed, because of their absence. A few Apulian Lamboglia 2 wine amphorae reached the Danube, though they may have arrived there with the Roman conquest.[34] Central Europe was awkwardly placed for direct exportation of wine from Campania and, indeed, Dressel 2-4s are rarely represented there.[35] However, there may have been a shift in the interests of some wine producers from the Tyrrhenian coast to northern Adriatic zones. The Istrian potteries of C. Laecanius Bassus, a man of Etrurian origin, possibly began operating around AD 15-20, producing containers to export wine principally to Central Europe. His son seems to have had estates in northern Campania, around Minturnae, which may have been passed down through the family.[36] Thus, purely hypothetically, it may be suggested that the Laecanii, who produced wine in northern Campania, shifted the centre of their activities to Istria under the early Empire so as to take advantage of new and alternative markets to those in Gaul. The Istrian workshop seem to have produced a small number of the typical Dressel 2-4 containers, familiar to Campania and the Tyrrhenian coast, while concentrating on the Adriatic form Dressel 6, believed to be an oil amphora.[37]

A few concluding remarks may be made. At the risk of simplification, it may be said that Campania, or at least Campanian landowners, in the later Republic could boast well-established connections with a number of strategically placed and privileged entrepôts that dictated routes for trade based principally on slaves, but also on metals and other valued goods. The evidence for such a system is now legion, ranging from literary sources, family ties and archaeological and numismatic finds. The opening-up of new territories and trade opportunities stimulated Campanian growth and led to strong competition for land which was evermore concentrated in the hands of the Roman élite and, eventually, in the Imperial *patrimonium*. Though the Gallic wars risked provoking a crisis in the Italian economy, market-minded entrepreneurs, including leading Roman statesmen, were able to expand into new market areas, thus staving off serious decline until the mid-first century AD. Interest in Campanian wine, which was noted for its quality, nonetheless remained strong enough to have sustained a diminished export trade well into the third century, as has been recently demonstrated by finds from Britain.[38]

NOTES

1. Quite aside from pottery and other traded imports, to complete the list of objects surviving in the archaeological record to yield indirect information on trade in agrarian produce from the East we might add the remains of clandestine rats, harbourers of the plague!

2. Few quantitative analyses have yet been carried out, though see the study by Fulford 1989, esp. figs. 6, 9 and 10, that give a good indication of Campania's eastern interests in Tripolitania and Cyrenaica. Local sigillata wares: Soricelli 1987. Jugs of Camulodunum form 139, Mortaria: Hartley 1973. Campanian Pompeian red ware exports are treated by Peacock 1977. Apparent kiln waste of Pompeian red ware has now been located in the pine wood just to the north of the acropolis of Cumae (*ex inf.* G. Soricelli). The other lid-seated pans include both Hellenistic/Republican types and their successors known as 'orlo bifido'.

3. Hesnard *et al.* 1989, 31 - stamp VALERIO from Minturnae, and earlier vessels may have been produced at Velia (Arthur 1990, 287).

4. Cunliffe 1988, 73-5.

5. Tchernia 1986; Cunliffe 1988, 139-40. For a similar pattern in Catalonia see Nolla and Nieto 1989.

6. Becker 1986, for both Dressel 1s and 2-4s; Laubenheimer, Odiot and Leclere 1987, for Dressel 1s. Desbat and Martin-Kilcher 1989, 355, claim that Falernian and Chian wines consumed along the Rhine had been imported as up-market brands for the officers. If this was so, I doubt that it can have been true for those wines imported prior to the conquest.

7. Duncan-Jones 1974, 46-8, discusses the problem of prices.

8. Tchernia, Pomey and Hesnard 1978, 106.

9. See Toynbee 1965, II, 303.

10. Some calculations are provided by Carandini 1980.

11. It may be noted that there is, as yet, no evidence that the amphorae passed Toulouse to travel down the Garonne and further.

12. Manacorda 1978; Lyding Will 1979; ibid. 1987, 205-6, where an unconvincing hypothesis of movement of the production centre from Cosa to Latium/Campania and Pompeii is advanced. Even if later products of the area were not stamped, it would seem that amphorae of type Dressel 2-4 were still being produced, though in very limited quantities with respect to earlier wine vessels going by finds from the *portus Cosanus* and Albinia.

13. Arthur 1991, 66-9 and 73.

14. Hesnard *et al.* 1989.

15. To these should be added the stamps already identified by Hesnard and by Amar and Liou. For L. EVMACHI see now van der Werff 1992, whose critique of Jongman's argument (1991) for Surrentum as origin of the group, is altogether convincing.

16. Lamboglia 1958, who already suggested a Campanian origin for the wreck.

17. Teanum: unpublished Dressel 2-4 wasters; Cales: Morel 1989; Melfa: *ex inf.* the late Edith Mary Wightman and John Hayes.

18. Cunliffe 1978, 65-8; ibid. 1987. On the later trade see Thomas 1988.

19. For example Millett 1990, 38, and on status gifts of Italian wine see, for example, the amphorae sent to King Herod of Judaea from the estates of L. Laenius, possibly located in the area of Brindisi: Cotton and Geiger 1989, 140-58.

20. Sealey 1985, 34, table 10.

21. Peacock 1981.

22. Sealey and Davies 1984.

23. Morel 1989.

24. Williams 1981.

25. Sealey 1985, 115.

26. A Rhodian amphora from the Lexden Tumulus is a sure pre-conquest import, though how many of the Graeco-Roman types listed in Peacock's 1971 seminal article are Italian Dressel 2-4s is still uncertain. On rates of exchange see Tchernia 1983, 99.

27. These amphorae had previously been identified as Tarraconensian: Tchernia 1986, 151.

28. Thierrin-Michael 1992.

29. Tchernia 1986, 150-1.

30. Sabratha: Fulford 1989; Benghazi: Riley 1981, 72-3.

31. I have seen some of the Arikamedu fragments that include Pompeian black sand Dressel 2-4s. See Tchernia 1986, 152-3; Wheeler 1946.

32. Harris 1980, 126.

33. Crawford 1977.

34. Cipriano and Carre 1989, 84, fig. 14.

35. On the conquest of Pannonia and Roman economic interests in Central Europe see generally Mócsy 1974, chap. 2.

36. Arthur 1991, 82, where perhaps I generate some confusion between the C. Laecani Bassi, father and son. The father seems to have established the Istrian potteries, which passed into the hands of his son, who died shortly before AD 78. The estate may then have passed into the Imperial patrimony - see Tassaux 1982.

37. Bezeczky 1987, 4. Hesnard 1980, 145, on a Dressel 2-4 with a stamp of C. Laecanius Bassus from the Magdalensberg.

38. Arthur and Williams 1992.

BIBLIOGRAPHY

Arthur, P. 1990. Amphorae. In, M. Gualtieri and H. Fracchia (eds.), *Roccagloriosa* I, 278-89. Centre Jean Bérard, Naples

Arthur, P. 1991. *Romans in Northern Campania: a study of settlement and land-use around the Massico and the Garigliano Basin.* The British School at Rome Monograph Series **1**. London

Arthur, P. and Williams, D.F. 1992. Campanian Wine, Roman Britain and the third century AD. *JRA* **5**, 250-60

Becker, C. 1986. Note sur un lot d'amphores régionales du 1er siècle ap. J.-C. à Lyon (Fouille de l'ilot 24). *Figlina* **7**, 147-50

Bezeczky, T. 1987. *Roman Amphorae from the Amber Route in Western Pannonia.* British Archaeological Reports International Series **386**, Oxford

Carandini, A. 1980. Il vigneto e la villa del fondo di Settefinestre nel Cosano: un caso di produzione agricola per il mercato transmarino. In, J.H. D'Arms and E.C. Kopff (eds.), The Seaborne Commerce of Ancient Rome: Studies in Archaeology and History. *MemAmAcc* **XXXVI**, 1-10

Cipriano, M.T. and Carre, M-B. 1989. Production et typologie des amphores sur la cote Adriatique de l'Italie. In, Amphores romaines et histoire économique, dix ans de recherche. *Collection Ecole Française de Rome* **114**, 67-104

Cotton, H.M. and Geiger, J. 1989. *Masada* II. *The Yigael Yadin Excavations 1963-1965 Final Reports.* Israel Exploration Society and The Hebrew University of Jerusalem

Crawford, M.H. 1977. Republican denarii in Romania: the suppression of piracy and the slave-trade. *JRS* **67**, 117-24

Cunliffe, B. 1978. *Hengistbury Head.* London

Cunliffe, B. 1987. *Hengistbury Head, Dorset* 1. *The Prehistoric and Roman Settlement, 3500 BC - AD 500.* Oxford

Cunliffe, B. 1987. *Greeks, Romans and Barbarians: spheres of interaction.* London

Desbat, A. and Martin-Kilcher, S. 1989. Les amphores sur l'axe Rhône-Rhin à l'epoque d'Auguste. In, Amphores romaines et histoire économique, dix ans de recherche. *CollEFR* **114**, 339-65

Duncan-Jones, R. 1974. *The Economy of the Roman Empire: Quantitative Studies.* Cambridge

Fitzpatrick, A. 1985. The distribution of Dressel 1 amphorae in Northwest Europe. *OJA* **4.3**, 305-40.

Fulford, M. 1989. To East and West: the Mediterranean Trade of Cyrenaica and Tripolitania in Antiquity. *Libyan Studies* **20**, 169-91

Harris, W.V. 1980. Towards a study of the Roman slave trade. In, J.H. D'Arms and E.C. Kopff (eds.), The Seaborne Commerce of Ancient Rome: Studies in Archaeology and History. *MemAmAcc* **XXXVI**, 117-40

Hartley, K. 1973. La diffusion des mortiers, tuiles et autres produits en provenance des fabriques Italiennes. *CahD'ArchSub* **II**, 49-60

Hesnard, A. 1980. Un dépôt augustéen d'amphores à La Longarina, Ostie. In, J.H. D'Arms and E.C. Kopff (eds.), The Seaborne Commerce of Ancient Rome: Studies in Archaeology and History. *MemAmAcc* **XXXVI**, 141-56

Hesnard, A., Ricq, M., Arthur, P., Picon, M. and Tchernia, A. 1989. Aires de production des gréco-italiques et des Dressel 1. In, Amphores romaines et histoire économique, dix ans de recherche. *CollEFR* **114**, 21-65

Jongman, W. 1991. *The Economy and Society of Pompeii*. Amsterdam

Lamboglia, N. 1958. La nave romana di Spargi. *Actes du IIième congrès international d'archeologie sous-marine*. Albenga

Laubenheimer, F., Odiot, T. and Leclere, H. 1987. Sous Auguste, un atelier de potiers italianisant à Saint-Just (Ardèche). *Mélanges P. Lévêque* **2**, 295-329

Lyding Will, E. 1979. The Sestius amphoras: a reappraisal. *JFA* **6.3**, 339-50

Lyding Will, E. 1987. The Roman Amphoras. In, A.M. McCann, J. Bourgeois, E.K. Gazda, J.P. Oleson and E. Lyding Will (eds.), *The Roman Port and Fishery of Cosa*, 171-220. Princeton

Manacorda, D. 1978. The ager Cosanus and the production of the amphorae of Sestius: new evidence and a reassessment. *JRS* **LXVIII**, 122-31

Millett, M. 1990. *The Romanization of Britain: An Essay in Archaeological Interpretation*. Cambridge

Mócsy, A. 1972. *Pannonia and Upper Moesia. A history of the Middle Danube Provinces of the Roman Empire*. London and Boston

Morel, J-P. 1989. Un atelier d'amphores Dressel 2/4 à Cales. In, Amphores romaines et histoire économique, dix ans de recherche. *CollEFR* **114**, 558-9

Nolla, J.M. and Nieto, F.J. 1989. La importaciòn de ànforas romanas en Cataluna durante el periodo tardo-republicano. In, Amphores romaines et histoire économique, dix ans de recherche. *CollEFR* **114**, 367-91

Peacock, D.P.S. 1971. Roman amphorae in pre-Roman Britain. In, M. Jesson and D. Hill (eds.), *The Iron Age and its Hillforts, 161-87*. Southampton

Peacock, D.P.S. 1977. Pompeian Red Ware. In, D.P.S. Peacock (ed.), *Pottery and Early Commerce*, 147-62. London

Peacock, D.P.S. 1981. The Amphorae. In, C. Partridge, *Skeleton Green, a Late Iron Age and Romano-British Site,* 199-204. London

Riley, J.A. 1981. Italy and the Eastern Mediterranean in the Hellenistic and early Roman periods: the evidence of coarse pottery. In, G. Barker and R. Hodges (eds.), *Archaeology and Itali an Society*, British Archaeological Reports International Series **102**, 69-78. Oxford

Sealey, P.R. 1985. *Amphoras from the 1970 Excavations at Colchester Sheepen*, British Archaeological Reports **142**. Oxford

Sealey, P.R. and Davies, G.M.R. 1984. Falernian wine at Roman Colchester. *Britannia* **XV**, 250-4

Soricelli, G. 1987. 'Tripolitanian sigillata': North African or Campanian?. *Libyan Studies* **18**, 73-88

Tassaux, F. 1982. Laecanii - Recherches sur une famille sénatoriele d'Istrie. *MEFRA* **94.1**, 227-69

Tchernia, A. 1986. *Le Vin de l'Italie Romaine*. Paris

Tchernia, A., Pomey, P., and Hesnard, A. 1978. L'épave romaine de la Madrague de Giens (Var), *Gallia* supp. **XXXIV**. Paris

Thierrin-Michael, G. 1992. *Römische Weinamphoren. Mineralogische und chemische Untersuchungen zur Klärung ihrer Herkunft und Herstellungsweise.* Dissertation Nr. 977, Universtität Freiburg Schweiz

Thomas, C. 1988. The context of Tintagel. A new model for the diffusion of post-Roman Mediterranean imports. *Cornish Archaeology* **27**, 7-25

Toynbee, A.J. 1965. *Hannibal's Legacy*. Oxford

van der Werff, J.H. 1992. L. EVMACHI - à propos d'une marque d'amphore trouvée à Nimègue. *Berichten van de Rijksdienst voor het Oudheidkundig Bodmonderzoek* 39, 357-76

Wheeler, R.E.M. 1946. Arikamedu, an Indo-Roman trading-station on the East coast of India. *Ancient India* **2**, 42-5

Williams, D.F. 1981. The Roman amphora trade with late Iron Age Britain. In, H. Howard and E.L. Morris (eds.), *Production and Distribution: a Ceramic Viewpoint*, British Archaeological Reports International Series **120**, 123-32. Oxford

Wilson, R.J.A. 1990. *Sicily under the Roman Empire. The Archaeology of a Roman Province, 36 BC-AD 535*. Warminster

PERIODS	V	VI	VII	VIII	IX	X
Marit. Villas	0	1	4	2	0	0
Villas	1	42	44	27	11	1
Farms*	9	68	69	42	14	1
Kilns	0	8	21	5	2	0
TOTALS	10	119	138	76	27	2

Key:

V   = Roman colonisation - Second Punic War
VI   = Late Republic
VII = Early Empire (*c.*1st BC - *c.*1st AD)
VIII = Mid Empire (*c.*2nd - *c.*3rd AD)
IX   = Late Empire (*c.*4th - *c.*early 5th AD)
X   = Late antiquity (*c.*5th - *c.*6th AD)

* inc. pottery scatters

Fig. 1   Habitation sites in northern Campania

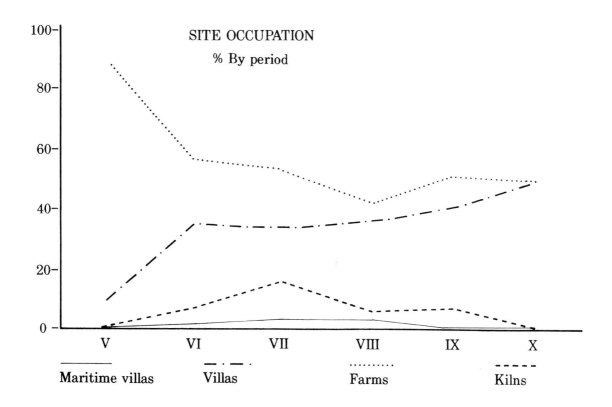

Fig. 2   Graph showing site types as percentage of total sites in northern Campania by period

251

Editors' Note: In recent years considerable interest has been aroused by reports in the press of excavations of burials of individuals of high status at the sites of Camulodunum (Colchester) and Verulamium (St Albans) in southeast Britain. The following three papers were commissioned to assess, in the light of such new evidence, the relationship of British communities in the late Iron Age to changing patterns of trade and social behaviour in continental Europe. The results are rather negative with regard to the extent of Italian trade in such objects as ceramics, but suggest some contact with Italy for the provision, perhaps as gifts, of objects of unusual status or material that could not be obtained from less distant sources.

ITALIC IMPORTS IN LATE IRON AGE BRITAIN: A SUMMARY OF THE EVIDENCE FROM 'CHIEFTAIN BURIALS'

Val Rigby

Department of Prehistoric and Romano-British Antiquities, The British Museum, London WC1B 3DG

'Chieftain Burials' of the late Iron Age and early Roman periods have been recognised in southern Britain since the last century.[1] The cremated dead were interred with a wealth of possessions, including metalwork, ceramics and glass imported from the Roman world. The rarity and rich variety of grave-goods in such burials naturally led to their interpretation as burials of a few individuals, at the apex of native society, who wished to demonstrate their assimilation of at least some aspects of Roman civilisation. Scientific and artefact researchers are gradually identifying the sources of the grave-goods, and it is clear that not all were actually made in Italy itself. Petrology and archaeology show that in the mid-first century BC the most plentiful Italic import was wine; in contrast, by the beginning of the first century AD, most of the fine pottery was made in Gaul, although the establishment of the workshops had Italian connections, for example the branch workshops of Gaius Ateius of Arezzo and Pisa at Lyons and La Graufesenque.[2] Detailed studies of the bronze vessels have produced some distribution maps which favour provincial manufacture. No workshops have been located, so caution is required when interpreting the evidence, since distribution maps notoriously favour areas of frequent archaeological activity with good publication records and good museums.

Rescue excavations in 1992 of other so-called 'Chieftain Burials' at Folly Lane, St Albans, Hertfordshire (Verulamium) and at Stanway, Colchester, Essex (Camulodunum) have provided valuable comparative data.[3] This survey is confined mainly to grave-goods because most of these were complete when deposited, and so provide the most reliable archaeological information.

There are differences between 'Chieftain Burials' of the first century BC found north and south of the river Thames. Those to the north are typified by burials found at Welwyn and Baldock, Hertfordshire, where the grave-goods include both imports and native products.[4]

The imports are associated with the preparation and consumption of wine and include wine amphorae (Fig. 2), silver drinking cups (Fig. 3), bronze pan and jug sets (Fig. 4) and a pedestal bowl; all are considered to have been produced in Italy, although recent research questions this for the jug and pan sets and suggests that production may have spread to Gallia Narbonensis.[5] South of the Thames, no wine amphorae have occurred in burials, yet there is one jug and pan set in the Aylesford Cemetery, Kent. Silver brooches found at Great Chesterford, Cambridgeshire, have been identified as Italian imports, but judgement is reserved on others found in burials at Folkestone and Faversham, Kent.[6] A pillar-moulded glass bowl in the burial at Hertford Heath, Hertfordshire, may be of eastern

Mediterranean origin, while the origins of the set of opaque glass gaming counters in the Welwyn Garden City Burial remain obscure.[7]   No gold objects have been recorded.

The accompanying native products required skilled metalworkers and are as impressive and rare as the imports. There are wooden buckets covered in decorated bronze bands and with helmeted-head handle-mounts, iron fire-dogs, a bronze cauldron with iron ring-handles and, on a more mundane level, numerous bronze- and iron-banded bowls and buckets, and local wheel-thrown pottery.

No Campanian ware has been found in Welwyn-type burials although the latest products are contemporary, and a sherd has been found at Ower, Dorset.[8] The earliest identified fine pottery, a lagoena and two platters in the Welwyn Garden City Burial, is from central Gaul, Gallia Lugdunensis, not from Italy.[9]

Grave-goods in the Lexden Tumulus, sited outside late Iron Age Camulodunum, and dated after 19 BC mark a change in the functional range of imported grave-goods and also the burial rite.[10] There are sherds from broken wine amphorae, representing more vessels than in any other British burial, but no metal or glass vessels for the preparation and consumption of wine have been identified: while the contents of the complete amphorae in Welwyn burials may have been for the deceased, those at Lexden are more likely to have been for the living. Cloth of gold, possibly the remains of a garment, silver-mounted furniture and bronze figurines, Roman if not Italic in their origins, were included in the grave-goods, and represent a luxurious lifestyle not hitherto represented in 'Chieftain Burials'. A silver medallion portraying Augustus may even have been a direct gift from the emperor himself, but the prototype coin is a Spanish issue, not Italian.[11] Native products include chain mail and an iron-bound casket or trunk, ornamented with bronze studs inlaid with red enamel. The fragmented state of grave-goods in the Lexden Tumulus has made identification and interpretation of the remains difficult, but it seems that in this burial the imports are more unusual and spectacular than insular products.

The tumulus at Mount Bures, Essex, and the Dorton Mirror Burial, Buckinghamshire, demonstrate both the continued decline of wine in the ritual and the decline in recognisable Italic imports.[12] The amphorae had been trimmed of their necks and handles before deposition, and of the five, only one is likely to be Italian. Fine imported pottery replaces metal equivalents often to the total exclusion of local pottery after *c.*10 BC. Decorative beakers and tablewares with precise functions in the Roman world - cups, platters and single-handled flagons and double-handled lagoenae - were chosen for the final meal or food-offering. Besides any symbolic attributes, such vessels were recognisably scarce; they were probably costly and unusual and outside the rather dull colour and finish range of native products by being clear red, blue and white or cream, and even decorated with glittering mica bands or covered with a glistening green glaze.

The King Harry Lane Cemetery, St Albans (Verulamium), Hertfordshire, provides the opportunity to compare imports of different types and from different sources available in the early- to mid-first century AD, although no burial was sufficiently rich in grave-goods to qualify as a 'Chieftain Burial'. In 463 burials there was one complete Italian wine amphora and sherds from four others, three Spanish olive oil and one Rhodian wine amphora.[13] One hundred and ninety-eight examples of imported ceramic fine wares were recognised, along with an array of brooches and other metal artefacts which would have been equally at home in contemporary burials in Gallia Belgica. Three amphorae, and half of the imported fine wares were in the burials richest in grave-goods, most located at the centre of ditched enclosures, or in 'family groups': for example, in Burial 241 all eight vessels were imports. Half of the imports were, however, in less rich burials in subordinate locations, implying that their use was not limited just to a few favoured families.

Limiting the comparison to cups and platters, 45 are in *terra rubra* and *terra nigra*, 3 in micaceous *terra nigra*, 4 in samian and 130 in grog-tempered wares; by source the totals amount to 1 Italian, 52 Gaulish and 130 local pieces.[14] The single Italian Arretine cup (Fig. 5), is one of only four recorded examples in cremations of the late Iron Age in Britain.[15] When a chronological factor is introduced and the sample limited to definite pre-Claudian imports there are sixteen Gaulish vessels and one Italian. The ratio of Italic and provincial Arretine to cups and platters in *terra rubra* and *terra nigra* is between 1:3 and 1:4. It is unlikely that such results demonstrate a specific preference for Gaulish pots in Britain; it is more likely an accidental effect of transport methods and routes.

Routes from the Mediterranean to Britain via the Rhône valley entailed an overland section with cargoes being loaded and unloaded at least twice. Non-perishable ceramic products were extremely versatile as space-fillers for cargoes: they could be replaced by perishable goods at any point in the journey, and either sold, or stored to await later shipment. Two routes crossing central Gaul to join the rivers Loire and Seine passed close to major potteries where fine tablewares were produced, and thus Italian pottery sold in Gaulish markets could easily be replaced. As a result, few traded Italian non-perishable goods reached southern Britain; most were off-loaded in Gaul where the market was larger and richer.

The most recent discoveries at Stanway and Folly Lane appear to support the King Harry Lane results, although processing is still under way, and there are more graves to be excavated at Stanway. With eighteen or nineteen cups and platters, the large vault at Stanway is the richest in imports yet recorded. There are four or five provincial Arretine vessels and an early south Gaulish dish, at least equalling the total from the King Harry Lane Cemetery; Gallo-Belgic imports are still more important with seven in *terra rubra* and six in *terra nigra*. In a burial which is up to a generation later, the only Gaulish imports are white pipe-clay lagoenae, while the cup and platter sets are from local sources. Other imports from the site include a fine amber-coloured glass bowl, considered to be Italian.

The vault of the Folly Lane Burial produced sherds from broken Italian amphorae, Dressel type 2-4, or Haltern 67, but the only fine wares are from Gaul, a Gallo-Belgic Butt Beaker and five samian platters from La Graufesenque; the remaining cups and platters were from local workshops. In a separate deposit, there was chain-mail decorated with silver, a horse-bit and toggle, both enamelled, all of native manufacture, accompanied by the burnt remains of a Roman couch, providing two parallels with the Lexden Tumulus, although up to fifty years may separate the burials.

The presence of rare and apparently costly items in 'Chieftain Burials' is typically explained by gift exchange: they are regarded as symbols of the esteem in which the recipient was held by outsiders, whether British, Gaulish or Roman, possibly as thanks for services rendered, or perhaps simply as bribes.   Yet compared to the products of British craftsmen with which they were associated, they are not particularly impressive, nor is their 'value' outstanding, and when compared to almost any torc in the Snettisham Hoards, never mind the 'Great Torc' itself, such so-called prestige gifts would appear to be unusual, but of limited intrinsic worth.[16]   Their value may have been symbolic, or possibly of ritual significance, but more probably demonstrated that the deceased and mourners recognised, and had adopted, civilised Roman manners.

It is impossible to put a value on rarity, but it is possible to estimate bullion value. Each of the silver cups weighs around 330 grams and so represents the weight of at least 220 silver British coins, or perhaps eighteen gold staters since the value of gold was about twelve times that of silver. Converted into human terms, each of the silver cups could represent eighteen Gallic mercenaries for an unspecified period (a reasonable household guard?), perhaps to be seen as a fair reward for services rendered.[17] An alternative Roman system uses the denarius containing about 4 grams of high purity silver as the basis of the calculation. Thanks to the literary evidence there is a wide variety of equivalences.[18]   Caesar doubled the annual pay of his legionaries to 225 denarii in the mid-first century BC.[19] The pair in Welwyn Grave A with the single cup in the Welwyn Garden City Burial represent one legionary for one year, by this method the donors of such grave goods were not being overly generous despite appearances to the contrary. Using a similar notional exchange rate for Gaulish slaves of one wine amphora for a slave, then Welwyn Grave B and the Welwyn Garden City

Burial also include the value of five slaves in the grave goods, here again the exchange rate seems to benefit the outsider who gains the energy value.

The late Iron Age imports to Britain, identified archaeologically, are luxury goods which were not produced in Britain for a variety of reasons - climatic, technological and cultural. The last seems most significant with regard to the metal vessels, for in technological terms British metalsmiths were sufficiently expert to produce them. The imports were manufactured within the boundaries of the early Roman Empire, and their distribution was facilitated by Empire-wide connections. By volume and accumulated value, Italian wine transported in amphorae has to be interpreted as the chief imported commodity in the mid-first century BC, but it can only be an interpretation, because the archaeological sample is not large. By 1986, Dressel 1A and B amphorae had been identified on seventy sites in Britain, and the minimum number of vessels was about 200, with a maximum of perhaps 2000.[20] From the evidence of various wrecks, it has been estimated that a ship could carry between 5800 and 7800 amphorae, so that all British amphora finds comprise at best about one-third of a single cargo, not obviously a major component in trade.[21] Metal vessels are too rare for consideration as traded items.

By the beginning of the first century AD, in simple numbers, ceramic tablewares from Gaul form the largest component, yet here again the problem of the sample size and reliability arises. While a lagoena could occupy as much space in the cargo-hold or cart as an amphora, but was much more fragile and had to be transported empty, cups and platters could be stacked in such a way that, even with packing materials, over a hundred vessels of mixed sizes occupied the space of just four amphorae, so that all the recorded assemblages of Gallo-Belgic imports from British sites for the whole of their period of import could easily be accommodated in a single cargo. Despite their fragility, imperishable ceramics are an obvious makeweight cargo, to be loaded and unloaded as, where and when necessary, so that it is unlikely that they arrived by the full boat-load. Their status as makeweight cargo may help to explain the varied types and sources represented in the early imports into Britain, and why Italic products are so rare, with most remaining in Gaul at their first point of unloading.

If Strabo had not listed the exports from Britain before the Roman occupation (slaves, cattle, corn, gold, silver and hunting dogs) it would be difficult to envisage how they could be deduced from archaeological evidence, even using modern techniques. But the corresponding list of imports has to be deduced entirely from the archaeological record, so it can be only partial. Inorganics will be markedly over-represented because organic materials and perishable goods will scarcely feature. Even when a list is compiled there is no method of establishing how the current archaeological sample relates to past actuality in order to achieve a reasonable basis for interpretation.

AUTHOR'S NOTE

This paper has been reconstructed from an outline in note-form prepared for the colloquium, which had to be reduced because of the exigencies of the timetable. The section on calculating the value of imports was not in the original outline.

Thanks are due to my colleagues Catherine Johns and Ian Stead for their helpful comments during preparation.

NOTES

1. Evans 1890; Smith 1912; Stead 1967; Laver 1927.
2. Peacock 1982, 116.
3. See Niblett this volume; Crummy this volume.
4. Stead 1967, 8-44; Stead and Rigby 1986.
5. Feugère and Rolley 1991, 23-45, 97-112.
6. Stead 1976; Stead 1984;
7. Hussen 1983, 9-11, pl. iv; Dr J. Price, *pers. comm.*; Stead 1967, 14-17, pl. 1.
8. Woodward 1987, 78.
9. Rigby and Freestone 1986.
10. Foster 1986.
11. Ibid., 90-2, pls. 19-20.
12. Roach Smith 1852; Farley 1983.
13. Stead and Rigby 1989.
14. Ibid., 113-14, 120-6, 145-6, for the fabric definitions.
15. Rigby, in press.
16. Stead 1991.
17. Nash 1981, 18.
18. Reece 1981, 26-7.
19. Watson 1969, 89.
20. Fitzpatrick 1985.
21. Greene 1986, 26.

BIBLIOGRAPHY

Evans, A.J. 1890. On a late Celtic Urnfield at Aylesford, Kent. *Archaeologia* **52**, 317-88

Farley, M.E. 1983. A mirror burial at Dorton, Buckinghamshire. *PPS* **49**, 269-302

Feugère, M. and Rolley, C. 1991. La vaisselle tardo-républicaine en bronze. *Actes de la table-ronde CNRS, Lattes. Avril 1990.* Publications de l'Université de Bourgogne, Centre de Recherches sur les Techniques Gréco-romaines, Dijon **13**

Fitzpatrick, A.P. 1985. The distribution of Dressel 1 Amphorae in north-west Europe. *Oxford Journal of Archaeology* **4**, 305-40

Foster, J. 1986. *The Lexden Tumulus: a re-appraisal of an Iron Age burial from Colchester, Essex.* British Archaeological Reports **156.** Oxford

Greene, K. 1986. *The Archaeology of the Roman Economy.* London

Hüssen, C.-M. 1983. *A rich late La Tène Burial at Hertford Heath, Hertfordshire.* British Museum Occasional Paper **44.** London

Laver, P.G. 1927. The excavation of a Tumulus at Lexden, Colchester. *Archaeologia* **26**, 241-54

Nash, D. 1981. Coinage and state development in central Gaul. In, B. Cunliffe (ed.), *Coinage and Society in Britain and Gaul*, 10-17. CBA Research Report **38**. London

Peacock, D.P.S. 1982. *Pottery in the Roman World*. London

Reece, R. 1981. Roman monetary impact on the Celtic world - thoughts and problems. In, B. Cunliffe (ed.), *Coinage and Society in Britain and Gaul*, 24-28. CBA Research Report **38**. London

Rigby, V. in press. The Pottery. In, K. Parfitt, *Iron Age Burials at Deal*.

Rigby V. and Freestone, I.C. 1986. The petrology and typology of the earliest identified Central Gaulish imports. *Journal of Roman Pottery Studies* **1**, 6-21

Roach Smith, C. 1852. Roman remains found at Mount Bures near Colchester. *Collectanea Antiqua* **II**, 25-36. London

Smith, R.A. 1912. On late-Celtic antiquities discovered at Welwyn, Herts. *Archaeologia* **63**, 1-30

Stead, I.M. 1967. A La Tène III burial at Welwyn Garden City. *Archaeologia* **101**, 1-62

Stead, I.M. 1976. The earliest burials of the Aylesford culture. In, G. de G. Sieveking, I.H. Longworth and K.E. Wilton (eds.), *Problems in Economic and Social Archaeology*, 401-16. London

Stead, I.M. 1984. Some notes on imported metalwork. In, S. Macready, and F.H. Thompson (eds.), *Cross Channel Trade between Gaul and Britain in the pre-Roman Iron Age,* 43-66. Society of Antiquaries of London Occasional Paper (new series) **4**. London

Stead, I.M. 1991. The Snettisham treasure: excavations in 1990. *Antiquity* **65**, 447-64

Stead, I.M. and Rigby, V. 1986. *Baldock: The Excavations of a Roman and pre-Roman settlement 1968-1972*. Britannia Monograph **7**, 51-61. Gloucester

Stead, I.M. and Rigby, V. 1989. *Verulamium: The King Harry Lane site*. Historic Buildings and Monuments Commission for England Archaeological Report **12**, 115-16.

Watson, G.R. 1969. *The Roman Soldier*. Bristol

Woodward, P.J. 1987. The excavation at a late Iron-Age trading settlement and Romano-British production site at Ower, Dorset. In, N. Sunter and P.J. Woodward, *Romano-British Industries in Purbeck*. Dorset Natural History and Archaeological Society Monograph Series **6**, 44-124. Dorchester

Photograph credits

All British Museum

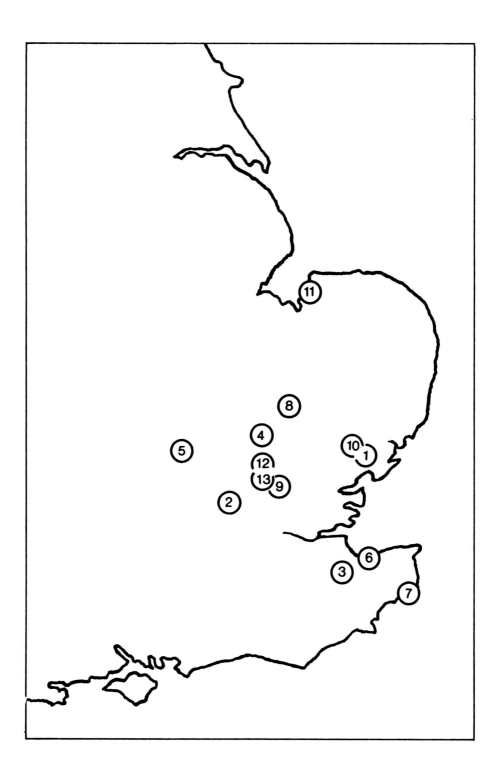

Fig. 1   Map showing place-names mentioned in the text

1   Stanway, Colchester (Camulodunum) Essex
2   Folly Lane, St. Albans (Verulamium) Herts.
3   Aylesford, Kent
4   Baldock, Herts.
5   Dorton, Bucks.
6   Faversham, Kent
7   Folkestone, Kent
8   Great Chesterford, Cambs.
9   Hertford Heath, Herts.
10   Mount Bures, Essex
11   Snettisham, Norfolk
12   Welwyn, Herts.
13   Welwyn Garden City, Herts.

2

3

Fig. 2   Dressel 1 amphora, one of five from the Welwyn Garden City Burial. British Museum
Fig. 3   Silver kantharos, one of a pair from Grave B at Welwyn. British Museum

260

4

5

Fig. 4   Bronze jug and pan found in the Aylesford Bucket cremation, Aylesford Cemetery. British Museum

Fig. 5   Cup, Loeschcke 8Aa, stamped AGATE. Made at Pozzuoli, Italy. From Burial 346, King Harry Lane Cemetery, St. Albans.

LATE IRON AGE BURIALS AT STANWAY, COLCHESTER

Philip Crummy

Colchester Archaeological Trust, 12 Lexden Road, Colchester, Essex CO3 3NF

Stanway seems to have originated as a middle Iron Age occupation site which in the late Iron Age became an important funerary place for individuals of high status who lived in Camulodunum.[1] The cremated remains were placed in large timber mortuary chambers set axially within large ditched enclosures (Fig. 1).

The Stanway site at Colchester, Essex, has been known from cropmarks since the 1930s. Excavation began in 1986 in advance of sand and gravel extraction. There were five enclosures set out in two rows, one of two and another of three (Fig. 2). By the end of 1993, Enclosures 1, 3 and 4 and the northern part of Enclosure 2 had been investigated. Excavation of the remaining areas is planned.

Three chambers have been examined so far. The grave-goods had been broken and fragments scattered throughout the backfills of their respective chambers. The cremated remains had been similarly treated. In at least one case (that of the largest), the chamber itself had been broken up, probably at the time of the cremation. Its associated grave-goods included at least twenty-four vessels (all of which had been imported) and a small detached copper-alloy base. The backfill of one of the other chambers contained over twenty vessels and beads from a necklace, the latter indicating that the cremated remains may have been of a female. The smallest of the chambers (in Enclosure 1) was also the earliest, with fragments of two pots indicating a date probably in the late first century BC. The apparent destruction of at least one of the chambers when the body associated with it was cremated suggests that the chambers were built as places in which to lay and keep the bodies until their cremation.

There were at least three secondary burials. In Enclosure 1, cremated remains had been placed inside a single unaccompanied pot set upright in a small pit. This is typical of many of the cremations of the late Iron Age at Camulodunum. In each of the other two cases, the cremated remains were placed on the floor of a square flat-bottomed pit containing no traces of a timber chamber. Both burials are post-conquest, dating to around the AD 50s. Although found crushed and broken, the grave-goods in both cases seem to have been intact at the time of the burial. The richest group, the so-called 'Warrior Burial', included at least fourteen ceramic vessels (mostly imported), a shallow, flat-handled pan of copper-alloy, a jug also of copper-alloy, a large glass bowl (Italian), two glass phials, a set of glass gaming counters, the remains of a probable gaming board, a spear, a probable shield, two Langton Down brooches, textile, a large copper-alloy armlet, a large glass bead, and a pile of cremated bone. The other burial was not so rich and contained a Hod Hill brooch, a flagon, a possible bucket or box, and an ink-pot.

The condition of the grave-goods associated with the chambered graves means that it is not possible to tell how rich the groups had been. Nevertheless it does seem that they would not have been comparable to those of the Lexden Tumulus[2] and thus the people concerned would not be of the very highest social order. However they must have been important since they were accorded a burial rite which plainly was reserved for very few. They were therefore presumably close relatives of Cunobelin. He lived at Camulodunum in the decades leading up to the Claudian invasion and was described by Suetonius as 'King of the Britons'.

The Stanway site is important for various reasons. It provides an example of a type of late Iron Age burial rite which was rare in Britain. It also suggests that mortuary chambers of this kind were intended to be temporary resting places for the body prior to cremation. Being a funerary site which seems to extend from the late first century BC to at least c. AD 60, it has implications for the understanding of the dynasty of which Cunobelin was part and of its relationships to Camulodunum and the southeast of England generally. Of equal interest is the light Stanway throws on the relationship between some members of this dynasty and their Roman overlords after AD 43.

NOTES

1. For brief interim accounts, see Crummy 1993a; also Crummy 1992, and Crummy 1993b (published by the Colchester Archaeological Trust).
2. Laver 1927; carefully reappraised by Foster 1986, who redates the burial to *c*. 15-10 BC and suggests that there is evidence for a wooden mortuary chamber.

BIBLIOGRAPHY

Crummy, P. 1992. Regal graves. *The Colchester Archaeologist* **5**, 1-5

Crummy, P. 1993a. Aristocratic graves at Colchester. *Current Archaeology* **132**, 492-7

Crummy, P. 1993b. Warrior burial. *The Colchester Archaeologist* **6**, 1-5

Foster, J. 1986. *The Lexden Tumulus*. British Archaeological Reports **156**. Oxford

Laver, P.G. 1927. The excavation of a tumulus at Lexden, Colchester. *Archaeologia* **26**, 241-54

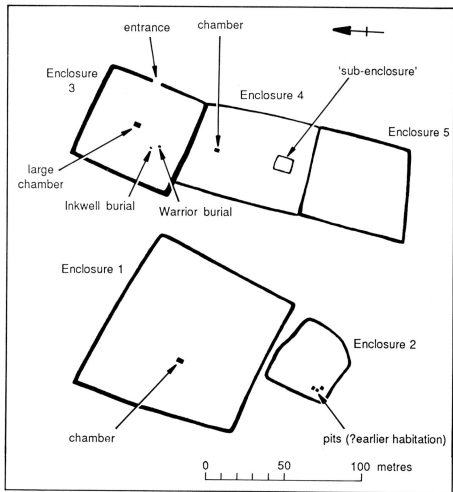

Fig. 1   Conjectural reconstruction of the Stanway site *c.* AD 60 during the cremation ceremony in Enclosure 5. Artist: Peter Froste

Fig. 2   Plan of the Stanway site, Colchester, Essex

A CHIEFTAIN'S BURIAL FROM VERULAMIUM

Rosalind Niblett
District Archaeologist, St. Albans District Council,
Kyngston House, Inkerman Road, St. Albans, Herts.

Early in 1992 rescue excavations on a site at Folly Lane, St Albans, on the line of the Roman road from Verulamium to Colchester, uncovered a high-status burial accompanied by an exceptionally rich collection of grave-goods.[1] The burial lay at the centre of a large rectilinear enclosure on the brow of a prominent hill, 500m outside the northeast gate of Verulamium, and within the area of the pre-Roman oppidum (Fig. 1).

In addition to the burial itself, evidence was recovered for an elaborate funeral ritual. A large pit (8m x 8m and nearly 3m deep) had been dug at the centre of the enclosure. The pit had been revetted with timber and a timber chamber erected on the pit floor. Strewn on the floor of the pit were fragments of iron, copper-alloy and silver, together with a few minute scraps of cremated bone and sherds from at least 33 pots. Half a metre east of the pit was a smaller pit which contained the cremation burial itself (Fig. 2). The wealth of the accompanying grave-goods together with evidence for complicated funeral ceremonial led to the identification of the burial as that of a pre-eminent native who was buried about AD 50.

In spite of the undoubted high status of the individual buried here, evidence for external trade was surprisingly sparse. It is true that the grave-goods had for the most part been placed on the pyre, and so rendered largely unrecognisable. A large deposit of solidified molten metal was found on the floor of the grave pit, including over 200 grams of molten silver. Whether some of this metal represents Mediterranean imports is now purely a matter for conjecture. The few objects that survived in identifiable form, including an iron mail tunic and various items of horse equipment, are either of British manufacture or items of Roman military equipment.

Most of the pottery was found on the floor of the timber chamber, although a small number of sherds, all of them burnt, were found in the filling of the grave. Apart from sherds from up to four Italian Dressel 2-4 amphorae, the pottery was either south Gaulish samian (15 vessels), Gallo-Belgic imports (1 vessel) or locally made imitations of Gallo-Belgic forms (14 vessels). Hence trade contacts seem to have been with Gaul rather than with Italy, and indeed it is in northern France that the closest continental parallels for the funerary rituals apparent at Folly Lane are to be found.[2]

There is, however, one item from the grave that may represent an Italian import. Among the broken and burnt fragments of copper-alloy on the top of the grave deposit were small fragments of turned ivory. Parts of at least three small objects were discernible. Two are simply represented by tiny scraps of flat, decorative discs or facings. The third and best-preserved object was a small, lathe-turned knob (Fig. 3 a,b), with traces of an iron spindle running through its centre. The initial identification as a dagger pommel was rejected in view of the absence of any blades, or indeed of any weapons, from the grave. There were, however, large quantities of decorative copper-alloy strips, rivets, small domed bosses and fragments of iron spindles, suggestive of an elaborate item of furniture. In addition, the knob is closely similar to the rather larger, bone mounts from a Roman funerary couch now in the Fitzwilliam Museum, Cambridge.[3] It is suggested therefore that the ivory fragments from Folly Lane are all that remain of an elaborate piece of furniture, imported from the Mediterranean world and largely destroyed in the funeral pyre. As such it presumably represents an exceptional import, brought here for the use of a particular, high-ranking individual. It may be that it should be regarded more as a diplomatic gift than as an item that found its way to Verulamium in the normal course of trade.

ACKNOWLEDGEMENTS

I am grateful to G.B. Dannell, C. Green and V. Rigby for their preliminary comments on the samian ware, amphorae and Gallo-Belgic ware respectively. I am also grateful to C. Green for drawing my attention to the couch in the Fitzwilliam Museum. The illustrations are the work of Alexandra Thorne.

NOTES

1. For a preliminary, interim account of the excavations see Niblett 1992.
2. For continental parallels see Bruneaux 1986; Pantreau 1991.
3. Nicholls 1979.

BIBLIOGRAPHY

Bruneaux, J. 1986. *Les Gaulois, sanctuaires et rites*. Collection des Hesperides, Paris

Niblett, R. 1992. A Catuvellaunian Chieftain's Burial from St Albans. *Antiquity* **66**, no. 253, 917-29

Nicholls, R.V. 1979. A Roman Couch in Cambridge. *Archaeologia* **106**, 1-32

Pantreau, J. 1991. Sépulture aristocratique Augustéenne, Antran (Vienne) - note préliminaire. *Archäologisches Korrespondenzblatt* **21**, 271-81

3a

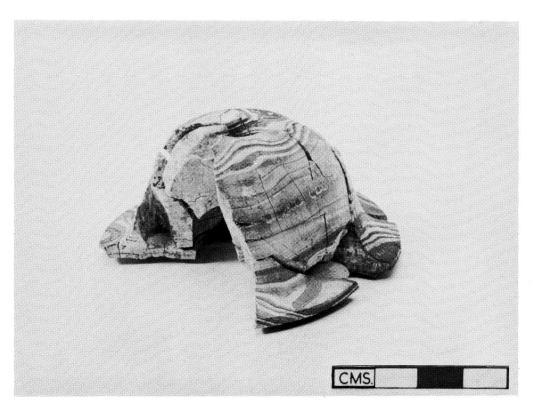

3b

Figs. 3a,b   Turned ivory knob, perhaps from a Roman funerary couch. Folly Lane
Photo courtesy of Verulamium Museum

269

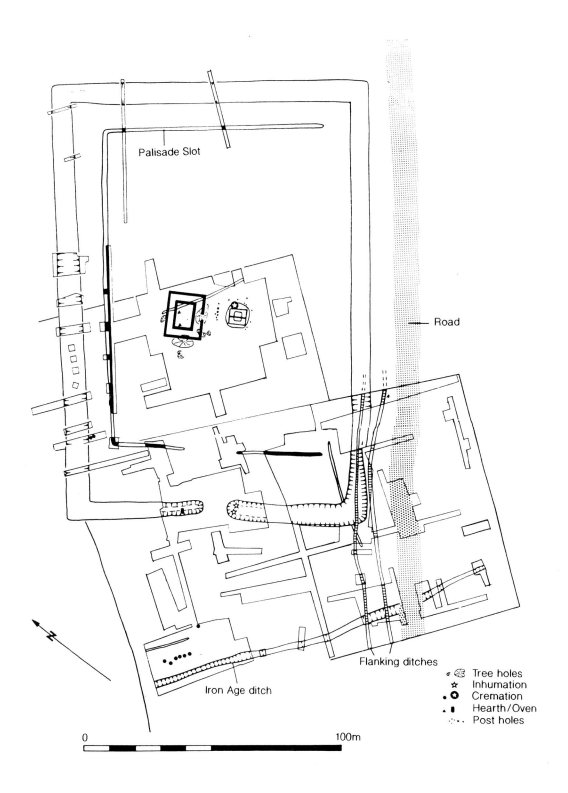

Palisade Slot

Road

Flanking ditches

Iron Age ditch

0   100m

Tree holes
Inhumation
Cremation
Hearth/Oven
Post holes

Fig. 2   Folly Lane: the chieftain's burial, funerary pit and later Romano-Celtic temple within the ditched enclosure. Photo courtesy of Verulamium Museum

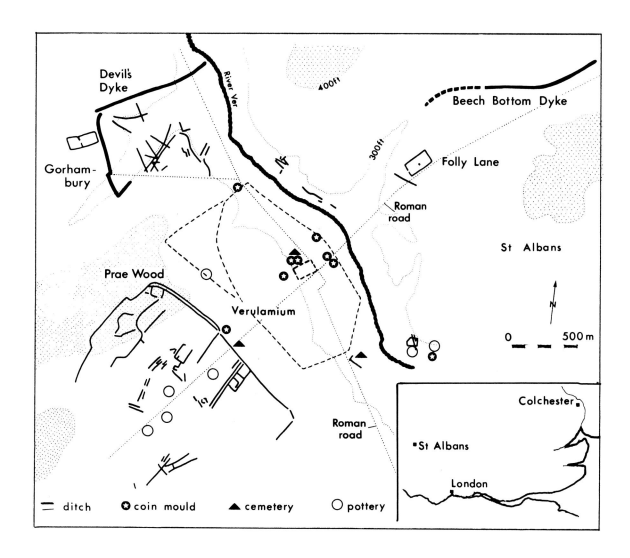

Fig. 1   The Folly Lane Site in relation to the Verulamium oppidum

ITALIAN BRONZE VESSELS IN TRANSDANUBIA BEFORE THE ROMAN CONQUEST

Klàra Szabó

Budapesti Történeti Múzeum, H-1250 Budapest, Szent Gyögy Tér 2

INTRODUCTION

The western part of the Carpathian Basin - modern Transdanubia, known to Greek authors as the land of the Pannonians - had already aroused the interest of Rome by the late Iron Age. Romans and native peoples were engaged in commercial exchange, though the intensity of this exchange was not constant, as collections of Roman imported objects prove. The findspots of ivory and vessels of pottery, glass and bronze, as well as articles for personal use, are located close to the amber route, the road along the Drave valley, and in proximity to other trade-routes. The most important finds are those which attest the farthest extent of Roman and native/Celtic trade; particularly important among these are bronze vessels, which were produced only in major centres. The variety of forms of this period is now quite well known as a result of the survey edited by Feugère and Rolley [1], and through several recent studies. The presentation of a typology of nearly thirty Transdanubian vessel types, their places of origin and their chronology, leads us to the conclusion that parts of Italy were in regular commercial contact with this region which, after the Roman conquest, was organised as the province of Pannonia. In addition, new information has been provided on the sources of Roman imports before the conquest.

Catalogues of late Iron Age bronze vessels from the Carpathian basin have been compiled by Werner and Breščak.[2] The typology for this period is now well established as a result of the excellent survey published by Feugère and Rolley. The present writer recently published a brief list[3] and now wishes to make a further contribution by adding new examples to those mentioned above. These are listed in the Catalogue below according to type.

The number of late Iron Age bronze vessels originating from the Transdanubian and the Save regions can be estimated at around sixty.[4] It should be noted, however, that this total is incomplete and it is almost certain that further pieces of the Republican period are as yet undiscovered in various museum stores. Nevertheless, the assembled material is quite representative and an archaeological assessment of it is necessary.

TOPOGRAPHICAL DIVISION

Of the sixty bronze vessels the findspots of thirteen are unknown, while the other forty-seven were unearthed at twenty-six locations (Fig. 1) concentrated in three areas: the Danube region (Vindobona, Brigetio, the bed of the Danube at Budapest, Intercisa, Szekszárd-Bakta-hill, Véménd), the northwestern part of Transdanubia and Burgenland (Sommerein, Oggau, Kőszegpatty, Velemszentvid), and the region between the bay of Trieste and the Save-Danube confluence (Trizisce pri Cerknici, Vrhnika-Nauportus, the river Ljubjanica, Novo Mesto, Smarjeta, Duboz, Sremska Mitrovica, Zemun, Vinkovci Dirov, Planina bei Dalj, Dalj, Sotin, Zmajevac, Brdovci, Siscia).

The finds rarely come from closed deposits. Only two graves of the late La Tène cemetery of Sotin and the cremation burial of Véménd can be included in this category.[5] The pieces from Velemszentvid, Segestike (Siscia) and Vinkovci were found in the *oppidum* and the La Tène settlement. Furthermore, other vessels were brought to light from the beds of the rivers Danube, Ljubjanica and Save.

PLACES OF ORIGIN AND MANUFACTURE OF THE INDIVIDUAL PIECES

The location of the workshops and manufacturing centres can be determined only according to region because their exact locations are not known. The E16 type buckets with cylindrical sides (Vindobona, Siscia, Sommerein, Oggau, Duboz, Kőszegpatty, see Fig. 1) were made in northern Italy,[6] while the E18-19 types were produced in northern or central Italy. They date to La Tène D 1-2, i.e. between 100/50 and 50/10 BC. Around ten examples of these types came to light in Transdanubia. The south Italian workshops are represented only by one bucket of Tarentum type, discovered in the bed of the river Danube at Budapest (Figs. 13a,b).[7] This example can be dated fifty years earlier than the previous ones.[8]

The single-handled jugs and glass vessels (eleven examples) unearthed in the region of the later province of Pannonia belong to the Kjaerumgaard, Kappel-Kelheim, Gallarate and Idria groups.[9] These vessels, like the above-mentioned buckets, came from northern and central Italian workshops and can be dated between 125/120 and 70/50 BC. The only exception is the Kjaerumgaard type jug in the Hungarian National Museum (Fig. 3),[10] which is undoubtedly of central Italian origin and dates to the period 25 BC - AD 25.

One example alone reached our region from the south Italian workshops (Figs. 11, 14a,b, MNM Inv. 44/1892-14). There are very few indications to date it, merely the characteristic grooving of the handle-band, the mediocre old Silenos head on the lower attachment, and the stylised bird-heads around the mouth of the vessel. Through these features it can be dated to around 100 BC.

The third group, comprising ladles and strainers, is the most numerous since these were needed most in everyday life. There are twenty-six vessels or fragments from our region.[11] There are no definite data which would indicate the manufacturing centre of the longest-lived vessel type of the late La Tène period.[12]

The manufacturing place of the Pescate type, produced between the second and the first century BC, was presumably situated in northern Italy. This type has several variations between the horizontal and vertical versions of the handle. The ladles with vertical handle were made in central Italy and most can be dated to around the second half of the first century BC. The ladles with horizontal handles were manufactured in northern Italy in the same period.[13] A special example of this type in the Hungarian National Museum (Figs. 4, 19a-d), has coin impressions of the Republican period on both ends of the handle, with a circular stamp in the middle. Only one other stamp of this type is known to me.[14] Parallel to the axis of the handle was punched decoration consisting of double circles (Fig. 19a). The piece dates to about the second half of the first century BC.

Four saucepans are known in our region of which the oldest was found in a grave at Szekszárd-Bakta Hill. Its rim is narrow and undecorated, the profile is nearly rectangular and its handle is triangular in shape (Fig. 5). Through these features the piece can be classified as the Montefortino-Scaldasole type and dated to the second century BC.[15] According to the typology of De Marinis only the saucepans of Véménd and the Hungarian National Museum (Inv. 94/1890-56) can be included as examples of the Aylesford type.[16] Another piece, published by Popović and unearthed presumably in the bed of the river Save, probably belongs - on the grounds of its long and oblique handle - to the same group,[17] although certain identification can be made only in the light of more detailed information.

Finally, it can be stated that in the late Republican period bronze vessels were regularly transported through marketing networks from the manufacturing centres of central and northern Italy to Transdanubia, Burgenland and the Save region (Fig. 1). In this period bronze vessels made in south Italy reached our region only sporadically (Figs. 13, 14).

In the case of the Gallarate jug, the finds of Transdanubia and the Save valley show numerous similarities to finds from Italy and the Alpine region (Figs. 2, 6, 18a,b).[18] The Kelheim jug (Figs. 8, 9, 15a,b, 16a,b) resembles some Italian and Gaulish pieces; the Kjaerumgaard jug (Fig. 3) resembles some European pieces, the Idrian cup (Fig. 12) resembles some European and North African pieces, and the Pescate simpulum (Fig. 10) resembles some north Italian and Alpine pieces.[19] In addition two more are quite unparalleled (Kappel-Kelheim jug handle: Fig. 7 and the strainer: Figs. 4, 19a-d).

The finds described above allow the following conclusion. After the foundation of Aquileia (181 BC) regular trade commenced along the amber road and the Save waterway, and in this commercial circulation of bronze vessels the workshops of central and northern Italy played the dominant role.

CATALOGUE

Buckets

TYPE = E 16, G 2 VARIANT[20]

Vindobona.[21] Historisches Museum der Stadt Wien Inv. 1866, (now missing).

Siscia (= Sisak): 3 examples, undecorated of which two are Roman.[22]

Nauportus (= Vrhnika): bed of the river Ljubljanica 1884; the findspot is reviewed by Breščak.[23]

TYPE E 16, G 3[24]

Sommerein. Wien, Niederösterreichisches Landesmuseum Inv. 1712; ht. 15.8cm, diam. of rim 22.4cm, diam. of base 18.6cm.[25]

TYPE E 16

Duboz = Doboj, Cirkvenica = near the the frontier.[26]

TYPE E 18

Komitat Pest. I have some doubts regarding the identification of the findspot.[27]

TYPE E 20

Bed of the River Ljubljanica 1884, Vrhnika = Nauportus.[28]

Ljubljana. Escutcheon. Ljubljana NM Inv. R 2212.[29]

TYPES E 21-22

Sisak, bed of the River Kulpa, Zagreb NM.[30]

Sotin. Zagreb Arch. Mus. Inv. 4166, 4185: 3 examples of buckets or cauldrons.[31]

TYPE ZAHLHAAS A

Bed of the River Danube, Magyar Nemzeti Múzeum, Budapest Inv. 175/1873-4. Ht. 42.5cm, diam. of rim 28.2cm, max. diam. of the body 14.1cm. The base is missing. Date, second century BC.[32]

Made in southern Italy. Fig. 13a,b.

Jugs

TYPE: GALLARATE JUG OR IDRIAN CUP [33]

Intercisa, Magyar Nemzeti Múzeum, Budapest Inv. 11/1912-7. Handle of jug or cup, cast. Length 8.2cm, width 6.2cm. Date, La Tène D1 = 125/120 - 70/50 BC.[34]

Production centre: central or northern Italy. Fig. 17.

TYPE: E 122, KJAERUMGAARD [35]

Findspot unspecified: Hungary. Magyar Nemzeti Múzeum, Budapest Inv. 10/1951-17. Bronze jug, made of sheet metal, handle missing but remains of solder indicating a voluted and leaf-shaped escutcheon. Three pairs of grooves on base, slight groove and ridge round lathe-mark at centre. Ht. 17.5cm, diam. of rim 9cm, diam. of base 8.6cm.

Date, 25 BC - AD 25. Possibly of central Italian manufacture.[36] Fig. 3.

TYPE: KAPPEL - KELHEIM[37]

Intercisa. Magyar Nemzeti Múzeum, Budapest Inv. 2/1950-202. Handle of jug cast and decorated with bird's heads at either end and two worn-away volutes on both sides along the mouth of the jug. In the centre of the top a raised, curled leaf with a knob. The lower part divides in two, where there is a female head. Length 14cm, width 9cm.

Date, LT D1 = 125/120 - 70 BC. Of north Italian manufacture.[38] Fig. 7.

TYPE: KELHEIM

Findspot unknown. Magyar Nemzeti Múzeum, Budapest Inv. 44/1892-12. Handle of jug, cast and decorated with two bird's heads at either end, and two volutes. The lower part divides into two on either side of a curled, ribbed leaf. Length: 11.1cm, width 8cm.

Date, La Tène D1 = 125/120 - 70 BC.[39] Believed to have been made in northern Italy. Figs. 8, 15.

Findspot unknown. Handle of another jug (as above). Magyar Nemzeti Múzeum, Budapest 44/1892-12. Length: 11.5cm, Width: 8.6cm.

Date and manufacture: as above. Figs. 9, 16.

TYPE: UNKNOWN

Findspot unknown. Magyar Nemzeti Múzeum, Budapest Inv. 44/1892-14. Handle of jug, hollow cast, with bird's heads at either end and a marked leaf in the centre. The middle section of the handle is grooved vertically at either end and the escutcheon has a Silenos head. Length 11.1cm, width 6cm.

Date, 100 BC. Possibly of south Italian manufacture. Figs. 11, 14a,b.

TYPE: GALLARATE JUG[40]

Findspot unknown. Magyar Nemzeti Múzeum, Budapest Inv. 44/1892-15. Handle of jug, cast, slightly curved, lower part leaf-shaped. Length: 12cm, width 8.3cm.
Date, 125/120 - 70 BC. Possibly of north or central Italian manufacture.[41] Figs. 6, 18a,b.

River Ljubljanica. Filozofska fakulteta, Ljubljana Inv. P 302. Length 12cm.
Date, 125/120 - 70 BC. Possibly of north or central Italian manufacture.[42] Fig. 2

TYPE: IDRIAN CUP

Velemszentvid. Naturhistorisches Museum, Wien Inv. 32439.[43] Handle, section with rounded edges. Lower part missing. Length 2.1cm, diam. of rim 4.5cm.
Date, 120 - 70/50 BC. Of north Italian manufacture. Fig. 12.

Trzisce pri Cerknici. Ljubljana NM Inv. P 3078.[44] Length 6.8cm.
Date, 120 - 70/50 BC. Of north Italian manufacture.

Ladles and strainers

TYPE: SIMPULUM TYPE B

Novo Mesto
Date: Second and first century BC. Produced in north Italy.[45]

TYPE: SIMPULUM TYPE A

Brigetio.[46] Kunsthistorisches Museum/Antikensammlung, Wien Inv. 3009. Vertical handle, cast and composed of three parts: the upper and the lower parts are flat, the middle is round. Decorated with small knots of bronze. Length 30cm, width 2cm. Fig. 10.

TYPE: PESCATE LADLE

Cibalae = Vinkovci, Dirov Brijeg, LT settlement. Bowl
Date, Second or first century BC. Manufactured in north Italy.

Sirmium = Sremska Mitrovica.[47] Date and manufacture see above.

TYPE: STRAINER[48]

Planina at Dalj. Date: middle of the second - middle of the first century BC. Italian manufacture.[49]

TYPE: STRAINER

Findspot unknown. Magyar Nemzeti Múzeum, Budapest Inv. 44/1892-19. This small strainer has a projecting rim with vertical lip. On the inside of the rim there is a large rib. The bowl is rounded, flattened and pierced. In the centre of the base there are numerous perforations. The handle is flat and proportionally long. Decoration: concentric circles and three busts. Figs. 4, 19a-d.

Saucepans

TYPE: SAUCEPAN E 130, POVEGLIANO - SCALDASOLE[50]

Szekszárd, Baktahegy, cemetery. Wosinsky Mór Múzeum, Szekszárd Inv. 15001. The rim is undecorated. The body is damaged and the handle is missing. Ht. 5.5cm, diam. of rim 21 x 18cm, diam. of base 20cm.
Date, Second century BC. Possibly of central or northern Italian manufacture.[51] Fig. 5.

TYPE: SAUCEPAN E 130, AYLESFORD[52]

Sremska Mitrovica, bed of the river Save. Muzej Srema, Sremska Mitrovica Inv. 1339.
Date, First century BC. Possibly of central or northern Italian manufacture.[53]

ACKNOWLEDGEMENTS

I am particularly obliged to the following museums: Magyar Nemzeti Múzeum, Budapest, Kunsthistorisches Museum/Antikensammlung, Wien, Naturhistorisches Museum, Wien, Historisches Museum der Stadt Wien, Niederösterreichisches Landesmuseum, Wien. I extend my thanks and appreciation to Mr L. Kocsis, Dr M. Nagy, Dr É.B. Bónis, Mr J. Isztl (Budapest), Dr K. Gschwantler, Univ.-Doz. Dr O. Harl, Dr R. Pohanka and Dr A. Kern (Wien). I also wish to express my gratitude for the help of Dr J. Swaddling, who encouraged me to write this paper.

NOTES

1. Feugère and Rolley 1991.
2. Werner 1954, 67-70, nos. Ac 15, B 9-10, C 20, D 19, 22, E 17-18, Fb 8-9, Fc 12; Breščak 1982, 16-23, nos. 43, 45-7, 60-1, 66-9, 114, 116, 147-9.
3. Feugère and Rolley 1991, 8-112; Szabó 1990, 132, 339.
4. Bolla *et al.* 1991; Castoldi and Feugère 1991; Boube and Guillaumet 1991; Feugère 1991; Guillaumet 1991; Majnarić-Pandžić 1973; Breščak 1982; Popović 1992.
5. Sotin: Majnarić-Pandžić 1973, 56-7. Véménd: Hunyady 1944, 106, 120.
6. Guillaumet 1991, 8-11.
7. Radnóti 1938, 105, pl. 39, 1.
8. Zahlhaas 1971, 47.
9. Boube and Guillaumet 1991, 31-45; Feugère 1991, 53-59.
10. Boube and Guillaumet 1991, 37-8 no. 12.
11. Castoldi and Feugère 1991; Guillaumet 1991, 61-95.
12. Guillaumet 1977, and in particular 1991, 92 suggests a date range between the second century BC and the annexation of Pannonia in AD 37.
13. Northern Italian Pescate type: Werner 1954, 70 Liste B. Variants: Castoldi and Feugère 1991, 61-72. With vertical handle: Feugère 1991, 72-88; with horizontal handle: Radnóti 1938, 70-4, pl. V, 22; Majnarić-Pandžić 1973, 56, pl. I, 7.
14. Feugère 1991, 106 fig. 6.
15. De Marinis 1991, 98-102; De Marinis and Feugère 1991, 106-8.
16. Feugère 1991, 112 nos. 84-5.
17. Popović 1992, 63 abb. 2.
18. Boube and Guillaumet 1991, 28 fig. 5, 32 fig. 9, 45 figs. 21-2.
19. Kelheim type jug: Boube and Guillaumet 1991, 39-42 figs. 16-17, 19. Kjaerumgard type jug: Boube and Guillaumet 1991, 37-9 fig. 15. Idrian type cup: Feugère 1991, 56 figs. 5-7. Pescate type simpulum: Castoldi 1991, 63-70 figs. 3, 10.
20. Bolla *et al.* 1991, 8.
21. Bolla *et al.* 1991, 11 no. 4.
22. Hoffiller 1908, 121 nos. 35-9. Roman examples: Radnóti 1938, 116; pl. XXXV, 1, 3.
23. Breščak 1982, 46 no. 51.
24. Guillaumet 1991, 8.
25. Guillaumet 1991, 11 no. 3; Radnóti 1938, 116; pl. XXXV, 5.
26. Guillaumet 1991, 11 no. 2; Radnóti 1938, 116 note 115.
27. Bolla *et. al.* 1991, 13-15 no. 38. Findspot: Glodariu 1979, 188-9, pl. 106, 16-18.
28. Breščak 1982, 47 no. 55.
29. Breščak 1982, 47 no. 61.
30. Hoffiller 1908, 120 nos. 17-33.
31. Majnarić-Pandžić 1973, pl. III, 7-8.
32. Zahlhaas 1971, 16, 47 A18. Date: Zahlhaas 1971, 47.
33. Boube and Guillaumet 1991, 23-45 fig. 2; Feugère 1991, 53-9, fig. 2,1.
34. Boube and Guillaumet 1991, 31 no. 18. Date: Boube and Guillaumet 1991, 25-7.
35. Boube and Guillaumet 1991, 33-8 fig. 10, no. 12.
36. Boube and Guillaumet 1991, 38.
37. Boube and Guillaumet 1991, 23 fig. 1.

38.   Radnóti 1957, 206, 223 no. 70, pl. XLI, 2. Place of manfacture: Boube and Guillaumet 1991, 40.
39.   Boube and Guillaumet 1991, 40.
40.   Boube and Guillaumet 1991, 23-7 fig. 5,21-22.
41.   Boube and Guillaumet 1991, 26-7.
42.   Popović 1992, 69-70, fig. 7,2. Place of manufacture: Boube and Guillaumet 1991, 26-27.
43.   Feugère 1991, 57 no. 35.
44.   Breščak 1982, 57 no. 147; Feugère 1991, 58 no. 36.
45.   Breščak 1982, 48 no. 66; Castoldi and Feugère 1991, 71 no. 75, with pp. 65-9.
46.   Castoldi and Feugère 1991, 71-2 no. 76.
47.   Ladles from Cibalae and Sirmium: Popović 1992, 64-5. Place of manufacture of Cibalae ladle: Castoldi and Feugère 1991, 65-9.
48.   Guillaumet 1991, 89-95 figs. 1, 3, 5.
49.   Popović 1992, 61-2.
50.   De Marinis 1991, 98-100 fig. 2; *contra* Feugère 1991, 112 no. 86.
51.   Feugère 1991, 105.
52.   De Marinis 1991, 98-100 fig. 2; Feugère 1991, 106-8.
53.   Popović 1992, 63 fig. 2; Feugère 1991, 106-8.

BIBLIOGRAPHY

Abbreviations in addition to those in Archäologischer Anzeiger:

ArchHung   *Archaeologia Hungarica (series)*

Bolla, M., Boube, C. and Guillaumet, J-P. 1991. Les situles. In, Feugère and Rolley 1991, 7-22.

Boube, C. and Guillaumet, J-P. 1991. Les cruches. In, Feugère and Rolley 1991, 23-45

Breščak, D. 1982. Antično bronasto posodje Slovenije - Roman bronze vessels in Slovenia. *Situla* **22/1**, 60

Castoldi, M. and Feugère, M. 1991. Les simpulums. In, Feugère and Rolley 1991, 61-88

Feugère, M. 1991. Les gobelets. In, Feugère and Rolley 1991, 53-9

Feugère, M. and Rolley, C. 1991. La vaisselle tardo-républicaine en bronze. *Actes de la table-ronde CNRS, Lattes. April 1990.* Publications de l'Université de Bourgogne, Centre de Recherches sur les Techniques Gréco-romaines, **13**. Dijon

Glodariu, I. 1979. Bronzes italiques en Dacie préromaine. In, E. Burkart (ed.), *Pénétration et diffusion, Actes du V*^e *Colloque International sur les bronzes antiques*, Cahiers d'Archéologie Romande 17, 185-9, pl. 109, 16-18. Lausanne

Guillaumet, J-P. 1991. Les passoires. In, Feugère and Rolley 1991, 89-95

Guillaumet, J-P. 1977. Les passoires de la fin de la Tène en Gaule et dans le monde celtique. *Gallia* 35, 239-48

Hoffiller, V. 1908. Antike Bronzegefäße aus Sissek. *ÖJh* 11, Bbl. 117-34

Hunyady, I. 1944. Kelták a Kárpát medencében - Die Kelten im Karpatenbeken. *DissPann II*, 18

Majnarić-Pandžić, N. 1973. Kasnolatenski keltski grobovi iz Sotina. *Vjesnik Hrvatskog Arheološkog Družtva* N A 6-7, 55-71, tav. I-V

De Marinis, R. and Feugère, M. 1991. Les Poêlons. In, Feugère and Rolley 1991, 97-112

Popović, P. 1992. Italische Bronzegefäße im Skordiskergebiet. *Germania* 70, 61-74

Radnóti, A 1938. Die römischen Bronzegefässe von Pannonien. *DissPann* II, 6. Budapest

Radnóti, A. 1957. Gefäße, Lampen und Tintenfässer aus Bronze. In, J. Borzsák (ed.), *Intercisa II. (Dunapentele) Geschichte der Stadt in der Römerzeit. ArchHung* XXXVI, 173-224

Szabó, Kl. 1990. Bronzipar Bronze industry. In, A. Mócsy, J. Fitz, and B. Lőrincz, (eds.) *Pannonia régészeti kézikonyve, Archaeological Handbook of Pannonia*, 130-51. Budapest

Werner, J. 1954. Die Bronzekanne von Kelheim. *BayVgbl* 20, 43-73

Zahlhaas, G 1971. *Großgriechische und römische Metalleimer*, 192. Munich

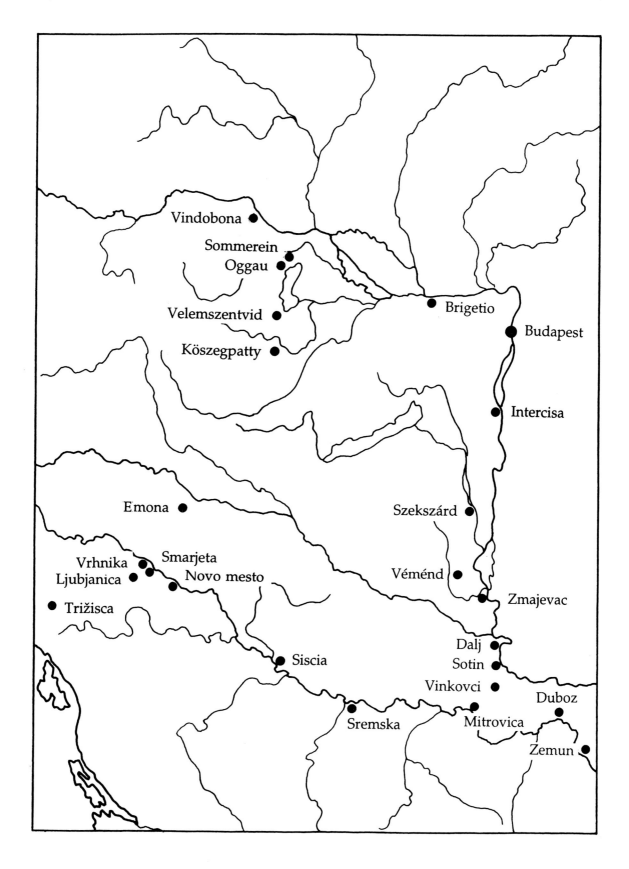

Fig. 1   Map of Transdanubia showing findspots of Italian bronze vessels dating to before the Roman conquest

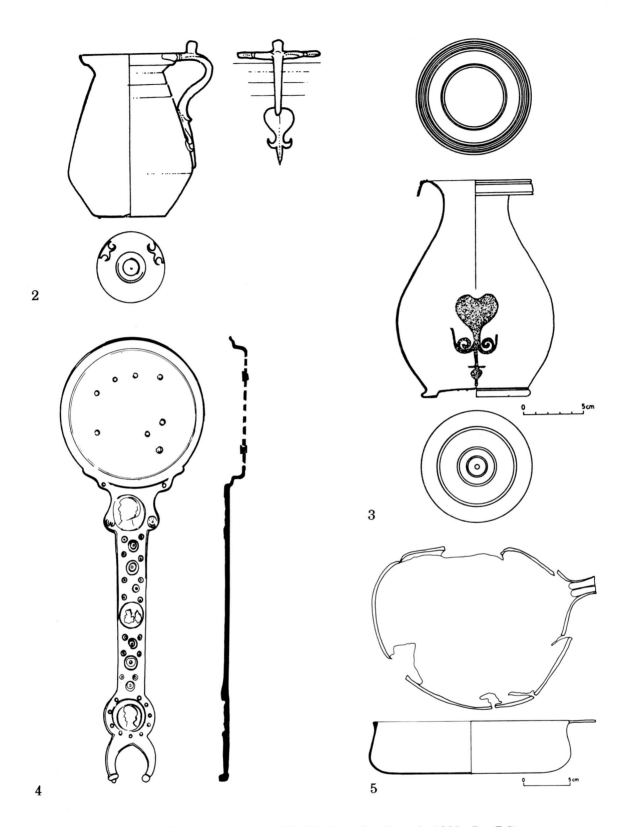

2

3

4

5

Fig. 2   Gallarate type jug, from the river Ljiubljanica (after Popovic 1992, fig. 7,2)
Fig. 3   Jug: type Kjaerumgaard E 122. Magyar Nemzeti Múzeum, MNM, Budapest 10/1951-17
Fig. 4   Strainer. MNM, Budapest 44/1892-19
Fig. 5   Saucepan: Povegliano-Scaldasole type, from Szekszárd-Baktahegy. Wosinsky Mór Múzeum,
         Szekszárd 15001

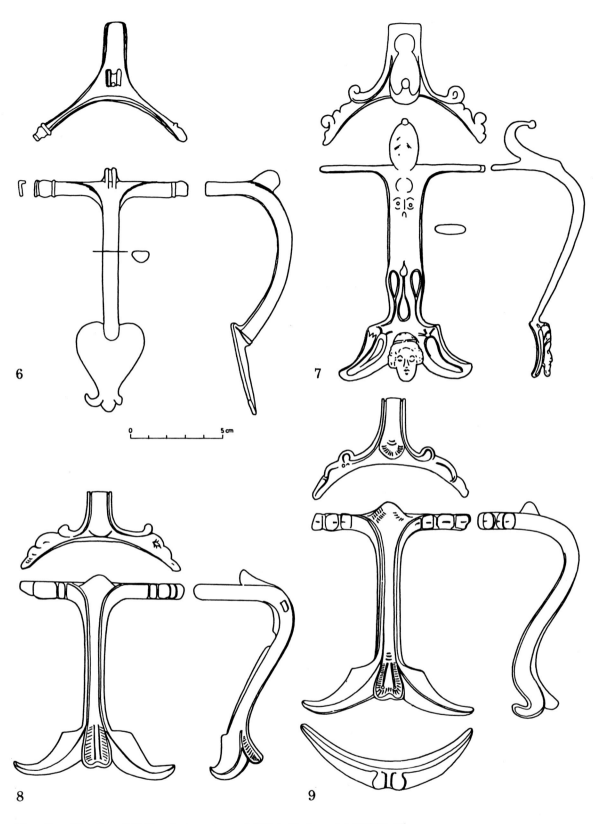

Fig. 6   Handle of Gallarate type jug. MNM, Budapest 44/1892-15
Fig. 7   Handle of Kappel-Kelheim type jug, from Intercisa. MNM, Budapest 2/1950-202
Fig. 8   Handle of Kelheim type jug. MNM, Budapest 44/1892-12
Fig. 9   Handle of Kelheim type jug. MNM, Budapest 44/1892-13

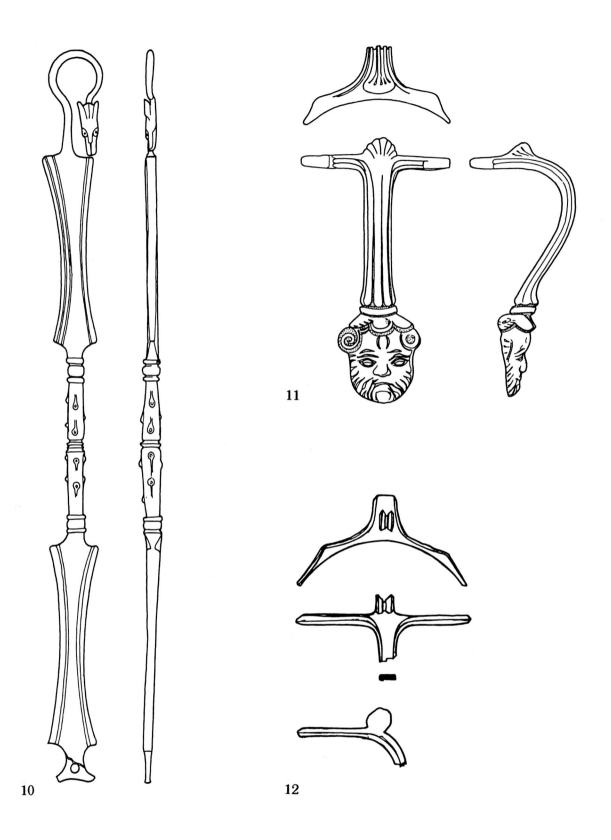

Fig. 10 Handle of Simpulum, type Castoldi A, from Brigetio. Kunsthistorisches Museum/Antikensammlung, Vienna 3009

Fig. 11 Handle of jug: type unknown. MNM, Budapest 44/1892-14

Fig. 12 Handle of Idrian cup, from Welemszentvid. Naturhistorisches Museum, Vienna 32439

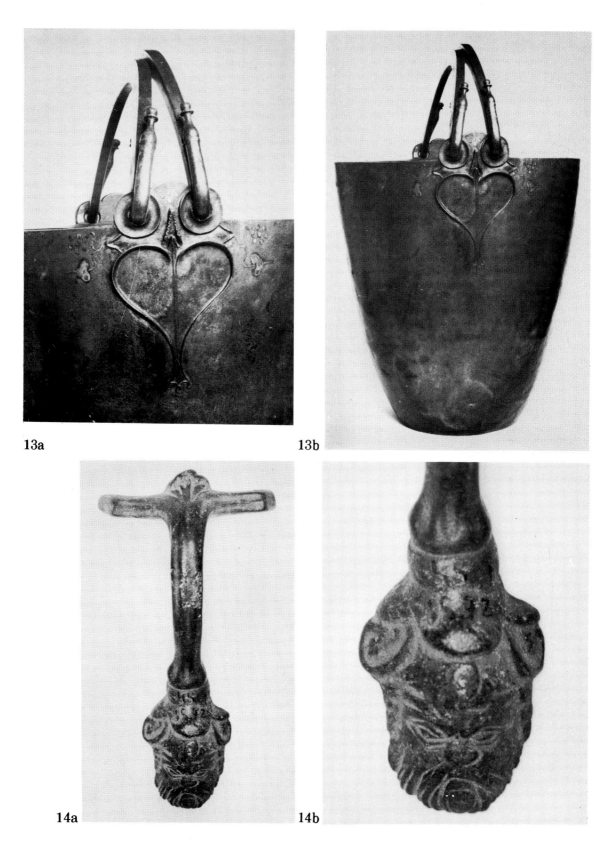

13a   13b

14a   14b

Fig. 13a,b   Bucket: type Zahlhaas A, from the bed of the river Danube. MNM, Budapest 175/1873-4
Fig. 14a,b   Handle of jug: type unknown. MNM, Budapest 44/1892-14

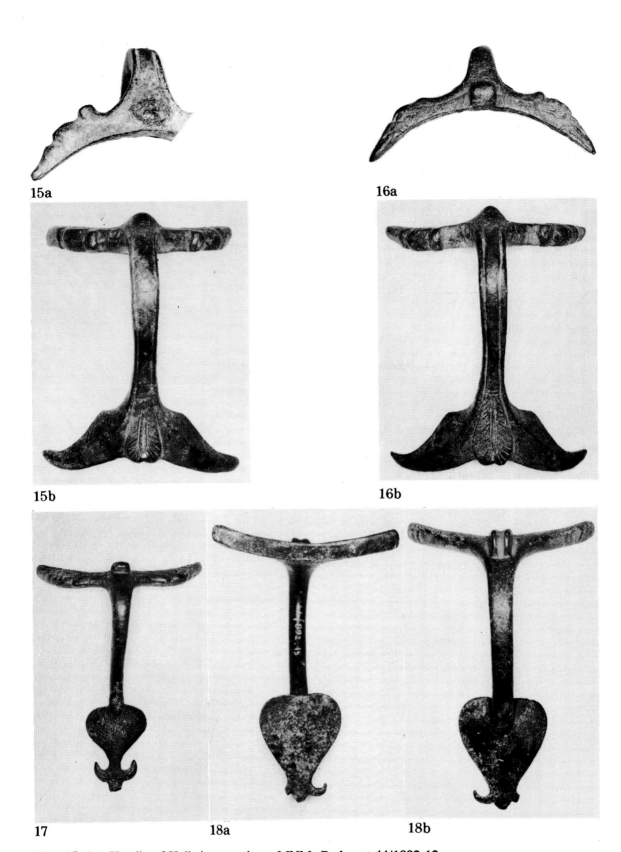

15a

16a

15b

16b

17   18a   18b

Fig. 15a,b Handle of Kelheim type jug. MNM, Budapest 44/1892-12
Fig. 16a,b Handle of Kelheim type jug. MNM, Budapest 44/1892-12
Fig. 17   Handle of Gallarate type jug or Idrian cup, from Intercisa. MNM, Budapest 11/1912-7
Fig. 18a,b Handle of Gallarate type jug. MNM, Budapest 44/1892-15

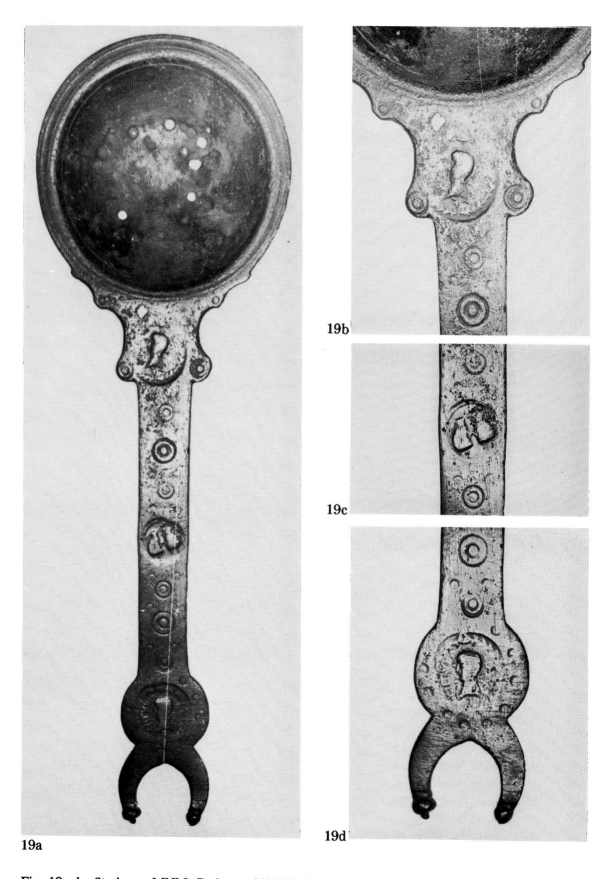

19a

19b

19c

19d

Fig. 19a-d   Strainer.   MNM, Budapest 44/1892-19

IMPORTS INTO DENMARK FROM PRE-ROMAN AND ROMAN ITALY

Helle Salskov Roberts

Institut for Græsk og Latin, Københavns Universitet, Copenhagen

The most spectacular pieces of evidence for contact between Denmark and the Italian peninsula in antiquity are indubitably large bronze vessels, especially cauldrons and other containers of liquid also known from many finds in other parts of Europe. The time of production of the earliest of these, i.e. the Langå cauldron (Figs. 3, 4), is the fifth century BC, but there are, in fact, a limited number of smaller finds such as fibulae that originate in an earlier period.

None of these finds, unfortunately, has come to light during controlled excavations. Reasonably reliable information, however, is available for a fibula with simple bow of the pre-Certosa type which was found by a farmer on the small island of Tåsinge off Funen (Map Fig. 1 no. 15) about a hundred years ago and which remained in his family until presented to the Svendborg and Omegns Museum in 1979 (Fig. 2).[1] The type is characteristic of the sixth century BC in the Picene area on the Adriatic coast, the present-day Marche.

A *navicella* fibula of a kind represented in Este from about 675-575 BC was found during ditch-digging at Iller Heath near Viborg in Jutland [2] and a *sanguisuga* fibula was found in Copenhagen, when the foundations for the present-day Central Station were dug.[3]

There are a few other such finds with more or less reliable information as to the circumstances of their discovery.[4] Of certain interest, however, is the occurrence of a pair of fibulae imitating the Certosa type in a cremation burial from Ulbjerg, near Viborg in Jutland.[5] That we are dealing with imitations is clear from the fact that the manufacturer had not mastered the function of the spring.

In 1882 J. Undset published a fragment of a horse-bit supposedly found in Denmark, but it has not been possible to verify this.[6]

These few small finds can hardly be interpreted as evidence of direct contact with their country of origin, but they may, of course, have arrived as items of exchange along the routes followed by the trade in amber and other luxury commodities or via the network of exchange that existed for centuries in Europe, as some scholars prefer to put it.[7]

The earliest major find is the rim of a large bronze cauldron with two well-preserved silenus mask-attachments from Langå on the island of Funen (Map Fig. 1 no. 1)and now in the Danish National Museum (Figs. 3, 4).[8] This cauldron was found in 1886 in a male burial of the pre-Roman Iron Age, i.e. the second part of the second or the first century BC, but it has been convincingly classified as an Etruscan work of about 475-450 BC, most likely originating in Etruscan Campania.

From the same site comes a bronze stamnos from the important bronze-working centre of Vulci and now in the Fyns Stiftsmuseum (Fig. 5).[9] The vessel was found in 1877 in a cremation burial of the same period as the cauldron. Similar stamnoi are known from finds in France at Bourges and Gurgy in mid-fifth century contexts, from tumulus I of La Motte-Saint-Valentin (Haute-Marne) with a red-figured kantharos from the beginning of the fifth century BC, as well as from Kleinaspergle in Germany, found with Attic kylikes of about 450 BC.[10] There are further examples from Weisskirchen in the Rhine province and from Tarnobrzeg in Poland and, of course, from sites in Italy itself.[11]

The shape of the Langå stamnos is close to those found in contexts of the first half of the fifth century BC. The handles, which may point to a fourth-century BC date, could be later additions by a smith or smiths who had some problem in fastening them and tried two different solutions, i.e. soldering and riveting respectively.

The Mosbæk cauldron, however, is a later creation of the third century BC (Fig. 7).[12] This cauldron was found upside-down in a peat bog in 1875. With its masks of a beardless Herakles it is a very unusual piece, but the Herakles face could well be a simplified version of the statuette in the Florence Archaeological Museum from Massa Marittima and it is also reminiscent of the Hermes head from the Vignale temple with regard to the strongly-pronounced eyelids, the eyes looking upwards, the long straight nose, full lips and round chin. Both these parallels are dated to the third century BC.[13]

In connection with these imports of Etruscan origin some other large cauldrons of foreign inspiration come to mind. From about the same period as the Mosbæk cauldron are the fragments of a huge vessel, consisting of an iron rim with a collar of bronze sheeting, three ring-handles of iron around which hollow bronze rings have been cast, three bronze attachments with the head of an owl and five bull's-head attachments and part of the lower body (Fig. 6).[14] The cauldron was found in 1952 at Brå near Horsens in Jutland, and had been deliberately broken before deposition (Map Fig. 1 no. 3). The attachments show distinct Celtic features, but the cauldron places itself in a long series known from temple deposits and burials in Italy and Greece and ultimately of Near Eastern inspiration.

Parts of another large cauldron with even more pronounced Celtic features were found at Rynkeby on Funen (Map Fig. 1 no. 24). It has attachments in the shape of ox-heads and human faces and is believed to date to *c*. 100 BC.[15]

From about the same time is the even more spectacular silver cauldron found in Himmerland at Gundestrup, decorated with repoussé plaques depicting deities, animals and warriors.[16] The cauldron had been dismantled before it was deposited on a dry piece of bog land. Its place of origin has been the object of much speculation, as it combines western Celtic features with Thracian technique. Lately, an area in Bulgaria near Thrace has been suggested, but northern Gaul has also found new support.[17] In the present context, however, it is more to the point that the depictions unequivocally indicate a ritual purpose for this large cauldron; this may in turn throw some light on the use of the Mosbæk cauldron, which was deposited in a rather similar way.

Although the Langå find comes from a burial presumably of the same period as the Gundestrup cauldron - and tomb gifts are usually thought to be indicative of status - it could still have served a ritual function, thereby giving status to the individual owning it.

Apart from cauldrons and the stamnos there are a few other containers of liquid of foreign origin found in Denmark. Found isolated, but near the site of 'Three Barrows' at Keldby on the island of Møn, comes a bronze bell situla from the end of the fourth century BC.[18] Since this piece was first brought to public notice in 1827 opinions have oscillated from 'of Greek taste' to 'of Greek workmanship', from 'South Italian' to 'Italic', from 'Hellenistic Etruria' to 'of Roman workmanship'. Riis in his study of the long list of bell situlae, of which some were ascribed to Corinth, ended up by classifying the Keldby piece as Tarentine. Lately, Shefton has settled for a North Peloponnesian workshop, mainly for technical reasons.[19] Be that as it may (the piece is not available for inspection at the moment), the Keldby situla no doubt came north via Italy, more specifically through the Etruscan trading-posts of the Po valley, where political circumstances from the end of the fourth century BC favoured trading links between the Etruscans and Gauls who, with the help of related tribes, furthered merchandise across the Alps, by the same route which the Langå and Mosbæk cauldrons may have followed.[20]

Apart from the bell situla there are other buckets with movable handles resting in rings, sometimes with a plastic mask-attachment underneath. A fine example was found in 1861 with fragments of a bronze casserole and a strainer on a hill slope at Søndre Jernløse (Knabstrup) on Zealand (Map Fig. 1 no. 4, Fig. 8).[21] Like the bell situla, it is derived from Greek metalwork of the second half of the fourth century BC.[22] Traditionally these buckets have been regarded as works from Roman Capua of the first century BC or first century AD. Recently, however, Poulsen has stressed certain features which seem typically Celtic as, for example, the horse's-head finials of the handles, on the basis of which he would ascribe the workshop to the eastern Alpine area.[23] Lund Hansen in her thorough analysis of Roman imports into Denmark accepts it as coming into that category, though she points out the complexity of determining the relationship between Roman products and their various derivations. She dates the bucket to AD 40-70 on the basis of the strainer found in the same context.[24] Whether the piece originates in Italy itself, or is a derived product from an Alpine region, the prototype must have come through Italy, most probably via the Po valley.

A bronze bucket with movable handle and human mask-attachment formed part of the tomb-group found at Hoby on the island of Lolland (Map Fig. 1 no. 17, Fig. 9)[25] The masks of the bucket should, no doubt, be taken as representing gorgoneia like those of the aforementioned situla in Thessalonike. Winged gorgoneia are quite common and the hairstyle, with a plait doubling back from the forehead, is well known from both sculpture and from the plaster casts of the victims of the Vesuvian eruption.[26] The setting of the Søndre Jernløse masks, usually described as vine-leaves, is likely to be a derivation of the wings.

Apart from local pottery and pieces of iron the burial, which was that of a male aged 20-35 years, contained a considerable number of imports: a bronze casserole stamped CN TREBELLI ROMANI, a bronze basin with relief medallion, a bronze oinochoe, two bronze fibulae, three silver fibulae, two silver fibulae with animal-heads, a silver cup with handle incorporating an animal-head,[27] a large bronze tray and, standing on this, the famous pair of silver cups with relief decoration depicting themes from Greek literature.

This pair of relief cups is unique in more than one respect. Quite apart from their aesthetic quality they have an artist's signature in Greek letters and language, indicating the nationality of the metalworker, and another signature identical to the first, except for the Roman lettering CHIRISOPHOS EPOI, thus pointing to the Roman market for which the cups were intended. Last, but not least, they have graffiti under the bases of the cups, giving the weight and the name of a one-time owner, SILIVS. Friis Johansen has convincingly identified this person as C. Silius A. Caecina Largus, who was *legatus exercitus Germaniae Superioris* in the years AD 14-21.[28] The Roman official may well have donated this fine drinking service to a person on the southern island of Lolland whose influence could be useful to the Romans, a practice mentioned by Tacitus (*Annals* I, 11). Such a diplomatic gift is likely to have been given during Silius' term of office and the Hoby burial may have taken place during the time of Tiberius, given the estimated age of the deceased.

The pair of drinking cups on a tray, the bucket, the casserole, the oinochoe and the relief bowl seem to form an original unit and it is natural to assume that they arrived together. Some of the smaller objects, such as fibulae, gold rings and a belt-buckle based on a Roman military type known from the *limes castella*, were not necessarily acquired in the same way. A study of the two most elaborate fibulae with animal-heads have shown them to be derivations of a type perhaps to be attributed to the eastern Alpine region (Fig. 11).

The typologically earlier phase is represented in a tomb-group found at Bendstrup in Jutland (Map Fig. 1 no. 16 and Fig. 10). The find, which was made in 1869 in the grounds of the manor Valbygaard, where it is still kept, included imported Roman bronze lion's-paw feet and part of a large bronze vessel, and shows evidence of personal international contacts.[29]

The following tomb-groups from the first half of the first century AD have Roman imports. An inhumation burial found at Stangerup on the island of Falster (Map Fig. 1 no. 18) had a shallow bronze bowl with movable handles, a bronze oinochoe, smaller than but similar to the Hoby specimen, and a casserole; at Byrsted in Jutland (Map Fig. 1 no. 19) there were found a bronze bowl with movable handle, two silver cups and various pieces of gold and silver jewellery. At Tombølgård on the island of Als (Map Fig. 1 no. 20) a cremation burial was found in 1932, containing a similar bowl, and a casserole as well as gold and silver jewellery, glass and amber beads, local pottery and so on, while from Balslev on Funen (Map Fig. 1 no. 21) comes another bronze bowl.[30]

Recently, an important new excavation at Hedegård near Horsens in Jutland (Map Fig. 1 no. 25) has added to the list of early Roman imports. The cremation burial A 1136 produced a rare type of bronze basin on a foot and adorned with vine-leaf handles (h. 28cm, diam. 42cm). In Germany only two examples are so far known, one from a tomb in Braunschweig and one from a bog in Mecklenburg,[31] and in Italy itself the type is rare, with only five specimens being recorded. These are dated to the first century BC and are regarded as being of Capuan workmanship. The Hedegård specimen is kept in the Horsens Museum, responsible for the excavation of the Roman Iron Age village and necropolis since 1986.[32]

So far only about a third of the necropolis has been dug and about one hundred tombs examined, consisting of cremation burials of about 50 BC to AD 50-150. Apart from the vine-leaf basin there are other more common imported bronzes, glass and gold beads, silver needles and fibulae of the same type as those from Bendstrup and Hoby. Analysis has shown a large iron ring to be made of imported metal but, even more significantly perhaps, iron slag and a furnace for iron extraction have been found. One tomb also contained a set of metalworking tools, best interpreted as belonging to a jeweller.[33]

At Hedegård we thus have evidence of metal workshops, which may indicate the economic basis for the wealth of this unusually large settlement. Local expertise may also point to the professional interest these smiths could have had in acquiring foreign metalware, to copy or to sell. The technology and the raw material came from the south, some of the finished products coming from as far away as Roman Capua. How far south the artisans working at Hedgård went personally to acquire their skills and materials we do not know. The evidence of contact, however, is indubitably there, a contact different from the 'diplomatic gift' exchange responsible for some Roman imports into Denmark, but perhaps more important for the economic and technological development of the area.

As for smaller objects, a few millefiori glass beads from Jutland and Funen should be mentioned, though they were unfortunately not found in context. Some are quite large, about 4cm in diameter, their specific purpose, although of obvious ornamental value, being unknown. In Celtic tombs further south large glass beads appear to be found mainly in tombs of children or young women and some believe them to be amulets.[34]

Finally, there is a modest number of Roman coins. The oldest is an as with a head of Janus on the obverse and a prow on the reverse, minted in Rome 179-170 BC, found at Fredericia in Jutland, followed by three denarii with the head of Dea Roma, from the second half of the second century BC, found at Vester Vedsted, Jutland (Map Fig. 1 no. 10), Lejre and Græsted on Zealand (Map Fig. 1 nos. 13 and 11), and a denarius with the head of Utica on the obverse and a trophy on the reverse from 47/46 BC found at Dankirke, Jutland (Map Fig. 1 no. 12).[35] Of greater interest is a hoard of twenty-five coins found behind the hearth of an Iron Age house at Ginnerup in northwest Jutland (Map Fig. 1 no. 14), covering the period 125 BC-AD 68, the last being a Neronian aureus (Figs. 13, 14).[36] The coins are obviously not evidence of trade based on payment in money, but are likely to have been collected for their metal value.

ACKNOWLEDGEMENTS

I should like to thank Dr Ulla Lund Hansen of the Institute of Prehistoric and Classical Archaeology, University of Copenhagen, as well as the staff of the Department of Danish Prehistory and of the Department of Coins and Medals at the Danish National Museum for their helpfulness during my work on this paper.

NOTES

1   Inv. 31312, Lavrsen and Randsborg 1982, 6-11.

2   Lavrsen 1958, 66 fig. 3.

3   Type Sundwall 1943, 179 no. F Ia b 16, from Vetulonia.

4   Lavrsen and Randsborg 1982, 10 n. 6.

5   Jensen 1965, 31-2.

6   Von Hase 1992, 240, with plate vol. fig. ll,6.

7   Jensen 1965; 1968, 101-2. Exchange network: Lund Hansen 1987, 219-20, 255.

8   Department of Danish Antiquities inv. C 5782. Diam. 36.6cm; ht. of attachment 11.8cm. See Riis 1959, 1-9; *Etrusques* 1992, 188-9.

9   Department of Prehistory D 1235: Riis 1959, 26-30, figs. 17-19; *Etrusques* 1992, 188-9.

10   Bourges: Gran-Aymerich 1992: 350 no. 6, 352, plate vol. fig. 9,2, and this volume. Gurgy: Gran-Aymerich 1992, 352, 358. La Motte-Saint-Valentin: *Etrusques* 1992, 263 no. 321. Kleinaspergle: *Celts* 1991, 127, 178-9; *Etrusques* 1992, 268 no. 343.

11   Riis 1959: 26-30; *Etrusques* 1992, 137-8 no. 148.

12   Danish National Museum, Department of Danish Antiquities inv. C 1968. Diam. at carination 49.5cm; inner diam. of rim 26.8cm; ht. 28.5cm. (Riis 1959, 10-16, figs. 9-11; *Etrusques* 1991, 188-9.

13   Massa Marittima: Inv. 5; *Etrusques* 1992, 80 colour fig. 143 no. 175. Vignale Hermes: Sprenger and Bartoloni 1977, fig. 244.

14   In Moesgaard, Forhistorisk Museum. Diam. 1.18m; original ht. *c.* 70cm; capacity *c.* 600 l. See *Celts* 1991, 375.

15   Danish National Museum, Department of Danish Antiquities inv. 8900. Diam. 70cm. See *Celts* 1991, 750, 770 no. 636.

16   Danish National Museum, Department of Danish Antiquities inv. C 6562. Diam. 69cm; ht. 42cm; weight 8,885 g. See *Celts* 1991, nos. 771, 430, 482, 504, 538, 646.

17   *Celts* 1991, 538. Northern Gaul: Hachmann 1991.

18   Danish National Museum, Department of Danish Antiquities inv. MCCCCLXXI. Riis 1959, 17-26.

19   Shefton 1985, 400-1, 409.

20   Vitale 1991, 222.

21   Danish National Museum, Department of Danish Antiquities inv. 19.471. Diam. of rim 24.2cm.

22   Cf. for example a situla with gorgoneion masks from Thessalonike: *Treasures*, 270, pl. 40.

23   Poulsen 1987, 103.

24   Lund Hansen 1987: 152-7. Strainer: Eggers type 162: Lund Hansen 1987, 401, 458, 30 fig. 10.

25   Danish National Museum, Department of Danish Antiquities inv. C 17.946-64. Friis Johansen 1923, 141-3; Lund Hansen 1987, 193, 403.

26   Sculpture: Ny Carlsberg Glyptotek: Poulsen 1962, nos. 34-41, pls. 52-69. Vesuvian victims: Grant 1971, 36.

27   Casserole: Eggers 1951, type 140. Basin: Eggers 1951, type 97; Friis Johansen 1923, 146 fig. 24. Oinochoe: Eggers 1951, type 126. Bronze fibulae: Almgren 1923, II, 26. Silver fibulae: Almgren 1923, II, 26. Silver fibulae with animal heads: Almgren 1923, IV, 71. Silver cup: Eggers 1951, type 166; Friis Johansen 1923, 150, fig. 28.

28   Friis Johansen 1923, 158, 164.

29   Hedeager and Kristiansen 1982, 150-62.

30   Stangerup bowl: Eggers 1951, type 92. Oinochoe: Eggers 1951, type 125. Casserole: Eggers 1951, type 140; Lund Hansen 1987, 402. Byrsted bowl: Eggers 1951, type 92. Cups: Eggers 1951, type 173. Jewellery: Lund Hansen 1987, 405. Tombølgård bowl: Eggers 1951, type 92. Casserole: Eggers 1951, type 140. Other finds: Lund Hansen 1987, 408. Balslev bowl: Eggers 1951, type 92; Lund Hansen 1987, 404.

31   Eggers 1951, type 94.

32   Madsen 1990, 23-5 with ill..

33   Ironworking: Voss 1988, 19-25. Jeweller's tools: Madsen 1990, 17.

34   Beads: Danish National Museum C 5191, C 4262, C 3353, C 706, C 262, 16.121, 1/26/75). Possibly amulets: Pauli 1975, 160-5.

35   Balling 1962, 6-11; Kromann 1984, 62, 64, 103. Dankirke coin type: Crawford 1974, 460/3.

36   Brøndsted 1960, 137, 175-6; Balling 1962, 6-9.

BIBLIOGRAPHY

Abbreviations in addition to those in *Archäologischer Anzeiger*:

AarbK   Aarbøger for nordisk oldkyndighed og historie
Kuml   Årbog for Jysk Arkaeologisk Selskab

Almgren, 0. 1923. *Studien über nordeuropäische Fibelformen*. 2nd ed. Leipzig

Balling, J. 1962. De romerske Møntfund fra Jylland. *Nordic Numismatic Journal* 1962, 5-78

Brøndsted, J. 1960. *Denmarks Oldtid* III. *Jernalderen*. Copenhagen

Celts 1991. *The Celts*. Exhibition Catalogue, Palazzo Grassi. Milan

Crawford, M. 1974. *Roman Republican Coinage*. Cambridge

Eggers, H.J. 1951. *Der römische Import im freien Germanien*. *Atlas der Urgeschichte* I. Hamburg/Glückstadt

Etrusques 1992. *Les Etrusques et l'Europe*. Exhibition Catalogue. La Réunion des musées nationaux. Paris

Friis Johansen, K. 1923. Hoby-Fundet. *Nordiske Fortidsminder* **II**, 3. Copenhagen

Gran-Aymerich, J. 1992. Les matériaux étrusques hors d'Etrurie. Le cas de la France et les travaux en cours a Bourges-Avaricum. In, L. Aigner-Foresti (ed.), *Akten des Symposions von Wien - Schloss Neuwaldegg 2.-5. Oktober 1989*, 329-59. Vienna

Grant, M. 1971. *Cities of Vesuvius*. London

Hachmann, R. 1991. Gundestrup Studien. *BerRGK* **71**, 1990, 2, 573-903

von Hase, F-W. 1992. Etrurien und Mitteleuropa - zur Bedeutung der ersten Italisch-Etruskischen Funde der späten Urnenfelder und frühen Hallstattzeit in Zentraleuropa. In, L. Aigner-Foresti (ed.), *Akten des Symposions von Wien - Schloss Neuwaldegg 2.-5. Oktober 1989*, 235-66. Vienna

Hedeager, L. and Kristiansen, K. 1982. Bendstrup en fyrstegrav fra den romerske Jernalder, dens sociale og historiske miljø. *Kuml* 1982, 81-164

Jensen, J. 1965. Ulbjerg-graven. *Kuml* 1965, 23-33

Jensen, J. 1968. Et jysk ravfund. Ravhandelen i den yngre bronzealder. *Kuml* 1968, 93f.

Kaul, F. 1991. The Gundestrup Cauldron. In, *Celts* 1991, 538-9

Kromann, A. 1984. Recent Roman coin finds from Denmark. *Nordic Numismatic Journal* 1983-84, 59-122

Kruta, V. 1992. Art étrusque et art celtique. In, *Etrusques* 1992, 206-13

Lavrsen, J. 1958. Votive finds from the end of the Bronze Age. *Kuml* 1958, 70-1

Lavrsen, J. and Randsborg, K. 1982. Italien på Tåsinge - omkring en fibel fra 6.årh.f.Kr. *Årbog 1981 for Svendborg and Omegns Museum*, 6-11

Lund Hansen, U. 1987. *Römischer Import im Norden. Warenaustausch zwischen dem römischen Reich und dem freien Germanien.* Copenhagen

Madsen, O. 1990. Hedegård - et jernalderaristokrati ved Skjern Å.Vejle.

Mortensen, P. 1991. The Brå Cauldron. In, *Celts* 1991, 375

Pauli, J. 1975. *Keltischer Volksglaube: Amulette und Sonderbestattungen am Dürrnberg bei Hallein und im eisenzeitlichen Mitteleuropa.* Munich

Poulsen, E. 1987. Kelto-romerske importer. *AarbKøb* 1987, 97-103

Poulsen, V. 1962. *Les portraits romains.* Copenhagen

Riis, P.J. 1959. The Danish bronze vessels of Greek, Early Campanian, and Etruscan manufacture. *ActaArch* **30**, 1-50

Shefton, B.B. 1985. Magna Grecia, Macedonia or neither? Some problems in 4th century BC metalwork. *AttiMGrecia* 1984, 399-410

Sprenger, M.A. and Bartoloni, G. 1977. *Die Etrusker. Kunst und Geschichte.* Munich

Strøm, I. 1992. Les relations transalpines au Danemark. In, *Etrusques* 1992, 188-9

Sundwall, J. 1943. *Die ältesten italischen Fibeln*. Berlin

Treasures. *Treasures of Ancient Macedonia*. Ministry of Culture and Science, Archaeological Museum of Thessalonike

Vitale, D. 1991. The Celts in Italy. In, *Celts* 1991, 220-35

Voss, O. 1988. Hedegård - et sjældent jernudvindingsanlæg fra ældre romersk jernalder. *Horsens Museum. Årskrift* 1987-1988, 19-25. Horsens

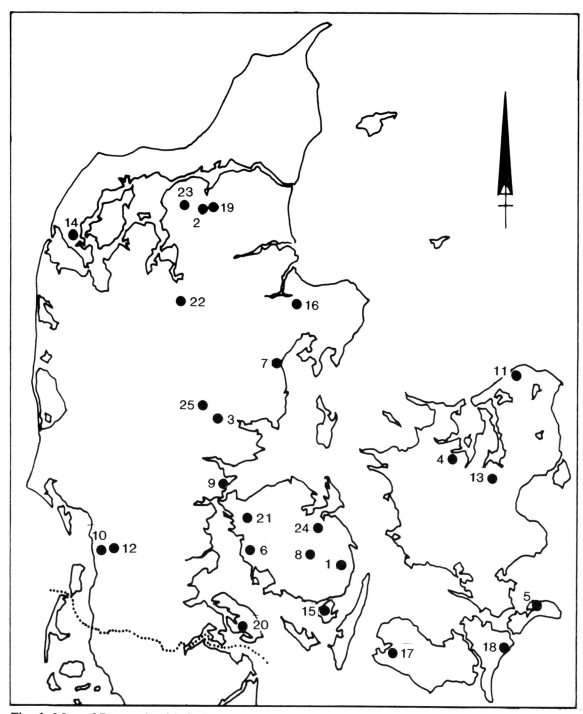

Fig. 1 Map of Denmark with findspots

1 Langå (Funen)
2 Mosbæk (Jutland)
3 Brå (Jutland)
4 Søndre Jernløse (Knabstrup)
    (Zealand)
5 Keldby (Møn)
6 Kærum (Funen)
7 Århus (Jutland)
8 Ringe (Funen)

9 Fredericia (Jutland)
10 Vester Vedsted (Jutland)
11 Græsted (Zealand)
12 Dankirke (Jutland)
13 Lejre (Zealand)
14 Ginnerup (Jutland)
15 Tåsinge (off Funen)
16 Bendstrup (Jutland)
17 Hoby (Lolland)

18 Stangerup (Falster)
19 Byrsted (Jutland)
20 Tombølgård (Jutland)
21 Balslev (Funen)
22 Viborg
23 Gundestrup
24 Rynkeby
25 Hedegård

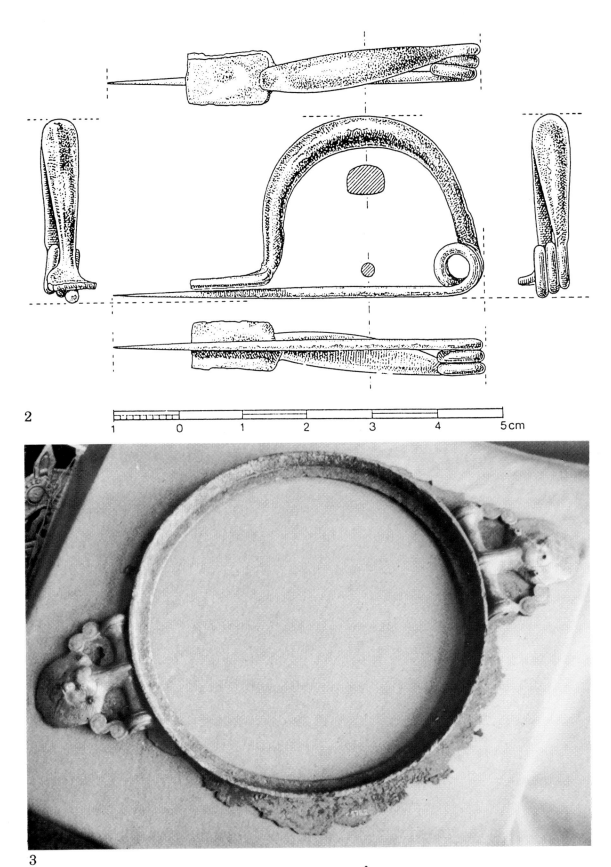

2

| 1 | | 0 | | 1 | | 2 | | 3 | | 4 | | 5 cm |

3

Fig. 2   Bronze fibula found on Tåsinge. After *Svenborg Årborg* 1981

Fig. 3   Rim of bronze cauldronfound at Langå

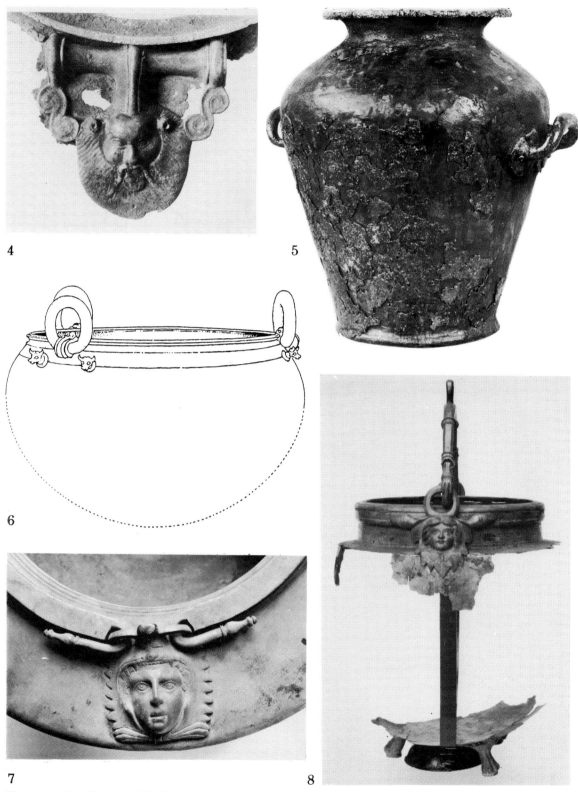

Fig. 4   Attachment with silenus mask, detail of Fig. 3. Photo Danish National Museum
Fig. 5   Bronze stamnos from Langå. Photo Odense Stiftsmuseum
Fig. 6   Reconstruction of bronze cauldron from Brå. After *Celts* 1991
Fig. 7   Bronze cauldron from Mosbæk. Photo Danish National Museum
Fig. 8   Bronze situla from Søndre Jernløse (Knabstrup). Photo Danish National Museum

301

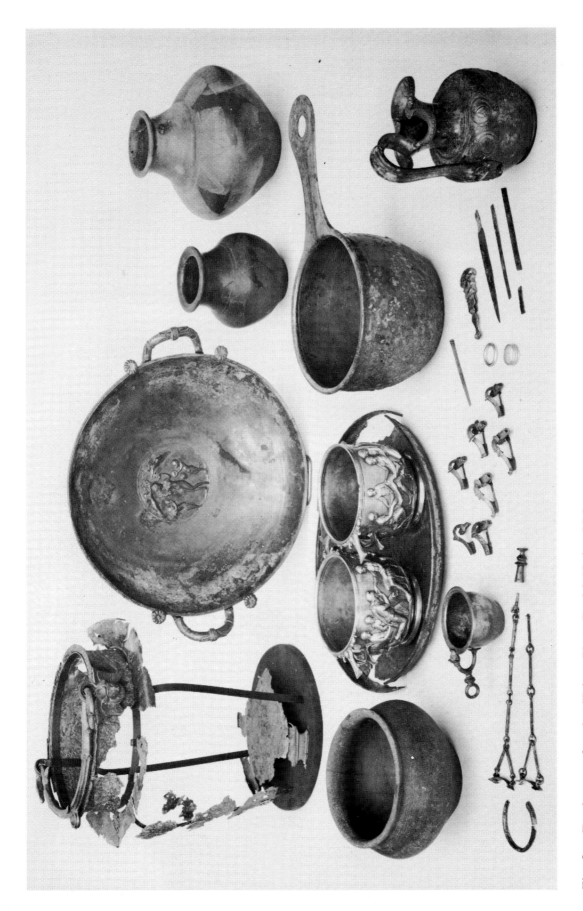

Fig. 9   Tomb group found at Hoby.   Photo Danish National Museum

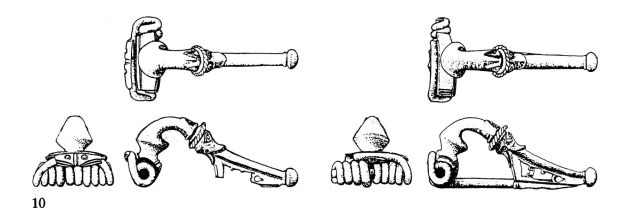

10

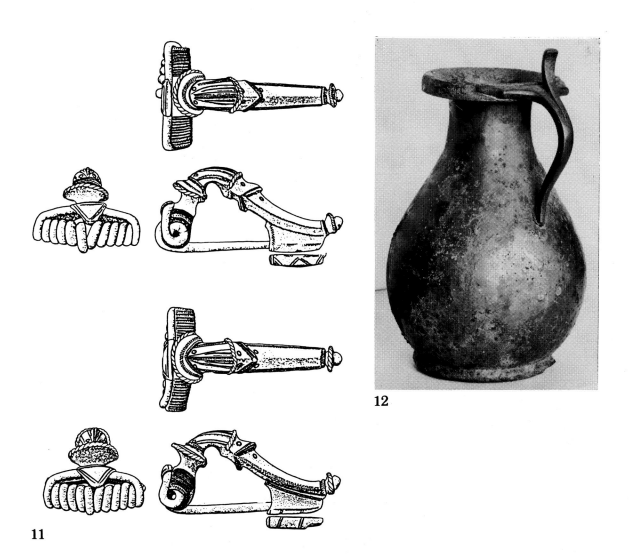

11

12

Fig. 10   Silver fibulae from Bendstrup. After *Kuml* 1981
Fig. 11   Silver fibulae from Hoby. After *Kuml* 1981
Fig. 12   Bronze olpe from Kærum. Photo Danish National Museum

14

13

Figs. 13,14   Hoard of coins from Ginnerup   13 = obverse   14 = reverse   Photo Danish National Museum

ROMAN FINANCIAL SYSTEMS

ITALY, EUROPE AND THE MEDITERRANEAN: RELATIONS IN BANKING AND BUSINESS DURING THE LAST CENTURIES BC

Jean Andreau

Directeur d'Etudes, EHESS, Centre de Recherches Historiques,
27 rue Masson, 78600 Maisons-Lafitte, France

Much has been written about Roman businessmen's activities in the Mediterranean area during the last centuries BC.[1] It is usual to insist on the part they played, after the conquest of the various provinces (and even, in some cases, before the conquest), in the exploitation of newly acquired territory, especially within the Greek world. It is also common practice to recall some substantial operations in which Senators and *Equites Romani* took part, such as Brutus' loan to the city of Salamis in Cyprus or Rabirius' mission in Egypt.

In this paper I shall try to make some general comments about those businessmen and, particularly, in accordance with the main topic of this colloquium, to consider the relations between them and the relations between their various activities. I should like to stress the point that, in my view, these relations must be studied and thought about in terms of what some sociologists and anthropologists call networks - that is , systems of mutual influences and relations, built up on purpose, between independent units, but in the frame of a single global, common structure. In the case-study we are now interested in, the networks have, I think, two main characteristics and results. On the one hand, they are an answer to the problem of the areas and distances under Roman rule, which grew very fast from decade to decade during the two last centuries BC. On the other hand, the networks are some kind of answer to the problem of understanding the structure of enterprises and of firms.[2] There is no need to connect Roman banks or money-lending businesses to the big Italian merchant companies of the Middle Ages; both are answers, and successful answers, to the same problem, but they are two different answers.

The peculiar characteristics of Roman financial and commercial networks partly explain the way in which activity in banking and business adapted itself with great flexibility after each conquest and the way in which it invaded every new province. The provinces were transformed, but the system stayed more or less the same. The flexibility of the system can help us to understand how, subsequently, the brightest and most sophisticated aspects of this business world lost their strength bit by bit and even seem to disappear. The first to disappear were the most prominent financial intermediaries, that is, those who put money-lenders in touch with borrowers,[3] as well as the big businessmen who were called *negotiatores* during the last century of the Republic. Then, in the second and third centuries AD, the professional bankers also disappeared - or at least the majority of them.[4]

Let us note that for the first half of the second century BC there is little evidence. I shall discuss mainly the second half of the second century BC and the Ciceronian period.

Every important notable or businessman organised around himself a large group of complex relationships which in some cases stretched over the whole Mediterranean. But the groups of relationships surrounding every major economic agent consisted of smaller segments, of links between several independent units, which formed the centre of a network.

The networks play, in commercial and financial life, the same role as the factions and alliances in Roman political life. And, just like the political factions, they were much more flexible and, in many cases, much less durable that one would think and hope (I say 'hope' because more rigid and lasting institutions are easier to understand and interpret).[5] They are the result of personal choices of the agents and of the sense of solidarity which they felt for certain groups.

Kinship plays a role in the building up of such segments; alliances by marriage play a role too, as well as political and private *amicitiae*. What the Latins call *propinqui* are both relatives or *adfines* and political or social friends. When Cicero writes that Q. Caecilius, Atticus' uncle, did not accept a better rate of interest from his *propinqui*, he does not refer only to his relatives.[6] In the same way, when the *Eques* C. Rabirius Postumus gave financial *partes* in the societies of publicans, he gave them to his *amici*, that is to the people with whom he was linked. Among those people, there were probably relatives, but there were friends too.[7]

From the first part of the second century BC to the middle of the first century, the Cossutii, who were studied some years ago by E. Rawson and M. Torelli,[8] were involved in architecture and sculpture, and they had large economic interests in marble quarrying and transportation. At the beginning of the first century BC, one of them entered the Roman Senate, and the line seems to disappear around 40 BC. Their vast *familia* of *liberti* carried on the trade, even after the disappearance of the line itself, with representatives known in areas connected with marble quarries and ports. In this case, enterprises lasted a long time, with inheritances within the same family line, though of course it does not mean that all the contemporary Cossutii took part in a single enterprise. But certainly they had mutual business relations.

The frontiers between the various networks are quite impossible to perceive, because of the nature of the evidence. The limit between a single enterprise and a network is not easy to perceive either. Everyone knows that many Italian aristocrats or big businessmen had agents in various regions. For instance, in 51 BC, T. Pomponius Atticus, Cicero's friend, had at least three main agents in Greece and Asia Minor: a freedman of his, Philogenes; a Roman citizen, Seius; and a peregrine, Xenon. At the same time, C. Curtius Mithres, who was very probably C. Rabirius Postumus' freedman, lived in Ephesus.[9] Some years before, the two Fufii brothers had sent an agent to *provincia Asia*, where they had lent money.[10]

In many such cases, it is very difficult or even impossible to distinguish direct agents, taking part in the same enterprise, from independent agents, who played the role of intermediaries, within the framework of several possible juridical relationships. Very often, however, it is easier to think of the second solution, that is a network of independent agents.

Of course, the word *procurator* (from the verb *procurare*) means that the agent's only role was to take care of the interests of the person he was representing. But such private *procuratores* (for instance, Pompey's *procuratores* in Cappadocia and Cilicia)[11] could fulfil this mission while managing their own businesses and lending their own, or other investors', money.

For instance, Lucius Oppius, who managed Egnatius Rufus' affairs in Asia (*negotia procurat*) and whom Cicero recommended to the proconsul of Asia, was himself doing his own business (*qui negotiatur*) at Philomelium in Phrygia, as an independent businessman.[12] In the same manner, the famous story of Marcus Scaptius and Publius Matinius who lent Brutus' money to the city of Salamis, cannot be understood if one supposes they were both Brutus' paid agents. The money belonged to Brutus, but they received a mandate to lend it, and so officially lent it as creditors themselves. In this way, no one knew that the actual creditor was Brutus, until he finally informed Cicero in a letter.[13]

Let me give you another example from Cicero. While he was staying in Brindisi and waiting for Caesar's forgiveness in 47 BC, Atticus, in Rome, managed to transfer to him some money through Cnaeus Sallustius, in Brindisi itself, and through the Tarentine Minucius. Minucius was Atticus' debtor; Sallustius had a correspondent and relative, Publius Sallustius, in Rome. P. Sallustius would receive the same amount of money as that given to Cicero in Brundisium. So in this case, too, they were independent agents, whether notables or specialised businessmen.[14]

In many cases, one must think of relationships between divided enterprises, some of them important, others smaller. When the agent was a freedman or even a slave, the enterprise, of course, could have been an independent one. When the slave received a *peculium*, he was professionally an independent entrepreneur (although he was still his master's property and depended on his master's money). However, in the financial world of the last centuries BC, freedmen and slaves seem to have been less numerous among businessmen than during the first centuries of the Empire.

Most of the financial networks were composed mainly of some particular social group: of these one may distinguish several categories.

The first one, the one we know best because of the nature of the evidence, was composed largely of aristocrats, Senators or *Equites*. Some of them had business deals to run: to transfer funds from the provinces to Italy or from Italy to the provinces; to try to borrow money, in order to pay off embarrassing loans by a *versura*; to exchange money; to purchase or to sell property; and so on. Others helped them to manage financial and more or less technical operations. The social rank of the second group was somewhat lower; some of them were *Equites*, while others were local notables or various businessmen and tradesmen.

A very prominent example of those who ran business on behalf of Senators was, of course, Atticus. According to Cornelius Nepos, he used to take care of the interests of several Senators and many Knights. The Senators whose businesses he used to manage were the two Cicero brothers, A. Manlius Torquatus, M. Porcius Cato and Hortensius.[15] Cicero's correspondence shows us very well how a prominent business friend such as Atticus could facilitate a Senator's domestic and financial life, for instance by providing him with financial assistance and services upon request, or by investing his surplus cash in profitable concerns. For such services, Cicero's brother Quintus appealed, not only to Atticus but also to L. Egnatius Rufus. And Atticus himself appealed to Lucius Cincius, especially when he had to leave Rome. So here is a business network, built up around Atticus and chiefly consisting of Senators and *Equites*, each of whom was in possession of a very important patrimony that implied, in some way, a major enterprise or rather a series of enterprises.

On the other hand, businessmen such as Atticus and L. Egnatius Rufus, who were in charge of Senators' interests, naturally expected a return, as Nick Rauh stressed some years ago in his paper, 'Cicero's business friendships'.[16] In many cases, as far as we know, this return was not money, but an obligation to protect the business interests of his friends whenever they clashed with Roman authority. Cicero's letters show that, in 51-50 BC, he refused to award military *praefecturae*,[17] and, moreover, Rauh's paper stresses the point that Cicero, when selecting his legates or the members of his *consilium*, took some private and financial interests into account. It seems, for instance, that his legate Lucius Tullius, the only one of his officers to disobey his orders about requisitioning amenities from the provincials, was chosen because of Atticus and, still more, because of Q. Titinius, a mutual friend and a Senator who happened to be a prominent financier.[18] Atticus' attitude toward Senators and other *Equites* certainly reflected philosophical and ethical thought, as M. Labate and E. Narducci showed,[19] but it was also a logical financial attitude, and Atticus was surely not, among aristocrats, a mere altruistic exception.

Another category of business networks consisted mainly of merchants and of financial intermediaries who collected money for them. We catch a glimpse of such networks through some Ciceronian texts, for instance some passages in the Verrines, and from inscriptions, either in the Greek world or in Puteoli. We also see something of them in the Murecine wax-tablets which date, however, from the Julio-Claudian period.[20] I have shown in other papers how important this role of the intermediaries of credit was at the end of the Republic.[21] We know half a dozen of them, not all of whom seem to be tightly linked with harbours and merchants. If Cicero and Atticus lent money to Cluvius and Vestorius, who lived in Puteoli and were involved without doubt in commercial operations, others belonged to the Knights' order and were *feneratores* within the aristocracy and for the aristocracy, without any visible relations either with ports or with provinces, at least as far as we know.

Q. Caecilius, for instance, a very grasping man who lent a lot of money, probably collected Senators' money as well, in order to lend it; Cicero's letter informs us that in, 65 BC, Caecilius was - together with Lucullus, Scipio and L. Pontius - one of the creditors of P. Varius, a Roman knight.[22] Besides, it is known that it was thanks to Lucullus that Caecilius had become *eques*,[23] and, when he died some years later public opinion blamed him greatly for having forgotten Lucullus in his last will. One may wonder whether Caecilius lent only his own money or if he collected other people's money as well; I would suppose that the latter is closer to the truth, and that he particularly used to lend Lucullus' funds.

Other intermediaries were involved in publicans' affairs, and collected money to invest in the *societates publicanorum*, most of which ran businesses in the provinces. For instance, we know, as I have said before, that C. Rabirius Postumus gave financial *partes* in the societies to his *amici*.[24]

Such intermediaries formed a network with their best and most regular investors and borrowers.

During the second and the first centuries BC, many *negotiatores* outside Italy were at the same time money-lenders and wholesale merchants. Some bankers, even if they had no direct commercial interests, used to lend money to merchants. Philostratus, for instance, active in Delos in the second half of the second century, was either involved in the slave-trade, or lent money to merchants.[25] But not all *negotiatores* were merchants and money-lenders at the same time and not all bankers lent money to merchants. Consequently, it is easy to understand that some networks were both commercial and financial, whereas others were only financial - all the more so since the commercial interests of Senators and Knights often consisted of loans to intermediaries, who then lent the money to merchants. For example, excavations in the shipwreck known as Planier III, near Marseilles, confirmed that Vestorius was not only involved in financial activity but also had commercial interests and was, moreover, a manufacturer of dyes. In his financial and commercial activities, he had relations with Tuccius Galeo and with Sempronius Rufus, a Senator,[26] probably the Senator who, according to Cicero, would often be seen at the harbour of Puteoli.[27] Thus, we perceive around Vestorius the existence of a network, both financial and commercial, whereas Atticus, when he gave money to Vestorius, did not himself participate in the commercial activity of the network.

Further examples could be given, but it is not necessary. Apart from those networks we have just considered, there were other categories more difficult to identify precisely. For instance, in various major Italian and provincial cities there were, by contrast, networks of professional bankers, mainly local or regional, as well as networks of notables.

Having distinguished several types of networks, I should like to stress four further points about them and about the larger groups of complex relations that surrounded every prominent economic agent.

We noted that, even if a network did not consist exclusively of Senators, or of Knights, or of merchants and so on, nevertheless each network consisted of dominant social groups. The same was true of the whole group of one's personal relations: a Senator naturally knew more Senators than merchants, but all the same the range of his personal acquaintances was wide and diverse. After all, a Senator had various needs, such as finding accommodation in a city where he had to stop overnight and so on, so many of them probably managed to have relationships, however superficial, in every social stratum.

The second point is that to bring in profit, money needed in most cases to pass from one network to another. When in 61 BC Cicero borrowed money to pay for his new house on the Palatine, he wrote that this money was *circumforaneum*: a play on words meaning that the money had been borrowed near the forum but also that it was mobile money, changing hands rapidly. ('Which moves from one place to another' is the actual sense of *circumforaneus*.[28]) The money usually went from less specialised rich aristocrats or notables to more specialised important persons and then, in a certain number of cases, to professionals, for example to merchants. To change hands, money needed intermediaries; without intermediaries, the system would not have worked in the same way.

Thirdly, it is possible that merchants' networks were specifically economic; it is as yet impossible to know precisely how they functioned. However, in the case of the more aristocratic networks, it is evident that they were never merely economic, never exclusively directed towards trade or manufacture, never, even, exclusively directed towards financial profit. I have already said that Atticus was both a successful *paterfamilias* with sophisticated financial activities and that he had a specific ethical and political attitude, an important point to recognise if his behaviour is to be understood. In the sixth Paradox of the Stoics, Cicero criticises Crassus and describes him as both *sumptuosus* and *quaestuosus*. *Sumptuosus* means the one who always tries to spend more whereas *quaestuosus* indicates the one who always needs more money and a larger fortune, whatever it may cost. In this passage itself, however, one can perceive that if Crassus was indeed continually looking for profit, his ways and his objectives were often more political than economic. We know also that the same Crassus was ready to lend money without interest to his friends, or when he understood that such a service could subsequently bring him political profit.[29] This is not at all surprising - an aristocrat's economic concerns, as we would call them, were always inextricably bound up with his whole political and social activity.

Finally, the existence of such networks and larger groups of relations was of course practically justified by the need to achieve some kind of division of labour in order to meet various individual needs. If a Senator wanted to transfer from a province to Italy a sum of money he had won while he was proconsul or propraetor, the societies of *publicani* were able to do this. But if it was a private financial transfer, completely independent from any public activity, let us say towards the eastern provinces, he had to find somebody who had property or important interests (commercial interests or money-lending) in Greece or in Asia Minor. When Cicero wanted to transfer money to Athens for his son or to Asia for himself, he was helped by Atticus, because Atticus had property in Athens and in Epirus. He had also lent money to the city of Sicyon and in the province of Asia itself, and he kept several agents in those regions, as we have seen before.

If Cicero or Atticus had money to invest, they might appeal to someone else, for instance Cluvius or Vestorius. If they needed to borrow money quickly, they appealed to another type of businessmen, the *feneratores*: Q. Caecilius, for instance, Atticus' uncle, or Q. Selicius, or Q. Considius.[30] If someone wanted to invest in *publica*, the right man might be Cn. Plancius or L. Lamia.

But in this aristocratic and amateurish world, such a division of labour was very flexible, so that it is impossible to divide known businessmen into four or five clear-cut categories. We saw that some groups were relatively solid and durable but apart from that, they depended on the nature of each precise business, and on the region in which it took place. From the financial point of view, every region of the Roman Empire seems to have been, during this period, organised more or less in the same way. We can find *negotiatores* in Gaul or in Africa as well as in Asia Minor; one cannot speak of clear differences between Mediterranean regions and continental European ones. What we read about T. Flavius Sabinus in Switzerland[31] could be said of M. Scaptius in Cyprus, though if one needed to transfer funds to Cyprus, one had to appeal of course to M. Scaptius, not to T. Flavius Sabinus.

In the framework of a flexible division of labour, however, there was a tendency towards duplication, a tendency to use several possible means and men for the same transaction. R. Bogaert stressed that in Egypt, about the middle of the third century BC, Zeno, the steward of Apollonius' *dorea* (estate) had, at the same time, relations with nine bankers, either royal bankers or private persons who had bid by auction for the banks belonging to the State. Royal bankers were less expert at exchange, while Zeno, in the *dorea*, used to pay the workers, every day, through an auctioned bank. But he had links with four royal and five other banks.[32] This multiplicity of links may be explained both by the geographical situation of the various banks and by the fact that it was the only way to be certain of obtaining money at the right time.

It is the same in the Roman period. If Senators and Knights, during the last century of the Republic and at the beginning of the Empire, do not seem to have been regular customers of the professional bankers, they knew several *feneratores* and several intermediaries to whom they might entrust money. Cicero entrusted money to Cluvius from Puteoli, but one part of Cicero's business with Egnatius entailed loans and deposits placed in his hands.[33] And in 43, Cicero recommended L. Aelius Lamia's interests in Africa to the provincial governor in the strongest possible terms: he requested that the governor should treat the *negotia, procuratores, liberti* and *familia* of Lamia as if they were Cicero's own.[34] One may suspect he had lent money to Lamia as well as to Cluvius (already dead in 43) and to Egnatius.

Very practical everyday concerns and strategic ones persuaded Senators and *Equites* not to put all their eggs in one basket!

In conclusion, I should like to stress that through networks we may understand some of the main characteristics of business life during the last centuries BC. The structure first explains how the Romans managed to control business during the second half of the second century BC. I have not examined here how Roman merchants and businessmen built up their own networks, but it is evident that they were backed by the Roman administration and by the aristocracy, with financial means. Native financiers, such as Greeks, might of course form part of these Roman networks but would always be subordinate, being less wealthy and without the backing of the Roman governor.

NOTES

1. See Hatzfeld 1919; Wilson 1966; Cassola 1971; Shatzman 1975; Delplace 1977; Barlow 1978; D'Arms 1981; Feuvrier Prévotat 1981; Maselli 1986.
2. See on this problem Andreau 1990.
3. Andreau 1983, 1985 and 1987b.
4. Andreau 1986 and 1987a; Petrucci 1991.
5. There are of course many books and papers about political factions and their relations with kinship; see for instance Hölkeskamp 1987, and Andreau and Bruhns 1990.
6. Cicero, *ad Att.*, 1, 12, 1; see Andreau 1978.
7. Cicero, *pro Rab. Post.*, 4; on Rabirius Postumus, see Nicolet 1974, 1000-2, and Shatzman 1975, 395-6.
8. Rawson 1975 and Torelli 1980.
9. Cicero, *ad Fam.*, 13, 69.
10. Cicero, *pro Flacco*, 46-8.
11. Cicero, *ad Att.*, 6, 1, 3 and 6, 3, 5; see for instance Shatzman 1975, 391.
12. Cicero, *ad Fam*, 13, 43, 1.
13. Cicero, *ad Att*, 5, 21, 10-13; 6, 1, 3-8; 6, 2, 7-9; 6, 3, 5-6; see Magie 1950, 385-9.
14. Cicero, *ad Att*, 11, 11, 2; 11, 14, 3; and 11, 15, 2.
15. Cornelius Nepos, *Att.* 15, 2-3.
16. Rauh 1986.
17. Cicero, *ad Att.* 5, 21, 10; 6, 1, 4-7 and 25; 6, 2, 8-9; 6, 3, 5-7.

18. Rauh 1986, 27.
19. Labate and Narducci 1981.
20. Camodeca 1992.
21. See above, note 3.
22. Cicero, *ad Att.*, 1, 1, 3.
23. Valerius Maximus, 7, 8, 5.
24. Cicero, *pro Rab. Post.*, 4.
25. See Mancinetti Santamaria 1982.
26. D'Arms 1981, 48-55 and Tchernia 1968-1970.
27. Cicero, *ad Att.*, 5, 2, 2; see D'Arms 1981, 48-55.
28. Cicero, *ad Att.*, 2, 1, 11.
29. See Shatzman 1975, 116-22 and 375-8.
30. Cicero, *ad Att.*, 1, 12, 1.
31. Suetonius, *Div. Vesp.*, 1, 4; Andreau 1987a, 380-2.
32. Bogaert 1991.
33. See Rauh 1986, 17-18.
34. Cicero, *ad Fam.*, 12, 29, 2.

BIBLIOGRAPHY

Andreau, J. 1978. Financiers de l'aristocratie à la fin de la République. In, E. Frézouls (ed.), *Le dernier siècle de la République et l'époque augustéenne*, 47-62. Strasbourg

Andreau, J. 1983. A propos de la vie financière à Pouzzoles: Cluvius et Vestorius. In, M. Cébeillac Gervasoni (ed.), *Les 'Bourgeoisies' municipales italiennes aux IIe et Ier siècles av. J-C.*, 9-20. Naples

Andreau, J. 1985. Modernité économique et statut des manieurs d'argent. *MEFRA* **97**, 373-410

Andreau, J. 1986. Declino e morte dei mestieri bancari nel Mediterraneo occidentale (II-IV d.C.). In, A. Giardina (ed.), *Società romana e impero tardoantico*, 1. *Istituzioni, ceti, economie*, 601-15. Rome and Bari

Andreau, J. 1987a. *La vie financière dans le monde romain: les métiers de manieurs d'argent (IVe siècle av. J.-C.- IIIe siècle ap. J.-C.).* Ecole Française de Rome, Rome

Andreau, J. 1987b. L'espace de la vie financière à Rome. In, *L'Urbs, Espace urbain et histoire (Ier siècle av. J.-C.-IIIe siècle ap. J.-C.)*, 157-74. Ecole Française de Rome, Rome

Andreau, J. and Bruhns, H. (eds.) 1990. *Parenté et stratégies familiales dans l'Antiquité romaine.* Ecole Française de Rome, Rome

Barlow, Ch. T. 1978. *Bankers, money-lenders and interest rates in the Roman Republic.* Ann Arbor and London

Bogaert, R. 1991. Zénon et ses banquiers. *Chronique d'Egypte* **66**, 308-15

Camodeca, G. 1992. *L'archivio puteolano dei Sulpici*. Naples

Cassola, F. 1971. Romani e italici in Oriente. *DArch* **4-5 (2-3)**, 305-22

D'Arms, J.H. 1981. *Commerce and Social Standing in Ancient Rome*. Harvard

Delplace, Chr. 1977. Publicains, trafiquants et financiers dans les provinces d'Asie Mineure sous la République. *Ktema* **2**, 233-52

Feuvrier Prévotat, Cl. 1981. *Negotiator* et *mercator* dans le discours cicéronien: essai de définition. *Dialogues d'Histoire ancienne* **7**, 367-405

Hatzfeld, J. 1919. *Les trafiquants italiens dans l'Orient hellénique*. Paris

Hölkeskamp, K-J. 1987. *Die Entstehung der Nobilität*. Stuttgart

Labate, M. and Narducci, E. 1981. Mobilità dei modelli etici e relativismo dei valori: il 'personaggio' di Attico. In, A. Giardina and A. Schiavone (eds.), *Società romana e produzione schiavistica 3. Modelli etici, diritto e trasformazioni sociali*, 127-82. Rome and Bari

Magie, D. 1950. *Roman Rule in Asia Minor*. Princeton

Mancinetti Santamaria, G. 1982. Filostrato di Ascalona, banchiere in Delo. *Opuscula Instituti Romani Finlandiae* **2**, 79-89

Maselli, G. 1986. *Argentaria*. Bari

Petrucci, A. 1991. *Mensam exercere. Studi sull'impresa finanziaria romana (II secolo a.C.-metà del III secolo d.C.)*. Naples

Rauh, N. 1986. Cicero's business friendships. *Aevum* **60 (1)**, 3-30

Rawson, E. 1975. Architecture and Sculpture, the Activities of the Cossutii. *BSR* **48**, 36-47

Shatzman, I. 1975. *Senatorial Wealth and Roman Politics*. Brussels

Tchernia, A. 1968-1970. Premiers résultats des fouilles de juin 1968 sur l'épave 3 de Planier. *Etudes classiques* (Aix) **3**, 51-82

Torelli, M. 1980. Industria estrattiva, lavoro artigianale, interessi economici: qualche appunto. *MemAmAc* **36**, 313-23

Wilson, A.J.N. 1966. *Emigration from Italy in the Republican Age of Rome*. Manchester

THE UNIFICATION OF THE MONETARY SYSTEM OF THE ROMAN WEST: ACCIDENT OR DESIGN?

Andrew Burnett

Department of Coins and Medals, The British Museum, London WC1B 3DG

To those who know little of Roman coinage, it is something of a surprise to learn that Roman expansion and conquest was not followed by the introduction of Roman coinage, and perhaps even more of a surprise to discover that the unification of the monetary system of the Roman world took as long as six hundred years. Roman coinage had begun in about 300 BC, but it was only with the reforms of Diocletian just before AD 300 that we find the same money in use throughout the whole Empire. This surprising fact prompts the questions I want to ask here. How did this transformation come about? Why was it so slow? What were the reasons for change?

This paper is not intended to answer these questions fully, and is only a part of a much larger theme, since it is confined to the western Empire.[1] Moreover, the process of unification was more or less complete in the west - as opposed to the east - by AD 50, the terminal date of this colloquium.

Before looking at the question in more detail, it is necessary, I think, to define more closely what we mean by the unification of the monetary system of the Roman world. We need to distinguish, first of all, between the unification of the *currency* system - using the same coins - and the unification of the *monetary* system - using the same denominations or units of account. This distinction is necessary because, as we shall see, the use of Roman coins and Roman denominations did not always coincide. Secondly we need to distinguish between the different coinage metals, since we find that the pattern is different for silver and bronze.[2] What I want to do is first indicate the way in which the use of the three elements - Roman silver denarii, Roman bronzes and Roman denominations - spread through the western Empire and replaced the locally produced coinages, and then, secondly, look at the reasons which may explain these changes and the speed at which they took place.

SILVER COINAGE

The Roman denarius was introduced in about 212 BC to replace the earlier third-century coinage of Rome. The existence of a long and well-known controversy about the exact *date* of the introduction of the denarius[3] has distracted attention from the reasons behind the change. The reform was prompted by the financial problems of Rome during the first half of the war against Hannibal, which resulted in the reduction in the weight of the bronze coinage, the reduction in the weight and purity of the silver coinage and, finally, the minting of an emergency gold coinage[4] - all measures intended to enable more coins to be minted from an insufficient stock of metal, since the need for coins exceeded the amount of bullion available.

But although these problems were severe, one should not exaggerate them. In the case of the silver coinage, for example, we know that the reduction in fineness of the pre-denarius coinage was not catastrophic - from about 97% to about 88%,[5] and accompanied by only a small decrease in weight. In view of this I think we should modify the traditional picture of monetary collapse which is usually painted for this period. Instead of *collapse*, we should think of financial *difficulty* followed by reform. The reform saw the introduction of the new, pure silver, denarius. But where, we may ask, did the new and plentiful supply of silver come from? Not from, for example, the silver resources of Spain, since it was at just this time that the Romans were having their greatest difficulties in Spain. In fact, the new source of silver was surely not newly mined silver at all, but rather melted down coinage from circulation - not just the earlier Roman coinage, but also the non-Roman and much larger silver coinages of the Greek cities of Italy like Taras and Naples. The earlier Sicilian coinages of Syracuse and Carthage were also removed from circulation and reminted as Roman coins; the same may also have happened to a more limited extent in Spain.

We should consider the possibility that this recoinage was an aggressive political act, to demonetise all the coins of the Italian cities and replace them with Roman ones, and that this decision was prompted by Hannibal's capture of Taras in 212 BC. This great setback for the Romans led to the defection of a number of south Italian cities like Metapontum from Rome to Hannibal, the very cities whose coins were removed by the reform.

With the introduction shortly before 210 BC of the new denarii, the Romans acquired a coinage which was to last some 450 years until the third century AD. But the circulation of the denarius was at first very restricted, and its use was confined to Italy, Sicily and parts of eastern Spain.[6] During the course of the second century BC the use of the denarius in Spain increased, and it began to be used in Africa and southern Gaul towards the end of the century. The change was gradual in the case of Gaul but sudden in the case of Africa: after the destruction of Carthage in 146 BC Carthaginian gold and silver coinage was taken out of circulation and replaced with Roman silver denarii. During the first century BC the denarius came to be used throughout Gaul, Germany and the Balkans and spread to Britain after the invasion of the island in AD 43. Thus by the end of the first century AD the denarius was the sole silver coin in use in the western part of the Empire, and the production and circulation of all other local silver coinages had ceased.

But we should not just think in terms of the gradual replacement of local silver coinages by the denarius. In two areas, at any rate, in Spain and Gaul, the picture is more complicated. Neither Spain nor Gaul had enjoyed, before the coming of the Romans, much in the way of silver coinage. In Spain, apart from the Punic coinage at the end of the third century, there had been no large-scale coinage throughout the peninsula, while in Gaul there were only a succession of small and isolated coinages. But in Spain in the second century BC and in Gaul in the early first century BC a uniform silver coinage appeared, produced over a wide geographical area and a reasonably long period of time. The coinages in question are the Iberian denarii and the Gallic quinarii.[7] There are differences between them - the types of the Gallic coins are varied whereas those of the Iberian denarii are uniform - yet there are strong similarities between the two coinages. They were both produced to a common model by a relatively large number of communities in an area subject to Rome. The uniformity of these coinages and their close relationship with those of Rome makes it inevitable, I think, that we should see Roman influence behind them. I would hesitate to say that they were *creations* of the Roman provincial authorities, since we do not know how they were organised, but it is difficult to see how they could have come into existence except as a response to the Roman presence and at least with the tacit toleration, if not the encouragement, of the Romans.

In the western part of the Empire, then, we see a picture of the gradual replacement of local coinages, including the newly created local coinages of Spain and Gaul, by Roman denarii; by the first century BC Roman denarii were the only silver coins being produced in the western Empire, and by the early principate, they were the principal silver coins in circulation.

BRONZE COINAGE

The bronze coinage exhibits a similar pattern, but one that takes place at a different time. Roman bronze coinage dominated the currency of Italy from about 200 BC; previously, in the third century, it had been only one of many bronze coinages circulating in the peninsula.[8] However, these, like the silver, were swept away by the reform of the denarius, and thereafter only a very few communities like Brundisium or Paestum made small issues of their own bronze to supplement the Roman issues. In the case of Paestum, these coins continued to be made until the reign of Tiberius, but they were always on a very small scale and cannot have accounted for more than a fraction of the coinage in circulation, of which the mint of Rome effectively had a monopoly.

But if the situation in Italy was similar for silver and bronze, this was not true of other areas of the western Empire. Even in Sicily, where large numbers of Roman bronzes circulated, there was still an extensive coinage of bronze from cities like Syracuse, Catania or Panormus throughout the Republican period;[9] as in Italy, they represented a very substantial proportion of the bronze coinage in circulation, as can be seen from the excavations at Morgantina, for example.[10] Spain in many ways seems to have resembled Sicily from the point of view of bronze currency, inasmuch as one finds a similar mixture of Roman and local bronzes; local issues continued to be made (probably on a larger scale than in Sicily) until the same time.[11] The other point to make about Spain is, of course, that presumably the same mechanism (whatever it was) that caused the creation of the Iberian denarii was also responsible for the creation of the similar Iberian bronzes minted by many different communities with the bearded head on the obverse and the horseman on the reverse.

There was no analogous creation of a Roman style bronze coinage in Gaul, where there is at first little trace of Roman bronze coinage.[12] The first century BC had seen the introduction and proliferation of Gallic bronzes, perhaps as a result of the increasing urbanisation of the Gallic communities, but there is no sign of any centralised organisation. Local bronze continued to circulate and dominate circulation until the Augustan age, when the new Augustan bronzes started to arrive in the area; in Britain we find a similar situation after the invasion of AD 43. In both Britain and Gaul the locally produced bronzes seem to have continued in circulation until the end of the first century AD.

In Africa,[13] as in other areas, local bronze continued to be produced by a number of cities down to the early Empire; the last ones were made under Tiberius. These city coinages seem, however, to have been produced on a fairly small scale. But the gap in bronze currency was not filled by Republican bronze - unlike Republican silver, Republican bronzes circulated in Africa only in tiny quantities. The bulk of the bronze currency was made up of Punic bronze; these coins had been produced in large numbers and, unlike Punic silver, they continued to circulate after the Roman conquest in 146 BC, remaining the dominant constituent of the bronze currency until the Imperial period, when they were eventually replaced by Roman bronzes.

So throughout the western Empire we have a number of different patterns in the bronze currency. In Italy, Roman bronze had a monopoly; in Sicily and Spain it was accompanied by locally produced bronzes until the early Empire, while in Africa it made little impact against the older Punic bronze until the Imperial period. Yet although each area shows a different pattern, they are all variations on the same theme, namely the replacement of locally produced bronze by Roman bronze and the cessation of minting by the cities during the first half of the first century AD.[14] In that sense the bronze of the western Empire undergoes a common transformation, and one analogous to that of the silver; but it took place in a different way and at different times from the silver.

DENOMINATIONS

Similar changes took place in denominations, but not at the same time as in those in the coinage and currency. In Italy it seems clear that Roman denominations were in use throughout from the time of the introduction of the denarius. We have no inscriptional evidence to the contrary, and the rare locally produced coinages all seem to use Roman denominations, such as at Paestum, Copia or

Brundisium.[15] One should perhaps observe that this evidence comes solely from Roman colonies, and in the case of the eastern Empire the evidence of colonies is not necessarily generally true for the whole region in which they were situated; but there is no reason to suppose that in Italy any local denominational systems continued in use.

The same seems to be generally true of Spain; as far as we know Roman denominations were in widespread use, and certainly in the city issues of Saguntum, Valentia or Carteia we find Roman denominations.[16]

In most other areas of the western Empire we are hampered by lack of information; we have no idea what denominations were used in most of Gaul and Britain, though the *lex Rubria* probably implies non-Roman ones in Cisalpine Gaul,[17] but from late in the first century BC we find that some Gallic bronzes use Roman denominations, like Nemausus, Cabellio or Lexovio, the last making coins inscribed SIMISSOS PVBLICOS, 'official semisses'.[18] In Africa, we have no direct evidence for denominations until the Augustan period, when the coinage of Lepti Minus has the value marks alpha, beta and delta, standing for 1, 2 and 4 asses.[19]

But though it seems in all these areas that mainly Roman denominations were used, we should be fairly cautious in assuming that they were the only ones in use. In Sicily, for example, the inscriptions from Tauromenium in the first century BC use a *nomos* worth forty litrai.[20] The *nomos* is the Roman denarius, but appears as a unit of account at Tauromenium only in the middle of the first century, some 150 years after it had come to play a monopolising role in the silver currency of the island. It is even more curious that there is no trace in the accounts of smaller units such as the *as*, which can indeed only be somewhat awkwardly accommodated in the system of litrai. In a similar way we also find some non-Roman denominations in Spain: some coins of Ebusus for instance have a numeral 50 in neo-Punic, which must presumably refer to some local system.[21] But even if some non-Roman systems survived, it seems clear that the system of Roman denominations was very dominant in the west: as Cicero wrote in his speech against Verres (referring to Sicily), 'How can there be an *agio* [commission for exchanging coins] when everyone uses the same kind of coins?' (*In Verrem* 3.181).

DISCUSSION

We therefore find a different pattern when we look at the change from the use of local silver to Roman silver coins; from local bronze to Roman bronze coins; and from local to Roman denominations. These differences can be observed in the western Empire and were even more pronounced in the east. How can we explain these different patterns and the different ways in which the changes came about?

First of all, it is clear that if the Romans had wished to impose denarii and asses throughout the Empire, they would have had no difficulty in doing so. The concept of a unified Imperial currency is implicit in the suggestion of Maecenas, according to Dio, that the cities of the Empire 'should not use their own coins and weights and measures, but use ours'.[22] In addition, the fleet coinage of Mark Antony, of the mid-30s BC, suggests that the idea of a uniform currency may have been current in the late first century, since the 'fleet coinage' embodies a system of different Roman denominations with the same types and same weight standards being used for three separate coinages produced at different mints in Greece and Cyprus or Syria.[23]

There can be no doubt that, had the Romans wished to impose the concept of such a single currency, they could have done so. In some cases we can see that when the Romans wished to intervene in the currency of an area they could do so with dramatic effect. As examples, I mention the reform which saw the introduction of the denarius, or the suppression of Punic gold and silver in

146 BC with the destruction of Carthage and the introduction of the denarius to Africa; in a similar way we read in Dio that the bronze coinage of Caligula was melted down by order of the Senate after his death.[24]

Some of these measures were of wider geographical effect than others; some were more profound than others; but most of them were fairly limited, and all were responses to specific circumstances. The demonetisation of Punic coinage can be seen in the same light as the aggressive attitude shown by Rome towards Carthage in the Third Punic War; 'delenda est Carthago' Cato had urged, and after its defeat Carthage was indeed destroyed, together with its precious metal coinage, a symbol of its wealth and power. Much the same is true of what happened to Caligula's coinage, although in this case it was a reaction to a hated emperor rather than a hated external power. So these cases of Roman intervention were responses to particular cases rather than a policy to reform the currency of the Empire.

There is then sufficient evidence to show that the Romans were aware of the possibility of unifying the monetary system of the Empire and that they had the power to do so if they had wished. But, except in the relatively isolated instances which I have mentioned, they did not, and the way in which they left the coinage of the areas unaffected is typical of Roman provincial government in many other fields; indeed it was this diversity in approach to control that gave the Roman Empire one of its strengths as a stable political unit. And, as we have seen in Spain and Gaul, the Romans might even occasionally take steps to continue or propagate the existence of local coinages, presumably because in these cases these were the easiest and cheapest options open to them.

Despite the fact that the Romans seem to have tried not to impose their own system of coinage and denominations - and indeed on occasion supported local ones - nevertheless there was a clear tendency for a gradual shift from the production and use of local silver to Roman silver; from local bronze to Roman bronze and from local denominations to Roman denominations. I have already described the diversity of these changes, and I stress now the slow and gradual process by which they took place. The minting of bronze coinage in the west stopped only slowly in the first century AD. Roman coin denominations were only gradually introduced into new areas, and often well after the relevant coins themselves. But what were the reasons that can have caused these changes?

Different explanations are important at different times. These reasons might be economic, administrative or political. There can be no doubt on the economic level that there is a connection between the Roman conquests and transfer of wealth from the provinces to Rome and the cessation of local silver coinage. But this cannot really be a sufficient explanation, since we can hardly believe that a rich city was really so impoverished that it was unable to produce even a small issue of silver if it had wanted to. There must have been other factors at work.

One relevant factor was the occurrence of civil wars. This would have affected the coinage of the Roman world in two main ways. In the first place the leaders of the various factions would have probably seized either directly or by taxation the wealth of the cities in the area which they occupied, and this would have exacerbated the impoverishment of those cities. Secondly there was a tendency for the leaders of civil wars to produce Roman style coins, particularly denarii, at mints outside Rome. This is most noticeable during the civil wars at the end of the Republic, when denarii were made in Spain, Gaul, Sicily, Africa and in the east. The production of denarii in these areas would have contributed to the spread of the denarius and encouraged the greater use of Roman denominations. In a similar way the war against Sertorius in Spain seems related to the end of the production of Iberian denarii.

A second cause was the growing presence of Romans, not just the soldiers or the businessmen or farmers attested in, for example, Gaul, without whose involvement according to Cicero no coins changed hands (*pro Fonteio* 11.2). We should not, however, attach too much importance to the presence of Romans, since a similar presence in the eastern Mediterranean did not have the same effect. But one aspect, important in this context, was the foundation of colonies. The best example comes from Greece, where the Caesarian colony at Corinth used Roman bronze denominations from its inception, and, because the coinage of Corinth was so dominant in (at least southern) Greece, this would have inevitably contributed to a greater use and awareness of Roman denominations.[25] In a different way the settlement of veterans in Cisalpine Gaul in around 100 BC and the minting of special issues of quinarii in connection with this settlement will have encouraged the use of Roman denominations there.

A third cause was taxation. The existence of Roman taxation and the holding of censuses as the basis for tax, and the keeping of *rationes imperii* or 'accounts of the Empire', as Suetonius calls them,[26] would have inevitably encouraged a greater use of Roman coins and denominations. In two of the specific cases in the east where the Romans intervened to change local to Roman denominations (at Thessaly and Palmyra), the changes were introduced in the context of taxation, and the Augustan changes in taxation have sometimes been seen as the cause of the change of the currency of areas like Gaul (the disappearance of Gallic quinarii from circulation).[27]

A fourth mechanism would have been the way in which a climate of opinion was formed in the early Empire. I have suggested elsewhere that we should see this as the explanation for some of the political changes which affected the coinage, such as the introduction of the Imperial portrait onto the civic coinage under Augustus or the cessation of the civic coinages in the western Empire in the early Imperial period.[28] It was a characteristic of Augustus and the early emperors to allow or encourage a consensus to emerge. Of course, when it was realised that some specific action by an individual or a city met with the emperor's approval, then other individuals and cities would adopt it, but this process might take time. This has been well discussed in other aspects of Roman life of the time, notably the way in which the prominent self-representation of senators gradually disappeared.[29] Even prominent Romans gradually found it inappropriate to put forward their own position rather than that of the emperor. In a similar way it may have come to seem appropriate to place the emperor's head on city coinages, or inappropriate for cities in the western Empire to continue to produce their own coinages.

To return to the question posed by the title. The answer should be clear. Although the Romans did on occasion suppress local coinages, their overall design was to leave things as they were and even to support local systems. Yet, despite this intention, the diversity of coinage and denominations gradually disappeared in the western part of the Empire. This has clear implications for our understanding of the nature and effectiveness of Roman monetary policy and allows us to see in one specific way how the processes of Romanisation might have worked.

NOTES

1. I hope to return to the wider theme on another occasion; the bibliography given here is therefore selective rather than complete.
2. I do not discuss gold here. Gold was minted regularly only in the last part of the period (the late first century BC and early first century AD) and was produced centrally at Rome (apart from the triumviral issues of gold which - like the contemporary denarii - were made around the Mediterranean in the years between 44 and 31 BC). There is one exception to this pattern, namely the Gallic and British gold produced in the late Iron Age. In this case, the gold disappeared from circulation at more or less the same time as the silver: see Scheers 1981.
3. There is a vast bibliography on this subject which is not central to the theme of this paper. One of the most recent contributions, with earlier bibliography, is Marchetti 1992. He argues

for a rather earlier date, but there is general agreement that the reform took place towards the middle of the Hannibalic war.

4. See, e.g. Crawford 1974, 32-3, 43-6.
5. Burnett and Hook 1989.
6. For the spread of the denarius, see, e.g. the map in Burnett 1987, 38.
7. For Iberian denarii, see Crawford 1985, 84-102.; for Gallic quinarii, loc.cit., 161-72. See also the distribution maps of Kent 1973.
8. See Burnett 1982.
9. For Sicily see Crawford 1987.
10. Buttrey *et al.* 1989.
11. Knapp 1987.
12. Nash 1987, 23-39.
13. Burnett 1987a.
14. For a fuller discussion of the end of civic coinage in the west in the first half of the first century AD, see RPC no. 18.
15. See n. 8.
16. Vives 1914 pls. XIX (Saguntum), CXXV (Valentia) and CXXVII (Carteia).
17. The law (*FIRA* I.19) distinguishes between *pecunia ... signata forma publica populei Romanei* and *omnei pecunia.*
18. de la Tour 1892, pl. XXVIII, nos. 7156, 7159 and 7166.
19. *RPC* nos. 784-91.
20. See n. 8.
21. Campo 1976, 33-4.
22. Dio, 52.30.9.
23. See *RPC* nos. 1453-70, 4088-93; and pp. 33, 37.
24. Dio, 60.22.3.
25. See *RPC*, p. 53.
26. Suetonius, *Augustus* 101.
27. *RPC*, 37.
28. *RPC*, 38-40.
29. See Wallace-Hadrill 1986, 79; Eck 1984.

BIBLIOGRAPHY

Burnett, A. 1982. The currency of Italy from the Hannibalic war to the reign of Augustus. *Annali dell'Istituto Italiano di Numismatica* **29**, 125-38

Burnett, A. 1987. *Coinage in the Roman World.* London

Burnett, A. 1987a. Africa. In Burnett and Crawford 1987, 175-85

Burnett A. and Crawford M. (eds.) 1987. *The Coinage of the Late Republic in the Roman World.* Oxford

Burnett A.M. and Hook, D.R. 1989. The fineness of silver coins in Italy and Rome during the late fourth and third centuries BC. *Quaderni ticinesi di numismatica e antichità classiche* **XVIII**, 151-67

Buttrey, T.V., Erim, K.T., Groves, T.D. and Holloway, R.R. 1989. *Morgantina Studies II. The Coins*. Princeton

Campo, M. 1976. *Las Monedas de Ebusus*. Barcelona

Crawford, M.H. 1974. *Roman Republican Coinage*. Cambridge

Crawford, M. 1985. *Coinage and Money under the Roman Republic*. London

Crawford, M. 1987. Sicily. In, Burnett and Crawford 1987, 43-51

Eck, W. 1984. Senatorial self-representation: Developments in the Augustan period. In, Millar F. and Segal, E. *Caesar Augustus*. *Seven Aspects*, 129-167. London

Kent, J. 1973. Les relations entre le monnayage des Romains et ceux des peuples voisins de l'ouest. *Cercle des Etudes Numismatiques Bulletin*, 2-10.

Knapp, R. 1987. Africa. In, Burnett and Crawford 1987, 9-37

Marchetti, P. 1992. Monnaies puniques en Sicile au cours de la deuxième guerre punique. In, T. Hackens and G. Moucharte (eds.), *Studia Phoenicia*. IX. *Numismatique et histoire économique phéniciennes et puniques*, 108-20. Louvain

Nash, D. 1987. *Coinage in the Celtic World*. London

RPC 1992. Burnett, A., Amandry M. and Ripollès, P.P. *Roman Provincial Coinage*. London (cited as *RPC*).

Scheers, S. 1981. The origins and evolution of coinage in Belgic Gaul. In, B. Cunliffe (ed.), *Coinage and Society in Britain and Gaul: some current problems*, 18-23. London

de la Tour, H. 1892. *Atlas des Monnaies Gauloises*. Paris

Vives, A. 1914. *La Moneda Hispánica*. Madrid

Wallace-Hadrill, A. 1986 Image and authority in the coinage of Augustus. *JRS* **66,** 66-87

TABLEWARE AS A SIGN OF ROMANISATION

GLASS IN ITALY[1]

Veronica Tatton-Brown

Department of Greek and Roman Antiquities, The British Museum, London WC1B 3DG

It now seems likely that glass was being worked, if not actually made, in Italy from the tenth or perhaps the eleventh century BC. Since I gave this paper at the colloquium, Dr. Macnamara has kindly drawn my attention to evidence for glassworking (and/or possibly making) at Frattesina di Fratta Polesina, near Rovigo and close to the Po delta, the location of a major source of fine sand.[2] Wound blue glass beads were found together with crucibles, or parts of crucibles, and glass waste. In their composition, these beads share the same technology as a group from Rathgall in Ireland. This raises far-reaching questions about origin and destinations, whose answers at present elude us. Suffice it to note that this early evidence pushes back the introduction of glass technology to Italy two centuries more than was previously thought.

This early tradition is remote from that employed by the Italian industry of the ninth and eighth centuries. Among its products were beads of dark colours decorated with marvered trails, and runners threaded on the bows of leech-shaped brooches (Fig. 1). While the brooches are found in Etruscan tombs of the eighth and seventh centuries, the beads are known over a wider area, notably the alpine region north of the province of Veneto and Greece.[3]

Both the beads of this type and the brooches were core-formed, and the most typical group of early Italian glass vessels were made in the same way. These are mostly trefoil-mouthed jugs, usually known as *oinochoai*, decorated with protruding scales with sharp points (Fig. 3) or flame-rounded knops.[4] A few other shapes are known, such as an alabastron in the Victoria and Albert Museum[5] and a squat jug (Fig. 2). My colleague Dyfri Williams, publishing pottery vessels from Etruria,[6] compares the scales of our glass examples with the protrusions on a painted multiple vase that he places in the second quarter of the seventh century BC. The glass examples in the British Museum all have scales rather than flame-rounded knops, while the alabastron in the Victoria and Albert Museum has both scales and knops; the largest group of jugs all have flame-rounded knops. The different forms of decoration now seem to have no chronological significance, and the series as a whole evidently dates from the mid-seventh into the beginning of the sixth century BC. Since those with known provenances come exclusively from Etruria, it is likely that they were the products of Etruscan glassmakers, though the exact location(s) or the glasshouse(s) is difficult to determine.[7]

Figure 4 illustrates a round aryballos, again core-formed, acquired by the British Museum in 1970. No convincing glass parallel can be quoted, but in form it is a close imitation of an Italo-Corinthian type of round aryballos of the later seventh and early sixth centuries.[8] Notable too is its disconnected zig-zag decoration. This occurs also on a core-formed jar from Ur in Mesopotamia[9] and on another oinochoe in the Vatican,[10] and on a series of cups of the sixth century BC from Santa Lucia di Tolmino in Slovenia.[11] These last, however, were not core-formed, but probably made by the slumping process.[12] Harden[13] places the British Museum aryballos in a glasshouse on the north Adriatic coast, close to the place of manufacture which he suggests for the Santa Lucia decorated series and related monochrome examples with vertical ribs.

We may now ask how the core-formed process for glassmaking reached Italy. As we have seen, the first products were decorated with marvered trails. Relevant here is a group of six small core-formed oinochoai, rather loosely allied in shape and marvered trail decoration.[14] Of these, two seem to have been found on Rhodes (including Fig. 5), one is from Crete and two are from Etruria;

the sixth has no known provenance. Although no comparable actual glass juglets are at present known from Mesopotamia, both the shape and style of our six have Mesopotamian connections. They were evidently made in the west, in Rhodes and/or possibly Italy. In addition, as will shortly become clear, neither the scales and knops, nor the separate zig-zag trails of early Italian glass vessels, were used by Rhodian glassmakers as decoration for their prolific series of core-formed vessels. It therefore seems most likely that the process was introduced to Italy directly from Mesopotamia. It is unlikely that Phoenicians were the intermediaries[15] as there is no evidence that core-formed glass was made in Phoenician glasshouses at this time.[16]

Luxurious glass vessels of clear monochrome glass, usually in natural greens or yellowish- or greenish-colourless glass, were evidently made by Phoenician glassmakers in the eighth, seventh and sixth centuries.[17] Occasional examples reached Italy, including a hemispherical bowl found in the Barberini tomb at Palestrina in Latium[18] and a two-handled flask of the sixth century from Bologna;[19] most common and widespread are handleless flasks, usually known as *alabastra*, of the seventh and sixth to fifth centuries (Fig. 6).[20]

We have already considered the early core-formed vessels produced in Italy, and made passing reference to the use of the technique in western Asia, notably Mesopotamia. By far the most numerous and widespread of the core-formed vessels are the products of Mediterranean workshops. Designed to contain perfumes, scented oils and cosmetics, they form a homogeneous group taking their shapes from the repertory of Greek vases in pottery and metal. Recent studies of the group as a whole[21] have identified three main divisions, assigned to about 550 to 440 BC, 340 to 200 BC and 150 to 50 BC. Rhodes is suggested as the location of the first workshops by the large numbers of the early group found in cemeteries on the island, and indeed by the concentration of such glass vessels in other areas of the Mediterranean and the Black Sea that were then in the *milieu* of Greek commercial activity. Also to be considered is the overwhelming Hellenic character of the early shapes as well as evidence for the production in Rhodes of scented oils and perfumes at this time which may well have stimulated the demand for glass vessels. A considerable number of these glasses reached Italy, particularly sites in Sicily, Campania and Etruria. It may be because of all these imported glasses that Etruscan glassworkers migrated to Slovenia to produce a series of brooch runners of the later sixth and fifth centuries, which have rounded protrusions similar to the scales or knops of their core-formed vessels.[22]

The Rhodian factories ceased production at the end of the fifth century BC. More than two generations passed before core-forming was revived in new glasshouses some time after the middle of the fourth century BC, the start of the era of Macedonian supremacy. Many fewer vessels were produced by this new industry and they are concentrated in Italy, especially Magna Graecia. Distinctive of the Italian finds are white speckles on the surface, the result of scum in the mixture, and it seems very likely that factories were established in southern Italy at this time.[23] However, recent discoveries of similar types in northern Greece and south Russia suggest that other workshops were located in Macedonia.[24] Many of the forms are more massive than before and new shapes were introduced. Miniature vessels were also made by Italian glassmakers (Figs. 7-9).

The final flowering of the Mediterranean core-formed industry lasted through the Hellenistic period, but the workshops of that era were located in the Levant. Meanwhile a purely Hellenistic style of glassware was emerging and the first group of Hellenistic vessels, made between the mid- or late third and mid-second century BC, is perhaps best represented by finds from Canosa in southern Italy.[25] To it belong some magnificent vessels of mosaic glass (Fig. 12), tableware of monochrome glass (Fig. 10) - often intentionally decolourised so that it has a greenish tinge, and decorated with fine linear-cut patterns - and some remarkable bowls of gold-sandwich glass (Fig. 11). The location of the glasshouses responsible for vessels of this high quality is a problem. Large mosaic glass plates (Fig. 12) and shallow dishes of similar glass, but dating from the second to first century BC, which have known findspots, come exclusively from Italy, mainly Magna Graecia and Etruria. Hemispherical bowls were made either of composite mosaic glass, like the plates and dishes, or of a new type of mosaic glass known as 'network' or 'lacework', consisting of canes of spirally twisted threads of different colours laid side by side.[26] Many of these date from the second century, though the type began in the third. Their findspots are more widespread than those of the plates and dishes. Examples are known from sites in Greece, the Aegean islands, Anatolia, Syria, Mesopotamia and Egypt, as well as southern Italy. However, all these areas were ready markets for luxury goods at this time and so do not shed any real light on the source of the glassware. Of the sandwich gold-glass bowls with known findspots, four come from southern Italy, and others are from Rhodes, Gordion, and Olbia on the Black Sea. The number of examples overall that come from southern Italy show at least that the inhabitants had a taste for fine glass tableware and the possibility of glasshouses being established there cannot be totally ruled out. Nevertheless, increasing numbers of these vessels are being found in the eastern Mediterranean, where evidence for Hellenistic glass factories comes from Delos and Rhodes. The former,[27] operating at the end of the second and the beginning of the first century BC, was making only beads. The Rhodian factory[28] was producing a variety of beads and pendants in the second half of the third century BC, and also it seems sandwich gold-glass bowls. It is in my opinion, however, impossible at present to identify with any certainty the manufacturing centre or centres for these splendid and innovative glass vessels.[29]

It was in the age of Augustus that the Roman glass industry was established.[30] It was then that important glassworks were set up in Rome itself and probably elsewhere in Italy, as many examples of glass of that period have been found on sites previously altogether devoid of glass. The importance of Rome is emphasised by the contemporary geographer Strabo, who ascribes to the Roman glassmakers certain innovations in colour and production.[31] In Latin as well, the word for glass, *vitrum*, appears nowhere in the extant literature before the sixties BC, but becomes exceedingly common in the Augustan period.[32]

Manufacture continued in the eastern Mediterranean and it is probable that migrant glassworkers from the east had arrived in Italy to establish the Augustan industry.[33] This is borne out by the fact that many of the types of non-blown glassware of the early Roman factories have their origins in the glass of the eastern Mediterranean of the preceding Hellenistic era, but innovations include a wider variety of patterns and more brilliant colours for mosaic glass vessels found almost exclusively on sites in Italy and the western Mediterranean. Certainly by the turn of the century the glass industry was being revolutionised by the invention of blowing, and by the close of the first century AD blown glass had become the norm, with the production of non-blown vessels having for the most part come to an end.[34] The Roman glassmakers participated in the blowing revolution, as we shall see, but first to be considered is the wide range of non-blown glassware that they made in the early years of the Empire.

Ribbed bowls were produced in large numbers, made of mosaic or, perhaps more often, of monochrome glass.[35] Distinguished from their Hellenistic predecessors by their evenly spaced ribs, they are often described as 'pillar-moulded.' The illustrated example of mosaic glass (Fig. 13), though found in Britain, was probably made in Italy. Indeed it is only one of a number of items of coloured mosaic glass of Italian origin found abroad, mainly in the northwest provinces of the Empire.[36] Unusual types of monochrome glass include model boats (Figs. 14, 15),[37] and some very large vessels such as a box, said to have contained ashes and so perhaps used as a cinerary urn.[38] A notable series of cups, plates, dishes and bowls, made either of single colours or of mosaic glass, resemble Roman vessels of fine pottery, and a particular carinated shape is known in silver too.[39] In several cases the glass versions predate the pottery. Innovations of the last phase of the Hellenistic period, namely coloured-band and gold-band glass, whereby canes of different single colours and sandwich gold-glass laid side by side were fused together, were readily adopted by the Italian glassmakers and used for little box-like receptacles and perfume bottles, as well as bowls of different shapes.[40] Lacework mosaic glass continued to be used as well.

The most far-reaching innovation in the manufacture of glass in antiquity was the invention of blowing. This happened in the first century BC, probably in the Syro-Palestinian area long associated with glassmaking,[41] but it seems not to have been before the closing years of that century that the technique was fully utilised, revolutionising the industry.[42] At present, the earliest known examples of true blown glass are for the most part small perfume bottles of coloured glass found chiefly on sites in Sicily, Italy and southern Switzerland and evidently produced in the newly founded Roman glass factories in central and northern Italy. They were found in contexts of the last quarter of the first century BC and the first decade of the first century AD. To the same period belong deposits from sites especially in Rome and its colony of Cosa which contained fragments of blown glass, together with non-blown glassware of the period.[43] This paper cannot survey all the early blown glass from the Italian factories, nor is it intended to give the impression that this revolution had not taken hold equally in the eastern Mediterranean, where it had all begun. It will concentrate instead on a few significant Roman products of this time.

It was probably in this experimental age, when the blowing technique was still in its infancy (the years around the turn of the first century BC/AD), that cameo-cut glass vessels were first made.[44] The majority being certainly blown[45] (and therefore not earlier than the time when the technique was properly practised) and demanding particular care and attention, they may well be seen as masterpieces from one or possibly more workshops exploring the potentials of a new technique. As such they were probably all made within a comparatively short period, not more than one or two generations. The best known is the Portland Vase.[46] The identification of its scene is much disputed, but the scenario seems to be one of love and marriage with a mythological theme in a marine setting. This famous vase is thought to come from Rome. Also from Italy, but from Pompeii, is a second cameo-glass vessel in the British Museum, known as the Auldjo jug after the lady who bequeathed part of it (Fig. 16).[47] The known findspots of the cameo-glass vessels being predominantly in Italy, the similarity of the designs of vine scrolls often used in their decoration with those of certain Roman monuments of the first century AD, together with the other evidence for a flourishing Roman blown glass industry at this time, make Italy and perhaps Rome itself the most likely source.

Some technically less elaborate glass vessels of the same era seem to imitate the cameo-cut series. These include a blown jar of wine-coloured glass with opaque white theatrical masks under the handles and white stripes embedded in the handles (Fig. 17).[48] It is said to be from Campania, where it may well have been made in the first century BC. The effect of the two colours recalls that of the cameo glass, but it would have been much simpler to make; blobs of white glass were applied and mould-pressed *in situ* to form the masks.

The evidence for glassmaking in Rome is discussed above; a passage in the elder Pliny, writing about sixty years later than Strabo, speaks of another factory in Campania.[49] Others must have existed in northern Italy in the Po valley, already noted as a source of fine sand, a prerequisite for the making of glass, and also at Aquileia;[50] numerous finds come from sites in that area as well as from Switzerland. One glassmaker, Sentia Secunda, records her origin as Aquileia on the base of two late first-century AD rectangular bottles found at Linz in Austria.[51] These provide, moreover, rare evidence for a female glassworker; other signatures are male and documentary evidence too suggests that glassmaking was generally a male preserve.[52]

Considering the products of these early Roman Italian factories as a whole, it is perhaps significant that to some extent the blown vessels seem to imitate the colours and decoration of their non-blown counterparts. This is true of a group decorated with white or coloured blobs embedded in the surface (Fig. 18). Less often the specks or blobs are in relief.[53] The many examples from Italy (and other western sites) were no doubt made there but others, including the example illustrated, from the Aegean and south Russia, must be eastern products. Production of the series as a whole does not seem to have lasted much later than AD 100. The lack of precise contexts giving firm dates for individual pieces makes it impossible to be certain, but it is tempting to award the accolade for the introduction of this attractive mode of decoration to Italian glassworkers.

Other close imitations of their non-blown counterparts from Italian glasshouses are blown glass bowls with pinched ribs decorated with white trails, found in particular in northern Italy and the nearby regions of Slovenia and Croatia.[54] Most like their non-blown contemporaries, however, are blown bottles of ribbon glass, for which the monochrome canes must have been fused together before being blown.[55]

This survey has now followed the story of glassmaking in Italy over a period of about a thousand years and it seems right to draw it to a close at the time when Rome was established as the capital of the known world.

NOTES

1. My thanks to the organisers and editors of the colloquium for inviting me to give this paper and for their help. I am particularly grateful to Dr D.B. Harden, Dr D. Grose and Dr J. Price for their help on many aspects of ancient glass.

2. My thanks also to the excavator, Anna Maria Bietti Sestieri, for providing me with further information. For the excavations in general see Bietti Sestieri 1975-80, especially 225, and Bietti Sestieri 1975, 1-14, especially 5. For the glass in particular see Biavati 1983, and Brill 1992.

3. Grose 1989, 81 and note 52, and 87, no. 35, colour pl. 70.

4. For the group as a whole see Harden 1981, 138-40, nos. 377-9, and Grose 1989, 82, and now also Martelli 1994, 75-88, 95-7 for a useful list of examples.

5. Haevernick 1981, 64, no. 11, pl. 3.3.

6. Williams 1986. I am grateful to Dr Williams for discussing these with me.

7. Martelli 1994, 83-8.

8. Harden 1981, 140.

9. Barag 1970, 157, no. 4, fig. 51 and 178 sv. shape 12; and cf. also Harden 1981, note 115.

10. Fremersdorf 1975, 29, no. 16, pl. 3 and col. pl. op. p. 80.

11. Haevernick 1981, 44-50.

12. For this process see Tait 1991, 219-21.

13. Harden 1981, 140.

14. Ibid. 55-56 and notes 62-3.

15. Martelli 1994, 88-9.

16. Barag 1985, 57, note 144; and Tatton-Brown 1985, 115.

17. Barag 1985, 57 with note 142 and 67-8.

18. Von Saldern 1970, 211, 225, no. 42, fig. 37; Martelli 1994, 90-3.

19. Ibid. 212, 225-6, no. 45, fig. 40.

20. This class was discussed as a whole by von Saldern 1970, 212, 226f., nos. 48-54a. Additions include *Luzern* 1981, 58, no. 136, pl. 9 and mention of two in von Saldern *et al.*, 1974, 92 with note 241. Close parallels to Fig. 6 include one certainly and another probably from Italy, von Saldern 1970, 227, no. 51, fig. 46 left (Pozzuoli) and 226, no. 448, fig. 44 right (see also Barag 1985, 67-8 and Goldstein 1979, 102, no. 200, pls. 12, 37).

21. For the group as a whole see Harden 1981, 58ff. and now Grose 1989, 109ff.

22. Williams 1986, 299. Related types are also known from the neighbouring area around Padua (Italy).
23. First suggested by Harden 1981, 103.
24. McCellan 1985, 34ff.; and 1992, 20.
25. First published by Harden 1968a, 21-47; recently, Grose 1984, 191-2 with extensive bibliography; to which add Corrente 1992; Gruzzo 1992; Stern and Schlick-Nolte 1994, especially 97-113..
26. For the making of network mosaic canes see Tait 1991, 219-20.
27. Nenna 1993, 19-21.
28. Weinberg 1969, 143-51; Weinberg 1983, 37; and Weinberg 1992, 22-3, note 16.
29. Cf. note 33 below.
30. For this in general see Grose 1983.
31. Strabo 16, 758. Cf. Trowbridge 1930, 104.
32. Ibid., 59ff.
33. Harden 1968b, 61-2 and 64 credits this to Alexandrian glassmakers whose output he continues to emphasise in 1980, 17-25. Doubts have since been thrown on the Alexandrian glass industry of this time, cf. Grose 1981, 64 and 1989, 188-9. It is, nonetheless, clear that mosaic glass was being produced in Egypt in the Hellenistic period (cf. Tait 1991, 51-2). Christine Insley-Green has also kindly drawn my attention to the output of Alexandrian workshops illustrated by items in the 'Per-Neb' collection, Christie's 1992 and 1993. Harden's championship of Alexandrian glassmakers, supported by references in ancient authors, admittedly mainly of Imperial date (Trowbridge 1930, 128-30), may yet be vindicated.
34. The production of Italian coloured mosaic glassware has been thought to have come to an end by about AD 50 (cf. Grose 1984, 242). However, increasing numbers of finds of mosaic glasses, evidently Italian in origin, in northwest provinces of the Roman Empire, particularly Britain, in contexts of the later first and second centuries, imply that production continued for at least another fifty years (cf. Harden and Price 1971, 323-6; and Price 1985, 468-70. Cf. also, Rutti 1991, 126-44. My thanks to Dr Jenny Price for discussing this problem with me.
35. For these see now Grose 1984, 245ff. with references.
36. Cf. note 34 above and also Price (forthcoming) for mosaic glass from Colchester.
37. BM GR 1869.6-24.20 said to be from Aquileia, and 1868.5-1.153 from Pompeii. Recently, Harden *et al.* 1987, 48, no. 24 and Tait 1992, 57 and pl. 69.
38. Recently, Harden *et al.,* 1987, 46, no. 22 and Tait 1991, 57 and pl. 70.
39. Cf. Grose 1989, 255-8 and cat. nos. 449-525.
40. For these techniques see Tait 1991, 217ff.
41. Recently, Israeli 1991.
42. Cf. Grose 1989, 262.
43. Grose 1979.
44. Most examples are described and illustrated in Goldstein and Rakow 1982; see also Whitehouse 1991, note 41. Fragments in the British Museum published inaccurately in Simon 1957, pls. 17-19, will appear in a forthcoming volume or catalogue on Greek and Roman glass in the British Museum.
45. Recently Harden 1983, 43 ff. with references to earlier work and cf. also Tait 1991, 227-8, figs. 98-108.
46. Extensively studied in Gudenrath *et al.* 1990, and for a recent discussion of the iconography see Painter and Whitehouse 1991. For the date given here see Tait 1991, 64-5.
47. Recently Harden *et al.* 1987, 79, no. 34.

48.   Harden *et al.* 1968, no. 75; Tait 1991, 86, pls. 83-4.
49.   Pliny, *Nat. Hist.* xxxvi.194.
50.   See Calvi 1969, 195ff.
51.   Harden 1970, 49 and note 25.
52.   Trowbridge 1930, 112ff.
53.   Cf. Harden *et al.*, 1987, 171 ff., group D, and for the technique Tait 1991, 226.
54.   Haevernick 1981, 171-9 and recently Biaggio Simona 1991, I, 71-4 with bibliography; cf. also Lightfoot 1993, 38.
55.   This group has been identified in Grose 1989, 261-2 and catalogue nos. 608-616.

BIBLIOGRAPHY

Barag, D. 1970. Mesopotamian core-formed glass vessels, 1500-500BC. In, A.L. Oppenheim *et al.*, *Glass and Glassmaking in Ancient Mesopotamia*, Corning Museum on Glass Monograph no. 3. New York

Barag, D. 1985. *Catalogue of Western Asiatic Glass in the British Museum,* I. London

Biaggio Simona, S. 1991. *I Vetri Romani proveninenti dalle terre dell'attuale cantone Ticino.* Locarno

Biavati, A. 1983. L'arte vetraria nella civiltà protovillanoviana di Frattesina, Fratta Polesine (Rovigo); analasi chimica dei reperti archeologici. *Padusa* V. **19**, 59-63

Bietti Sestieri, A.M. 1975. Elementi per lo studio dell'abitatio protostorico di Frattesina di Fratta Polesine (Rovigo). *Padusa* **XI 1-4**, 1-14

Brill, R.H. 1992. Chemical analyses of some glasses from Frattesina. *JGS* **XXXIV**, 11-22

Calvi, M.C. 1968. *I Vetri Romani del Museo di Aquileia.* Aquileia

Christie's, 1992. *The 'Per-Neb' Collection.* Christie's, 9 December

Christie's, 1993. *The 'Per-Neb' Collection* (2). Christie's, 7 July and 8 December

Corrente, M. 1992. La tomba degli ori. In, R. Cassano (ed.), *Principi Imperatori Vescori due mila anni di Storia a Canosa,* Exhibition Catalogue Bari, 337-45. Bari

Fremersdorf, F. 1975. *Antikes, Islamisches und Mittelalterliches Glas in den Vaticanischen Sammlungen Roms,* Catalogo del Museo Sacro V. Vatican

Goldstein, S. 1979. *Pre-Roman and Early Roman Glass in the Corning Museum of Glass.* Corning

Goldstein, S. and Rakow, L. and J. 1982. *Cameo Glass. Masterpieces from 2000 years of Glassmaking,* Exhibition Catalogue. Corning

Grose, D.F. 1977. Early blown glass: the western evidence. *JGS* **XIX,** 9-29

Grose, D.F. 1981. The Hellenistic glass industry reconsidered. *Annales du 8e Congrès de l'AIHV,* 61-72. Liège

Grose, D.F. 1983. The formation of the Roman Glass Industry. *Archaeology* **XXXV no. 7,** 38-45

Grose, D.F. 1989. *Early Ancient Glass. The Toledo Museum of Art.* New York

Gudenrath, W., Painter K. and Whitehouse D. 1990. The Portland Vase. *JGS* **XXXII**

Guzzo, G. 1992. Gli Ori. In, R. Cassano (ed.), *Principi, Imperatori, Vescovi, duemila anni di Storia a Canosa,* Exhibition Catalogue Bari, 530-41. Bari

Haevernick, T.E. 1981. *Beiträge zur Glasforschung.* Mainz

Harden, D.B. 1968a. The Canosa group of Hellenistic glasses in the British Museum. *JGS* **X,** 21-47

Harden, D.B. 1968b. Ancient Glass I: Pre-Roman. *ArchJ* **CXXV,** 46-72

Harden, D.B. 1969. Ancient Glass II: Roman. *ArchJ* **CXXVI,** 44-77

Harden, D.B. 1980. A Hellenistic footed glass bowl of Alexandrine origin. *Toledo Museum of Art News* **22,** 17-25

Harden, D.B. 1981. *Catalogue of the Greek and Roman Glass in the British Museum,* I. London

Harden, D.B. 1983. New light on the history and technique of the Portland and Auldjo Cameo vessels. *JGS* **XXV,** 43-54

Harden, D.B. *et al.* 1987. *Glass of the Caesars.* Exhibition Catalogue, Milan

Harden, D.B. *et al.* 1968. *Masterpieces of Glass.* Exhibition Catalogue, London

Harden, D.B. and Price, J. 1971. The Glass. In, B. Cunliffe (ed.) *Excavations at Fishbourne 1961-9,* II, Reports of the Research Committee of the Society of Antiquaries of London **XXVII,** 323-6. London

Israeli, Y. 1991. The invention of blowing. In, M. Newby and F. Painter (eds.), *Roman Glass. Two centuries of Art and Invention,* 46-55. Society of Antiquaries of London, Occasional Paper **XIII.** London

Lightfoot, C. 1993. Some examples of ancient cast and ribbed bowls in Turkey. *JGS* **XXXV,** 22-38.

Luzern, 1981. *3,000 Jahre Glaskunst* Kunstmuseum Luzern, Exhibiton Catalogue. Luzern

Martelli, M. 1994. Sulla produzione di vetri orientallizanti. In, M. Martelli (ed.), *Tyrrhenoi Philotechnoi*, Atti della Giornata di Studio, Viterbo 1990, 75-97. Rome

McClellan, M. 1985. Ancient glass perfume vessels; the collection of the Museum of Art and Archaeology. *Muse* **XIX**, 34-43

McClellan, M. 1992. Core-formed glass vessels 525 BC to 10 AD. In, Weinberg 1992, 19-23, 80-94

Nenna, M.D. 1993. La verrerie d'époque hellénistique à Delos. *JGS* **XXXV**, 11-21

Painter, K. and Whitehouse, D. 1991. The Portland Vase. In, M. Newby and K. Painter (eds.), *Roman Glass: Two centuries of Art and Invention*, 33-43. Society of Antiquaries of London Occasional Paper no. **XIII**. London

Price, J. 1985. Two Pieces of Polychrome Mosaic Glass Tableware from Roman Britain. In, Exhibits at Ballots. *Antiq.J.* **LXV**, 468-71

Rütti, B. 1991. *Die römischer Gläser in Augst und Kaiseraugst*. Forschungen in Augst, 13. Augst

Simon, E. 1957. *Die Portland vase*. Mainz

Stern, E.M. and Schlick-Nolte, B. 1994. *Early Glass of the Ancient World. The Ernesto Wolf Collection*. Ostfildern

Tait, H. (ed.) 1991. *Five Thousand Years of Glass*. London

Tatton-Brown, V. 1985. Rod-formed pendants. In, Barag 1985, 115-7

Trowbridge, M.L. 1930. Philological Studies in ancient Glass. In, University of Illinois Studies in Language and Literature **XIII** (1928)

von Saldern, A. 1970. Other Mesopotamian glass vessels. In, A.L. Oppenheim, R.H. Brill and D. Barag, *Glass and Glassmaking in Ancient Mesopotamia*, 203-28. Corning Museum of Glass Monograph no. **3**. New York

von Saldern, A., Nolte B., La Baume P. and Haevernick T.A. 1974. *Gläser der Antike - Sammlungen Oppenländer*, Exhibition Catalogue. Hamburg

Weinberg, G.D. 1969. Glass manufacture in Hellenistic Rhodes. *ADelt* **XXIV**, 143-51

Weinberg, G.D. 1983. A Hellenistic glass factory on Rhodes: Progress report. *JGS* **XXV**, 37

Weinberg, G.D. 1992. *Glass Vessels in Ancient Greece. Their history illustrated from the Collection of the National Archaeological Museum, Athens*. Publications of the Archaeologikon Deltion no. **47**. Athens

Whitehouse, D. 1991. Cameo Glass. In, M. Newby and K. Painter (eds.), *Roman Glass. Two Centuries of Art and Invention*, 19-32. Society of Antiquaries of London, Occasional Paper **XIII**. London

Williams, D. 1986. Greek potters and their descendants in Campania and southern Etruria, *c.* 720-630 BC. In, J. Swaddling (ed.), *Italian Iron Age Artefacts in the British Museum*, Papers of the Sixth British Museum Classical Colloquium, 295-304. London

Illustration credits

All items in the British Museum. My thanks to Mr. P. Nicholls for the photographs, published by courtesy of the Trustees of the British Museum.

Fig. 1   GR 1846.6-8.1. Fibula with core-formed glass runner decorated with marvered trails
              forming a feather pattern. Given by the Marquis of Northampton. Length of glass tip
              to tip 7.5cm

Figs. 2-3   Glass 379 and 377. Core-formed jugs decorated with scales. Ht. of taller jug
              7cm

Fig. 4   Glass 380. Core-formed aryballos, translucent dark blue with opaque white zig-zag
              decoration. Ht. 4.4cm.

5

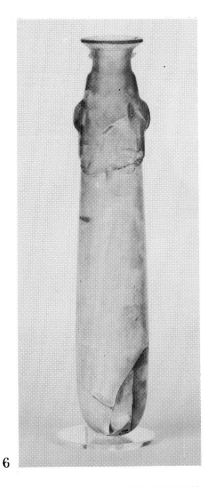

6

7,8,9

Fig. 5   Glass 82. Core-formed glass jug decorated with a continuous trail forming spirals on the
             neck and festoons on the body. From Camirus, Rhodes. Ht. as extant 8.3cm
Fig. 6   GR 1869.6-24.16. Tall alabastron of sea-green glass, said to be from Pozzuoli (ancient
             Puteoli). Ht. 21.1cm
Figs. 7-9   Glass 295, 311 and 297. Three miniature core-formed glass vessels, the jug and globular
             flask from Ruvo di Apulia (ancient Rubi). Ht. of jug 4.7cm

10

11

12

Fig. 10   GR 1871.5-18.9. Wing-handled cup from Canosa. Ht. 11.1cm
Fig. 11   GR 1871.5-18.2. Gold-glass bowl from Canosa. Ht. 11.4cm
Fig. 12   GR 1871.5-18.3. Mosaic glass plate from Canosa. D. 30.8cm

13

14,15

16

Fig. 13   PRB 1923.6-5.1. 'Pillar-moulded' bowl of marbled mosaic glass. From a cremation
              burial at Radnage, Buckinghamshire, England. Ht. 4.7cm.; D. 16.8cm
Figs. 14,15   GR 1869.6-24.20 and GR 1868.5-1.153. Two model boats. The example on the left,
              of blue glass, said to be from Aquileia; that on the right, of green glass, from
              Pompeii. L. of blue boat 7.7cm
Fig. 16   GR 1859.2-16.1 and 1840.12-15.41. Cameo-glass jug, from the House of the Faun
              at Pompeii. The neck and handle (1859.2-16.1) bequeathed by Miss Auldjo. Ht.
              including handle 22.8cm

17

18

Fig. 17   GR 1856.12-26.1122. Blown glass jar with theatrical masks at the handles.
           Said to be from Santelpido, near the ancient Atella (Campania); bequeathed by William
           Temple. Ht. 24.8cm
Fig. 18   GR 1868.5-1.85. Blown glass jug of yellowish-brown glass decorated with embedded
           opaque white blobs. Said to have been found on one of the Aegean islands; bequeathed
           by Felix Slade. Ht. 23.8cm

FOUR GROUPS OF THIN-WALLED POTTERY
IN THE BRITISH MUSEUM

Susan Walker, John Hayes and Paul Roberts
Susan Walker and Paul Roberts, Department of Greek and Roman Antiquities, The British
Museum, London WC1B 3DG;
Dr. John Hayes, 9 Linton Road, Oxford, U.K.

Roman thin-walled ware, visually attractive to those with a taste for the finer type of modern ceramic, is also of considerable archaeological interest. The chronological development of thin-walled pottery runs parallel to that of the so-called Hellenisation of Italy, and yet in origin at least thin-walled drinking cups patently have nothing to do with Greek traditions.

In general, current understanding of the production of thin-walled wares is patchy. They are thought to originate in northern Italy, where they appear to imitate late La Tène metal goods, and perhaps also drinking habits, for thin-walled wares comprise almost exclusively drinking vessels, at first beakers or mugs, and, later, more open shapes with lower walls.[1] The potters of thin-walled wares then appear to multiply, and their products are represented at a wide range of sites, not confined to the western Empire. Most pots discussed below appear to be of local manufacture, or at least potted in a distinctive clay exclusive to each regional group. But while the clays appear distinctive, the shapes of the vessels and their decoration enjoyed a wider currency, and from the first century BC displayed an evident dependence upon late Hellenistic metal and glassware. Then and in the succeeding century, a relationship with Campanian A and other fine wares inevitably developed, yet the thin-walled genre retained a separate identity, often appearing as an alternative at the same sites as the better known (but not necessarily more expensive) wares.

On this occasion, four groups of thin-walled vessels have been selected from the Departmental reserves. Though they cannot be said to have an archaeological provenance, all the vessels have some association through a collector or dealer with a named site (Map: Fig. 1).

A. POTTERY FROM TOSCANIA

The first of these groups was acquired in 1839 from the dealer Campanari as part of a larger group of fifty objects, including thirteen bronzes, all said to have been 'excavated in Toscania'. Discussion is here confined to the thin-walled pottery, as there seems little point in building a house of cards upon such minimal indications.

The six vessels (Figs. 2-6, 11-16) are all potted in orange clay, more or less micaceous, with variation in firing resulting in differentiated tones. The range of dates represented in the Toscania group runs from about 100 BC to AD 50. Two of the earlier forms are evidently closely related, and represent an attempt to translate late Hellenistic metal forms into clay (Figs. 2, 11-12). These are, firstly, a two-handled cup of roundish profile not unlike the first-century BC silver cup from Boscoreale decorated with an olive branch around the bowl.[2] The form is known at Cosa, where it appears with an inscription on the thumb-rest of the handle.[3] Secondly, an ovoid ciborium with looped handles and plain thumb-rests: a grander version of this with moulded foot was found at Cosa in a context of 75-50 BC.[4] This shape, which is derived from the Attic *kantharos*, appears in silver, glass and other types of pottery, notably Campanian A, lead-glazed ware and, in rare instances, Pontic and Arretine sigillata.[5]

An unusual cup with rounded lower wall and tall everted top (Figs. 3, 13) does not appear at Cosa, but is paralleled by another in the collections excavated at a tomb in Tharros, Sardinia, and dated to the first century BC or AD.[6] Research by Mayet has defined the shape (Form VIII) and its currency (the isles of the western Mediterranean, notably the Balearics), and narrowed the date range to the second half of the first century BC.[7]

A two-handled cup with carinated base and sloping high walls (Figs. 4, 14) is most likely a local version of a type known from various sites, including Cosa and Tharros and locations in the eastern Mediterranean. The form is not greatly diffused before the first century AD; this version may be Tiberian.[8] An unglazed bowl of slightly irregular form with low foot and incised horizontal line on the body (Figs. 5, 15) is a standard widely known type of the first half of the first century AD. It is most likely a local version of a type originating in the Po Valley, represented in grey ware at another site discussed below, Ventimiglia (Figs. 5, 8, 19).[9]

Finally, a very thin-walled vessel with two handles and incised decoration below grooves at the shoulder (Figs. 6, 16) probably also comes from this group, though the record is not entirely clear on this point. It is difficult to see how such a delicate vessel could have been produced in significant numbers without recourse to a mould. The clay is less orange than that of the other members of the group, and the cup may originate in northern Italy. It may be a much finer version of the carinated cups that appear at Ventimiglia and Herpes (C and D below).

B. TWO VESSELS FROM RIO TINTO, BAETICA

The two-handled cups (Figs. 7, 17, 18) presented to the department in 1935 were said by the donor to come from the site of the famous mines at Rio Tinto in southern Spain. One has a rolled rim and carinated body decorated with barbotine leaves with tendrils and dots above and below them; the other, its handles lost, has a stamped pattern of dots over the body. The clay and its treatment are typically Spanish, being pinkish buff with a metallic brown slip. The first cup is clearly derived from Gaulish models, and both may date to the Claudian/Neronian or the early Flavian period. The types are well published by Mayet and López Mullor, and indeed one of these vessels is illustrated in Kevin Greene's volume on the pre-Flavian fine wares from Usk.[10]

C. POTTERY FROM VENTIMIGLIA

Four vessels (Figs. 8, 19-22) were selected from a large mixed group of Roman date collected by Mackay MacDonald and given in 1905 to the Victoria and Albert Museum, whence they were transferred to the British Museum in 1980. The pottery is said to have been unearthed near Ventimiglia, about a mile on the Italian side of the frontier between the Roja and the Nervia valleys. In a strict sense, not all of this is thin-walled, and most of it falls beyond the chronological bounds of this colloquium. Nonetheless it is included here because the vessels are of interest to the development and diffusion of the genre.

Besides the grey bowl mentioned above, the group includes three vessels of bright orange clay, unevenly fired. Two of these (Figs. 21, 22) are the globular cups known as *urnette/boccalini a collarino* and commonly found on sites in Italy and the Aegean area. The series begins around AD 60 and continues into the early third century; the British Museum pair comprise an early and a later version, the latter semi-vitrified and with a graffito.[11] Lastly, a red ware cup (Fig. 20) with two handles (one lost) compares in shape (but for the indented collar) if not in superficial treatment with two cups of different size from the site of Herpes in the Charente, northeast of Bordeaux (Fig. 10).

A vessel of similar form but without handles was unearthed in the excavations at Rue des Farges (Lyon) in a Flavian context.[12]

D. HERPES (AQUITANIA)

At Herpes were found some 900 tombs, located on either side of a paved Roman road. The site was excavated by Pierre Delemain, who published his findings in 1892.[13] When his collection was acquired by the British Museum in 1905, it was found to contain Roman as well as Merovingian material. Eleven lamps have been dated from the mid-first to the mid-third century AD and are thought to be of Gaulish or Spanish manufacture.[14] The pottery (Figs. 9, 23-27) offers a similar conspectus. Besides the bowls related to the vessel from Ventimiglia, there is an indented beaker evidently imitating a glass shape, of the first or second century AD, and two cups of similar shape to the first pair, but without handles and decorated with barbotine horseshoes in a fashion well documented in Spain (Figs. 26, 27).[15]

CONCLUSION

The provincial material represents the continuation of the thin-walled tradition in areas beyond the Mediterranean, where the shapes and decoration of thin-walled vessels were strongly influenced by the flourishing sigillata industries of central and southern Gaul. It must surely be the case that the spread of thin-walled ware, in the examples we have seen not so much exported as imitated locally, was driven by the expansion of Rome and Roman tastes. The genre thus takes its place among other forms of Roman tableware of more obviously Hellenistic Greek inspiration. We see here perhaps a glimpse of Rome as the agent of cultural change, as indeed she served in respect of better-known tablewares in various media.

CATALOGUE

A. Pottery from Toscania

A1. GR.1839.11-9.14b = Campanari 2076 (Figs. 2, 11). Ovoid ciborium with looped handles and plain thumb-rests. Ht. 85mm; diam. 86mm. Orange clay: the interior is pinkish-red and slightly micaceous. The fabric is quite close to A3. Unslipped and undecorated.
Cosa Form XXVIII is comparable, but has a higher elaborately moulded foot. The form is dated to 75-50 BC, i.e. contemporary with the peak in popularity of the silver version of this form. The shape, derived from the Attic *kantharos*, appears in other classes of pottery (see note 5); glass versions were also made.[16] Mayet illustrates the distribution of the thin-walled version with complex moulded foot (Form IX): finds are heavily concentrated in western Italy, southern Gaul, the Balearics and Spain.[17] The date of the example from Toscania is probably within the range 100-25 BC.

A2. GR.1839.11-9.14a = Campanari 2085 (Figs. 2, 12). Two-handled cup, the handles decorated with incised lines and curved motifs. Ht. 75mm; diam. 92mm. Orange clay, reddish-brown towards the base and foot. Unslipped. Close to A5.

Comparable to Cosa Form XXIX, but with a sharper carination. Cosa no. 140 has a rounder body decorated with parallel grooves and the inscription CICLOPS on the thumb-rest of the handle. The form imitates silver vessels of the type found at Boscoreale; it also appears in contemporary glassware.[18] The origin of this form is uncertain; the date is likely to be near 50 BC.

A3. GR.1839.11-9.16b = Campanari 2078 (Figs. 3, 13). Cup with rounded lower wall and tall everted top with incised rim and a line defining the two sectors of the body. Ht. 90mm; diam. 70mm. Reddish-orange clay with rosy patches. Less mica than A5.
A similar vessel is known from Tharros; see also Mayet Form VIII; heavier or variant forms are found at Pompeii/Herculaneum and Ornavasso.[19] Made from about 50 BC until the early first century AD. An origin has been proposed in the western Po plain, influencing subsequent production in the Balearics.[20]

A4. GR.1839.11-9.1 = Campanari 2086 (Figs. 4, 14). Two-handled cup with carinated sloping base below the handles, and high walls, sloping slightly inward. Ht. 67mm; diam. 80mm. Micaceous orange clay.
Form not much diffused before the first century AD. Probably of local manufacture: the form resembles Cosa Form XXXIII (without handles) and XL (with lower walls), both of which are dated to the Augustan period.[21]

A5. GR.1839.11-9.16a = Campanari 2079 (Figs. 5, 15). Cup of slightly irregular form with incised horizontal line around the body and a low foot. Ht. 67mm; diam. 102mm. Micaceous orange clay. No slip.
A standard shape of the first half of the first century AD, comparable to Cosa Form XXXVI and Mayet Form XXXIII.[22] This example could be a local version of a type made in the Po Valley (see C1 below). Several workshops apparently existed in Italy, producing vessels in grey, black or orange clay; the type was very popular in coastal areas of the Western Mediterranean and is also thought to have been made at La Muette, near Lyon.[23]

A6. GR.1839.11-12.2 = Campanari 2080 (Figs. 6, 16). Probably Campanari and mistakenly recorded as Castellani. Two-handled cup with incised decoration below grooves at the shoulder. Ht. 60mm; diam. 85mm. Very fine walls. Unglazed.
Though A6 is much finer, the form may be influenced by Mayet Form XLIII (mid-first to early second century AD).[24] Technically related to the Aco beaker and Sarius cup, and also probably thrown in a mould.[25] Probably made in northern Italy, perhaps in the Po Valley.

B. Two Vessels from Rio Tinto (Baetica)

B1. GR.1935.6-10.2. Two-handled cup (Figs. 7, 17). Ht. 60mm; diam. 100mm. Rolled rim, carinated body and barbotine leaf decoration, with tendrils and dots above and below. Double folds on handles. Pinkish-buff clay with brick-red slip; extremely worn.
Very similar shape to Mayet Form XXXVIII, and especially to nos. 455-457 from Baetica.[26] See also López Mullor Form XXXVII 8h (form); 8j (decoration).[27] Claudian/Neronian and continuing into the Flavian period; derived from Gaulish sigillata.

B2. GR.1935.6-10.3 (Figs. 7, 18). Cup with rolled rim and carinated body. Ht. 67mm; diam. 73mm. Handles lost. Stamped pattern. Very worn. More orange a clay than B1, with a metallic orange-brown glaze.
Same decoration as Mayet Form XXXVII (from Belo, Baetica); López Mullor Form XXXVIII B, 3b. Related types are known from Rio Tinto.[28] Mid-first century AD.

C. Pottery from Ventimiglia

C1. GR.1980.10-14.6 = V&A 1068-1905 (Figs. 8, 19). Cup without handles, lines or grooves. Ht. 54mm; diam. 107mm. Micaceous grey clay, darker towards base. Greenish tinge above, with black inclusions.
Comparable to Cosa Form XXXVI, Mayet Form XXXIII and Ricci Types 2/232 and 2/405.[29] Known to have been made in the Po Valley, the type was widely exported through northern Italy into Switzerland and the Rhineland; to Spain, north Africa and by the Adriatic as far as Greece.[30] AD 1-50.

C2. GR.1980.10-14.3 = V&A 1062-1903 (Figs. 8, 20). Carinated cup with two handles, one lost. Ht. 97mm; diam. 150mm. Bright orange clay with rosy red slip. Very uneven colour.
Similar to Mayet Form XLIII, though none of Mayet's examples has such a sharp carination or tall rim.[31] Mid-first to early second century AD.

C3. GR.1980.10-14.9 = V&A 1076-1901 (Figs. 8, 21). One-handled cup with collar at base of rim. Ht. 92mm; diam. 79mm. Bright orange clay, with some mica; firing ring on base from rim of vessel below.
Urnetta/boccalino a collarino, a form originating in north Aegean perhaps Thracian workshops and common on sites in Italy and the Aegean (but not in Spain) from the late first to the mid-third century AD.[32] A more carinated version from Ventimiglia is in the Royal Ontario Museum.[33] This is an early example of the genre.

C4. GR.1980.10-14-10 = V&A 1077-1901 (Figs. 8, 22). Globular cup. Ht. 92mm; diam. 60mm. Mouth damaged, graffito below neck. Orange clay, redder than the norm: over-fired and semi-vitrified. Base and interior as C3.
A late example of the *urnetta/boccalino a collarino* shape, probably made at the turn of the second and third centuries AD.

D. Pottery from Herpes (Charente)

D1. GR.1905.5-20.135 (Figs. 9, 23). Indented beaker. Ht. 82mm; diam. 76mm. Sandy micaceous clay with all-over pale yellow/orange slip. Vertical burnishing on upper wall.
Comparable to Mayet Form VI, though these have thinner walls and a more elaborate rim.[34] Originating in the mid-first century BC, possibly in metal or glass, the technique of indenting vessels was apparently common in Italy and the western Mediterranean until the second century AD.[35]

D2. GR.1905.5-20.139 (Figs. 9, 24). Carinated two-handled cup. Ht. 87mm; diam. 125mm. Two deep grooves below carination and another above the foot. Handles have rolled edges and are grooved on the interior surface. Sandy buff clay with ochre slip, unevenly fired.
A local version of a Provençal type? Compare Mayet Form XLIII, especially nos. 535, 538.[36] Although antecedents of this form may be detectable at Cosa (e.g. Form LXIII), the broader, shallower proportions of D2 and D3 seem to belong to the mid-first to early second centuries AD. The form is common in Spain, the Balearics, southern France and Tyrrhenian Italy.[37]

D3. GR.1905.5-20.140 (Figs. 9, 25). Carinated two-handled cup, as D2 but smaller. Ht. 79mm; diam. 125mm. Sandy white clay with orange/red slip, unevenly fired and patchy towards the top of the vessel.
Compare Mayet Form XLIII, especially no. 535.[38.] Mid-first to early second centuries: see also D2 (above).

D4. GR.1905.5-20.128 (Figs. 9, 26). Cup, with broken rim. Ht. 84mm; diam. 125mm. Horseshoe decoration in barbotine and a deep groove below the carination. Whitish clay, with a yellow-ochre/orange slip; worn on upper wall.
Comparable to Mayet Form XLIV.[39] Although Mayet distinguishes the more rounded Form XLIV from the carinated Form XLIII, there seems little if any difference in date (mid-first to early second centuries AD). The horseshoe decoration is typical of Spanish, in particular Lusitanian, production.

D5. GR.1905.5-20.137 (Figs. 9, 27). Cup, a smaller version of D4. Ht. 65mm; diam. 82mm. Sandy white clay with yellow/orange slip, very unevenly fired and pinkish towards the top.
Compare Mayet Form XLIII.[40] Mid-first to early second centuries AD. Decoration as D4.

NOTES

1. On the origins and development of thin-walled wares, see Marabini Moevs esp. pp. 35-45, and Mayet 1980, 201-21.
2. See recently Baratte 1986, 53 and 91 (Louvre Bj 1915-16).
3. Marabini Moevs 1973, Form XXIX no. 140, pls. 13, 63.
4. Marabini Moevs 1973, Form XXVIII nos. 134-9, pls. 12,13,62; see p. 87 for the context.
5. Campana A: Morel 1981, 253 nos. 3156a and 3161a, and pl. 89; lead-glazed ware: Hochuli-Gysel 1977, 33 no. S45 and pl. 11; 'Pontic' one example from Olbia: Knipowitsch 1929, 24, Type 18, and pl. 1; Arretine sigillata: Dragendorff and C. Watzinger 1948, 25, Type 7, fig. 2, pl. 7 nos. 70 a-b. For a similar form, but with plain foot see *CVA USA VIII Fogg Museum* 71, no. 13. pl. XL.
6. Sparkes 1987, 244, Tomb 53 no. 4, and pl. 142.
7. Mayet 1975, 39 no. 89, and pl. XII.
8. Marabini Moevs 1973, Form XXXIII nos. 169-71, pls. 16, 64 and p. 102, where the form is considered typical of the Augustan period.
9. Mayet 1975, 136 Map 6 shows the distribution of this type.
10. GR. 1935.6-10.2. See Greene 1979, 68 no. 3 with fig. 30 p. 69.
11. Carandini *et al.* 1968, 65-7, and pl. 7, figs. 143-9; pl. 61, figs. 792-840; Hayes 1976, 11, no. 44 and fig. 6.
12. Grataloup 1988, Type LXX p. 102 and 178 no. 249.

13. Delemain 1892.
14. Bailey 1988, 151, 161, Q1531, Q1533, Q1540; 162, Q1547; 163, Q1567; 164, Q1572; 175, Q1668, Q1669; 176, Q1671; 187, Q1690; 193, Q1747 MLA.
15. Mayet 1975, Forms XLIII-XLIV, pp. 103-5, nos. 545-54, pls. LXVI-LXVII.
16. For example the blue glass cup now in the Corning Museum of Glass (CMG 70.1.29) see Harden 1987, 38 no. 14, dated 50-1 BC.
17. Mayet 1975, 131 carte 3 nos. 1-11 *bis*.
18. Cosa no. 140: Marabini Moevs 1973, 274, pls. 13, 63. For silver versions see Baratte 1986, 36, 43, 53 (below), 89; for glass see Harden 1987, 189 no. 99; and Isings 1957, 55, form 39. The shape is often called a skyphos from the form of the handles; it is in fact a hybrid of a kantharos bowl with handles more appropriate to a skyphos.
19. Barnett and Mendelson (eds.) 1987, Tomb 53, no. 4, p. 244 and pls. 20, 142; Mayet 1975, Form VIII, p. 39 and pl. XII no. 89 from Majorca. Ornavasso: Bianchetti 1895, pl. XXI no. 12. Pompeii: Carandini 1977, p. 28, tav. XVII, nos. 67-8.
20. Ricci 1985, 278.
21. Cosa Form XXXIII: Marabini Moevs 1973, 176 nos. 314-15, pls. 35 and 76. Form XL: pp. 113-14, nos. 202-5, pls. 20 and 67.
22. Cosa Form XXXVI: Marabini Moevs 1973, 159-60, 176-9, nos. 316-32; pls. 35, 36, 76-8; Mayet 1975, 67-8, nos. 256-74, pls. XXXIII, XXXIV.
23. Grataloup 1988, 39-40, Type VIII no. 89. Grataloup suggests the workshop of la Muette as the provenance, and emphasises the influence of north Italian models on this product.
24. Mayet Form XLIII; Mayet 1975, 98-108, nos. 503-87, pls. LXII-LXIX.
25. Ettlinger *et al.* 1990, 182, Taf. 60; use of moulds, Bermond Montanari 1972, 65-76, esp. 66, fig. 1.
26. Mayet 1975, 72-94, pls. XXXVIII-LVII; Baetica (Osuna): p. 93, pl. LV.
27. López Mullor 1990, 348-50, 371, no. 4 (8h), p. 373, no. 1 (8j).
28. Mayet 1975, 86, pl. XLVIII; López Mullor 1990, 388-390; Rio Tinto examples: Mayet 1975, 86, nos. 397, 403, pls. XLVII-XLVIII.
29. Marabini Moevs 1973, 106-11, nos. 180-94, pls. 18, 19, 65, 66; Mayet 1975, 67-8, nos. 256-74, pls. XXXIII, XXXIV; Ricci 1985, 286-7, tav. XCII.
30. Ricci 1985, 287.
31. Mayet 1975, pls. LXII-LXV; López Mullor 1990, pl. 280, no. 2.
32. Cosa Form LXVIII; Marabini Moevs 1973, 237-8, nos. 431-3, pls. 46, 85; on p. 238 the appearance of the form from the mid-first century AD is noted and a link with La Tène cooking wares is suggested. However a preponderance of the type amongst recent finds at Ainos and Troy suggests a source on the Thracian coast. Painted examples in the typical fabric appear at Ostia in the earlier third century: Carandini 1968, 65-7, nos. 143-9, tav. LXI, nos. 792-840. From this time onward the shape was much copied in the Athenian workshops. Ricci 1985, 267-8, Type 1/122 (bibl.); tav. LXXXV.
33. Hayes 1976, 11, no. 44, fig. 6.
34. Mayet 1975, 37-8, nos. 82-6, pl. XI.
35. Marabini Moevs 1973, 86 suggests that indented decoration in general, and specifically on Cosa Form XXVII, was inspired by prototypes in other media, in particular metal.
36. Mayet 1975, 102, no. 535, pl. LXIV (from Alto Alentejo); 103, no. 538, pl. LXV (from Mérida, whose products are found throughout Baetica, Lusitania and northwest Africa.
37. Marabini Moevs 1973, 252-3, nos. 459-69, pls. 49, 50, 87, 88. For the distribution of Mayet Form XLIII, see López Mullor 1990, 410.
38. Mayet 1975, 102, no. 535, pl. LXIV; D3 has a less ribbed handle.

39.   Mayet 1975, 105, no. 554, pl. LXVI.
40.   Mayet 1975, 104, nos. 551-2, pl. LXVI.

BIBLIOGRAPHY

Bailey, D.M. 1988. *A Catalogue of the Lamps in the British Museum*, III. *Roman Provincial Lamps* London

Baratte, F. 1986. *Le Trésor d'Orfèvrerie Romaine de Boscoréale*. Paris

Bermond Montanari, G. 1972. Pozzi a sud ovest di Ravenna e nuove scoperte di officine ceramiche. In, G. Bovini, and G.A. Mansuelli (eds.), *I problemi della ceramica romana di Ravenna della Valle Padana e dell'Alto Adriatico*, 65-76. Bologna

Bianchetti, E. 1895. I sepolcreti di Ornavasso, *Atti della Società di Archeologia e Belle Arti per la Provincia di Torino* **VI**

Carandini, A. *et al.* 1968. *Ostia*. Studi Miscellanei 13. Rome

Carandini, A. 1977. *La ceramica a pareti sottili*. In, A. Carandini (ed.), *L'instrumentum domesticum di Ercolano e Pompei nella prima età imperiale*. *Quaderni di cultura materiale* **I**, 25-31

Delemain, P. 1892. *Le Cimitière d'Herpes*. Angoulême

Dragendorff, H. and Watzinger, C. 1948. *Arretinische Reliefkeramik mit Beschreibung der Sammlung in Tübingen*. Reutlingen

Ettlinger, E. *et al.* 1990. *Conspectus formarum terrae sigillatae Italico modo confectae*. Bonn

Grataloup, C. 1988. *Les céramiques à parois fines: Rue des Farges à Lyon*. British Archaeological Reports International Series 457. Oxford

Greene, K. 1979. *Report on the Excavations at Usk, 1965-76. The Pre-Flavian Fine Wares*. Cardiff

Harden, D.B. (ed.) 1987. *Glass of the Caesars*. Milan

Hayes, J.W. 1976. *Roman Pottery in the Royal Ontario Museum. A Catalogue*. Toronto

Hochuli-Gysel, A. 1977. Kleinasiatische glasierte Reliefkeramik. *Acta Bernensia* **VII**. Bern

Isings, C. 1957. *Roman Glass from Dated Finds*. Groningen

Knipowitsch, T. 1929. *Materialien zur römisch-germanischen Keramik*, IV. Frankfurt/Main

López Mullor, A. 1990. *Las cerámicas Romanas de paredes finas en Cataluña*. Zaragoza

Marabini Moevs, M.T. 1973. The Roman Thin-Walled Pottery from Cosa (1948-1954). *MemAmAc* **XXXII**

Mayet, F. 1980. Les céramiques à parois fines: état de la question. In, P. Lévêque and J.-P. Morel (eds.), *Céramiques Hellénistiques et Romaines*. Centre de Recherches d'Histoire Ancienne Vol. **36**/Annales Littéraires de l'Université de Besançon **242,** 201-29. Paris

Mayet, F. 1975. *Les Céramiques à parois fines dans la Péninsule Ibérique*. Paris

Morel, J.-P. 1981. *La Céramique Campanienne: les formes*. Rome

Ricci, A. 1985. *Atlante delle forme ceramiche,* **II**. Enciclopedia dell'Arte Antica, supplement, 231-357 s.v. Ceramica a pareti sottili. Rome

Sparkes, B.A. 1987. Pottery: Greek and Roman. In, R.D. Barnett, and C. Mendleson, (eds.), *Tharros: a Catalogue of Material in the British Museum from Phoenician and other Tombs at Tharros, Sardinia*, 59-70. London

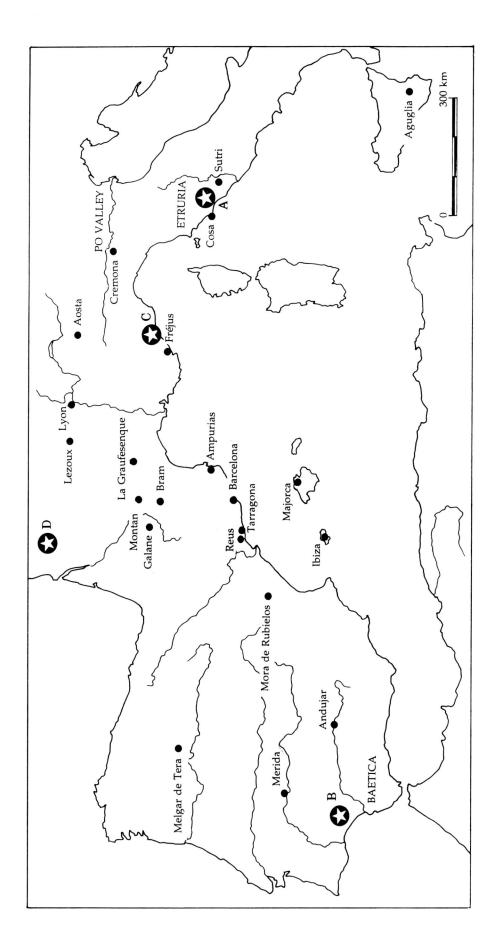

Fig. 1   Map of sites discussed in the text and other sites producing thin-walled wares
A Toscania   B Rio Tinto   C Ventimiglia   D Herpes

347

2

3

4

Fig. 2   Toscania: Vases A1 (r.) and A2 (l.)
Fig. 3   Toscania: Vase A3
Fig. 4   Toscania: Vase A4

348

5

6

7

Fig. 5   Toscania: Vase A5 (r.) and Ventimiglia Vase C1 (l.)
Fig. 6   Toscania: Vase A6
Fig. 7   Rio Tinto: Vases B1, B2

8

9

10

Fig. 8   Ventimiglia: Vases C1-4
Fig. 9   Herpes: Vases D1-5
Fig. 10   Ventimiglia: Vase C4 (r.) and Herpes Vases D3 (l.) and D2

350

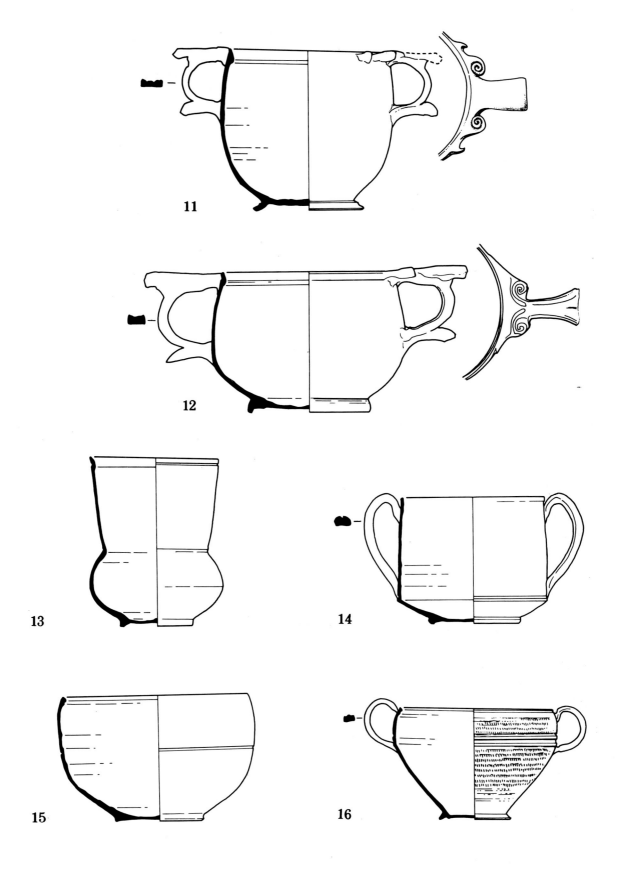

Figs. 11-16   Drawings of vases from Toscania

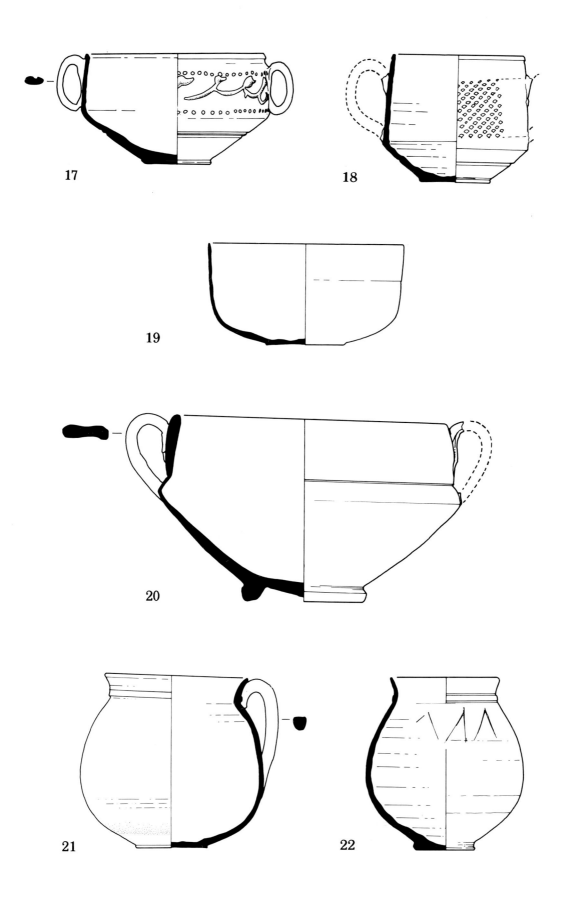

Figs. 17-22   Drawings of vases from Rio Tinto (17,18) and Ventimiglia (19-22)

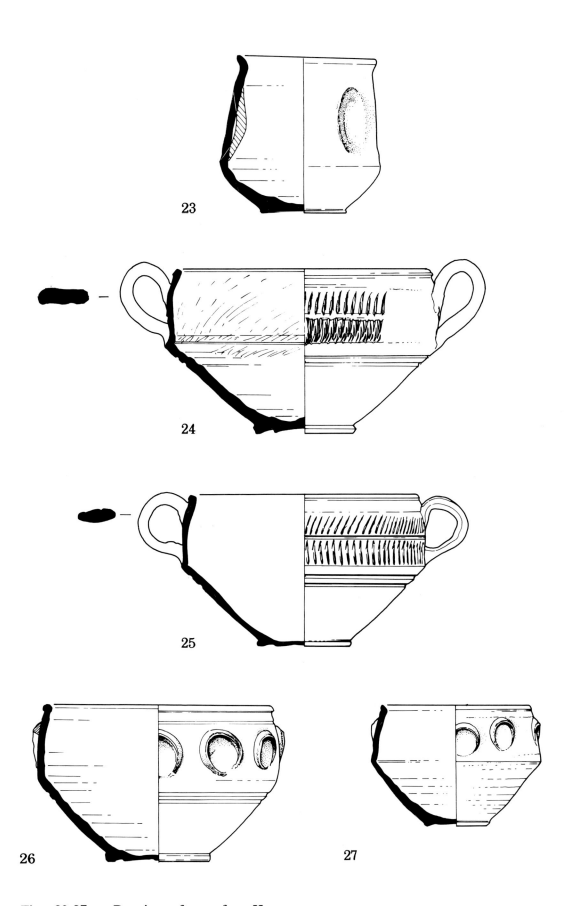

23

24

25

26

27

Figs. 23-27   Drawings of vases from Herpes